Interpreting Minds

Interpreting Minds   Radu J. Bogdan

The Evolution of a Practice

A Bradford Book
The MIT Press
Cambridge, Massachusetts
London, England

This book was set in Times Roman on the Monotype "Prism Plus" PostScript Imagesetter by Asco Trade Typesetting Ltd., Hong Kong, and was printed and bound in the United States of America.

First printing, 1997.

Library of Congress Cataloging-in-Publication Data

Bogdan, Radu J.
 Interpreting minds : the evolution of a practice / Radu J. Bogdan.
     p.   cm.
 "A Bradford book."
 Includes bibliographical references and index.
 ISBN 0-262-02419-5 (hc : alk. paper)
 1. Philosophy. 2. Psychology. I. Title.
B29.B585   1997
121'.68—dc21   96-45207
                                                            CIP

To the memory of Alexandru
Vianu, Bob McCann, and Norton
Nelkin

Contents

Contents

Acknowledgments

The topic and arguments of this book straddle several fields, most notably philosophy of mind, animal and developmental psychology, and evolutionary theory. As a philosopher, I note this with humility but also with a sense of inevitability, for I think there is no other cogent way to seriously study commonsense psychology or interpretation, as I will call it. Fortunately, I was not alone on this road. For many years, but not enough, I was surrounded by kindred spirits in our small but lively community in New Orleans: philosophers who knew from their work that bold interdisciplinary speculation becomes imperative as the questions about the mind probe deeper and wider. I am thinking of Harvey Green, Carolyn Morillo, and Norton Nelkin. The four of us were "the mind people," and what a difference that made to my mind and work. The interaction was so constant and thorough that I find it hard now to single out specific inputs. All have seen, heard, and commented on parts of this work. Carolyn also took a careful and critical look at an advanced draft and followed up with further questions. Norton left us more than a year ago, a loss still hard to accept, but his lively mind and iconoclastic questions have continued to watch over my thinking and writing. My heartfelt and already nostalgic gratitude goes to these good friends. In the last few years I was privileged to know and exchange ideas with Daniel Povinelli, a wide-ranging evolutionary and comparative psychologist whose work and insights have been so helpful. Danny read and commented on an entire draft, and I warmly thank him for that. Other people in town have reacted to various interim reports. I thank Robert Berman, Bruce Brower, Ronna Burger, Jim Stone, and my doctoral student Tian Ping. I am also much indebted to people in other towns where I got into the habit of stopping frequently to talk about my work, particularly to my students and colleagues at the University of

Bucharest and my friends at CREA (Centre de Recherche en Épistémologie Apliquée) in Paris, among whom are Pascal Engel, Pierre Jacob, Joelle Proust, François Recanati, and especially Dan Sperber.

A few other colleagues and friends have left their mark on this book. I begin with Dan Dennett. A pioneer analyst of the evolution of interpretation and a courageous intruder in closely guarded domains of science, Dan's example fortified my resolve to dare and speculate. Dan also took the time to read an early draft and provided excellent criticisms and suggestions, for which I am so grateful. Over several years I benefited from direct and written exchanges with other philosophers, some not likely to approve of the final result but helpful in reaching it. I am thinking of Paul Churchland, Martin Davies, Jerry Fodor, Alvin Goldman, and Keith Lehrer.

All of the above would not have materialized in a book without the help of many people at the MIT Press. I single out for praise and warmest thanks Dr. Amy Brand, a superb editor, very knowledgeable and efficient, and very supportive of my work, and Alan Thwaits for his erudite, sensitive, and fine editing.

During my work on this book, three close friends passed away. Each epitomizes a chapter of my life: Alexandru Vianu, a professor of history at the University of Bucharest, was a mentor of my adolescence; Bob McCann, in my eyes the quintessential American, eased Catalina and me with grace, warmth, and humor into a new life on a new continent; and Norton Nelkin, whose friendship and philosophical companionship brightened my years in New Orleans. I dedicate the book to these departed and much beloved friends.

Interpreting Minds

Chapter 1
The Project

This essay is about commonsense psychology, also known in philosophy as folk psychology and in psychology as theory of mind or mind reading. I opt for the term *interpretation* as the attribution relation between an *interpreter* and a *subject*. I motivate this choice later in this chapter. First, I outline the background of the main topic in section 1, distinguish several stances on it, and extricate the one that matters to interpretation. With the territory so delineated, I preview in section 2 the main argument of the essay and conclude in section 3 with a word about terminological policies.

1 Background

The stances Interpretation is a competence that allows primates to make sense spontaneously and effectively of each other in terms of behavioral dispositions and psychological attributes, such as character traits, emotions, feelings, and attitudes. This essay seeks to contribute to an explanation of the nature of the competence, its history, and its job. Because of its evolutionary rationale, reflected in its job, interpretation has a privileged relation to the mind interpreted. I phrase the point diplomatically because the nature of the relation is much contested. This is why it is helpful from the outset to separate interpretation from other stances on the mind.

There are four stances worth distinguishing: naive, folkloric, ideological, and scientific (Dennett 1987, chapter 3; 1991b; also Bogdan 1991b, 1993a). Interpretation is a sort of *naive psychology*, programmed innately and exercised spontaneously (Humphrey 1988). The elucidation of its nature is the object of this essay. There is also a *naive phenomenology*, which provides unreflective and immediate access to the phenomenal data of mental life. The relation of this phenomenology to interpretation is still subject to inquiry and debate.

The *folklore of the mind* is a collection of popular notions and conceptions, some universal, others specific to a culture. This psychofolklore has many sources: interpretation and naive phenomenology, myth and religion, philosophical and artistic views that spread in a population and survive across generations, linguistic practices and social expectations, and ordinary observations about people and their behaviors that find their way into the general mentality. The notion of soul is folkloric (sources: myth, religion, philosophy), and so are the ordinary observations that people tend to act on their desires and beliefs (source: interpretation), that pain is unpleasant (source: naive phenomenology) and that people tend to believe what they say (sources: linguistic practice, social expectation, interpretation).

The *ideology of the mind* originates in myth, religion, folklore, and philosophy, and encompasses notions and conceptions that construe the mind not as a result of a search for the truth (science) or on the basis of ordinary observation (folklore) but according to religious, moral, social, or political views, implications, or prejudices. An ideological conception comes close to being wishful thinking, though it is not always detrimental. Freud suggested that the notion of an immortal soul may have been a clever concoction to maintain the mental health and motivation of the tribe confronted with the realization of impending death. Such a notion would be ideological. Equally ideological are the a priori notions that the human mind is unique, special, with no animal pedigree. That ideology is independent of interpretation is often seen in the fact that individuals may hold the silliest views about the mind (as the history of folklore and philosophy abundantly testify) while managing quite well in interpreting their conspecifics. Interpretation is one thing; false consciousness about the mind another thing.

The last stance is that of *science*. There are many sciences of the mind, nowadays collected under the label of 'cognitive science'. Their aim is to figure out and explain the design and operation of the mind, from its neural mechanisms (neuroscience) to its various programs (psychology, linguistics, philosophy of mind). Whatever their angle on the mind, it is their methodology and objectives that radically distinguish the sciences of the mind from each of the other stances.

This essay is exclusively about interpretation as a naive psychology— although the word 'psychology' is merely a concession to current usage, for the argument developed below is that interpretation is neither a (naive) *logos* nor literally about the *psyche*. The notion that it is literally though naively a logos of the psyche draws on preconceptions nurtured by the other stances. This is why keeping these intrusive stances at bay requires constant vigilance.

Motivation   There are several reasons why I thought this project worth pursuing. If I were to single out the most motivating ones, I would choose three. The first is the desire to get *to the roots* of interpretation. At least since the emergence of philosophical behaviorism a few decades ago, there has been much talk about interpretation but relatively little effort to uncover its roots and reasons. Some views seemed to get things right, others didn't, but there wasn't a firm sense that one knew why. Dominating the debate were linguistic and introspective intuitions, views about the nature of psychology, semantic analyses of attributional sentences, and the metaphysics of mind. Even if these were the right levels of analysis (which I doubt), we were not told why. Turning to the psychology of interpretation, which rapidly became a new and dynamic research program, one discovers a larger theoretical horizon, robust data, and impressive experiments. And yet one retains the sense that the roots of interpretation remain elusive, not so much for lack of data but for lack of further theoretical probing.

Hence the second reason for this project: the prospect of *proximate impasse*. Current views tend to talk past each other, assigning to interpretation different and often conflicting domains, aims, and skills, or else they debate the same issues with no resolution in sight. Here is a sample of what I mean. Interpretation is (a) innate, no, learned; (b) modular and specialized, no, general-purpose; (c.1) procedural, no, more like an explicit theory; (c.2) neither procedural nor theorylike but rather projection or simulation; (d) naively true of the mind, no, totally false; (e) uniquely human, no, with animal precedents; (f) about the mind, no, about behavior only; and so on. There will be occasions later to label and explain these views. Now I stress their inconclusive oppositions. What is wrong with that, you would ask. Isn't science progressing in this way? Is there a better formula, you ask. The problem (I reply) is not with disagreement and debate but with the *level* of theorizing. The oppositions just noted are all proximate, that is, concerned with programs and their use, not with why the programs are there in the first place, which would be an explanation of the ultimate or evolutionary sort. Some of the questions cited (early in the list) may be settled by further data and insightful proximate research. Other questions (down the list) might not be so easy.

Thus I come to the third reason for this project, the *need for evolution*. I argue in chapter 3 that the domain and job of interpretation cannot be easily figured out without evolution. The competencies (so far) best understood in cognitive science without appeal to evolution, namely, vision and grammar, are *producers* of representations. Interpretation, however, is one level up on the processing ladder, being mostly a *categorization* capability. Such capabilities—from concepts to meaning representations—are notoriously hard to fathom. In interpretation, they are even harder to pin down without asking why they evolved, under what pressures, and in what contexts of selection. Once evolution is brought into the picture, it emerges that the domain and job of interpretation are different from what the mainstream positions hold. Or so I will argue.

Yet before embarking on an evolutionary venture, I acknowledge the formidable obstacles facing it. Antievolutionism, still rampant in philosophy and cognitive science, is animated by two chief prejudices. One is that complex mental abilities—and interpretation is one—did not evolve by natural selection, or even if they did, this fact need not illuminate their design. The other prejudice is that we will never know whether such abilities evolved and, even if they did, we would not know how. Brains do not fossilize; new functions can emerge without precedents; and the primate mind, the only candidate for interpretation, is simply too recent and complex to allow a coherent and verifiable evolutionary story.

Neither prejudice is as substantial as it sounds. But I find their methodological message depressing and rather reactionary, for they tread on mysterianism and lack of firm evidence. Neither is a good reason not to probe and speculate. One learns from mistakes but not from mysteries. This is when a handicap may turn into an asset. My handicap is that I am a philosopher of mind, not a psychologist or evolutionary theorist. My evolutionary ideas and arguments are those of an amateur who took some time to appreciate their force and relevance. Philosophers can be good at brainstorming and integrative speculation—an institutional adaptedness, if you like. The study of mind and interpretation needs that, and this is something appreciated nowadays in neighboring disciplines. Recent avenues of research on interpretation (e.g., its form of theory, innateness, false-belief recognition, simulation) have been suggested or even initiated by philosophers. Good omens to continue in the same spirit. Even if the case for the evolution of interpretation is not as tight or plausible as one may wish, attempting to make the case and show what this reveals about the design of interpretation is a heuristic journey worth making in the quest for new clues and insights. There is nothing to lose, except some reading time. My sense, though, is that the journey is more than heuristic. The following, very briefly, explains why.

2 The Argument

From why to what   At the heart of this essay is the notion that the *why* of interpretation illuminates its *what*, meaning that its *evolutionary reasons* can constrain and even specify its *job*. The quest for evolutionary reasons is a quest for the forces that shaped the goals and tasks of interpretation, or the design of its job. The why-to-what, or rationale-to-job, syllogism goes like this. If interpretation first evolved by natural selection, then it is an adaptation. If an adaptation, then it is a competence or family of skills good at doing something that serves the interpreter's goals and ultimately promotes her biological prosperity. Good-at-doing-something indicates the goals and tasks, or job design, of the competence. The job design of a competence is in turn the best avenue to understanding its operation.

On this view, identifying the selective pressures under which interpretation evolved provides the constraints on what interpretation is good at and hence on what its adaptedness consists of. I distinguish three families of such pressures—*communal* (cooperation, family life), *epistemic* (education, communication) and *political* (manipulation, deception)—and show that they are at work throughout the evolution of interpretation. At each evolutionary turn, these pressures correlate systematically with key properties of the respective form of interpretation. Such correlations not only show that interpretation is the outcome of evolution, which is one major aim of this essay, but also pave the ground for applying evolutionary insights to the analysis of the job of interpretation, which is the other major aim.

For this explanatory strategy to work, I need to identify the evolutionary *environments of selection* as the contexts where the forces of selection produce interpretive skills as adaptations. This identification yields clues to the specificity of the forces involved and of the skills they produce, and also to the common pattern of adaptedness found in the evolution of interpretation as a distinct competence. This pattern is displayed by (what I call) the *goal setting for interpretation*, where the satisfaction of the interpreter's goals depends on figuring out and doing something about the goals of the interpreted; that is what selects for interpretation.

Practice   What goal settings make manifest and motivate is that interpretive skills were selected as *effective strategies* to do something about
the subject's goals and behaviors when they interfered with or had consequences for those of the interpreter. Interpretation thus evolved as
a cognitive instrument with practical import. The most salient insight
provided by evolution is that interpretation is practical in two senses: it
operates as a practice and has practical aims. It operates as a practice in
that it conceives of and handles the subject's psychological attributes and
behaviors in terms of effective strategies of engagement, intervention, and
reaction, or in short, *involvement.* And it has practical aims because it
picks up and categorizes those subject-world relations that allow such
effective strategies.

The practical effectiveness of interpretation depends on the interpreter's
correctly parsing the subject's relations to and actions on the world into
units that afford opportunities for involvement, whether by incremental
interception or alteration or influence or reaction, and that also afford
opportunities for control of the whole process by fine-tuned expectations,
predictions, and feedback. Thus emerges the leading theme of this essay,
according to which the interpretive categories of psychological attributes
are practical in nature, for they operate as parsers of the sort just sketched.
Put simply, to interpret a subject's attributes is to know what to do about
them.

To sum up, there are communal, epistemic, and political pressures for
practical involvement in the subject's affairs. This translates into selection
for skills to influence causally or take advantage of a subject by executing
tasks that parse his relations to the world in a practical format. On this
line of analysis I propose to explain the phylogenetic and ontogenetic
differences in the job design of interpretation in terms of the accord between the epistemic, communal, and political demands of social life and
the potential of the interpretive skills to affect the subject practically at
joints where effective strategies of involvement are possible and successful.
When that accord snaps, evolution ends up changing the rules of the
game. The resulting historical pattern would look as follows.

Evolutionary turns   I distinguish two major phases in the evolution
of interpretation, one called *early* or *situated* interpretation, the other
advanced or *unsituated* interpretation. The former is a reflex or instinctive
interpretation, steeped in the immediacy of perception and behavioral
response; the latter a thoughtful or reflective interpretation that ranges

across space, time, and imagined possibilities. The former is shaped mostly by natural selection, the latter mostly by culture. Within each major phase I distinguish several evolutionary turns, sufficiently distinct in terms of epistemic, political, and communal pressures and the skills they pressured for.

The first turn is *natural teleology*. It is the earliest and simplest form of interpretation. It responds to the crude agency of subjects and their basic goals. When pressured to identify specific goals, basic and nonbasic, by clues that reflect more than physiological propensities for fixed behavioral patterns, interpretation turns *psychobehavioral*. When pressured to share information and experiences, interpretation takes a uniquely human *psychosocial* turn, first in an infant version. Although different in terms of evolutionary pressures-skills packages, all these forms of interpretation are situated and reflex in manner. It is only at the *metarepresentational* turn, in early childhood, that interpretation moves beyond its perceptual and behavioral immediacy and becomes unsituated and able to attribute basic propositional attitudes, such as desire, belief, and intention. In disagreement with prevailing views, I think that evolution does not stop at this ontogenetic phase and has one more turn to take. *Reconstructive* interpretation becomes fully reflective, since it is based, on thinking, and takes the form of adult commonsense psychology.

The mind deal   Interpretation is a practice evolved in response to distinct selective pressures, first natural and later cultural. It is a practice in the service of the interpreter's goals and ultimately of her biological fitness. As a result, interpretation is not a probe or reader or theory of minds but a pragmatic policy of tracking the subject's relations to the world to the extent that they affect the interpreter. Yet to be effective along these lines, interpretation evolves to factor in and exploit the subject's mental and behavioral propensities and their affordances for practical involvement. This need not yield an explicit knowledge of minds. At no evolutionary stage do interpretive skills generate explicit representations about the subject's mental architectures (functional resources and programs), data structures (in the case of attitudes), or other functional configurations (in the case of affects, feelings, and traits). Nor are any of the latter tracked implicitly but systematically. What interpretation tracks systematically, whether explicitly or implicitly, are the subject's *relations* to the world and their *external relata*. This is the only intentionality that interpretation cares about. Many theorists may agree with this position, in which case the debate is about how to analyze the mind-world relations picked out in interpretation. My proposal is that the systematic tracking of subject-world relations is motivated and formatted by the practical interests of the interpreter, even in adult human interpretation, where there is much greater freedom to interpret beyond immediate needs. As a result, the interpreter has a practical knowledge of minds, mostly implicit and limited to the aspects that afford practical involvement. The success of such knowledge in various applications (prediction, control, manipulation, explanation) is secured by evolutionary arrangements, natural and cultural, and not by the interpreter's knowledge of minds.

To sum up, then, there are three main and tightly interwoven lines of argument, with ample polemical fuse, to be developed in this essay. One is the evolutionary hypothesis—the selection of interpretation. Another is its practicality—a tool to secure the interests of the interpreter and ultimately her biological prosperity. The third is the subject-world-interpreter relation at the heart of the domain of interpretation.

The plan Part I makes the general case for the evolution of interpretation. Chapter 2 argues that interpretation is a competence selected epistemically, communally, and politically. Chapter 3 holds that interpretation is distinct and, being in the categorization business, needs an evolutionary reading of its goals and tasks. The second part of the book focuses on situated interpretation, whose forms are in the direct grip of natural selection. Chapter 4 surveys the main forms and inquires into the selective pressures responsible for them. Chapter 5 takes its clues from a comparison between selective pressures and the skills they called for, and ventures a hypothesis about the design of the job of early interpretation. This is where I articulate the notion of interpretation as a practice consisting of effective strategies of involvement in the subject's affairs. Against the current consensus, chapter 6 suggests that the metarepresentational turn, when unsituated attitudes come under interpretation, is a transient phase that grounds what evolves next. Part III turns to reconstruction, the adult form of human interpretation. Chapter 7 retraces the chief evolutionary sources of reconstruction: the development of thinking and its cultural regimentation. Drawing on these evolutionary data, chapter 8 explores the job design of reconstruction. In the process, it argues that reconstruction remains practically motivated and operated, a feature reflected in its categorizations and attributions; that content ascriptions map aspects of practical interest to the interpreter into functional roles those aspects play in the interpreter's thinking and acting; that intentional explanation is a creature of culture, attuned mostly to its norms, not to psychological regularities; and that the evolutionary plausibility of simulation may be more modest than thought by both its proponents and detractors. The final chapter 9 puts two and two together to reach a few conclusions.

Evolutionist credits Given the evolutionist thrust of this work, I salute at this point fellow travelers who have often guided my journey. (Other intellectual debts and points of reference are noted throughout this essay and in further detail in chapter 9, section 3.) My work stands and builds on many evolutionists' shoulders. Following the pioneering insights of Humphrey (1988) and the work of Premack and Woodruff (1978), many psychologists have turned in recent years to animal and child interpretation. It is an indication of the explosion of creative work in the last two decades that it is hard to list all those whose data and hypotheses provided grounds and guidelines for many ideas developed in these pages. Several excellent collections of papers sample these contributions and get due recognition later (Baron-Cohen, Tager-Flusberg, and Cohen 1993; Byrne and Whiten 1988; Carruthers and Smith 1996; Lewis and Mitchell 1994; Moore and Dunham 1995; Whiten 1991a). Although many students of interpretation have gestured toward evolution, few have adopted an explicit evolutionary stance, and even fewer have systematically explored interpretation with the tools of evolutionary analysis. Just doing animal or developmental psychology, even comparatively, is not yet doing evolutionary psychology. The latter requires explaining systematically the history and design of abilities in terms of selective forces or other evolutionary causes. Nothing less will do.

Yet there are notable exceptions. In philosophy, Dan Dennett has not only been the evolutionist par excellence but has also contributed significant evolutionary analyses of interpretation. Besides developing the concept of the intentional stance, so central to interpretation, and boldly defending adaptationism as a method of studying the mind, Dennett has allied the two in a new and influential look at animal interpretation (Dennett 1987). There are a few other (alas, too few) philosophical attempts to inject evolution more thoroughly into accounts of interpretation. I cite in particular those of Bennett (1976, 1991a, 1991b), Clark (1989), Graham (1987), and Levin (1984).

In animal and child psychology, several authors have turned more than occasionally to evolution. I am thinking of Baron-Cohen (1995b), Cheyney and Seyfarth (1990), Humphrey (1988), Mitchell (1994), de Waal (1982, 1989), Whiten (1993), Whiten and Byrne (1988a, 1988c), and the more programmatic Daniel Povinelli (1993, 1996, Povinelli and Eddy 1996). Last but not least, I acknowledge the influence of the methodological program for evolutionary psychology articulated by Leda Cosmides and John Tooby (Cosmides and Tooby 1987; Tooby and Cosmides 1990b, 1992) and the conceptual tools with which they link the notions of selection and adaptation with the top-down analysis in cognitive science. Much as I have learned from these illustrious precedents, I found some room left for further probing, particularly in the direction of a systematic and comprehensive argument going from the evolutionary rationale of interpretation to the design of its job. I hope this essay will show why this argument is necessary and useful, and why interpretation may have evolved as a practice of involvement, not as mind reading.

3 Words

The term 'interpretation' is employed in many fields, from literary theory to hermeneutics, logic, and semantics. Yet the notion I so label is antecedent to all others in the order of history and explanation. Without organisms making sense of each other in contexts where this matters biologically—the Ursense of interpretation, if you like—there would be no other kind of interpretation. If the coevolutionary link between interpretation and primate cognition is validated, as I expect it to be, then the other senses of interpretation can be seen to depend historically on the one deemed the most basic in this work.

My choice also has terminological motivation, for I need a compact and convenient word that takes verb, adjective, and adverb forms easily and naturally; the other candidates don't. I also get to name the termini of an interpretation relation. The interpreted organism is *subject*, and the one who interprets is *interpreter*. To keep track pronominally of who is who, across species, I stipulate that *she* is the interpreter and *he* the interpreted, unless the context says otherwise. I use the adjective 'interpretive' for what pertains to the use or functioning of interpretation, as in 'interpretive skills or concepts', and (unless I get confused) reserve the adjective 'interpretational' for what pertains to a theory, analysis, or language of interpretation.

Words matter in another crucial respect. The ordinary words 'belief', 'desire', 'intention' (and such like) belong to two equally busy and valid vocabularies, which I call 'ambivalent' and 'dedicated' respectively. These vocabularies must be distinguished and the distinction respected, lest confusion engulf us. The *ambivalent* vocabulary does not discriminate between naively cognitivist concepts of forms and outputs of information processing (studied by cognitive science) and purely interpretive concepts. The latter belong to a vocabulary *dedicated* to interpretation. Throughout this essay I stick to the dedicated vocabulary and, whenever possible, replace the ambivalent vocabulary with cognitive-scientific paraphrases. To illustrate, 'belief' used dedicatedly means a subject-world relation as categorized by an interpreter; 'belief' used ambivalently may mean either the former or (as so often) an information state or process of the sort investigated by cognitive science.

All this may look pedantic, but it pays off methodologically. Mighty philosophical views and many intense debates have suffered from the confusion and begged many questions. Perhaps the worst question begging is to assume that interpretation is about the mind. It could be, but that determination ought to be the conclusion of an arduous inquiry, not its unmotivated starting point. Equally counterproductive is the use of the ambivalent vocabulary—with meanings imported from metaphysics, mental causation, physicalist reduction, and relation to various sciences—to make points about interpretation. The trouble is further compounded when one ambivalently identifies both naively cognitivist and interpretive concepts from the viewpoint of introspection and naive phenomenology—a misguided tactic that goes back to Descartes and the British empiricists and from which philosophy of mind has not yet fully recovered.

The dangers just signaled explain not only a terminological policy but also a methodological policy. Philosophers initiate and conduct arguments from inside a shared though contested territory of assumptions, vocabularies, and problems. Given the way I intend to map out the territory of interpretation, there is not much common ground around which to place the usual philosophical fencing. Few philosophical inquiries have taken the evolutionary route as far as I intend to, and few begin by separating what is going on in the mind (the naive-cognitivist reading) from how the interpreter relates to a subject (the dedicated reading). As a result, playing the good old philosophical game would not be very productive, which is why I opt for a fresh start.

PART I

The Case for Evolution

If interpretation is the solution, what was the problem?

Chapter 2

A Selected Competence

Interpretation is an evolutionary phenomenon. It is the outcome of natural selection, at least in its initial and basic properties, and was selected for reasons that reflect durable pressures on interpreting species. The pressures explain the reasons for interpretation and the patterns found in its phylogeny and ontogeny. The appeal to evolution can help identify important properties of interpretation not visible from a proximate stance. The appeal to evolution takes the form of the following argument. If interpretation was naturally selected, then it is an adaptation. If an adaptation, then it is a competence good at doing something, for the selection must have been for tasks performed to reach goals that resulted in enhanced fitness. Specific tasks being performed to reach specific goals is what I mean by a competence being good at doing something. Later in the book I construe the tasks and goals that interpretation is good at as the *design* of its job. The thrust of my argument in this first part is that it was natural selection that shaped that design, at least in its early contours. Later contours are outside the direct reach of natural selection and genetic heritage, and show instead the impact of cultural forces.

I begin the argument, in section 1, with a sample of the facts supporting the notion that interpretation was naturally selected among primates as a basic and innately programmed competence. The notion of selection needed to understand interpretation is spelled out in section 2. The case for the selection of interpretation as an adaptation is made in section 3. If interpretation is an adaptation and selectionism explains it best, then interpretation must have been selected for distinct evolutionary reasons. This is what section 4 speculates about. Section 5 finds grounds to believe that, so selected, interpretation is the work of a distinct set of skills, a competence apart.

1 Facts

Monkeys do it (perhaps), chimps do it (almost certainly), with relish and expertise. Human infants begin very early to exercise it and get better and better at it as they mature, before getting better at anything else of intellectual import. Human adults do it most of the time, naturally and spontaneously, with the same ease with which they talk or think. To give a flavor of the facts that receive most attention in the next chapters, I choose a few examples from the ethological and psychological literature and let them stand inductively for the entire class. I begin with some quotations.

Apes "A monkey that may require lengthy pre-training and adaptation to an apparatus as well as 20 to 100 trials to solve one two-choice object-discrimination problem will, in a matter of seconds or at most minutes, become thoroughly adapted to a particular dominance status when introduced for the first time to a social situation with three or four cage-mates" (Zimmerman and Torrey 1965, quoted by Jolly 1988a, 28). Also, "the problem with chimpanzees is that they do remarkably little most of the time. They move slowly, eat grass, sleep for a long while, groom one another. On the other hand, when the chimpanzees do wake up and cause some social ripples, there is no way an observer can record with pencil and paper all that is going on.... Chimpanzees have memories like the proverbial elephants, and are capable of planning ahead; observation of their social life suggests that they use these capacities all the time" (de Waal 1989, 36, 38).

Children "Some recent work suggests that the central components of commonsense psychology and commonsense metaphysics are developed between 2 and 5. This may, indeed, be the central cognitive achievement of this period" (Forguson and Gopnik 1988, 231). "Data suggest that the three year old child may be working on a theory of mind virtually all his waking hours. And quite possibly many of his sleeping hours as well" (Gopnik and Wellman 1992, 167).

Properties Primates interpret each other in ways that are

- universal or species-wide,
- ontogenetically scheduled,

- impaired through genetic deficit,
- spontaneous and unreflective,
- quick and efficient,
- based on fragmentary data,
- successful most of the time,
- irrespective of culture, talent, motivation, education,
- invariant during the history of the species.

One recognizes here many of the properties invoked on behalf of the species-universality and innateness of grammar. Our discussion will identify other properties, most notably modularity, that also indicate that interpretation begins as an innate, deep-seated, and instinctive competence. At the same time, in its human version, interpretation displays further properties, at variance with those in the former group, such as

- marked distinctions among individual interpreters,
- creativity and improvisation,
- interfaces with other abilities,
- learning and reliance on explicit knowledge (a database),
- cultural indoctrination and compliance.

It is common knowledge that some people interpret better than others. Artists, advertisers, German-accented shrinks, political manipulators, as well as sensitive and thoughtful people, women more often than men and older people more often than younger ones, are thought to be better than the rest at interpretation. Many of these differences show up in creative and improvised interpretations. In most cases, the differences in interpretation result from bringing in other skills, such as imagination, linguistic dexterity, or different experiences. It is also common knowledge that human interpretation is in many respects shaped by culture, construed broadly as a public matrix of ways of doing things in society. Cultural shaping, through parental guidance, instruction, play, imitation, and schooling, goes beyond what is innate, and thus predetermined, in interpretation, and to this extent culturally determined forms of interpretation are different from simpler forms of interpretation. Nevertheless, the results of *these* forms of cultural coercion show signs of uniformity, spontaneity, efficiency, and consistent success, hence the impact of pervasive shaping forces.

So what is going on here? It looks as though the facts quoted at the beginning of the section and the first set of properties point to a tightly regimented competence, evolved in some manner, whereas the second set of properties point to a general-purpose ability, like learning, having little, if anything, in common with the former and with evolution. This, I think, would be a wrong reading. The entire picture points unmistakably to evolution, specifically, to a competence evolved as a distinct adaptation and shaped by selection, first tightly and directly and later more loosely and indirectly, through cultural substitutes. Given what is known about the work of natural and cultural selection and what interpretation is supposed to do, it would be very odd if it were otherwise. So I argue next.

2 Selection, Generally

The selection of interpretive skills is a complex and often messy affair, and nature has only variable grip on the results. Consequently, the analysis must be selectionist in spirit but liberal and modest in letter. Even so, it can deliver a workable notion of adaptation. Thus goes the argument of the present section. First, the larger picture.

Evolution   Evolution is a generous history maker. It allows for traits of organisms, including cognitive ones, to emerge over time in a variety of ways—through selection, mutation, sexual recombination, genetic drift, or migration in and out of a population—as long as there is a change in gene frequencies. It is when we ask why and how a trait has invaded and maintained itself in a population that a tighter explanation is needed. This is when selection becomes the only contender for being an explanation. Selection can be natural (on which more anon) or sexual (when the evolution of a trait increases fertility but not viability) or cultural (when genetic inheritance is replaced by the cultural formation and transmission of a trait across generations). Selection matters explanatorily because of this simple fact: Whereas the origin of a trait is fortuitous and arbitrary, its resilience and universality are not. There must be a *reason* for them, particularly if the trait shows a complexity of design that fits a specific environment. The thought is that the design must have survived and spread because its functions were beneficial to the organisms possessing it. According to Darwinism, there is only one mechanism of evolution that can systematically explain the functions and benefits of a complex design in its ecological niche, and that is natural selection (Williams 1966, Dawkins 1986, Dennett 1995). On this view, if the competence for interpretation displays complex design, is typical of a species, and fits a specific environment, it is likely (or, carefully put, more likely than on any competing explanation) that the competence is the outcome of natural selection, on account of having fitness-enhancing benefits. The story, of course, is not this simple and uncontroversial, but we will worry about that later. What is needed right now is a handy synopsis of evolution by natural selection.

Natural selection   For a trait to evolve by natural selection, certain conditions must be met. Three stand out. One is the *variation* condition: there is variation in phenotypic traits among the reproducing members of a species. Another is the *inheritance* condition: the trait variations are heritable, so that offspring are more like their parents with respect to the trait than they are like the unrelated rest of the species. The third is the *differential-fitness* or reproductive-success condition: different variants leave different numbers of offspring in succeeding generations.

The first condition is explicated by population biology and the second by genetics. It is the third condition that forms the object of the theory of natural selection, Darwin's major contribution to evolutionary thinking (Lewontin 1984, Brandon 1990). Influenced by Malthus's notion of the struggle for existence, Darwin came to understand the fitness condition in competitive terms. Species tend to reproduce in excess of the resources available, which is why the struggle over resources is won by those individuals whose phenotype secures a greater share of the resources, or survive and reproduce on a lower level of resources, or utilize resources unsuitable for their competitors, or the like (Lewontin 1984, 245). Needless to say, evolution by natural selection is an exceedingly complex phenomenon, much contested and far from being fully understood. Given the task of this essay, the focus is on those aspects that matter to interpretation. One such aspect is the wide scope of natural selection, and another is its "delegation of power" to culture in species that interpret. These aspects in turn suggest a modest and liberal selectionism that goes for coarse-grained selection.

The wide scope of selection   Organisms live in an environment, which is why natural selection tends to reward or punish the *entire* arrangement. Although the variation and inheritance conditions require innate mechanisms, the differential-fitness condition requires fitness to an environment. The fit results from clues that guide the right (adaptive) development or behavior. Such clues may be ecological, situational, or cultural. Eco-logical clues secure a relatively fixed relation to an environment, situa-tional clues track fast-changing environments, and cultural clues respond to social artifacts, such as collective habits, public norms, and the like. Ecological and situational clues play a major role in situated interpreta-tion, with natural selection very much in charge. Cultural clues dominate unsituated interpretation. The general idea is that for natural selection, "it does not matter whether a strategy is activated by a gene, an environ-mental cue or a cognitive assessment of a situation. All that matters is that the innate mechanism is designed such that the right alternative is activated under the right circumstances" (Tooby and Cosmides 1990a, 43). Clues to the right circumstances are part of a package that natural selection acts upon.

Most environments do not stay put. Changes and variability are the rule rather than the exception. As a result, natural selection rewards flexible strategies that secure alternative fit. Examples abound. The cleaner fish, *Labroides dimidiata*, begins as a female and turns into a male when it becomes the largest in the group. Different diets transform a female ant into a worker or a queen. Less drastic features of development also respond to changing environments. Organisms with access to less food stay small; it is easier to survive this way. In general, the fact that in many species, sex, labor profile, or developmental shape are environ-mentally determined shows that these facultative responses must have been selected because one version is advantageous in some environ-ments and others in different environments (Sober 1984a, 209; Tooby and Cosmides 1990b).

The point I need is this. Natural selection operates on larger organism-environment arrangements, often with built-in alternative strategies cued to appropriate signals. Think of these strategies as conditional rules of the form 'If x, then y'. The selection, then, is not literally for one trait or another, such as being a female or male fish, but rather for a conditional rule, such as 'Change to male if you are the largest conspecific in the group; remain female if you are not' (Tooby and Cosmides 1990b). Alternative strategies, construed as conditional rules, turn out to be cru-cial to interpretation. The reason is simple. The environments of inter-pretation are highly socialized, and hence teeming with fast-changing situations that keep modifying interindividual interactions in real time. Each new situation opens up multiple possibilities for still other sit-uations, and so on. As a result, one's reading of a situation and one's response strategy to it, and eventually the fitness consequence of this exercise, depend essentially on, and must be scaled to, the readings and behavioral strategies of others (Chisholm 1988).

It is natural, in these conditions, that the selection of interpretive skills is going to be a selection for batteries of sophisticated conditional strategies that respond to situational clues of the environment of social interaction and to one's assessment of a situation. In human societies, the conditional strategies must also respond not just to fast-changing environmental situations but also to culturally defined situations, signaled by their own clues. This generates enormous pressures for a mental and cultural redesign of interpretation, as explained in chapters 7 and 8. The net effect of these evolvements is that natural selection leaves room for a cultural evolution whose results are not genetically expressed. Human development (on which more anon) and in particular the development of interpretation vividly exemplify the transition from simpler conditional rules cued to ecological signals to more complex rules cued to social situations, and finally to very sophisticated batteries of rules cued culturally to the ways things are done in society. Far from undermining selectionism, this trend can be best explained on selectionist grounds. Outcomes of selection (adaptations) are contracts between genes and environment, natural and cultural; what changes along the phylogenetic and ontogenetic routes are the form, the terms, and the scope of the contract.

Modest selectionism   The many ways in which selection operates and the wide scope of its operation suggest a modest, liberal, prudent selectionism as an explanatory stance. Later in this section I will outline the working notions that characterize this stance. At this point I need to motivate the stance. To begin with, many biological phenomena do not bear the imprint of selection in any *direct* way; they may be exaptations (new functions for old structures), free riders or accidental concomitants (spandrels) of adaptations, and so on. Furthermore, there are complex cognitive competencies, such as language and interpretation, which are shaped during a delayed *development* under a variety of selective forces. Development generates two sorts of pressures (natural as well as cultural) that interact constantly: those of doing well at a given stage to make it to the next and those of preparing the ground for further structural and functional changes (Williams 1966). It is not easy to tease out which novel acquisitions and which of their functions respond to which set of specific pressures (Bonner 1988, Bowlby 1982, Chisholm 1988, Frazier 1990).

Cultural pressures add complications when grafting culturally useful skills onto naturally selected instincts. An example is the emotional cuing of the child to its mother as a strategy to do well at a given stage, which also helps formatting the skills for linguistic reference (Bruner 1983; Hobson 1993a).

In sum, there is no easy way to retrieve the selective forces acting on complex cognitive competencies, such as language or interpretation. The forces operate in environments of selection whose complexity and evolutionary dynamics are still elusive. Yet this should be no reason for despair or for an antiselectionist mysterianism that preaches that it's all a puzzle that's beyond us, a cosmic accident, an arbitrary emergence, a physical fluke, the miracle of life or of the brain, and then that counsels against any historical investigation, labeling attempts at such investigations "just-so stories." (Dennett [1995] examines this attitude in great detail and with much verve.) Even just-so stories, when bold, systematic, and sensitive to evidence, are better than no stories at all. One learns from mistakes and speculations; one does not learn from untouchable mysteries.

Selectionist accounts should always be given a chance because, when applicable and plausible, they are fruitful and informative in virtue of the systematic links between traits of organisms and features of environments. Such links are the stuff the best biological explanations are made of. Even when ascertaining general properties and correlations, which is not that often, nonselectionist accounts fail to relate them to how organisms systematically interact with their habitats. It is this systematic interaction that motivates selectionism and gives it preeminence within evolutionism. Selectionism also has the advantage of being more testable than its competitors—a fact recognized even by its detractors (West-Eberhard 1992, 18). Yet it always remains wise to test the limits of selectionist explanations, compare them with alternative accounts, and when the latter do better, adopt them.

Selection as durable fixer   Against this background of tempered optimism, let me tailor a few working notions to fit my modest and liberal selectionism and to help with the ensuing inquiry. There are two major views about how natural selection installs traits in a population. One views natural selection as sculptor of traits, the other as stabilizer and maintainer of traits. The *sculptor* sense is that over time natural selection shapes organisms in ways that increase their differential fitness by retaining the traits that have this effect and weeding out those that don't—I assume that there is agreement about the time span and the nature of the traits. Because there is trait variability in any population and for any trait, the sculpting process actually never ends. So where does one draw the line? Sculpting makes some sense for simple and specific traits, such as length of the neck. In a very few cases, such as melanism in British moths and finches' beaks, sculpting has been empirically proven. These are fairly simple traits, with unique functions and little interference from other functions. They constitute cases where one hopes to establish a systematic correlation between the pressures of selection and the trait selected—the selectionist's dream. It is such "ambitious Darwinian histories" that identify with precision the causes of evolutionary change and manage with systematic rigor to rule out alternative histories (Kitcher 1985, 68–72). Ambitious selectionism goes hand in hand with the sculpting sense of natural selection.

If the case for selectionism rested solely on such cases and such an ambitious reading of natural selection, selectionism would be close to hopeless. Ambitious selectionism cannot handle complex traits, such as language or interpretation. For reasons noted earlier in this section, the sculpting does not make much sense in these cases, nor do the fine-grained one-to-one correlations between selective pressures and resulting traits. In such complex cases the *stabilization and maintenance* role of natural selection is the only realistic option. By parity of reasoning, the stabilization and maintenance effect of natural selection can be parsed only in a liberal and coarse-grained manner. If the time span granted to the natural selection of a trait is long enough to cover both the sculpting process and the fixation and maintenance of its result in a population, then we have a distinction without much of a difference. Although my liberalism favors spread and maintenance, it allows for, but does not count on, sculpting. To mark this inclusiveness I call natural selection a *durable fixer*, for it is the evolutionary mechanism that fixes a trait in a population and keeps it there over time. What is important for selectionism is that one identifies the forces that did the selecting and ascertains that these forces have a history and that their work is done.

My liberalism on the history of selection resonates to the evolution of interpretation. Its basic rudiments, such as recognition of goals or of informational access, were selected ancestrally for clear and often unique functions, possibly even by sculpting. In this area correlations between selective pressures and traits selected could have been univocal and fine-grained. As complications pile up on the rudiments, the selectionist stance gradually shifts in the other direction, toward trait stabilization and maintenance and a coarse-grained identification of selective pressures. Let me amplify.

The forces   Talk of selective forces typically bears on physical pressures as well as interspecific or socially competitive interactions within a species that selected for a trait, be it a behavioral disposition (e.g., running fast), external trait (colored red), mechanism (heart), or competence (vision, interpretation). One is hard pressed to find formal definitions of the forces of selection. The one I found and like is Elliott Sober's. He notes that selection can be said to *act as a force or pressure* on organisms whenever it has the effect that there is some physical (phenotypic) property, expressed genetically, which causally affects the organisms' fitness (Sober 1984b, 201).[1] I take Sober's definition to accommodate both macroforces and microforces of selection. *Macroforces* are coarse-grained pressures on organisms to come up with classes of responses that would satisfy the conditions on natural selection without necessarily correlating with any particular function and therefore without sculpting any particular trait. By contrast, *microforces* are fine-grained selective pressures that correlate with specific functions, perhaps uniquely, and whose effects could have been sculpted. If the famed correlation between food high in the trees and the giraffe's long neck deserves a microstory, then in interpretation so does the correlation between basic goals and gaze recognition.

Except for such rudiments of interpretation, the selectionist stories I favor are macrostories of the coarse-grained sort. In the giraffe's case, a macrostory could go as follows. If, for some reason, food became bountiful at higher altitudes (the macroforce), then those individuals who genetically mutated means to get there (by growing long necks, or jumping up and down, or flying, or whatever it takes) and managed to spread these acquisitions in the population became adapted in a general sense. It is only when additional constraints are brought in (e.g., jumping up and down is not recommended on mountains) that one can use a macroforce story to pin down more specific adaptations. That is not going to happen often in the macrostories of interpretation. Although selectionism ultimately depends on systematic links between microforces of selection and specific traits, the absence of an account of such links need not be held against the coarse-grained version practiced here. Many species move by jet propulsion or flying, and biologists find coarse-grained evolutionary reasons why they do so, without attending to the details of how they implement their general locomotion strategies. My angle on interpretation is similar.

Adaptation, liberally　Neither the concept of evolution nor that of natural selection say anything direct about a trait being an adaptation.[2] Yet selectionism would be incomplete if not pointless without adaptation. Saying that selection increases the representation of a trait in a population states a historical truth but does not tell us the reason for it. Why would that happen? In virtue of what properties does selection do that? The notion of adaptation fills this explanatory gap. I need the notion for the specific job of linking selection to the design of interpretation. The features of adaptation needed for my story can be packaged as follows.

A trait is deemed an *adaptation* if historically there was selection for it, as a result of which the trait got fixed and maintained in a population in virtue of promoting increased fitness among its possessors. I link selection with adaptation without yet fingering the explanatory force of the latter concept. The linkage carries the liberalism of macroselection to that of adaptation. It is important to stress this implication because one would tend to associate adaptation with the ambitious Darwinism of microselection. I don't buy that association if I can help it.

I take selection to be a durable fixer, natural or cultural. An adapted trait, for which there was selection, could subsequently acquire another function that also confers some reproductive advantage. An adapted trait may even have a nonselected current utility that confers a reproductive advantage, just as a trait may have been an adaptation that is useless in new conditions.[3] I do not assume a fine-grained individuation of adaptations as objects of selection, and I am ready to accept macroadaptations as packages of traits, only some of which have a distinct and retrievable selection history.[4] And I do not construe adaptation as optimal. I do neither assume nor exclude the possibility that selection may increase the relative fitness of descendants relative to ancestors in some objective and measurable sense. Such an optimization view assumes that the selective forces remain relatively stable over long periods of time (for a careful and sobering discussion of optimization models, see Kitcher 1985, chapter 9). This is not likely for primates and their interpretive skills.

With this background in place and these caveats out of the way, I want to explain now in more detail why I need the notion of adaptation. Biologists view an adaptation as a trait selected for performing a *task* (Sober 1984a, 1993a; West-Eberhard 1992). The notion of a task is a crucial concept here because it acts as a bridge between the forces of selection and the resulting design. An analysis of tasks reveals the design of the job of a competence, for which it was selected as an adaptation. By *job design* (or profile) I mean not the nuts and bolts (the how, the architecture) of the competence but rather the things done with it (the what). My evolutionary argument goes from adaptation to tasks to job design, and pretty much stops there. Clearly, then, the notion of task-defining adaptation is the fulcrum of the entire enterprise.

Given the definitional relation between task and adaptation, one can redescribe the latter in terms of the former. For, strictly, it is the task execution that accomplishes goals that have effects on differential fitness and meet the test of natural selection. In taking this unorthodox line in evolutionary thinking (*que Dieu me protége!*), I am bringing natural selection and its forces specifically to bear explanatorily on the job design of a competence, not on its specific programs. That is also why my selectionism and adaptationism have to be liberal and modest. The programs executing the tasks and the functional mechanisms running the programs are less significant, for there could be various mechanisms with various programs doing the same job. It is the job parameters (goals and tasks) that signal an adaptation because they best reflect the nature of the responses to the selective pressures.

3   Interpretation as Adaptation

The next step is to show that interpretation can be, and is worthy of being, treated as an adaptation. Although it is beyond my intention and competence to provide a complete and fully documented and defended evolutionary analysis of interpretation, I will do my best to identify and occasionally analyze the evolutionary components of such an analysis, as they are known to me from the biological, ethological, and psychological literature. So here we go.

The visible hand of selection   If the selection of situated interpretation was natural, as I think it largely was, then it must satisfy the conditions of variation, inheritance, and differential fitness. The last condition is met only if adaptedness resulted from the selection for skills good at handling the goals and tasks of interpretation. The facts surveyed in section 1 anticipate that much. A closer look at the conditions confirms this anticipation.

According to the first condition, there must have been *genetic variation* among individuals with respect to their ability to interpret. Apes and humans vary in their innate abilities to interpret. Autistic persons lack in interpretive skills because of brain deficits that are often organic and hence genetic (Frith 1989). The genetic variations must also be *heritable* (the second condition). This is how genetic variations responsible for new interpretive skills pass from one generation to another. This is also how deficits in interpretation are passed on; autism may be transmitted genetically though not directly (few autistic persons have children, yet the probability of autism in identical twins or siblings is much above chance). Finally, heritable variations must impact the *differential fitness* of descendants (the third condition). Variations in interpretive prowess must have resulted in better fitness and, for that reason, must have spread in the population. That should not be difficult to imagine, at least when it comes to basics. Knowing what a rival is up to and how to outsmart him have clear survival and reproductive advantages, particularly in sexual competition. It must be shown, of course, that such differences in reproductive fitness originate in some interpretive skills being better adapted than others to the conditions that selected for them. And, as just noted, autistic people rarely marry and leave offspring, largely because of their interpretive deficits.

The invisible hand There are other conditions, some implicit in what was said so far, that also point to the selection of interpretation.[5] Early interpretation looks like an adaptation. Primate interpretation has enough functional complexity of design to satisfy Williams's (1966) expectation of an adaptation. It is hard to see how such complexity, with attending costs in neural circuitry and cognitive effort, could have maintained itself without being an adaptation. But there is more to the case for interpretation as an adaptation. Its core skills, narrowly specialized for distinct jobs, such as gaze recognition or goal identification, must have been ancestrally selected as survival-securing adaptations. The *form* of the adaptations also strengthens the case for the selection of interpretation. The specialized programs for basic interpretation are modular (Baron-Cohen 1995a; Baron-Cohen and Ring 1994; Leslie 1988, 1994). They show not only domain-specificity and informational autarchy but also clear phenotypic expression, automatized performance, and distinct breakdowns. These are reliable symptoms of modularity, with selection as a primary cause.

Another reason why interpretation is likely to have started as a family of adaptations is the fact (documented in the next section) that many of its basic skills had evolved primarily (though not exclusively) out of conflict, manipulation, and exploitation. These often are life-and-death or sex-sensitive situations, hence directly bearing on reproductive fitness. A related reason is that the selective forces unleashed by conflict and manipulation escalate into an arms race, which in general is a major installer of adaptations. I return to this matter later on.[6] Furthermore, in many cases, particularly in human ontogeny, interpretation shows a local and variable adjustment to surrounding conditions by letting specific stimuli activate one but not another of the available programs. As in other biological instances cited earlier, such environment-sensitive alternative policies are a sign of adaptation (variable fit) and cannot be easily explained on nonselectionist grounds, such as learning (Bowlby 1982, Tooby and Cosmides 1990a). Add to this the powerful evidence that the ontogeny of child interpretation follows a well-timed schedule of maturation. That could not happen without some genetic priming caused by selective forces originating in the child's environment and in the multifarious constraints on her physical and mental development. There are so many indications, then, that basic interpretive skills have a genetic expression that may have been durably fixed by selective forces.

Aping the apes?   The case for selection is also strengthened on the *phyletic* side, where interpretive skills show some similarities of broadly construed goals and tasks (though not necessarily of programs) in the species suspected of interpretation—the primates. These species live under largely similar social and political pressures not found in other species. For all we know, there was enough evolutionary time and genomic space separating primates from other species, and humans from great apes, to enable transitions and modifications to occur. (This is another important requirement of selection.) There are plenty of opportunities, then, for selection to do its work on interpretation. Yet the fact that interpretation is naturally selected in several species for some of the same reasons need not entail nor exclude that the adaptations evolved are similar, related, or overlapping. These matters must be settled empirically; judging from the state of the evidence and of the theoretical debates, it's not going to be easy.

The chimpanzees, deemed to be among the interpreting primates closest to humans, may lack the resources that evolved in the latter. The chimpanzees may be among our direct ancestors or may have evolved after humans separated from an earlier common line. If there were one or more missing links, they may have vanished, while the chimpanzees may have evolved since the split, whenever that occurred.[7] Yet the possibility of never finding the missing links should not be used against selectionism. This would be like judging the big bang theory in terms of not being able to witness the big-bang or its immediate aftermath. Missing links are an evidential nuisance but not an insurmountable handicap. Yet even if all the links were confirmed, it would still not be easy to ascertain continuities and discontinuities in interpretation.

Think of the ontogeny of human interpretation. It contains some breaks, like that around age three to four, when the enterprise becomes unsituated and children begin to see that others can misrepresent. Prior to this insight, young children may live in a different universe of interpretation than older children and adults (Povinelli 1993). Caution and an open mind are therefore needed in this comparative business. The general point, though, is that dramatic divides need not speak against selectionism or its use in ferreting out the design of interpretation. Selection can be choppy or smooth or in-between. It can still tell us lots about the designs it brought about, however different or similar they may be.

4 Reasons for Interpretation

Why interpret? Suppose that situated interpretation was selected naturally and its unsituated successor culturally. Why would interpretation be selected one way or another? Why interpret other organisms? What consequences does interpretation have, what benefits does it confer, to make it selectable? I am not asking about fitness-enhancing benefits, for that is what defines interpretation as adaptation. I am now asking a more basic question about what interpretation enables an organism *to do* so that fitness-enhancing benefits and adaptedness ensue.

Phrased very roughly, the answer is that interpretation evolves as a specialized form of cognition because goal-pursuing organisms, operating as independent and versatile agents, interact with other such agents in social patterns where the interaction among their goals ultimately affects the viability and fertility of the interactors. To be effective, the social interactions require that the goals and behaviors of one party be recognized and factored into the goal strategies of the other party. Interpretation will turn out to be that recognitional and factoring instrumentality. We have in this preliminary sketch three *generic* conditions for interpretation: (a) the teleological autonomy (agency) and versatility of the parties to interpretation, (b) the interpreter's recognition of the other's versatile agency, and (c) a situation of goal interaction that calls for factoring the subject's goals and behaviors into the interpreter's. Treating the subject as teleologically autonomous and versatile (i.e., capable of context-sensitive improvisation and planning) is an enduring propensity exercised in a variety of situations. The contrast intended here is with organisms that are primed or learn to interact along fixed patterns. The latter sort of interaction, typical of most of the animal world, need not select for interpretation.

Recognizing and factoring the subject's goals into the interpreter's means that the latter evolved specialized categorizations and inferences apt to guide her plans and response actions. It is such plans and actions that rely on, and thus call for, interpretation. To anticipate, this connection between plans, actions, and interpretation explains why the latter is not spectatorial contemplation of a subject's mind but a modality selected for *doing* something about a subject's goals and behaviors. In chapter 5, I translate this crucial idea into the concept of interpretive skills as *effective strategies* of involvement in the subject's affairs and into the notion of interpretation as *practical*, and I argue that breaks in the evolution of interpretation are likely to revolve around new and pervasive challenges to do something about the subject's goals and behaviors by means of effective strategies with practical import. This is quite different from construing interpretation as mere representation or understanding the subject's mind and behavior—a position taken by most students of interpretation.

The generic conditions on interpretation sketched above are centered on interpreter and subject (what sort of agents they are) and their typical relations (goal interference, goal recognition, and goal factoring). Although necessary for interpretation, these conditions do not suffice to select for interpretation. Many species made up of teleologically independent agents interfere with each other in the pursuit of their goals, yet very few interpret. The conditions by themselves do not have evolutionary potency. They do not yet select for anything but rather delineate the frame (i.e., an agency that takes account of and interferes with another) in which the forces of selection would act. It is only when we embed the frame in the *right environments* that we see evolutionary action. To select for interpretation, those environments must display a communal organization rife with education and enculturation, exchange of information, self-regulation, various collaborative activities, and also politics, lots and lots of it. The conditions to be discussed next describe such environments apt to spawn selective pressures for interpretation. We need *both* sets of conditions, generic and environmentally selective, to get interpretation going as an evolutionary phenomenon. I do not exclude further conditions, but I doubt that fewer will do.

Three basic reasons   I single out three major *evolutionary reasons* why one agent would find it worthwhile to interpret another. These are not the only reasons, but I think they are so basic, obvious, and apt to induce pressures for basic interpretive skills as to require little justification and elaboration. Interpretation is evolutionarily worthwhile, if not vital, whenever a subject is (a) a source or receiver of information about matters relevant to the interpreter, (b) a partner in a joint activity, or (c) an exploitable tool, a competitor to be handled in some advantageous way, or an enemy to be countered. I call these *epistemic, communal*, and *political* reasons for interpretation. They operate as macroforces of selection, so I take the liberty of talking generally of epistemic, communal, or political forces or—when the process itself is considered—of epistemic, communal, or political selection. The fine line among these reasons is hard to draw. In real primate life they operate in intricate and often hardly distinguishable patterns. Yet a working distinction is worth a try.

Communal selection   Communal activities secure the integrity, well being, and continuity of groups and ultimately of the participating individuals. Collective foraging, tool making and use, and cooperation against predation are among the key benefits that individuals derive from communality. In these joint activities the participants exchange information, get attuned to each other, and coordinate goals and behaviors. All of these call for interpretation. The communal life of higher primates is different from that of other species in ways that directly affect the selection for interpretation. Group living and joint activities are common to numerous species, including insects, and very common among vertebrates, from birds to mammals. If the pressures of group life and joint activities were enough to spawn interpretation, why are all species, except the primates, uninterpretive? Bees, for example, are essentially social (they can't manage otherwise), have common goals, share plenty of information, yet do not interpret each other. They are primed to access and share information by innate but noninterpretive algorithms. They read each other's behavior (the famous dancing) for information about the world (e.g., food location) pretty much the way our vision reads light patterns for data on distal objects.

What is missing in most nonprimate but communal species are the forms of social learning and social commerce that we find in primates. These forms display the teleological autonomy and the planning versatility of the participants, which are manifested in education or behavioral coordination and therefore are apt to be reflected in how the participants factor the goals and plans of others into their own. This is pressure for interpretation. Being merely communal and having group goals does not yet select for interpretation, as the case of bees suggests. In dancing their way to food, the bees are not autonomous and versatile goal systems but functional cogs in a collective goal-directed system. So they are not, and need not be, interpreters.[8] Yet communally exercised teleological autonomy and versatility are not enough for interpretation, either. Elephants and dolphins live in complex and hierarchical clans that recognize not only kin but ad hoc groups (in temporary alliances) as a basis of communal interaction (Cheney and Seyfarth 1990, 298–299). Still, neither elephants nor dolphins appear on the list of interpreting species drawn by ethologists and animal psychologists. Why not? Because it also takes a group whose frequent interindividual interactions among both kin and nonkin display those properties that, for lack of a better word, may be thought of as political. This is another major evolutionary reason for interpretation.

Political selection This form of selection is defined by competition, exploitation, deception, and tactical alliances against competitors. In this sense, there is politics in most social mammals (Povinelli, personal communication), and there is politics within the family, between parents and offspring and among siblings. The latter may shape and sharpen basic interpretive skills and provide early rehearsal for things to come. As with the other conditions on interpretation, politics by itself would not suffice to select for interpretation. My guess is that the potency of primate politics for interpretation resides in (a) the mix with other conditions, (b) the quality of the primate politics (specifically, the fast-changing power relations through very temporary alliances), and (c) the ability of primate politics to generate an arms race in interpretation. All this is worth explaining in some detail.

Let me begin with the family. Infants of most species, particularly mammals, are helpless in both obtaining food and defending themselves against predators and natural accidents. They need constant attention and help from, and hence proximity to, their parents. These are potent forces selecting for attachment (Bowlby 1982, Bremner 1988). At some point during infancy (the periodization being debated and revised in the literature), infants get political to maintain attachment and its benefits. Parents often are reluctant helpers. The offspring must compete with their parents' attention, energy, and willingness to share time and resources. Given their limitations, how do the offspring do it? By a sort of psychological warfare. This is how they induce more investment than the parents are naturally inclined to give. The offspring produce overt signs of satisfaction or distress when their needs are met or not, respectively. The parents are attuned to these signs and react accordingly. The offspring then become attuned to the parents' attuning and end up exploiting it. For example, the infant's not smiling at the parent may induce the latter to come up with more food or attention. The parent proceeds to learn how to read through that lovely deception, and an arms race is on (Trivers 1985, 155–159; also Dunn 1988, 1991).

Is this mixture of communal (group, family) dependence and domestic competition enough for interpretation? If it were, then (on Trivers's account at least) offspring-parent relations in many species, not just primates, should select for interpretation. Yet that did not happen. The arms race between offspring and parent could be explained by learning new dependencies between what the offspring does at a stage and how the parent responds at the next. This is not interpretation. Why not? Because only when the domestic competition between infants and parents forces the former to recognize the latter's goals and factor them into their goal policies can we say that domestic politics stimulates interpretation. Psychologists agree that at some point in their cognitive development, toddlers begin to treat others as distinct individuals with goals, such as the need for food or rest (Baron-Cohen 1993a; Wellman 1990). If attachment, needed for obtaining resources or providing defense, can be secured and maintained by knowing and manipulating the goals of others, then it could be a potent pressure for interpretation. Since the goals of others cannot always be recognized from their facial expressions, voices, or behavior and since it is often imperative to anticipate those goals, the infant interpreter comes under pressure to find further clues that deliver such an anticipation.

Outside the family, politics selects for interpretation when a small and stable group with numerous communal interactions allows for *nonkin* interaction that mixes competition with cooperation, manipulation with alliances, and allows power, status, and access to resources to flow not only from brute force and kinship relations but also from political games. There is political selection for interpretation when the group enjoys a (relatively) open politics with a (relatively) fair chance for high office. A comparative look at highly communal species like elephants, dolphins, and primates shows that the communal life of the latter, in contrast to those of the former two, are permeated with a lively and continuous politics of fast power shifts and tactical alliances among scheming individuals, and these features selected for interpretation.

The role of politics in the selection of interpretation is particularly visible in *reciprocal altruism*. This phenomenon is so important that it has been thought to have fueled not only interpretation but primate intelligence itself (Trivers 1985; see also Alexander 1990; Beer 1986; Cheney and Seyfarth 1990, chapter 2). Although found in nonprimates, reciprocal altruism seems to me to acquire political significance in primates because of what I take to be their unique style of politicking. Reciprocal altruism operates when one organism helps another not related to it on the assumption that the other will reciprocate, should the need arise. The altruist takes risks or spends energy, which would not make evolutionary sense unless there is a good chance that the effort will be reciprocated in the future. Reciprocal altruism is said to be selected only if the differential fitness of altruists exceeds that of nonaltruists. Outside kinship relations, however, the attraction of cheating is high. The containment of cheating requires two conditions relevant to interpretation. One is that the groups be small enough, so that the members know each other well, and stable enough, so that a repeated give and take of aid can occur and be monitored. These go together with individual recognition, keeping score, and forming tactical alliances, all of which deter cheating. Given the possibility and occasional advantage of cheating even in small groups, there will still be inducement for clever cheating, so the other condition is that the altruists evolve skills to read through the cheater's new tricks. These will be interpretive skills. Reciprocal altruism and containment of cheating may be indispensable for the well-being of social groups larger than family yet small and stable enough to sustain an open political life. The groups that require reciprocal altruism and open politics are those most likely to be made of interpreters. They are to be found among the primates.

Epistemic selection   Members of all species pursue their goals by monitoring what other organisms are up to. But gathering information would not suffice to select for interpretation. Epistemic selection for interpretation springs from a communal and political life in which gathering social information, imparting it, and using it to further one's goals bear ultimately on biological prosperity. This is the case in education, communication, cognitive and behavioral collaboration, division of labor and knowledge, and regulation of one's cognition and behavior by means of social information (e.g., what would others think and say). These are all contexts in which the traffic of social information affects the pursuit of one's goals, with eventual impact on viability and fertility. The point, then, is that the epistemic selection operates in environments *already* shaped by communal and political forces. Lots of noninterpreting species exchange information and monitor information access, but these epistemic feats are not channeled communally and politically, as they are in interpreting species. Social information gathering, exchange, and use under communal and political constraints require interpretation because these activities cannot be carried out without the participants' ability to read and accommodate each other's goals and other attributes (Rogoff 1990; Tomasello, Kruger, and Ratner 1993). This pattern of selection is confirmed by the observation (documented in chapter 4) that the more complex the forms of learning, enculturation, communication, or self-regulation, the stronger the epistemic pressures for interpretation.

In primate societies the young enjoy unusually long periods of education and enculturation in the ways of the group. In its key forms, such as imitation, instruction, and collaboration, social learning requires interpretation (Tomasello, Kruger, and Ratner 1993). The forms of such learning and the interpretive skills needed to carry them out remain life-long acquisitions constantly put to use. Primate societies and particularly its human version operate effectively only by division of labor and knowledge. This operation would also be impossible without interpretation.

Summing up   The moral is that it takes a mixture of conditions to select for interpretation. A few are generic but not apt to trigger evolutionary developments. One is the teleological autonomy and versatility of the agents involved. Another is the recognition of such autonomy and versatility. The third and most critical is factoring the subject's goals into the interpreter's goals and responses. The next three conditions add evolutionary potency. The epistemic condition reflects the requirements for information gathering and exchange in social learning, enculturation, and collaboration. The latter activities reflect forms of communal organization —another condition for interpretation. Finally, the political condition probably best explains the evolutionary dynamics, which takes the form of an arms race, responsible for the escalation of interpretation. It takes the evolutionary fine tuning of all these conditions, in the right mix and proportion, to yield interpretation. This essay has no ambition and no means to capture this evolutionary drama. Its brush is broad and mostly suggestive of the spirit, not the letter, of a selectionist story of interpretation.

5   A Competence Apart

What was said so far could still leave room for the skeptic to counter that interpretation may be the output of other skills with other functions, ancestrally selected for different reasons, or else the outcome of learning. Either option would be detrimental to selectionism, the second more than the first, and to the idea that interpretation is a distinct competence evolved for reasons of its own. This section aims to challenge these options and vindicate the evolutionary integrity and functional autonomy of interpretation.

By other means   Traditional but still influential is the view that primate intelligence evolved as a result of foraging or tool making. It is then possible that some of the programs that evolved to handle foraging or tool making became at some point available for interpretation. In that case, interpretation is deployed by a specialized competence that was selected for different reasons and over time was pirated to do another job in another domain. This possibility is tempered by two observations. One is that some researchers think that most primates were not (and are not) very much into either foraging or tool making, at least not as intensely as they were (and are) into other interpretation-based activities, such as education, playing, family life, and politics (Dunbar 1993, Humphrey 1988, de Waal 1989).[9] The other observation is that neither foraging nor tool making seem apt to trigger and sustain the arms race that is supposed to have pushed primate interpretation to higher complexity. Tools do not retaliate, but conspecifics do.

If anything, foraging and tool making might explain the primate *conative* intelligence in the form of very simple planning—say, thinking of x in order to do y and thus achieve z. Yet even if such planning were effective in foraging or tool making, by itself it need not stimulate interpretation. What must also be shown is that such planning is utilized in *social* interactions among primates, but this would bring communal life and politics back into the picture. Only so constrained might a simple planning ability have selected for a certain form of interpretation. This is plausible, as suggested in chapter 4, section 4. Even if a puritan work ethic is responsible for the planning conation, it takes riotous Machiavellian politics and other facets of communal life to make it relevant to interpretation.[10]

The learning option   The standard behaviorist challenge to any functionally dedicated and domain-specific cognitive competence is to reduce it to a general-purpose learning ability. The reduction starts from the benign truth that any organism adjusts its innate programs to an environment by learning, and also learns to recognize new dependencies observed between distinct events. Behaviorism goes further, however, and replaces innate programs with some vague propensity for learning. On this weakened basis, behaviorism then proposes that when it looks as though an organism interprets, what actually happens is that it learns dependencies that allow it to predict or exploit another organism's behavior. If so, then interpretation is not a functionally dedicated and domain-specific competence, it could not have been naturally selected as such, and hence there is nothing to learn about its domain and modus operandi from a selectionist analysis. What parades as interpretation is actually a family of applications of a general learning ability.

Before I sketch an answer to this objection, let me stress its impact. The literature on interpretation is rife with worries about interpretation being nothing but learning. The worries deepen in experimental contexts where apes and children inevitably learn new dependencies associated with new and unusual tasks and experimental setups. Thus it becomes imperative yet hard to distinguish between what they learn and what they know by evolutionary programming. A further methodological problem is raised by the deservedly respected principle of economy in explanation, which is often taken to favor behaviorism. Perhaps the best expression of the principle is Lloyd Morgan's law of parsimony: "In no case may we interpret an action as the outcome of a higher psychical faculty, if it can be interpreted as the outcome of one which stands lower in the psychological scale" (quoted from Gregory 1987, 496; see also Bennett 1991a; Dennett 1987, 246–248). As a ubiquitous ability, learning is always on hand to explain more economically. Or so it seems.

A first step in countering the learning option is to undermine the idea of an open-ended and general learning ability. There are good reasons to think that organisms do not have such an ability. They learn specific things and fail to learn so many others. What organisms learn is the tip of an iceberg made of prior instincts that delineate and constrain the domain and often the nature of the dependencies to be learned. Children learn Romanian or English but do not learn the universal principles of grammar. Even when they learn a specific language, children need to be exposed to definite types of input (phonetic) structures, or else no learning ensues. The universal grammar constrains and structures what children learn in a specific language yet allows enough freedom of adjustment to the peculiarities of a specific language. In cognition, generally, something must be in place in order for something new to be added. Learning builds on innate skills.

For any competence, this is the sort of picture that makes more sense of learning than the notion of a blank slate of vague dispositions ready to be imprinted whichever way. The notion of learning based on and constrained by prior structure squares with evolutionary data. Most adaptations represent finely tuned and often variable trade-offs between prior constraint and environmental adjustment. Furthermore, open-ended learning is not the sort of ability that natural selection likes or indeed knows how to install; most adaptations are very specialized (Piatelli-Palmarini 1989; Pinker and Bloom 1990; Cosmides and Tooby 1987, 1992). If there is learning in interpretation, as there must be, there is a good chance that it is domain-specific and constrained by prior programs that adjust their parameters to an environment and/or stage of development.

This conclusion pushes the behaviorist one step backward but not yet off the mat. His new objection may be that all an interpreter does is register environment-behavior dependencies. True but so incomplete. The 'all' is the spoiler. (Behaviorism often mistakes such dependencies for the whole story.) The dependencies may be what the interpreter registers but not what she *interprets*. The visual cortex registers myriads of dependencies among light patterns and retinal configurations, but these are only a part of the process that generates a visual image. Registration of dependencies is not yet vision and is not yet interpretation. The nature and scope of interpretation are fixed not by the dependencies registered sensorily but by the larger cognitive and behavioral frame in which they play a role.[11] For example, the goals of the subject are part of this larger frame. Goals are often assumed, hence are not explicitly indicated by those dependencies, and yet are vital to interpretation. Just as the visual cortex is programmed to read the correlations between light and retinal patterns for information on distal outlay, so the interpretive cortex is programmed to read the correlations between environmental and behavioral patterns for information on goals.

The arguments against open-ended learning and the sufficiency of registered dependencies are necessary but not sufficient to make the selectionist case for interpretation as an innate competence. The learning buff may retreat further but still flail his arms, grinning mischievously. He may be willing to minimize the role of learning but put forward the possibility that what looks like interpretation may actually be the accomplishment of *another* capability, such as sensorimotor coordination, with *its* domain-specific learning. This time the objection is not that interpretation has pirated another competence (an option noted earlier) but that the limited learning it relies on might draw on a competence that has nothing to do with interpretation. That competence would simply be adjusted to a new domain of facts. As noted in later chapters, the idea of interpretation as a competence apart is compatible with the exploitation of other resources for interpretive jobs. The point now is that the exploitation is not by random or occasional learning but is constrained by what interpretation was selected to do, by its functions. The question, then, is how to tell the difference, how to read the evidence for clues about which competence is at work, which is exploited, and under what constraints.

The answer, my dear Watson, is the pattern, always the pattern! From Holmes to Dennett, any pattern freak knows that a pattern requires a theory or stance to makes it visible and analyzable.[12] A first step would be to identify the structure of the environment of ancestral adaptedness whose instances, registered by the interpreter, trigger interpretation. Roughly, these are instances where the subject's goals and behaviors interfere with and must be accommodated by the goal policies of the interpreter. The accommodation in turn reveals further patterns, in the form of specific goals and tasks of interpretation. In chapter 5, section 3, I characterize the structure of the environments of ancestral adaptedness whose instances trigger interpretations, as goal settings for interpretation.

The anticipation I need now is that what sets interpretation apart as a competence selected for a distinct job is that it is an *adaptation* relative to a type of goal setting. It is in a goal setting that we find what interpretation is *good at*. When the interpreter finds herself in a situation that instantiates a goal setting, her cognition goes into an interpretive mode and works according to historically selected patterns. Here, for illustration, is one such pattern that indicates what is innately primed by selection and what is allowed as local adjustment. Suppose that an interpreter knows how to track goals by monitoring the subject's gaze and then improves her performance by learning also how to check bodily posture. This improvement would not be intelligible as interpretation if construed as mere summation of registrations of separate dependencies. Why not? Because as avenues to interpretation, gaze-world correlations are related to posture-world correlations *only if* the interpreter is already primed to check gaze for goals; then when she stumbles upon a new way of spotting goals and finds that it meshes with the older trick, her interpretation is enriched. What is learned makes sense as, that is, has the pattern of, interpretation because it fits a prior competence. Learning to interpret in a particular way depends on being able to interpret at all.

Chapter 3

Why Evolution Matters

The previous chapter made the case for the natural selection of interpretation as a competence apart, with a distinct evolutionary rationale and history. Suppose that this is true. Why would this truth matter, scientifically and philosophically? Many competencies—including vision, memory, and grammar—may have an evolutionary pedigree, yet it does not seem (so far, at least) that their scientific understanding owes anything substantive to evolutionary insights about their histories. Why would interpretation be different? Because interpretation *is* different. So argues section 1. Interpretation begins phylogenetically and ontogenetically as a modular competence, but not of the sort exemplified by vision or grammar. As a result, argues section 2, interpretation cannot be fathomed solely by the classical and evolution-indifferent top-down approach that works well in vision and grammar. This is why interpretation also needs a selectionist analysis for insights about its design. There is, however, another hurdle to face. If evolution matters in understanding the design of interpretation, then the question is how to go about chasing the right evolutionary insights and where. Scientific research on interpretation is divided, often irreconcilably, between field work and naturalist observation, on the one hand, and laboratory experiments, on the other hand. Most empirical data come from these two sources, yet the sources often diverge on how they judge the data and the conclusions they draw from them. So one must tread carefully and wisely. It turns out that this diplomatic exercise has methodological benefits. I sense pluses and minuses on each side and suggest, in section 3, a division of labor between nature and lab. Nature hints at the action of the forces of selection and thus provides clues as to what interpretation is up to. The lab tests tease out, compare, and measure the skills involved and provide operational detail to the evolutionary hypotheses about such skills. Section 4 addresses some worries that my analysis is bound to generate.

1   Interpretation Is Different

If interpretation is a competence apart, with its history of selection and
its ontogenetic schedule, it is likely to have an innate and modular
core. What sort of innateness and modularity? The answers to these
questions make all the difference to understanding the design of situated
interpretation.

Innate and modular   A survey of the evolutionary and developmental
data leaves little doubt that the basic interpretive skills of primates are
innate. Their universality in a species and the well-paced rhythm of their
development point to genetic priming; so does the presence of interpretive
deficits. I doubt that learning could account for such facts. Perhaps I have
not searched enough, but I have still to find a serious student of situated
interpretation that dismisses its innateness. The real question is how to
construe it.

There are two main options on offer, a "modularity nativism" and a
"starting-state nativism" (Meltzoff and Gopnik 1993). *Modularity nativism*, inspired by Fodor 1983, takes as evidence of modularity facts such
as these: interpretation is species-wide, innate, subject to well-sequenced
developmental patterns, operates spontaneously, unreflectively, fast, and
successfully, has its own domain, apparently draws on a proprietary
database not shared with other faculties, is immune to the influence of
other cognitive traits, such as talent, motivation, or intelligence, and, as
autism shows, is subject to organic deficits. Among child psychologists,
Leslie (1991, 1994), Baron-Cohen (1995b) and Baron-Cohen and Ring
(1994) have argued for the strong modularity of interpretation (see also
Fodor 1992). Baron-Cohen (1995b) and Baron-Cohen and Ring (1994)
have distinguished several modules, independent but cooperative: an
intentionality detector, an eye-direction detector, a shared-attention
module, and a theory-of-mind module (ToMM) that handles attitude
attributions. This is a strong modularity nativism because it allocates
the chief functions of interpretation to functionally distinct mechanisms
dedicated to interpretation, assumes fixed and unchanging architectural
constraints on the form taken by the interpretive competence, and connects these architectural constraints with definite brain locations with
specific functions.

Starting-state nativism allows for innate "starting states" of an unspe-
cified sort that could but need not be modular, and can be modified

by evidence and learning (Astington and Gopnik 1991, Gopnik 1993, Gopnik and Wellman 1994, Meltzoff and Gopnik 1993, Wellman 1990). This view takes seriously the notion that interpretation is close to being literally a *theory* of mind in three crucial respects: *organization* (theoretical constructs that animate lawlike generalizations going beyond the behavioral evidence and applying subsumptively to particular cases), *change* (revision of concepts and generalizations in the light of new evidence), and *utilization* (explaining and predicting facts in terms of general kinds and by derivation from the lawlike correlations among kinds).

Although modularity and starting-state nativists are often lumped together as theory-of-mind theorists and although the empirical evidence so far cannot always separate their views (Gopnik and Wellman 1994), a distinction must be maintained (Leslie and German 1995). For terminological clarity, the theory-of-mind view based on starting-state nativism will be abbreviated as 'ToM', and the strong modularity position as 'MoM' (from modules of minds). ToM and MoM can overlap. Modules might engage in theorylike interpretation (Baron-Cohen 1995b; Baron-Cohen and Ring 1994; Leslie 1994), and theorylike interpretations might have modular origins (Gopnik and Wellman 1994). Such a compromise, for example, emerges when ToM theorists allow interpretation to tap already existing modules. Meltzoff and Gopnik (1993) take the simplest recognition of attitudes to be projected from the interpreter's motor plans (more on this in chapter 5, section 5). Yet in the final analysis, one option is less plausible than the other. Here is why.

Rather MoM   It is ToM nativism that fares less well, at least on current evidence and theorizing about situated interpretation. (The balance seems to change in unsituated interpretation, but we are not yet there.) There are few if any grounds to think that early interpreters "theorize" as the ToM view says they do. These interpreters follow simple instructions for, say, how gaze or posture reveals goals or predicts behaviors. Their interpretive knowledge need not be explicitly represented, and its application to particular cases is not derivational, as the analogy with scientific theory would require. In general, simple interpreters do not appear to revise their knowledge in the face of recalcitrant evidence, as the ToM model predicts (but see Gopnik, Slaughter, and Meltzoff 1994 on young children). If there were revision based on evidence, as in learning, it should occur in different individuals at different times and in different formats because the exposure to evidence temporally varies from individual to individual and may yield different revisions, given the variability of evidence and of stored experience. Yet nothing of the sort seems to happen. Changes in interpretive know-how, when they occur, are paced roughly in the same order and follow a rather uniform schedule, resulting in similar skills. In this respect, apes and very young children do not follow the example of (say) Kepler's theory revising or replacing Brahe's. There are no biologically constrained necessities for the latter, yet there seems to be such a necessity in the evolution of early interpretation. The previous chapter suggested reasons for this fact and the reasons favor a MoM nativism over a ToM nativism.

Part of the problem with ToM nativism, as with behaviorism, is its vagueness about what is innate. Perhaps this is inevitable at the present stage of knowledge, but it does not help. To say, with Meltzoff and Gopnik (1993, 359), that what is innate is "the very idea of mentalism itself" or that "children are innately equipped with certain kinds of information about the nature of persons" is not very substantive. It would be hard to see how innate skills could be installed by evolution in programs other than modular ones and hard to see how evolution could install mere states or data structures in the way learning can (Bogdan 1994, chapter 9). The story is bound to be more complex: modular programs have access not only to a proprietary and unshared database containing templates and recognition patterns but also and essentially to instructions or rules. To accommodate this complexity, when I talk of competence or skills throughout this essay, I have in mind programs with rules or instructions *and* their databases.

Yet I do not think this is what ToM theorists have in mind. They seem to link the ability to interpret to an *explicit* database formed by learning and by exposure to examples. Vigorous defenders of ToM nativism, such as Gopnik and Wellman (1994, 285), cite data about variable conceptualization in young children as suggesting theory change forced by evidence. The data indicate, for example, that children surrounded by intense talk about mental states or by competitive siblings do better on false-belief tasks than those deprived of either. I find this relevant to the epistemic or political pressures on interpretation but admit that they may affect the fixation of open parameters of some innate programs rather than indicate conceptual revision. Most biological adaptations are like this. So what looks like evidence for theory change may in fact point to a selective pressure acting as a *trigger* for the maturation or deployment of an innate skill. If, within the window of opportunity, the trigger acts earlier, the skill gets to work earlier.

MoM nativism has evolutionary theorizing behind it. Natural selection prefers instinctive skills as domain-specific adaptations, and situated interpretation was naturally selected, so it is very likely modular. MoM nativism also seems to have neurological facts on its side. Baron-Cohen and Ring (1994) point to the facts that the (attitude-attribution) ToMM module and executive functions, such as planning and response inhibition, are neurally close and share impairments, as in autism. Other interpretive modules have a neural basis (specific brain cells have been found to respond to direction of gaze), and the interpretive deficits in autism are robustly associated with lesions in the orbitofrontal cortex and dysfunctions in the amygdala.

The higher modularity of interpretation If situated interpretation is modular, what *sort* of modularity is it? The question is critical because I think the classical view of modularity, summarized and analyzed so influentially by Fodor (1983), is about the sort of modules whose understanding might not always need evolutionary help. Yet I do not think these are the sort of modules that interpret. The analysis of those that do interpret would benefit from such help. To see why, here is a serviceable reminder about the flowchart of cognition.

The first stage of information processing in cognition consists of transducers that transform the proximal input (light or sound) into internal forms of energy (electrical, biochemical) specific to the nervous system. In so doing, the transducers encode the input in a format appropriate for the next functional stage, that of the computational programs. These programs produce data structures that are further categorized and utilized mentally and/or behaviorally. So one can distinguish *three* stages of cognitive processing in terms of their tasks: production, categorization, and utilization of data structures. In vision, for example, both transductive and computational programs are in production; they generate visual images. At the next stage, the categorization programs discriminate, recognize, classify, conceptualize. Finally, the utilization programs, both mental and behavioral, employ categorized data structures (images, conceptual structures) for various purposes. At each processing stage the programs *can* be modular, insofar as they satisfy the modularity criteria. In early vision, the transductive, computational, and categorization programs are modular, as are most behavioral routines. These are the territory of sensorimotor cognition, of which simple interpretation is a distinguished form. In contrast, the thinking programs in humans are widely assumed to be either nonmodular or partly modular or perhaps modular in totally new arrangements, although the debate on these matters is just heating up.

With this background to help, let us return to interpretation. My reading of the data suggests that interpretation is *not* production. It does not seem to work like vision or grammar, nor does it seem to have a production role or rationale. Identifying gaze presupposes vision and categorizes the outputs of vision in a certain format. In general, one interprets *after* seeing or hearing or smelling something and even *after* categorizing that thing as (say) physical object in motion or fellow conspecific or predator. Interpretation thus *re*categorizes the relation to a conspecific or predator in its domain-specific terms (goals, attributes, and so on). Interpretation, then, is not a generator but rather a (re)categorizer and utilizer of data structures.

By saying that interpretation is a recategorizer I mean that it is a *domain-specific* or *dedicated* categorizer. This nuance is critical to my argument that understanding the design of interpretation benefits from evolutionary guidance. When an interpreter sees a subject, the first categorizations of the latter as having a shape, being in motion, being a physical object, and the like, are done by the visual and naive-physics modules. The subject classified as conspecific or predator may be the output of a naive-biology module. Nothing interpretational so far. All these categorizations originate in domain-specific and functionally dedicated skills but are not interpretive. The tasks of some such categorizing skills, I suggest below, may be fathomed without evolutionary help (visual categorization and perhaps the naively physical are good candidates). With others we have no such luck, and interpretation is one such task.

The interpretive skills that kick in earliest in the functional pipeline may look productive but need not be. Baron-Cohen and Ring characterize the intentionality or basic agency detector as a perceptual mechanism "that interprets self-propelling stimuli in terms of ... goal or desire. That is, it reads directional stimuli as volitional. In this system, 'goal' is defined as the target of an action, and 'desire' is defined as a movement towards or away from target" (1994, 185). They also note that their notion of intentionality detector is similar to one proposed by Premack (1990) as built into the visual system, and add that the detector generates representations of behavior. The same point is made about another functionally early interpretive module, the eye-direction detector. Leslie talks of an early theory-of-body module as mapping visual "descriptions that make explicit the geometry of objects contained in a scene, their arrangement and their motions" into "the mechanical properties of the scenario. In doing this [the module] interprets the motions, arrangements and geometry of the objects in terms of the sources and fates—the dynamics —of *force*" (1994, 128).

Perceptual mechanism, reading stimuli, hardwired in the visual system, mapping visual descriptions—all these concepts may suggest that functionally early interpretive skills are in the production business, as early vision is. That would be a mistake. Early vision is not entire vision and contains not the only modules that read stimuli, map descriptions, and are hardwired. There is also high-level vision, and its main business is categorization (Marr 1982, Hildreth and Ullman 1989). As I construe them, the analyses of Baron-Cohen and Ring (1994) and Leslie (1994) regard the functionally early interpretive modules as relying on early vision for their inputs. (Leslie is quite explicit on this.) Premack's suggestion (1990, Premack and Dasser 1991) that the perception of agency is hardwired as part of vision can only mean hardwired as part of the *high-level* vision involved in *pattern* recognition. In my story, this is categorization, not production. So I conclude that if interpretation is instinctive or modular, it is at processing levels *higher* than production, that is, categorization and utilization.

Categorization modularity   Is this a coherent hypothesis? Not if one assimilates categorization and utilization to thinking and then takes the line—Fodor's (1983)—that thinking is not modular.[1] Yet this is not the only choice, and it is not mine. The option I favor combines three ideas. One is that categorization and utilization *could* be modular. This is a hypothesis ably defended by Sperber (1994). The second idea is that categorization and utilization cover *more* than thinking. The third is that interpretation belongs to the *unthinking* territory of categorization and utilization, at least in its situated forms. Let me amplify.

A good deal of categorization could be modular on grounds of innateness. There are innate categories ranging from sensory discrimination (say, among colors), pattern recognition (of faces), domain-specific object recognition (agent, predator), specialized sensorimotor routines (flight from serpents) to sundry concepts. These categories classify the data structures generated at the production stage in forms that allow further utilization, typically behavioral. Organisms are born with such categorization skills, and even those learned or compiled can operate like modules. Such skills are domain-specific (take in only definite types of input), informationally autarchic (process the input relative solely to their specialized and isolated knowledge bases), and cognitively impenetrable (process the data irrespective of what other faculties do)—to list the most critical criteria of modularity. Since the inputs to categorization modules originates in production, we have a first layer of postproduction modules that categorize but not conceptually.

I mention this *preconceptual* option because I think it applies to situated interpretation, as I argue in chapter 5. Its modules follow preset instructions, not explicit and flexible rules, and are directly tied to behavior. Concepts, in contrast, are a late phylogenetic acquisition underlying thinking, are not necessarily tied to behavior, and can be utilized mentally, as in planning or imagining.[2] Simple species categorize nonconceptually relative to one or more types of input. An interpretive module, such as the intentionality detector, can categorize a goal or desire relative to a wide range of inputs, such as touch or sound structure or visual images (Baron-Cohen and Ring 1994). Categorization domains need not match perceptual domains to remain specific, which is a modularity requirement (Sperber 1994). Domain-specificity is a generous concept. Information from several perceptual domains, and only from them, can be categorized and integrated along definite dimensions and relative to an unshared database, and the subsystem can still be domain-specific.

Concepts, by the way, can also be modular (Sperber 1994), and that may be true of basic interpretive concepts, such as belief and intention, which seem uniquely human and emerge later in childhood according to a rather tight ontogenetic schedule. That might mean that the arm of natural selection reaches even into unsituated interpretation. In addition, it appears that apes and very young children are prone to feed their categorizations of sensory inputs directly into behavior, without much, if any, mental ratiocination. That makes situated interpretation an instinctive enterprise, in which case its modularity would cover not only categorization but also utilization.

Suppose that all this makes sense and is corroborated empirically. Does the theory of interpretation need to turn to evolution to figure out the goals and tasks of interpretive modules? Or could it go the good old verified way of classical cognitive science and, as in the case of vision or grammar, do well without evolution? These are the questions to be taken up next.

2 Beyond Classicism

Antievolutionism   No, the study of cognitive modules need not appeal to evolution, says a position that has been singularly effective in deciphering modular cognition; so effective in fact that it has been, for several decades now, the *classical* position in cognitive science. My loyalties are divided. I like classicism in general. I also like it in cognitive science for having whipped and shaped the field into a very exciting enterprise, where philosophers often work as equal partners (but less well paid). What I like less is its lapses into programmatic antievolutionism; in matters of interpretation I find these lapses counterproductive.

The argument of the antievolutionist classicist might go as follows: It is good to know that interpretation may have evolved as a modular competence. But it does not follow that appeal to evolution is needed to figure out its design. Evolutionary data are often elusive or inconclusive, and evolutionary hypotheses almost always in danger of looking ad hoc, speculative, and too individualized, as if manufactured to fit the specific facts under consideration. So, avoiding appeal to evolution would be a plus, not a minus. More to the point, the most spectacular successes in cognitive science come precisely from theories of modular competencies, such as vision and grammar, which have *not* appealed to evolution and indeed have rejected evolution as explanatory. Why would interpretation be different?

Because, I answer, evolution makes a difference to the understanding of interpretation in ways in which it does not, or does not to the same extent, for other modular competencies, particularly those of the production sort. Let me explain why.

The ICM method   Classicism in cognitive science starts from the insight that to understand how an information-processing mechanism works, one must first understand the programs it runs, and thus the competence they define, and to understand a program, one must antecedently identify the information tasks the program executes and the problems encountered and solved in the execution. The analysis thus proceeds top-down: from Information tasks to Competence programs executing the tasks to the functional Mechanisms that run the programs. For brevity, I call this the *ICM method.* In recent decades, thanks to the very influential work of Noam Chomsky on language, David Marr on vision, and Allen Newell on artificial intelligence (to cite the pioneers), the ICM method has been clearly and forcefully articulated and applied successfully to a variety of cognitive competencies. This is how the ICM method has become the classical way of doing cognitive science (Chomsky 1975, 1980; Marr 1982; Newell 1982; for a foundational synthesis, see Pylyshyn 1984; for a defense of the ICM method relevant to evolution and cognition, see Dennett 1978a, 1987, 1991a; also Bogdan 1994).

Being a form of cognition, interpretation could be treated in the same classical ICM way as vision or grammar. One wishes things were so simple, but I fear they aren't. Interpretation is not like vision or grammar, for good evolutionary reasons, which is why its goals and tasks (the starting points of the ICM approach) are not as *transparent* as they are in vision or grammar, and why I think help from evolution is needed. To sharpen the contrast, I need to clarify the sense in which the goals and tasks of vision or grammar may (or appear to) be transparent without evolutionary light.

Production modularity: transparent without evolution   Vision and grammar were said to be production modules. The classicist position is that theories of modular production do not need help from evolution. Several arguments could be invoked on behalf of this position. One is *historical*. It is historically true that revolutionary insights into the design of vision and grammar were not fueled or backed by evolutionary data. Consider grammar. The much debated function of a human language— communication versus thought calculation and expression—did not affect Chomsky's theory of grammar. This may suggest the irrelevance of evolution to understanding grammar. And so may the fact that one can accept Chomsky's theory without taking a position on the function of language. This is not to deny that evolution may have shaped grammar. It did, according to Pinker and Bloom (1990). The point, rather, is that, whatever the role of evolution, it was not needed for *understanding* the design of grammar.

That, opines the classicist, cannot be fortuitous. *Systematic* arguments can explain why. To simplify, vision and grammar are production modules that run programs whose inputs are sensory stimuli and whose outputs are semantic representations. Vision takes light input and delivers representations of distal items; grammar takes phonetic or graphic input and delivers representations of meaning. So construed, the input-output relations are apt to reveal fairly directly the *goal* of processing, which is to map the input into what the output represents. The goal in turn constrains, and thus hints at, the nature of the tasks, which is to extract from the input, incrementally, cumulatively, and combinatorially, what is needed for the output. One does not need evolution to see this.

In a further and ironic twist, the antievolutionist classicist can turn the tables on the evolutionist and exploit to his benefit an argument usually made on behalf of evolutionism. I am thinking of the *reverse engineering* argument. Here is an intuitive version of the argument. Imagine that you find an artifact you know nothing about; assuming it has a function, you take it apart and analyze its architecture in terms of the problems solved and the constraints respected in carrying out its function. (Replace 'artifact' with 'cognitive organ' and 'taking apart' with 'dissecting theoretically' and you have the classical top-down method described earlier.) So far, so classical. Now "biologize" the artifact, turning it into a real organ, think of its function in terms of some biological utility shaped by natural selection, and think of the latter as a clever natural engineer. The classicist's spin on the argument would be that the rational top-down analysis of the organ's architecture would approximate the work of natural selection, under some utility maximization strictures. It's classicism that helps evolutionism, not the other way around!

Think now of cognition. What this argument purports to show is that once the inputs and outputs of production are fixed historically in the form now known (light to images and sound to meaning representations, respectively), a classical theory of production enables one to guess rationally that natural selection must have implemented the theory, more or less, if vision or grammar were to be possible at all and efficient. Put this way, when evolution begets a cognitive competence, its design is *first* intelligible to a classical ICM analysis, and through it, so is the work of natural selection. The classical analysis thus comes out on top and the selectionist one ends up in a subordinate role.[3] Funny reversal.

A reverse-engineering analysis of the sort just contemplated works best on production modules, the cognitive organs best understood by the classical ICM method (Bogdan 1994, 188–192). Indeed, the work of Pinker and Bloom (1990) goes *from* the classical insights into the design of grammar *to* the estimate that natural selection must have caused it. Following some of Dawkins's hints (1986, chapter 2), one might try to do the same with Marr's classical ICM analysis of vision. The irony in all this, of course, is that the reverse-engineering analysis is anathema to some of the pioneers, like Chomsky, whose work (on this story) made it possible in the first place.

Finally, one could invoke a sort of *reach-of-selection* argument on behalf of classicism. According to it, natural selection works on programs in virtue of their behavioral effects. In cognition those effects are closer to categorization and utilization than production.[4] As long as categorization and utilization do an adaptive job, it does not much matter how production works and why it works one way rather than another. Production could be a total evolutionary fluke, and thus be outside the reach of natural selection. If it enables categorization to map the world in ways beneficial to behavior, all is fine. This is why grammar and possibly vision may have little to do with the long-range and incremental work of natural selection.

Note that the different antievolutionist arguments on behalf of classicism have something in common: they do not have much bite outside production. But interpretation is categorization, not production, and hence is rather immune to this line of thought. Being categorization, interpretation could not guide behavior as directly as it does, particularly in its situated versions, without undergoing the constant scrutiny of natural selection. The classicist would have to agree to that. The selectionist game is still on.

A prescientific stage?   Yet there is still a nagging doubt. What if the time of an ICM analysis of interpretation has not come yet. After all, the design of vision or grammar was not always transparent to scientific analysis; it became so when theorists like Chomsky or Marr and their colleagues and students came along and did some of the things noted earlier. Aren't we witnessing the same prescientific stage in understanding interpretation and awaiting similar breakthroughs of the ICM sort?

True, until recently the psychological study of interpretation as a cognitive competence was in a prescientific phase. Yet the last 20 years or so have seen rapid progress, particularly in animal and child psychology. That may presage a theoretical breakthrough. Would this breakthrough, if and when it comes, follow the sheer accumulation of empirical results? Or a flash of rational insight? Or both? Hard to tell, but do not bet on these. I doubt that empirical data or armchair insight or both would suffice to identify the goals and tasks of interpretation, and without goals and tasks, there is no ICM method to apply and no constraints to organize the empirical data. The design of interpretation is not that transparent. Some of the reasons were noted earlier. Another hint that things are not that easy comes from recent history. Mighty efforts notwith-

standing, the classical ICM method has been visibly less successful outside
the production stage of cognition. It may be because categorization and
utilization are not modular, as Fodor (1983) surmises. I think the failure
is not so much due to the putative (but still unproven) unmodularity of
categorization and utilization as to the fact that neither displays a *production* modularity. The latter, so far, is the only modularity intelligible to
the classical ICM method (Bogdan 1994, 182–189, 196–208).[5]

Summing up I have argued so far that in the flowchart of cognition,
interpretation is categorization and utilization, not production. The classical ICM analysis works best on production, much less so on categorization and utilization. As categorization and behavioral utilization,
situated interpretation is under the direct watch of natural selection,
which fact in turn is probably expressed in its modular organization. All
these considerations suggest bringing evolutionary considerations aboard.
But how? The evolutionary hints must be backed by the empirical data
provided by psychological research, for it is only such data that indicate
what animal and human interpreters do and do not do, and also what
they can and cannot do by way of interpretation. The question is which
sorts of data best reveal these facts and therefore best map evolutionary
insights into concrete analyses of the design of interpretation. This turns
out to be a delicate question, yet one that, if carefully handled, can yield
further clues to the sort of competence interpretation is likely to be. Hence
the next topic.

3 Nature versus Lab

Your place or mine? Nature versus lab is the methodological question of
where and how to study interpretation best. At the metaevolutionary
level, adopted here, the question is which sort of research best picks out
the design of interpretation and gives kibitzers like me a good reading of
the evolutionary patterns responsible for the design. The discussion of this
question goes beyond methodology and brings out other important issues
about interpretation.

The nature-versus-lab question finds its sharpest expression in the
debate on whether primate intelligence can best be studied from field
observations and anecdotes (naturalistically) or from carefully and
ingeniously crafted experiments (artificially). Let me encapsulate the spirit
of this debate in the form of a dilemma. On the one hand, primates (apes

and children in particular) are interpreters at their best in their natural habitats, but there they can be investigated with little precision. On the other hand, in the lab, where careful controls and generalizable tests can be implemented, primates can be better investigated but not necessarily in evolutionarily revealing contexts. In one case scientists know what to study but cannot study it well; in the other they study it well but are less likely to get its nature right. I will argue that this is a dilemma only if we opt for methodological imperialism, that is, one single method for one single object of inquiry. Otherwise, the dilemma dissolves or at least becomes less threatening. I first elaborate on the first but unwanted version of the dilemma, where nature competes head on with the lab, before seeing a way out.

Different results   Experiment and natural observation can yield significantly different results about interpretive skills. Let us consider chimpanzees first. Gallup (1970) has shown in the lab that chimpanzees can recognize themselves in a mirror; no such result was confirmed in the wild. It has also been claimed that "in the case of chimpanzees, advanced cognition would appear to be largely a laboratory phenomenon. For only the chimpanzee who has been specially trained—exposed to the culture of a species more evolved than itself—shows analogical reasoning. Here is an interesting irony. Most of the deceit described in anecdotal reports from the fields is probably based on simple learning, whereas advanced cognition, such as analogical reasoning, is confined to the laboratory" (Premack 1988, 171–172; also Povinelli and Eddy 1996). Similarly, an evolutionist pioneer of animal interpretation notes that "it has been repeatedly demonstrated in the artificial situations of the psychological laboratory that anthropoid apes possess impressive powers of creative reasoning, yet these feats of intelligence seem simply to not have any parallels in the behavior of the same animals in their natural environment" (Humphrey 1988, 17).

Aside from the fact that neither analogical nor creative reasoning may have much to do with interpretation and (at least according to Humphrey) may actually have piggybacked on interpretive skills, we have further confirmation that the lab may be tapping into skills that are not exhibited in nature, or not exhibited in the same ways, or (perhaps less plausibly) even absent in nature. This tapping strategy may be queried for hints as to how culture may have grafted new utilizations onto old skills, from reading and writing to new interpretation gambits. For it is possible that what happens to individual chimps in the lab is an ephemeral and low-grade initiation into the culture of artificial symbols and symbolic communication (as in Kanzi's case, described in Savage-Rumbaugh and Lewin 1994). The difference is that human culture acts constantly and universally as a new form of selection of skills, whereas in the lab it is just an occasional and individual shaper of new skills.

The argument could also go in the direction that favors nature over lab. Nature taps into (since it has selected for) skills that are not fully employed in the lab, if at all. Tool making and use is one example. Chimps employ tools to do all sorts of things (termite fishing, ant dipping, nut cracking, leaf clipping, etc.) that they are less inclined to do in captivity. Against the views quoted previously, one naturalist researcher writes, "The wild chimpanzees live in a permanent training condition where survival and reproductive success are the teachers and I would expect them to be more intelligent than their captive counterparts" (Boesch 1993, 514). Related discrepancies were found in the case of children as well. Experiments place the onset of deception at the age of five, whereas natural observation places it much earlier (Dunn 1991, Sodian and Frith 1993). Lab tests place the onset of the recognition of false belief around three to four, whereas naturalist observation finds it earlier (Chandler and Hala 1994, Mitchell 1994, Sodian and Frith 1993). There are other examples in both groups, but I trust the polemical pattern is clear. If lab and nature were on a collision course, competing as the sole access to interpretation, then such discrepancies of results and the limits inherent in each approach would bode ill for the entire enterprise. But I do not think this is the only reading of the case.

Division of labor   I think the relation between experiment and naturalist observation exemplifies—in part, but this is the part that counts here—the distinction between the proximate study of a competence and its evolutionary explanation. If we so look at the matter, we see that experiment and natural observation can be complementary. Experiment is in principle better at the proximate identification and analysis of a competence and its modus operandi; natural observation in principle better at feeding into an ultimate explanation data that sample the environment of ancestral selection. In so doing, natural observation can help the evolutionist and the experimenter identify critical features of the design of interpretation less visible in the lab. The two strategies clash, however, when they compete for the proximate identification of skills and the proximate explanation of their work.

In saying that naturalist observation is good at providing the input to evolutionary explanations, I am not suggesting that field workers necessarily or often engage in evolutionary reconstructions. Most don't.[6] The point, rather, is that their data could identify the sorts of *settings* where interpretation occurs naturally as instances of the environments of ancestral selection. From such data the evolutionary psychologist can guess the selective pressures that operated ancestrally and/or continue to do so, and thus begin to answer the why questions: why that competence, why at that age, why in that form, and so on. The why questions, however, are not the only questions that naturalist research can help answer. There are other questions that pertain either directly to the design of interpretation or indirectly but importantly to (what we may call) the *enabling* conditions of interpretation. Let me work my way toward these questions by comparing more closely the virtues and handicaps of lab research. For it is the handicaps that reveal evolutionary clues to the design of interpretation.

Lab virtues   Laboratory tests are better than naturalist data gathering at spotting and analyzing a skill, for two reasons. One is the *generalization test*. Only in the lab can one challenge an ape or child with a task never encountered in real life, or never encountered in that form or in familiar contexts, and thus test the power and scope of a skill. This is how one finds out whether the skill generalizes to a variety of performances, and is therefore a genuine capability, or is merely a result of habituation. Without human pressure, the chimpanzee or child might not have bothered to use her skills to handle new tasks, thus frustrating the generalization test.

The other reason is *control*. Tests can be crafted to filter out unwanted interferences. Natural observations and even naturally implemented experiments are not reliably good at identifying, let alone analyzing, skills because they cannot filter out such noise very effectively.[7] The irony is that there is noise in the lab as well, inevitably self-inflicted, because of the the interaction between experimenters and subjects. The methodological worry here is whether the subjects display the genuine interpretation under test or an (unanticipated) interpretation meant to figure out what the experimenter wants or, finally, simply learn how to please the experimenter and get the goodies. This is why experiments get ever more sophisticated in order to filter out not only environmental noises but also those created by the experimental setup. (Who knows, if we give this laboratory game enough evolutionary time, and funding, to play itself out, it may trigger its own arms race and take primate and child intelligence on a possibly new path.)

Lab handicaps What is it that labs do not do, or do not do very well? Saying that they rarely if ever exemplify the natural contexts of interpretation is obvious but not very illuminating. We want to know why that exemplification is important to a theory of interpretation. We know that the laboratory contexts are not always likely to offer instances of the selective pressures manifested in the environments of ancestral adaptedness. In the lab, and perhaps even in captivity in general, apes do not always enjoy the rich and fast changing patterns of communal, sexual, political, and other interactions found in the wild. The question is whether we are missing something else, besides the selective pressures themselves and their current manifestations, something important to a theory of interpretation. I think we are.

To begin with, missed may be the *enabling conditions* of the exercise of interpretive skills. Any skill is exercised when certain conditions are right. If they are not, the exercise is obstructed or else is simplified or crippled. The absence of a natural setting is apt to create either opportunity. Here are some examples. It has been speculated that chimps might interpret at a higher level of sophistication when confronted with conspecifics in natural interactions but either lower their standards when dealing with humans (Povinelli and Eddy 1996) or else resort to ad hoc solutions, such as learning or attempting to please. The very training for a test may generate interesting habits parading as deep-seated skills (Dennett 1978b). In either of these cases the proper (selected) competence is not really tested. It may even be, as Cheney and Seyfarth (1992) fear, that having human trainers as part of the experiments is not very helpful, because apes do not respond naturally and therefore do not activate or fully use skills selected for conspecific interaction.[8]

The child picture is not that different. Autistic children and normal three-year-olds, for example, are known to fail to attribute false beliefs to others. The consensus is that they lack the requisite aptitude. Some critics argue, however, that the laboratory task of "attributing beliefs to story figures (or even to real people) may in itself be too computationally complex or not motivating enough for very young children. These children may nevertheless display a genuine understanding of belief when given an opportunity to *manipulate* other persons' beliefs in highly motivating contexts" (Sodian and Frith 1993, 159).[9] This observation ties in with another hinting that belief attribution is exercised earlier if there are pressures to that effect, such as sibling rivalry (Perner, Ruffman, and Leekam 1994). Another diagnosis, equally critical of the lab setup, is that children fail the false-belief test because they do not "grasp the causal texture of the false belief narrative" (Lewis 1994, 462). Lewis's idea, congenial to the argument of chapter 7, is that three-year-olds are already protoreconstructors; he cites data suggesting that boosting the narrative comprehension of children and facilitating their reconstruction of the false-belief stories yield superior results on the test. If these diagnoses are on the right track, the differences noted in the false-belief tests may concern enabling conditions rather than having or not having the belief-attribution skill. The distinction is crucial. Failure to pay heed to enabling conditions may prevent the lab work from doing what it is supposed to do best, which is to identify a competence and analyze its modus operandi. So let us take a closer look at enabling conditions. They are essential for understanding the design of interpretation.

Enabling conditions   One notable enabling condition, well known in cognitive science, is the *window of opportunity*. Young children not exposed to language in the early years will not develop grammar. It is conceivable that apes isolated in captivity may miss the window of opportunity, or the part of it, required for developing interpretive skills. This possibility, no matter how remote, ought to be kept in mind. *Clues* are also critical as ongoing triggers of interpretation skills. The interpreter must be attuned to certain sensory patterns involving subject (his gaze, bodily posture, demeanor), other individuals, and states of the world. Such clues signal that a setting for interpretation is present, thus putting the interpreter's cognition in the appropriate functional mode. It is conceivable that occasionally such clues are missing in the lab tests. Whatever their specificity, the natural settings also prompt *active involvement*, a critical enabling condition that points to a major thesis of this essay, namely, the practicality of interpretation. Interpretation makes sense for primates and is motivated in contexts where the interpreter is a *protagonist*—an agent, a victim, an accomplice (I am quoting Bruner [1990, 85], who refers to the naturalist work of Dunn, especially 1988). Being a protagonist not only motivates interpretation and activates other enabling conditions; as Bruner (1990) also notes, it *frames* interpretation around a protagonist or agent, an action, its object and repercussions. This almost literally solves the "frame problem" for interpretation by structuring its domain in standard patterns. Lab tests may often fail to provide such frames, thus missing an indispensable enabling condition.[10]

There are also the enabling conditions of motivation and cost-benefit assessments, which in turn connect with those of cognitive effort and relevance. Interpretation occurs when one needs to factor into one's goal policies the goals of others. Once we bring the *interpreter's goals* into the picture, as I argue we should, then her *motivation* must also be brought in. Motivation marks the presence and strength of a goal policy, because it is the latter that initiates a behavioral response. This response is calibrated by a *cost-benefit analysis* that compares effort, from energy expenditure to cognitive travail, to what must be accomplished as a goal. Against these enabling conditions, *relevance* measures the worth of integrating new information (including what a conspecific or the experimenter proposes) into that already available to the interpreter (Sperber and Wilson 1986, chapter 1, section 9).

Like other forms of cognition, interpretation depends on such enabling conditions and probably others. Apes and children may find a context not motivating and relevant enough to warrant the cognitive effort needed for interpretation. False-belief attribution seems to be a candidate for high motivation and massive cognitive effort, and the same may be true even of simpler tasks, such as knowledge assessments.[11] If the motivational and relevance values of a laboratory task are small, the processing costs high, and the benefits (even in the form of sweet goodies) not terrific and not commensurate with the efforts, then apes and children may fail to perform as expected, despite having the ability to do so.[12] In short, the impact of enabling conditions must be taken into account in the debate between lab and nature.

Let me now go one step further and put the story of enabling conditions in a larger perspective. A competence is an adaptation. An adaptation consists in adjusting a program to enduring and occurrent conditions of an environment. This, we noted, is how the universal grammar adjusts to a Chinese or Portuguese environment, or how some fish species are genetically instructed to turn female if the water is warm, male if cold, or how plants alternate growth policies relative to weather. We also noted that this adjustment policy is itself the outcome of selection, as part of an adaptation package. Enabling conditions are ingredients in this adjustment policy and selected as part of the package. Thus the window of opportunity encompasses the period when the core program adjusts its parameters to enduring traits of an environment; sensitivity to clues is a contextual adjustment needed to activate the program; motivation and cost-benefit calculation are also contextual adjustments that indicate degrees of program activation; and so on. The lab tests may fail to instantiate such enabling conditions by failing to capture key facets of the environment of adaptedness.[13] The failure may be even more serious and affect the nature of what is studied.

It is also conceivable that some tests considerably weaken the assumed conditions under which the tested programs have evolved and which are needed for proper operation. Here is an example that comes to mind. In a series of fascinating experiments, Povinelli and Eddy (1996) tested chimpanzees for attentional focus of gaze. In one experiment eye holes were cut inside circular cardboard screens with which the experimenters cover their faces; only their eyes were visible, open or closed. Povinelli and Eddy conclude that the chimpanzees are unable to track attentional gaze with specific targets; they also conclude that the chimpanzees only learn certain rules about faces and eyes. Both conclusions seem plausible. But for the sake of the argument made in this section, let me gesture at another reading. A question that may arise is whether the chimp's gaze-monitoring programs operate on the assumption that an entire or partial face is visible. The cardboard test may violate a face-eye assumption, so that the subjects improvise a solution by learning—the experimenters' conclusion—given other features of the experiment (e.g., rewards). This does not necessarily show lack of a skill; it may show that not all conditions are in place for the skill to be exercised. I am not denying that other tests are designed to check these possibilities. I am simply calling attention to the role of enabling conditions as triggers of interpretation. But, as I say, I speculate. Now I must also anticipate.

Summing up: reflective equilibrium   In the next two parts of this essay I will argue that interpretation was selected as a practice of informational and behavioral involvement in the subject's affairs. So I view the domain of interpretation as configured according to the demands of the practice. The categorization prism through which the interpreter views an interpretable context articulates a network of nodes and routes of practical involvement along which the tasks needed to satisfy practical goals are defined and executed. It is in terms of such a network that the interpreter parses the subject's relations and attitudes, his behavior and its context.

This being my line, which I take to be supported by evidence about epistemic, communal, and political selection, it should come as no surprise that I take *so* seriously the lab-nature debate and look for a solution based on wise reflective equilibrium (Dennett 1987, chapter 7). The practicality of interpretation may easily be missed in the wrong context (the risk of the lab) or with the wrong methodological tools (the risk of naturalist observation). On balance, my metaevolutionary inclination is to have naturalist research first define the proper domain of interpretation in terms close to the settings of ancestral selection. Then it takes experiment, more than observation, to reveal the nuts and bolts of interpretive skills and the fine articulation of joints of the practical involvement that configures interpretation tasks. Outside the natural settings, the experimenter can, of course, detect many features of the competence for interpretation, but not necessarily the practical configurations that constrain its natural exercise and thus illuminate its design. Without experiment, the naturalist can, of course, detect the practical contexts where interpretation is deployed but fail to discern the fine "grammar" of deployment. In a word, reminiscent of Kant's, experiment without natural observation can be blind, but natural observation without experiment can be empty. This is also reminiscent of the relation, examined earlier, between the classical ICM method in cognitive science (closer to the lab) and evolutionism (closer to naturalism). Lab and nature complement each other. The study of interpretation needs both. The next chapters follow this policy of reflective equilibrium.

4 Pacifying Prejudices

By taking the evolutionary line outlined so far, I am stepping into a much contested territory that occasionally becomes a conceptual and ideological minefield. No precaution can pacify a strong prejudice, and there are many such prejudices against selectionism, evolutionary psychology, and their use in interpretation. Yet a few clarifications can do no harm and may even fortify the arguments of this essay.

Competence, performance, and domain To begin with, I honor scrupulously the distinction between competence and performance. My analysis intends to capture only the evolutionary macroreasons for having a competence for interpretation, *not* its uses in one context or another. There is no selection for performances, although there is selection *through* performances; there is selection only for programs and mechanisms, and the two sides rarely if ever stand in fixed one-to-one correlation. A competence can be used in all sorts of nonepistemic, noncommunal, or nonpolitical, or generally noninterpretational, applications. This has nothing to do with what brought the competence about, as a matter of selection.

I also honor scrupulously the distinction between the proper and actual domain of a competence. I follow Sperber (1994) and construe the *proper* domain of a cognitive competence as containing the sort of information the competence was selected to process; the *actual* domain may contain information for whose processing there was no selection. The human eye was selected to make out the distal layout, not to read, or read Hegel in particular, yet some people spend most of their time reading Hegel. (Young Hegelians did, which is how we got Marx, and the historical rest we all know.) The latter venture (reading Hegel) operates in an actual, not proper domain.

From these two distinctions it follows, importantly, that a selected competence cannot be inferred from its uses, nor can a proper domain be inferred from actual successors. As a result, one should not say that, historically, interpretation had (say) no political bite, because now Jane uses it (as performance in new and actual domains) to prove mathematical theorems and John to write novels. A competence can be put to new uses in new domains for which there was no selection. Likewise, interpretation may have been selected for its practical uses in epistemic or political domains, despite later nonpractical uses in other domains. There is, therefore, no conflict between interpretation allowing empathy or fostering love or writing novels or doing mathematics, as uses of the competence, and the competence itself having been selected for communal or political reasons.

Several other truths about the relation between competence and performance are worth recalling. A competence is necessary but not sufficient for performance; the latter also depends on the right environment, the right triggering and enabling conditions, and the operation of other competencies. Furthermore, a competence is selected to adjust its open parameters to the environment of operation, which often is not predetermined, certainly not in detail. The performances of the competence necessarily reflect such adjustments. The more sophisticated a cognizer, the more intricate the interplay among triggers, cooperating competencies, and environmental adjustments. Primates are sophisticated cognizers. They are sophisticated (partly) because they have a long ontogenesis during which these interfering factors have more latitude to diverge. This brings further variability into the picture.

Finally, it is important to separate competence—in the case of interpretation, like that of language, consisting of a knowledge base and programs operating on it—from an *ability* to activate and use the competence. This is a finer-grained distinction than the one between competence and performance (Chomsky 1975, chapter 1; 1980, chapter 2; Leslie and German 1995, section 1). Performance is a manifestation of the competence; the activating ability, on the other hand, concerns getting the competence to perform in the first place. Injury can prevent one from exercising a competence, say for biking, speaking, or interpreting. What is injured is an ability to access and use the competence, not the competence itself.[14] Hard as it may be methodologically to tell when a deficit affects a competence or the ability to use it, the distinction must be respected. My analysis is about the competence, not the ability to use it.

These reminders are intended to extricate the global reasons for interpretation from the surrounding array of enabling conditions of use, interaction, and parameter adjustment. There is no point in using facts about the latter against an analysis of the former—alas, a tactic often adopted by opponents. One does not argue against universal grammar by pointing out that English is different from Turkish, or that many people make grammatical mistakes, or that some use grammar elegantly, even poetically, and most don't, or that some (autistic individuals, for example) use it only for monologue or brief exchanges and not for full communication.

Politics need not be that bad The role of politics in interpretation need not entail aggressiveness or moral wickedness or other such depressing traits. It is crucial to understand this point. The argument about politics in interpretation draws on the political form of primate sociality and gives it a role in the selection of interpretation. This has nothing to do with primates and their societies being or not being intrinsically aggressive or bad or manipulative. Making tactical alliances and getting elected to office is neither intrinsically aggressive nor bad; indeed, it looks like the sort of political process that is much admired and emulated these days. One could argue, not implausibly, that by being openly political, primate societies are less murderous than those that are not (compare Yeltsin's Russia with Stalin's). Political competition takes the pressure off its nakedly physical counterpart. Politics matters to selectionism because it may be the most dynamic selector of interpretation, thanks to its ability to fuel and sustain an escalating arms race. Primates are precisely the species known for intricate and fast-moving political life. Although epistemic and communal selection may suffice in selecting for interpretation in some form or another, they probably fail to trigger and sustain its advances in primates, particularly great apes and humans.

At the risk of reawakening prejudices in a section meant to appease them, here is an intriguing analogy. To some historians and many amateurs, the intellectual wonders of ancient Athens are attributable largely to its political life. Its relative and narrow democracy—with open competition for office, but only for propertied nonslave males, and the resulting exploitation of the opponent's failures, tactical coalitions, and whatever else goes with the game—culturally "selected for" (in the relevant social groups) such intellectual skills as rhetorical verve, argumentative prowess, critical scrutiny of positions, and so on. These skills in turn called for critical pedagogy, logic as a theory of argument, and philosophy among the intellectual practices that produce and refine such skills. The rest, as we know and debate fiercely, is history.

Now there is nothing in this story that assumes (or excludes) that the political Athenians were aggressive or bad or good or innately competitive or whatever. As individuals, they were no different from their contemporaries in Sparta or China. Nor does this story assume that communal and epistemic conditions in Athens and elsewhere did not contribute to intellectual and cultural development. The point, rather, is that the form of political involvement and interaction in ancient Athens may explain important differences, at least according to the line of analysis caricatured here. Chimpanzees and early humans lived in a bush version of political Athens. Current thought has begun to wonder whether this fact may have had something to do with their unique ability to make sense of each other, and whether this ability in turn may explain their intelligence. And if the answers are 'Yes' or at least 'Possibly', then the question is 'Why?' If history teaches a lesson, from the bush to ancient Athens to eighteenth-century Paris to 1917 St. Petersburg, it is never to underestimate the role of politics in shaping minds.

Finally, what about the same conclusions without evolution? It may occur to a reader sympathetic to the spirit of this essay but wary of evolutionary stories that the main claims defended here might stand on their own, without appeal to evolution. In particular, one could accept that the practicalist hypothesis plausibly explains the facts known so far about interpretive skills and their domain, and does so better than alternative hypotheses. This should suffice. Even consideration of epistemic, communal, and political contexts and phylogenetic and ontogenetic comparisons need not commit one to any substantial evolutionary story. Those who can't stomach the relation between mind and evolution may want to take this shortcut. I do not mind it, as long as the same conclusions are reached. But I say this much about the shortcut. The intellectual discomfort about evolutionary stories of the mind is usually motivated by the fact that such stories, especially when selectionist, are evidentially weak and speculative. But what about the deepest theoretical stories in particle physics or cosmology dealing with the ultimate elements and configurations (superstrings, 10-dimensional or multiple universes, and so on) and their origins? Aren't these too evidentially weak and speculative—at least as much as most selectionist stories? And yet (almost) nobody seems to mind it. How much evidence did Einstein have when making his relativity claims? And how much evidence is there today about strings or even black holes? Prior to conclusive evidence, isn't it all a matter of theoretical coherence? Or does one smell here a faint scent of double methodological standards? Let me conclude this line of questioning somewhat rhetorically: If not evolution, then what? What is the alternative? And if evolution, then what else but natural selection? What other alternative would explain a phenomenon such as interpretation with clear individual benefits and social scope and with a long history of service among primates?

Yet one should not conclude from these remarks and questions that appeal to evolution in general and selection in particular is to be viewed merely as a legitimate heuristic or a logical exercise in coherence or a methodological ploy. Earlier I noted more weighty reasons for adopting an evolutionary stance on interpretation, such as inquisitive curiosity about a phenomenon with a powerful pedigree and influence in primate life, the threat of impasse if we limit ourselves to a proximate stance, and the explanatory promise of evolutionary hypotheses in the domain of categorization where interpretation operates. I trust that the chapters that follow will vindicate this decision.

PART II
Instinctive Practice

The point is not to understand the mind but to change it.
Marxist paraphrase

Interference and interaction are the stuff of reality.
Ian Hacking

Chapter 4

Situated Interpretation

The last two chapters have argued for the selection of interpretation as a competence apart, owing mostly to three types of macroforces (communal, political, and epistemic). This chapter puts the arguments in historical motion in order to see how, by operating in different environments of selection and on different species at different developmental stages, the macroforces selected for distinct interpretive skills. The case for selection is firmed up by identifying patterns of nonaccidental correlations among selective forces and features of interpretation. These correlations are queried for clues to the job design of interpretation. The clue-chasing strategy is explained in section 1. Then we are on to history. I discern several major turns in the evolution of interpretation. The empirical record is set out in section 2. The first turn, examined in section 3, results in a natural teleology that responds to the crude agency of subjects and their basic goals. When pressured to identify specific goals, basic and nonbasic, by clues that reflect more than physiological propensities for fixed behavioral patterns, the interpreter turns psychobehavioral, according to section 4. When pressured to share information, emotions, and experiences, interpretation takes a uniquely human psychosocial turn. So argues section 5. During all these evolutionary turns, interpretation remains thoroughly situated.

1 Looking for Clues

What follows is not an evolutionary movie but rather a disjointed series of sketchy and still takes, distilled from the ethological, evolutionary, and psychological literature, and peppered with some of my speculations. I need these takes for two reasons. One is to pursue the cause of selectionism by correlating at critical junctures selective pressures with properties of interpretation. The other reason is to query these properties and other evolutionary patterns for clues about the job design of interpretation. Faithful to a liberal selectionism, I propose to pair a sample of macro-selective forces with packages of properties of interpretation and occasionally to signal similarities of such properties across evolutionary turns, whenever the selective pressures and the behavioral data are supportive. Here is how my strategy is meant to work.

My evolutionary takes on force-outcome correlations sample at each evolutionary turn the dimensions of interpretation that bear the mark of selection *and* could reveal the job of interpretation. In most cases I divide these dimensions into accomplishments, operating parameters, and symptoms. Recognizing goals or emotions is an *accomplishment*. Being stimulus-driven or interpreting from current motivation is an *operating parameter*. A *symptom*, finally, is a mental or behavioral performance in which interpretation has a direct hand, as in communication or education. The dimensions to be sampled below are picked mostly from the psychological literature. Their list is partial. Inclusion in the list has to do with supporting the case for selectionism and providing useful guidance to the design of interpretation.

The mapping from evolutionary clues to design will proceed as follows. The empirical evidence offers instances of interpretive skills at work in a species or at a developmental stage. Observations or tests reveal dimensions of some sort, such as gaze monitoring (accomplishment) or communication by joint attention (symptom). Although the selection is not for dimensions but for the skills behind them, evidentially the latter are retrieved from, because manifested in, the former. The skills in turn are constituted by programs and their knowledge bases, but my strategy is to conceptualize them in terms of what they are good at (i.e., selected for) doing, that is, in terms of their goals and tasks. This leaves open, though it may constrain, the nature of their program execution.

In the previous chapter I argued that evolution helps discern the job design of interpretation. How? Basically, as follows. The first step, taken in this chapter, is to distinguish several evolutionary turns in situated interpretation and then, at each such turn, pair macroforces of selection with dimensions of interpretation. This would show that the skills behind the dimensions have a history of, and reasons for, selection. The second step, taken in the next chapter, is to identify how the skills respond to specific patterns of communal, epistemic, and political interaction and thus approximate their job design. The same overall gambit will be at work in the study of unsituated interpretation, in chapters 6 through 8.

2 The Empirical Record

Next I set out the general evidence for the proposed sequence of evolutionary turns. Then, at each turn, further empirical support will be brought aboard.

Natural teleology Most primate species interpret by means of a simple interpretation of crude agency (Cheney and Seyfarth 1990). This is *natural teleology*. The same may be true, but only partly, of human infants (Baron-Cohen 1993a; Premack and Dasser 1991; Gopnik, Slaughter, and Meltzoff 1994; Poulin-Dubois and Shultz 1988; Wellman 1990, chapter 8). They appear not to switch to a higher-power interpretation before fifteen months or so. Human infants are inveterate gaze watchers. The ability to monitor the subject's gaze and thus anticipate basic goals (as objects and events in the visual field) may function as the simplest and earliest form of interpretation (Baron-Cohen 1993a; Butterworth 1991). Until two years of age, the young child's use of language also shows exclusive focus on the observable features of the subject's behavior, with little if any awareness of its psychological origins (Wellman 1990, 224–225, reporting on work by Huttonlocher and Smiley). I take these data to provide reasonable room for natural teleology. There is debate about where to place the chimpanzees. Some authors believe that they are capable of more than natural teleology (Byrne and Whiten 1988, Whiten 1991b); others deny it (Povinelli 1996, Povinelli and Eddy 1996). The debate focuses mostly on the interpretation of cognition (gaze, attention, seeing), while I see the earlier part of the psychological revolution in interpretation, at least in apes, as being mostly about conation. In fact, I am ready to risk a proposal.

Two psychologies My proposal is that the *psychological turn* is actually made of two distinct turns, one *psychobehavioral*, typical of chimpanzees and possibly (but only partially) typical of human infants, and another *psychosocial*, found in humans alone. The former responds to the simple planning conation and visible cognition of the subject; the latter to sharing and communicating experiences, emotions, and attitudes with others. The classifications that come closest to mine are those of Wellman (1990, particularly 209–210, 233–234; also 1991), Perner (1991, 283–284), Gopnik, Slaughter, and Meltzoff (1994), and Baron-Cohen (1993a, 77). Turn by evolutionary turn, I note other similarities. Natural teleology overlaps with Wellman's (1990, 1991) notion of "behaviorism" and with Baron-Cohen's (1993a, 1995a) notion of "attention-goal psychology." The psychobehavioral interpretation overlaps considerably with Wellman's (1990, 1991) notion of "simple desire psychology," practiced by children older than fifteen months but younger than three. Psychosocial interpretation is most visible in the analyses of joint-attention sharing, social referencing, and communication (Bruner 1983, 1990; Hobson 1994; Gomez, Sarria, and Tamarit 1993; Mundy, Sigman, and Kasari 1993).

Metarepresentation   Despite disagreements about dating and the extent and depth of what it brings about (on which more later), the *metarepresentational turn* is acknowledged by most students of child interpretation. For many of them, this turn begins between three and four years of age, when the rudiments of desire-belief psychology get assembled. Whatever happens at this turn, for whatever reasons, is only an interim phase leading to a new and increasingly reconstructive format, as the older child marches on to adolescence. So I argue in chapter 6.

Reconstruction   The *reconstructional turn* is possibly the least recognized and studied yet the most important in human interpretation. It has often been assimilated to story telling and comprehension as well as conversation (see Britton and Pellegrini 1990 for a survey). There are now more hopeful signs of recognition of the distinct identity of reconstructive interpretation, and there is even a sense that in fact it is gradually assembled since infancy along psychosocial lines (Bruner 1983, 1986, 1990; Bruner and Feldman 1993; Carrithers 1991; Lewis 1994; Siegal and Peterson 1994). This is a position that I find congenial. I view reconstruction as closest to the pretheoretical notion of commonsense psychology, whether implicit in spontaneous attributions and predictions or explicit in mental rehearsals of social interactions, conversation, story telling, or dialogue with the self. Adult interpretation has been extensively studied in social psychology, mostly in attribution theory (see Fiske and Taylor 1991 for a survey) and philosophy of mind (Davidson 1984, Dennett 1987, Fodor 1987, Quine 1960, Stich 1983, to list a few notable positions). Yet aside from those just noted in psychology, few attempts have been made so far to view interpretation as reconstruction and examine it systematically in this posture (Morton 1980 being a notable exception in philosophy).

With this satellite view of the territory to guide us, let us descend and take in some details, turn by turn by turn by turn.

3 The Teleological Turn

Beginning with goals   Organisms have goals. They are genetically primed to pursue basic goals that revolve around food, sex, rest, power, and avoidance of danger. Since they live among other creatures, the satisfaction of their goals depends on what others do to satisfy their own goals. This simple fact compels most, if not all, organisms to evolve ways and means to recognize and treat others *as goal-directed*. This is a recognition of crude agency. It means, for example, that an organism expects another to pursue a course of action persistently and often with variations due to context until an end state is reached; the same organism would not expect the mechanical behavior of a physical object to display such features. Organisms that failed to register the agency of others (say by treating them as inert or lacking self causation or not aiming at producing end states with persistence and behavioral variation) and that also failed to connect it to their own goals must have flunked the test of natural selection, which is why it is hard to find them. Recognition of crude agency need not draw on a concept or explicit attribution. It is simply a perceptual ability to spot and monitor behavioral patterns in interaction with the world (Premack and Dasser 1991).

Recognizing crude agency may be necessary but not sufficient for interpretation. Many species recognize crude agency. Yet the empirical record hints that only primates are natural teleologists. How does one draw the line? Very, very cautiously and with an eye to the larger picture of the environments of and the pressures for selection. Agency recognition must be functionally specialized and must serve the interpreter's goal policies in a variety of situations. These factors jointly suggest that there was selection for a simple but specialized interpretation of agency. According to chapter 2, only some primate societies have the potential to generate such a selection. The potential turns into reality when the strategies of agency recognition, most notably gaze watching, evolved into dedicated skills.

Accomplishments   The ethological and psychological literature reveals several key dimensions of natural teleology. Here is a representative sample of accomplishments:

• *Basic goals* The natural teleologist views the subject as related to basic goals, such as objects to eat, avoid, mate with, attack, play with, and the like, in an appropriate surround. I call the latter *goal situations* to indicate that the interpreter construes the subject as related not merely to things but to things to be acted upon or things to be placed in a relation or things undergoing change or things undergoing displacement in a context.

• *Indicators of basic goals* Relations to basic goals are viewed as expressed by behavior, bodily posture, facial expression, emotional intensity, and gaze.

• *Subjects as reactors* The natural teleologist views the subject as being (durably) disposed to react directly to states of the environment and the behavior of other organisms. Behavior prediction and manipulation are based on such an understanding, and so is deception and other interpretive accomplishments.

• *Goal-based epistemology* Natural teleology does not track the subject's cognitive relations to the world to determine information access. The subject's gaze is monitored solely as a clue to basic goals, not as evidence of access. Other clues, such as bodily posture, which could reveal access, are also treated as goal indicators rather than as cognition indicators. This explains why gaze watchers may be oblivious to the attentional implications of the gaze (Povinelli and Eddy 1996). It also suggests the coarse-grained character of the basic goals disclosed by gaze watching, as opposed to the finer-grained and more specific character of the nonbasic goals identified by monitoring attention at later evolutionary turns.

Operating parameters Here is representative sample of operating parameters:

• *Innate recognition of basic agency* All interpreters innately recognize crude agency, possibly by means of a domain-specific perception that picks up indicators of basic goals. It is important to emphasize the presence of this ability as early as natural teleology because its simplicity and coarseness may mislead in suggesting mere learning of what other organisms do, as opposed to a readiness to recognize what they aim at as agents. How does one prove such readiness? By theory and data. Since Plato, the innateness argument has been that if the recognition of a property is based not on repeated experience but on stimulation acting as a trigger and associated with environmental adjustment, then the recognition is innate. The empirical task is to calibrate observations and devise tests that reveal the role of stimulation as trigger, not as learning. That is what Premack and Dasser (1991) have shown in the case of young human infants and apes. Baron-Cohen and Ring talk of an intentionality detector as an innate and "primitive perceptual mechanism ... that interprets self-propelling stimuli in terms of that stimulus' goal or desire" (1994, 185).

• *Tracking goals by assumptions, not explicitly* Although the natural teleologist innately recognizes crude agency, she explicitly registers and monitors the subject's behavior, gaze, posture, and environment. Unlike her evolutionary successors, the natural teleologist does not systematically track the subject's goals by way of specialized programs evolved for that function. The basic goals are tracked by *assumptions*.[1] That is, the programs register environmental and behavioral clues under assumptions, installed by evolution, to the effect that such clues link systematically with basic goals.[2]

• *Out of sight, out of interpretation* The spatiotemporal stance of natural teleology is one of total immediacy and immersion in the here and now, and is based exclusively on the interpreter's direct and continuous sensory tracking of the subject's behavior. This is what makes early interpretation *situated*. To borrow a notion of Perner's (1991, 45), this is interpretation by means of a single updating cognitive model constantly tied to a perceived situation.[3] There may be brief gaps in the model (say when the object watched disappears from view briefly), but the model can manage the gaps as long as they pertain to the *same* properties of the object. Such gaps trigger an information update. The single updating model encodes and maintains only the information about the same properties of a topic of ongoing perceptual interest and cannot accommodate conflicting information about different properties. When conflicting data show up (say that the object now looks red whereas before it looked yellow), the old data are simply erased and replaced by the new (Perner 1991, 47). The same is true of *past* information. Although young children remember past episodes, they do not remember their own or others' attitudes toward those episodes. They are memorizers but not interpreters of the past (Astington and Gopnik 1988, 205; Perner, Baker, and Hutton 1994, 278–280). Out of sight means out of interpretation; a subject interpreted is a body in sight. From birth until around 18 months, infants interpret with single updating models that pick up information only from the accessible visual field (Butterworth 1991, 225–227; Perner 1991, 46–47).

Symptoms   A symptom of natural teleology is the following:

• *Protoimperative communication*   Natural teleologists communicate instrumentally by protoimperatives. These are typically requests for action, either by direct physical means or through gaze coordination.

This symptom and other dimensions are partly shared with interpreters at the next turn. So I will continue their identification in the next section and turn now to the factors that may have selected for natural teleology.

Conditions for selection   Perhaps the most important interpretive gambit in natural teleology is the one that links gaze to basic goals. So I take it as representative for our discussion. What would be the selective pressures for a goal-gaze link? Consider two groups of presumed natural teleologists, apes and human infants. Both benefit from establishing that a subject wants something when gazing in a direction, and locating the goal by following his gaze. Gaze provides important data on food, mates, and impending social interactions. Who is looking at whom could inform not only on the basic goals of the participants but also on their relations and possible conflicts. These data have an impact on the interpreter's goals. Particularly in the wild, there is also the need to anticipate predators; a sudden shift in the gaze of an organism can signal imminent danger to another.

Communication, cooperation, and simple learning—all powerful communal and epistemic forces—also select for gaze reading. Apes and infants who want something and want others to do something to get it for them would first look in the direction of their goal, then at those who could help (trainers, adults, conspecifics), and then again at their goals. They could learn such tricks but if a gaze-following algorithm is already in place (for other reasons), it would probably be enlisted for these jobs as well. Politics would also select for gaze watching. Manipulation of behavior or, at the other extreme, reconciliation depend on eye contact and mutual gaze watching. (These examples come mostly from Gomez 1991).

Another dimension of natural teleology was said to be its implicit, assumption-based recognition of basic goals. It makes selectionist sense if one is persuaded, as I am, by the following argument. As evolutionary tricks, assumptions capture gross, constant, and pervasive features. Think of the solidity of the ground assumed by walking skills or of air pressure assumed by flying skills. If the job of a competence such as natural teleology is to recognize gross, constant, and pervasive features of the environment, then the job can be done by assumptions. Suppose that gaze monitoring is run by a program such as the eye-direction detector proposed by Baron-Cohen and Ring (1994). The program may instruct the interpreter to follow gaze until a recognizable object or situation is encountered; that would be the subject's basic goal (Povinelli and Eddy 1996). Goal determination can be construed as a rule operating on the assumption that gaze links regularly with basic goals and behaviors directed at them. The gaze-monitoring program does not pick up basic goals explicitly (for there are no program features that covary systematically with goals) but triangulates them from assumptions and clues about the direction of gaze, according to rules like the one just suggested. The question is why.

Here is the sketch of an answer. A reason why gaze is *systematically* tracked by a specialized program, while basic goals are merely assumed, is that gaze, unlike basic goals, displays a *richness* and *variety* of instances and of behavior-revealing patterns (in predation, imitative learning, cooperation, deception, etc.) that could not be captured otherwise.[4] There is thus selection for a *specialized* program that systematically tracks gaze across various contexts. (More on this notion in the next chapter, section 4.) When the subject's goals turn nonbasic (as in doing x to get y to reach z), they also become too numerous, specific, richly instantiated, and fast changing (hence no longer gross, constant, and pervasive) to be worth assuming or to be assumable at all; as in the case of gaze, this is when the pressure mounts for skills (programs and databases) that track goals systematically. This is when, for the interpreter, gaze turns into attention and attention patterns reveal nonbasic goals—a psychobehavioral accomplishment.

Another reason for systematic tracking is causation, or more exactly, *causal influence*. Interpretation is selected to serve the interpreter's goals in contexts of practical involvement. The communal, epistemic, and political conditions of life ensure that primates *deliberately* influence each other in a variety of interactions. There is thus an evolutionary premium on the ability to cause someone else to do things that further one's goals. That ability translates into (what I call in the next chapter) *effective strategies* of carrying out the interpreter's goals by taking causal advantage of the subject's relation to the world. Causal influence (as in misinforming or inducing a desire) is effective and beneficial only if the link between what one does and how another responds is recognized and utilized in a rich *variety* of circumstances, often with little else in common.

In such circumstances innate skills often afford better and more effective strategies of causal intervention in the subject's affairs than learning the right dependencies.

A crucial selectionist syllogism   We have now the elements of a selectionist syllogism that is at the heart of my stance on interpretation as an evolved practice. (Undivided attention is kindly requested.) The syllogism goes as follows: (a) There is communal, epistemic, and political selection for causal intervention of a behavioral or informational sort in social interactions open to interpretation. (b) This translates into selection for skills to influence causally or take advantage of a subject. How? (c) By evolving programs and databases that systematically track the subject's relations to the world. Hence the connection between (b) and (c): an interpreter can causally influence or take advantage only of those subject-world relations that can be systematically tracked by specialized programs and their databases.

This syllogism predicts that at each evolutionary turn there would be selective pressures for skills that systematically identify those subject-world relations that can be causally influenced. Gaze and its correlate, basic goals, are the relations of choice in natural teleology; attention and its conative correlate, simple desire, the relations of choice in psychobehavioral interpretation, and so on. In short, the relations and attributes most interpreted at an evolutionary turn are those in which the interpreter has the highest practical interest and for which she therefore evolves effective strategies of involvement. Put colloquially, one interprets a relation or attribute if one can do something about it. This practicality theme will be taken up in the next chapter.

The evolutionary syllogism just sketched also offers a retrodictive reading. If one has reasons to think that a species shows signs of having such skills, then one can guess backwards that there may have been selective pressures for effective strategies of causal intervention. This is useful information about the communal, epistemic, and political environment where such pressures emerged. No wonder, then, that situated interpretation is so much geared to gaze. Apes and human infants live in a cognitive world of gazing and gaze exchanges. Gaze is the attitude of choice in natural teleology not merely because it connects with basic goals but particularly because the latter can be causally engaged by an interpreter who knows how to read and handle gaze. Gaze is not a window to the mind but to basic goals out there in the world. Although many species use gaze to figure out what others are up to, and even to frustrate their inimical aims (Ristau 1986, 1991), only primates seem to use gaze *causally* as effective strategy of intervention. At least, this is how I read the gaze exploits of apes and infants surveyed in the literature (Byrne and Whiten 1991, Butterworth 1991, Gomez 1991, Povinelli 1996, Whiten and Byrne 1988a).

Comparable selection To sharpen our grasp of the correlations between selection and interpretation at this evolutionary turn, I turn to some interspecies comparisons, an exercise that stirs many passions, as witnessed by the lively debates around Cheney and Seyfarth 1992. I think the reason such comparisons make sense and can be insightful is that many cognitive abilities, including those for interpretation, can be retained alongside new developments. Every primate, from monkeys to humans, is a watcher of gaze and bodily posture, often for the same evolutionary reasons. Every human is occasionally a natural teleologist.

This general truth being acknowledged, let us focus on one stimulating though admittedly risky comparison between autistic children and monkeys (Happé and Frith 1992).[5] Like monkeys, apes, and infants, autistic children communicate by protoimperatives. Both autistic children and monkeys are known to resort to sabotage (simple manipulation of behavior) and to manipulation of seeing in order to conceal information (requiring only an awareness of an external access relation such as seeing) but not to genuine deception (requiring manipulation of belief). The point, of course, is not that sabotage or concealment of information, as political pressures, select for autism. The reading should go in the other direction, from autism to its political manifestations.

Autism is a brain deficit in interpretive skills and allows for no more than sabotage in the political domain. This reading has the following import. Significant correlations are found in child autism between interpretive (also communicational) skills and certain political games. Related correlations are found in monkeys or hand-reared apes. One speculates that in monkeys the pressures for interpretive skills were communal and political, some displayed in sabotage, concealment of information, and utilization of others as tools. Comparing autistic children and monkeys along these lines reveals correlations from opposites poles, namely, politics as cause and politics as effect. The diagram of influences ($\rightarrow$) and vague similarities or parallels ($\approx$) might look as follows:

monkey politics → selective pressures → interpretive skills in monkeys ≈
interpretive skills in autistic children → autistic politics ≈ monkey politics

Knowing what sort of politics selected for specific interpretive skills in
monkeys and knowing that those skills resemble the autists' allows one to
guess that the political utilization of autistic skills cannot be much different from that of monkeys. The same reasoning may apply to forms of
communication and learning in both groups, in light of the links among
these accomplishments, interpretive skills, and communal and epistemic
pressures. Another dividend of this comparative gambit is that it allows us
to use knowledge about the level of interpretation of one group to elucidate the level of interpretation of the other. The monkey-autism comparison provides insightful suggestions about where natural teleology comes
from and what uses it has in communication and politics. Those uses in
turn signal properties of the competence that made them possible.

This has been just a sketch of some of the pressures that might have
(macro)selected for key dimensions of natural teleology. In the belief that
it conveys the general picture, I turn now to a polemical defense of natural teleology. The case for natural teleology would not be complete without considering and countering objections. This critical exercise sharpens
the contours of natural teleology and pays dividends later when similar
issues pop up in the discussion of other forms of interpretation. Question
and answer period, then.

Pro and cons   The first question I hear coming is whether natural teleology is *really* interpretation. If the assumption behind the question is that
interpretation can only be human, because only humans have a "theory of
mind" or can "simulate" others and in either modality interpretation
captures the mental states of others, then the question begs the entire
evolutionary issue. It may turn out that only humans interpret psychologically. This is a reasonable possibility. It does not follow that there
cannot be *pre*psychological interpretation. It may also turn out that the
gap between the two forms of interpretation is truly enormous. This is
also likely. Yet enormity of difference does not speak against rudiments
of interpretation. What I think must be avoided, in making such comparative judgments, is the expectation that interpretation must be directed
at mental states to be genuine. This is not only question-begging at this
stage in the inquiry but is also wrong even for advanced interpretation, as
I argue later. My reading of the evolutionary evidence points in a different

direction. This is worth anticipating at this point because it affects the entire argument of this essay.

The mind of the subject enters the interpretation equation only as a set of variables to be valued indirectly and externally. At no evolutionary juncture is the equation about minds, in any reasonable sense of about-ness; it is always about subject-world relations as they impinge on the interpreter's goals. The gaze tracked by natural teleology is about basic goals in the world and the behaviors directed at them, not about the mind that initiates the gazing. Psychobehavioral interpretation turns to attention and simple desires, and so takes in "more" of the subject's mind, but still only indirectly, because it can no longer solve the equation with the old means—specifically, it cannot evolve effective strategies of practical involvement in any other way. Yet even then, attention and simple desires are windows to the subject's nonbasic goals and behavioral relations to the world (i.e., externalities), not to the details of his mind. The new windows do reflect more mental constraints on goals and other relations to the world than was the case in natural teleology, but this is different from saying that they produce more probing representations of the mind. Recall that the defining conditions for interpretation (agency, goal factoring, and the conditions of selection) do not *require* literal mind reading of either architectures (programs, functional mechanisms) or occurrent data structures and other neural configurations (pains, feelings, etc.). Nor should they. The evolutionary conditions define a job to be done, as adaptation, not the means of doing it.

Given the evolutionary role of interpretation in survival and reproduction, its phylogenetic stages are unlikely to come out of nowhere. Interpretation is more like vision than like grammar; many species have vision but see differently, though only one has grammar. Interpretation begins (almost literally) as an "eye" on other organisms' relations to the world, not as a "grammar" for social hermeneutics. The latter role shows up late in evolution. It may be that most prehuman primates interpret by natural teleology—or not at all, if the latter turns out not to be genuine interpretation. It is the chimpanzees (and other great apes) that we need to worry about. On some accounts, they have interpretive flashes that lower primates don't. Yet at the same time, chimpanzees share many properties with lower primates, particularly conditions of selection. So we should be prepared for some continuities in interpretation. Think again of the eye.

When not begging the issue, the question 'Is natural teleology really interpretation?' may aim at something else that is important. The issue may be that natural teleology is too simple and perhaps not specialized enough to rate as interpretation. In principle, how interpretation is done is an open question. It is *what* is being done—the job—and for what reasons that distinguish interpretation and its forms, not *how* it is done, by what specific processing. So simplicity or complexity of processing is not an issue. Nevertheless, as argued a chapter ago, the job requires skills with functional specialization (for that sets interpretation apart as a competence), and natural teleology seems to fit the bill.

Finally, there is the matter of the parallel tracks. I noted that monkeys, great apes, very young infants, and possibly autistic children may share some interpretive skills pertaining to natural teleology. This would indicate that interpretation may evolve along parallel tracks, since we know that at the same time chimpanzees and human children engage in higher-grade interpretational exploits. So when I said that infants begin as mere gaze watchers and hence natural teleologists, I did not mean that this is *all* the interpretation they are capable of. They also use gaze in psychosocial sharing of experience, which is a quite novel evolutionary path. Other parallel tracks show up at other evolutionary turns. When selected as adaptations, many early acquisitions find a way to coexist with more advanced acquisitions and prove their worth in the right contexts.

Interpretation goes to the dogs   I would like to sum up this critical examination of natural teleology with an example that portrays vividly the clash of intuitions and prejudices about natural teleology. Consider simple deception. There is strategic deception, such as camouflage by imitating features of the environment or mimicry of some other species, and there is tactical deception, whereby an animal conveys contextually misleading information and even alternates it with honest information (Byrne and Whiten 1991). It is the latter that I want to examine for our critical exercise. Here is how Krebs and Dawkins (1984) parse it. Dog *A* bares its teeth, thus appearing to signal attack. Instead, *A* deceives and forces dog *B* into retreating. *A* allows *B* to read *A*'s behavior and predict attack, as a result of which *B* retreats.[6]

How does this work as interpretation? It doesn't, but let us suppose it does. Imagine that *A*'s goal is to eat in peace. Nuisance happens. *B* shows up looking envious at *A*'s food. *A* forms the *B*-regarding goal of scaring *B* away through deception. Interpretation is in order. To carry out the deception, *A* needs to establish what *B* is up to (eating something). To do that, she may read *B*'s gaze and bodily posture and proceed to identify *B*'s goal. *A* could use the same readings to rank *B*'s basic goals (e.g., avoiding being attacked by a bigger dog normally ranks higher than eating). With data on *B*'s goals and their ranking, *A* can proceed to predict *B*'s response. According to Krebs and Dawkins, the prediction relies on statistical correlations assumed by the "interpreting" dog. *B*'s behavior obeys statistical regularities that can be assumed and exploited by *A*. The sensory clues furnished by *B*'s behavior provide *A* with evidence for activating the statistical assumptions backing her prediction of behavior.

If this were interpretation, our dogs would be natural teleologists. In that case, lots of species would be in the same league—a fact that begins to smack of a *reductio*. Many species use elements of gaze watching (e.g., line of regard) not only for gathering information but also for behavior prediction, often in the service of tactical deception. Birds are deep into this ploy. Piping plovers, for example, engage in deception (the broken wing display) or alter their behavior depending on the determination of the subject's direction of gaze; they appear to triangulate gaze from the orientation of eyes and head as well as bodily posture and direction of movement (Ristau 1991).

There is also deception that uses gaze monitoring and connects it to behavior prediction and manipulation but still fails to be interpretation. Why? My answer would be that several criteria of interpretation are not met. As far as I can tell, neither dogs nor birds nor most other animal species are subject to epistemic, communal, and political selection, as characterized in chapter 2.[7] Their skills have not been selected for having factored the goals and attributes of their subjects into their own goal policies in a variety of situations of causal involvement calling for interpretation. Such a variety of involvements is crucial to interpretation. Dogs, birds, and other creatures connect elements of the gaze relation with some behavioral patterns in a few stable patterns. Gaze at an object may mean a basic goal (typically pursued by aggression), avoiding a gaze may mean retreat. In such cases gaze monitoring may be a defense program, or it could be a learned adjustment of a defense program to new contexts. The deliberate and versatile causal use of others' goals and attributes indicates effective strategies of practical involvement. Sorry, but the grinning dog is not into that. Or so it seems to me. His manipulative gimmick of baring his teeth works in one single context, relative to one assumption. (Even two or three assumptions wouldn't help much.) This is adjustment and exploitation of a regularity, so often found in the animal world, not a flexible strategy effective across contexts.

My guess is that the reason that primates evolve gaze monitoring as a specialized skill for interpretation is that they are pressured into using it in rather complex patterns of education, communication, courtship, defense, deception, alliances, and so on, where causal manipulation is at a premium. Given this explosion of causal uses, one would think that at some point neither pirating another program nor learning limited to specific contexts and statistical assumptions are going to do the job efficiently. A better solution is a specialized skill that would recognize goals and other attributes in a variety of manifestations and would be able to sustain practical involvement. Hence natural teleology.

4   The Psychobehavioral Turn

Interpretation turns psychological because and to the extent that aspects of the psyche of the subject become important to the interpreter and must be recognized and factored into her goal policies. It does not follow that the interpreter has access to or insight into the subject's psyche. The interpreter evolves skills to discriminate and respond to the subject's relations to the world and his behavioral patterns in ways suggesting that her skills assume the subject's psychological propensities, such as simple planning.

The great divide   My reading of the literature suggests two independent psychological turns, one psychobehavioral, the other psychosocial. The psycho*behavioral* turn reflects mostly the pressures of coping with simple planning and simple desires. The psycho*social* turn reflects the pressures of sharing information, experiences, and emotions. As far as I can tell, these turns mark the grand evolutionary divide in interpretation between humans and other primates. I see several reasons to group them together as psychological. One is that both go beyond natural teleology, its domain of basic goals, and its assumptions of physiological reflexes. Another reason is that great apes and infants may share some psychobehavioral dimensions, for some common epistemic and communal (though not political) reasons. Infants in part and older children in general develop psychosocial skills for reasons (in the beginning, mostly epistemic and communal) not shared with the apes. Another supporting consideration is that autistic children have brain deficits that prevent them from practicing vigorous psychosocial interpretation yet their interpretation surely goes beyond natural teleology, so I rate it as at least psychobehavioral.

Finally, to look at the matter this way is to allow a general pattern whereby evolutionary changes may result from the convergence of separate developments. All interpreters recognize agency. Only higher primates plan and recognize some planning in others, make and use tools, and treat others as tools, often in a planning manner. These primates may interpret psychobehaviorally by joining recognition of agency, recognition of simple planning, and the ability to use tools. Some earlier forms of psychosocial interpretation may have emerged from the confluence of means-ends planning and interpersonal coordination, while later forms may have issued from recognition of agency allied with that of subjective orientation. I return to these matters below. The point now is that the evolution of many cognitive and interpretive skills shows disorderly patterns of interferences and confluences. We need zigzagging classifications (so to speak) to map out such patterns. It is in this sprit that I propose mine.

Accomplishments   The following is, again, a partial but representative list of accomplishments drawn from the literature on ape and child interpretation in areas of sufficient consensus.

• *Nonbasic goals*   Psychobehavioral interpretation can pick out goals other than basic. These are instrumental goals that secure the basic ones. The subject's relations to nonbasic goals are treated as simple desires (Wellman 1990).

• *Anchoring interpretation in the subject's conation*   Like natural teleology, psychobehavioral interpretation is anchored in and usually starts from the subject's goals. One speculation is that the attribution of the evolutionarily earliest and simplest desires is modeled on the motor plans of the interpreter (Gomez 1991, Meltzoff and Gopnik 1993).

• *Tracking simple desires*   Nonbasic goals are no longer assumed, as basic goals were in natural teleology, but rather are often systematically tracked through patterns of clues by programs selected for this task. Among such clues are attention to an object or situation, linked to behavioral posture in a direction; emotional reaction of pleasure when object or situation is obtained, disappointment when not obtained; and so on (Wellman 1993; Gomez, Sarria, and Tamarit 1993).

• *Transparency* Simple desires are construed transparently as situations desired, and perceptions as situations perceived. Desires or perceptions are individuated in terms of relevant situations—current, future, or possible. Like its predecessor, psychobehavioral interpretation uses the world, parsed into situations, to identify and track the subject's relations to it, yet unlike natural teleology, it can countenance more than current situations desired here and now (Perner 1991, Baron-Cohen 1993a). By contrast, the subject's cognition remains interpreted here and now.

• *A desire epistemology* Like natural teleologists, the psychobehavioral interpreters understand the subject's informational access to a situation in terms of behavioral indicators of his interest in and desires for a situation (Povinelli and Eddy 1996; the work on children is reported from Lyon 1993). The monitoring of perception thus appears constrained by the interpretation of desires.

• *Monitoring access* To the extent revealed by his desires, the subject's informational access is monitored solely in the present, typically as perception or attention. Monitoring attention is finer-grained and more specific for recovering nonbasic goals than monitoring gaze. The psychobehavioral interpreter does not seem to acknowledge or act on the longer-term retention and implications of the data of attention or perception as knowledge (Povinelli and Eddy 1996).

• *Specificity of information* Psychobehavioral interpretation is sensitive to specific information because nonbasic goals can be specific. The monitoring of attention is an expression of this sensitivity.

• *Exclusive interest in behavior* Like natural teleologists, psychobehaviorists interpret with an exclusive interest in the subject's behavior (Gomez 1991, Povinelli and Eddy 1996). This limitation squares with the here-and-now frame of their interpretation, and also with the next dimension.

• *Joint-attention behavior* This is a class of behaviors used to direct attention to situations and objects of interest. It includes convergent or coreferential looking (one looks at what another looks at or attempts to get another to look at what one looks at by using one's direction of gaze or gestures such as showing or pointing in a direction or at an object). This is the dimension that most clearly reveals the effective strategies of psychobehavioral interpretation. The world being visually shared between interpreter and subject, joint-attention behavior is used not only to figure out what the subject is up to but also to get him to attend to something or do something desired by the interpreter. Yet the subject is not treated mechanically but rather as a means-ends agent capable of planning (Baron-Cohen 1991; Butterworth 1991; Butterworth 1994; Hobson 1994; Gomez 1991; Gomez, Sarria, and Tamarit 1993; Mundy, Sigman, and Kasari 1993).

Operating parameters   Here is a sample of operating parameters:

• *Multiple but reality-bound models*   Natural teleology interprets by a single updating model of the subject's relations to the world. Children older than 18 months and apparently chimpanzees do better than that, when necessary. They resort to *multiple models* that encode data about situations desired by the subject, current or future. These situations are viewed as related directly to the subject but not to his mental condition (not as represented). This dimension receives indirect support from other accomplishments at this stage, such as tool making and (at least in children) understanding external media of representation, such as photographs, which require separate models (Perner 1991, 47).

• *Interpreting from the motivational present*   The psychobehavioral interpreter shares with the natural teleologist a narrow and immediate motivational horizon. Both interpret from their current conative stance because they live in the motivational present, animated by present goals, from where they look at the world and act. The difference is that the psychobehavioral interpreter can track the subject's simple planning, whereas the natural teleologist cannot.

• *Interpreting from the cognitive present*   The cognitive frame of interpretation continues to be one of spatial and temporal immediacy (Wellman 1993, 27), as it was in natural teleology. (The multiple models that reach into the future or hypothetical situations engage desires alone.) The key difference at this turn is that the here-and-now stance on the subject's cognition serves the multiple-models interpretation of the planning conation. As Humphrey notes (1988, 19), primates calculate in contexts where the evidence is ephemeral, because it is tied to the flying present. Their decision tree, capable of forward planning, has its roots in a current situation. This makes psychobehavioral interpretation more like a game of chess played with fixed opening moves (the interpreter's goals) made from the same positions anchored in the here-and-now (identifying the subject's basic goals) and from where subsequent moves branch out (identifying his nonbasic goals) by deploying multiple models.

Symptoms The symptoms of psychobehavioral interpretation are manifested in social activities that rely on interpretation and therefore express
what the latter can and cannot do. Indirectly, then, the symptoms reflect
the selective pressures for the form of interpretation in question. Communication is a good example because interpretation is massively implicated in it and because it is a vital group activity for which interpretation
gets selected.[8]

• *Protoimperative communication* Simple interpreters communicate
instrumentally by protoimperatives. These are usually requests for action.
The interpreter use signals, gestures, or utterances to get a subject to do
something physically. This sort of communication is a substitute for
pushing one or taking one's hand or gazing and pointing in a direction in
order to get the other to do something—activities typical of very young
children, older but autistic children, and apes (Cheney and Seyfarth 1990,
173, 1992, 174; Baron-Cohen 1992, 148; Gomez 1991; Gomez, Sarria,
and Tamarit 1933; Mundy, Sigman, and Kasari 1993).

• *Simple learning* Apes, infants, and very young children learn new
behaviors. Often what they learn are new affordances of objects, new
things to do with them. This does not require interpretation. But there are
forms of learning new behaviors that require coordinating one's attention with what others do and with the goals of their actions. The agency
of others must be factored into that of the learner. Interpretation is then
required. Imitative learning is an example. Infants are capable of it. Following the teacher's focus of attention is a prerequisite of imitative
learning (Tomasello, Kruger, and Ratner 1993, section 2.1). As for
chimpanzees, the verdict is not yet in. On some views, chimpanzees are
capable not only of imitative learning but also of simple instructional
learning (Boesch 1993).

Conditions for selection Why would the psychobehavioral aspects of a
subject's relations to the world be worth interpreting, worth that considerable evolutionary investment? What is it about interactions among primates at this evolutionary turn that would invite this sort of
interpretation? These questions call for checking out the evolutionary
action and retrieving the selective macroforces that correlate with psychobehavioral dimensions.

The general answer is that the subject's relations to the world are worth
interpreting when he is viewed as having goals other than basic ones and

when these goals make an epistemic, communal, and political difference. To get more specific, we need to ask how far this form of interpretation extends phylogenetically. There is debate on whether chimpanzees graduate to psychological interpretation. My bifurcation hypothesis allows that chimpanzees might do *some* psychobehavioral interpretation. They display a few pertinent dimensions and symptoms, for good evolutionary reasons. This is the line I will explore (amateurishly, of course). On the surface, the epistemic, communal, and political life of chimpanzees does not seem to differ much from that of other primates. That would suggest natural teleology. Yet there are also signs that chimpanzees are inveterate planners, apparently more so than other primates. Factored into their epistemic, communal, and political life, this fact could invite psychobehavioral interpretation. I may be wrong, but the thought is not that far out. This is how I would argue for it.

Ape planning   More than any other nonhuman primates, chimpanzees manufacture and use tools. Tool use in particular requires positing interim goals in order to reach further goals. The chimpanzees' use of tools and their learning how to make and use tools is a communal affair (Cheney and Seyfarth 1990, 295–298). Two things follow. One is that chimps possess some planning conation. The other is that in learning tool manufacture and use, chimpanzees rely on imitative learning and this may provide clues to interpreting others (e.g., what they are up to when doing certain things). In either case, their interpretation must respond to the planning conation of conspecifics.

A nice example that combines tool use with foresight and planning is that of the chimpanzees who travel for miles to find good but hard-shelled nuts. There are no rocks in the area to crack the nuts, so the chimpanzees bring rocks with them. Likewise, if there are no good flat rocks where the nuts are, chimpanzees would again travel for miles to find the rocks and bring them back (Cheney and Seyfarth 1990, 297). Other examples of conative intelligence of this instrumental sort involve tool use (using sticks to flush out termites from trees) or logistical problem solving (the notorious Sultan, who used a stick to get a banana behind the bars of his cage). Another important feature of chimpanzee's planning is its *specific* focus. Cheney and Seyfarth note that "chimpanzees who fish for termites and use hammers to crack open nuts are the only primates that select particular objects as tools, modify them appropriately, and do so in a way that shows foresight" (1990, 297).[9]

Calculating conation and the specificity of planning hint at what chimpanzee interpretation is up against, if the right epistemic, communal, and political pressures are on. For the same calculating and finely targeted conation that we find in tool use may be reproduced in learning and also used against another individual (Whiten and Byrne 1991). The chimpanzee planning to take rocks on the journey to the cherished nuts could also be the one who resorts to deception. This possibility is vividly encapsulated by a refined case of counterdeception (told by Whiten and Byrne 1988a, 220). One chimpanzee is about to fetch a banana from a metal box when another shows up at the border of the clearing. The first chimp quickly closes the box, walks away several meters, sits down, and looks around as if nothing happened. The second chimp leaves the area but, as soon as he is out of sight, he hides behind a tree and looks at the first chimp. When the latter approaches the metal box, the hiding chimp rushes toward it and fetches the banana. (Don't we all, older and newer primates, do things like this? And not only with bananas?)

The main reason a planning conation and specific nonbasic goals pose such a challenge to interpretation is that unlike basic goals, nonbasic goals can change rapidly, as the context of action and interaction shifts. It would be hard and impractical for evolution to install durable assumptions about nonbasic goals, as it did in natural teleology about basic goals. This is why we find a selection for specialized programs that can anticipate and track specific nonbasic goals from a variety of clues, most prominently attention, through models of current and future situations. Furthermore, with planning conation in charge, the chimp behavior becomes less predictable from external stimuli (Mitchell 1994). A world perceptually shared by interpreter and subject no longer suffices to constrain what would happen next. Some reliable sense of the subject's simple desires could help.

At the same time, the planning limitations of chimpanzees make psychobehavioral interpretation manageable. The planning and specificity of nonbasic goals can be handled as long as the subject desires and acts relative to a *current* frame of basic conation and cognition—a limitation that all situated interpreters share. Recall the chimps who travel to distant lands to find hard-shelled nuts and bring with them rocks they cannot find there. Intelligent and far-sighted as it is, the plan to take rocks (a nonbasic goal) is confined and related directly to the current urge of getting the nuts (a basic goal). This script portrays the subject as a planner who starts from the motivational present, is anchored in a basic goal, and linearly or treelike plots his future moves. The interpreter responds (evolutionarily) by finding ways to read the subject's basic goals and to counter his next moves (nonbasic goals), as in a simple chess game (Humphrey 1988; Whiten and Byrne 1988b). Such anchoring in current motivation is a planning limitation not shared by older children and adults, for they can foresee getting thirsty (a change of basic goals) while looking for the nuts and bring water with them (another nonbasic goal linked to the anticipated basic goal), although at the moment of planning they are not thirsty (Perner 1991, 313, reporting on the work of Norbert Bischof). This sort of planning would confront psychobehavioral interpretation with a combinatorial explosion it cannot handle, which is another effective reason for the next evolutionary turn.

Ape life   A planning conation poses additional pressures for the epistemic, communal, and political selection of psychobehavioral interpretation. Most primate species have a vibrant and intricate public life that combines family care, learning, socializing, playing, and politicking. Chimpanzees engage in imitative learning. Tool making and use, which in turn rely on planning, are learned this way. This would be a notable epistemic pressure for psychobehavioral interpretation. Some researchers think that only chimpanzees enculturated by humans show signs of joint-attention behavior, which implies that wild chimpanzees join other primate species in using gaze as a clue to goals and behaviors (Tomasello, Kruger, and Ratner 1993). That may be so. The point then is that the enculturated chimpanzees evolve this ability under artificial pressures of "socialization of attention" generated by "being raised in an environment in which joint attention to objects is a regular and important part of their social lives with their human caregivers.... When chimpanzees are raised in ways that enhance their social-cognitive abilities, their imitative learning abilities are enhanced as a result" (Tomasello, Kruger, and Ratner 1993, 507). That is the selection-skill correlation that we are after at this point.

Yet it is probably the group politics where interpretation is shaped most vigorously. Political primates are known to engage in complicated and frequently shifting patterns of dominance and submission, temporary alliances, and power plays (for comprehensive surveys, see Byrne and Whiten 1988, Cheney and Seyfarth 1990, Whiten and Byrne 1991). Chimpanzees, in particular, are great masters at this kind of politics. De Waal's works (1982, 1989) contain a wealth of cases in which political competitors for the dominant male position jockey for support by extending favors and threats right and left, and are seen by their opponents as doing so, with counterfavors or threats offered in response. Although most primate species do such things, for the same reasons, the chimpanzees again are singular in a respect that may also call for psychobehavioral interpretation. Communal and political selection for interpretation (for natural teleology, in particular) works best in primate groups that are relatively small and stable. Imagine a group that operates this way part the time, so that the pressures will be there, but also splits often enough into smaller units whose composition is fluid. This would require the individuals new to a group to be able to figure out the others fast and reliably. Interpretive speed and acuity are now at a premium (Cheney and Seyfarth 1990; Dennett 1987, 275–276). Almost alone among primates, chimpanzees fit this description.[10] In short, planning, tool making and use, some specificity of information, and the epistemic, communal, and political pressure cooker in which these new ingredients are mixed may explain some of the psychobehavioral accomplishments of chimpanzee interpretation.

Child life   Simple planning in children may also call for fragments of psychobehavioral interpretation. Children younger than three are capable of such planning and also of recognizing it in others. As Wellman (1990, 212–217) reports, young children make successful predictions about the actions of others aimed at interim and final goals, based on assumptions about the latter's desire dispositions and the state of the world. The prediction schema is that if the world contains an object somewhere and the subject shows the behavioral patterns indicative of a desire for that sort of object, then the subject will do a number of specific things to get the object. The interpreter's memory of similar past situations and the reading of clues from the subject's behavior and the world help anticipate which things (nonbasic goals) will be attempted.

Now the larger picture of selection. Family relations form a potent environment of epistemic, communal, and political selection. Young children engage in imitative learning, which epistemically favors psychobehavioral interpretation, as does playing, which combines epistemic, communal, and occasionally political pressures. Child politics also accelerates interpretation. The evidence says that children with siblings become better interpreters earlier than those without. Why? One explanation cites the competition among siblings for the parents' attention and resources.

This can provide fertile ground for sharpening one's interpretive wits.[11] Of all the social settings where children interpret others, the one where the child's self interest is threatened and manipulation becomes a defense is also the earliest and possibly the most important setting selecting for advanced interpretation and a better understanding of the social world (Dunn 1991, Reddy 1991). As with chimpanzees, when a planning co-nation must be interpreted under new epistemic, communal, and political conditions, the outcome is likely to be psychobehavioral interpretation. This comparison raises an interesting issue for a selectionist analysis. Its discussion rounds out the evolutionary case for psychobehavioral interpretation.

Comparable selection? Do children and chimpanzees share some dimensions of interpretation and some selective pressures for them? To some researchers, chimpanzees seem to fall in between natural teleology and psychosocial interpretation. I construed that intermediate position as psychobehavioral interpretation and speculated that young children might also practice it to some extent. Is this overlap reflected in the conditions of selection? Chimpanzees plan, cognize, and act in the present, from a current motivational and perceptual state, which is a limitation they share with very young children. One would expect, then, that both groups would be pressured to recognize simple desires as means to accomplish current goals. (Knowing that you want food, now and badly, and that you are a schemer, I recognize that you may form a simple desire, such as distracting my attention, which will get you the food.) What this interpretive policy does not afford is viewing subjects as form-ing future desires with future plans for action (intentions) or viewing subjects as different in how they construe and pursue their desires (rep-resentational desires). The latter developments occur after five or six years of age (Wellman 1990, 290, 292). Interpreting subjects as intending something responds to the fact that older children, unlike younger chil-dren or chimpanzees, are capable of complex planning, including antici-pation of future desires.

Are there other similarities in selection that take account of the subject's planning conation? Communal relations may provide a clue. Chimpan-zees and children have a rich and protected family life, enjoy an extended period of initiation and imitative education, communicate in the present and always with an eye toward action (protoimperatively), and play a lot. There is a rich shared ground for selection here. What about politics?

Unlike the adult chimp, the young child knows about neither sex nor competition for it nor courtship nor ruthless group politics. Yet the young child plays some politics, first with parents, then with siblings and other children. These political differences could occur at the level of the micro-forces of selection, leaving the macroforces more alike in some respects. The political macroforces call for behavioral deception and other forms of manipulation of behavior, simple desires, and attention. It is a matter of microforces, and hence of evolutionary implementation, as to whether the shared political macroforces are expressed in fun and nasty Machiavellianism, in chimps, or in tamer political relations to parents, siblings, and peers, in young children.

5   The Psychosocial Turn

This is a uniquely human turn, or rather series of turns, in interpretation. My reading of the evidence suggests a possible division into *three* ontogenetic phases: one situatedly psychosocial, a second metarepresentational, and a third reconstructional, the latter two being unsituated. They share a core of psychosocial dimensions and selective pressures for it, which is what appears to distinguish human interpretation so radically from earlier forms of primate interpretation.

The psychosocial core   This core can be characterized as *engaging others psychologically in sharing experiences, information, and affects.* Psychosocial interpretation evolves as the set of skills that make such sharing possible and effective. The ontogenetic unfolding of the initial core is slow and goes through several distinct turns, each with its additional dimensions and symptoms and, on the selection side, its own set of pressures. I see the first two psychosocial turns as transitory and preparing the ground for the third. The *metarepresentational turn* in particular may be a computational adjustment of the situated policies of early psychosocial interpretation to the unsituated parameters of adult minds, social life, and public language. The *reconstructional turn* appears to be a subsequent adjustment to cultural constraints and language-based mentation. Viewed from a long ontogenetic perspective, the psychosocial turn thus looks like a gradual insertion of mental sharing into the fabric of culture, sophisticated linguistic communication, and language-based thinking. After outlining the ingredients of the psychosocial core, my expose will follow this ontogenetic schedule.

Accomplishments   Here are some key accomplishments that distinguish situated psychosocial interpretation from its predecessors and form the core of later developments.

• *Mental sharing*   Like other primates, humans interact epistemically, communally, and politically in a shared world, whether actual or future, imagined or counterfactual. What is new in human ontogeny is that this interaction is accomplished *psychosocially* by reciprocally engaging the participants' emotions, experiences, and attitudes. For simplicity, I call this reciprocal psychological engagement *mental sharing*.[12] If there are two participants (interpreter and subject) and a shared world, we have what Hobson calls a "relatedness triangle" (Hobson 1993b, 141.) Mental sharing, apparently, is something other primates do not do. Chimpanzees may probe the simple desires of others, but that is a one-way street, from interpreter to subject, traveled exclusively for behavioral purposes, such as prediction or mischief. Mental sharing is a two-way street on which the participants constantly travel back and forth as they organize their mental states and actions and fix the relations of these states and actions to the world.[13] It is the epistemic, political, and communal demands on mental sharing that select for psychosocial interpretation, in all its ontogenetic versions.

• *Mental take*   Mental sharing relies on recognizing someone else's subjective stance toward some event or situation. This recognition is stronger than that of a simple relation to a goal situation, typical of earlier forms of interpretation, but weaker than that of representation-based attributes emerging later. Mental take is a sort of protoattitude, if you like. It is a category that takes time and sweat to put together, as does that of attitude, which is why the initial psychosocial and metarepresentational turns are essentially formative. What I find intriguing and consequential is that the category of mental take requires mental sharing and is shaped as an instrument of mental sharing. It is not as though the infant first develops a sense of the other's mental take on the world, by watching how the other relates to the world, and then uses this acquisition to share information and experiences with the other. The pressure for sharing comes *first*, and it alerts the infant to the mental take of the other, forcing her to discover what features of the other best ensure sharing. This realization in turn formats the infant's understanding of mental takes and later of attitudes.

This hypothesis can be momentous. It suggests that the evolutionary cauldron where the understanding of mental takes and attitudes is cooked up has favored not the distant and spectatorial recognition of a subject's intentional relation to the world (the standard view criticized here) but a *give-and-take format* of sharing, within whose confines the mentality of the other is recognized indirectly in sundry practical ways. We need to advert to *this* format to understand the job for which the categories of mental take and attitude were selected. Evolution being an improvising cook, we should expect it over time to have poured other ingredients into the cauldron to come up with skills to recognize mental takes and attitudes. Yet whatever else goes into those skills—such as recognizing agency and intentionality and means-ends relations (Hobson 1994)—the sharing format seems to have been preeminent. The next two accomplishments afford a closer look at it.

• *Joint-attention sharing*   Joint-attention behaviors such as looking or pointing, often associated with expressions of emotion (such as happiness or distress), can be used to share and communicate general awareness or specific experiences of the world other than purely conative or cognitive (e.g., evaluative, such as pleasure or disappointment) by commenting behaviorally or verbally on a shared portion of the world. This is joint-attention sharing. It requires that the subject be treated as an experiencing agent, not merely as a tool or planner. To this extent, joint-attention sharing goes beyond a grasp of nonbasic conation and regards the subject as a locus of experiences, emotions, and other mental takes on the shared world and on the interpreter herself (Baron-Cohen 1991; Bruner 1983; Bruner and Feldman 1993; Butterworth 1991; Hobson 1993b, 1994; Mundy, Sigman, and Kasari 1993).

• *Topic-comment format*   The psychological cooperation that secures joint-attention sharing works only if the interpreter establishes that the subject acknowledges her focus of attention and attends to what she does and how she reacts to the subject's acknowledgment. Sharing a focus of attention identifies a topic of common interest and allows various mental takes on the topic to be expressed and evaluated as comments (see the same literature as above).

• *Plot script*   Joint-attention sharing operates in time and involves an exchange of several comments about one or more topics. The sharing process is normally generated by a new interest or development that polarizes the attention of the participants, creating a "dramatic" or "plotlike" script for interpretation. The latter confers unity and coherence upon the process of mental sharing. In prelinguistic interpretation, such a plot script can be caricaturized as follows: child sees object, adult sees object, child looks at adult, then at object, so does the adult, child smiles, adult smiles back, object is valuable to child, adult has noticed this, child is happy that adult has noticed, and so on. The topic is the object, one comment is its value, still another comment is its value for the child being recognized by the adult, and so on. The plot is what motivates this hierarchical topic-comment sequence, is what gets the adult to see the topic, approve of the comment, and react to how the child reacts to the approval of the comment. The plot script will become standard in language-based interpretation and interpretation-assisted communication (Bruner 1983, Hickman 1987).

• *Emotion, affect*   Mental sharing in general and joint-attention sharing in particular rest on the recognition that the subject psychologically engages the interpreter by taking him to have a mental take on a shared situation. This recognition first extends to feelings, emotions, affects. These are the primary and earliest attributes whose recognition secures social referencing and mental sharing and prepares the ground for the linguistic mechanisms that secure attitude recognition and so much more. In the prelinguistic phase, infants and young children manage to communicate and interpret essentially by tracking emotions and feelings as expressions of mental take (Bruner 1983; Hobson 1993b, 1994; Rogoff 1990; Trevarthen 1979).

• *Bias toward desires and emotions*   Not only the behavioral evidence of interpretation but also its language indicates that early psychosocial interpretation remains firmly anchored in conation and emotion. The young child's use of action verbs and modal expressions is aligned with agency and desires rather than belief or thought, and so is her understanding of emotions (Wellman 1990, 225–226). Also, the interpreter's memory of her past conations seems to be better than of past cognitions (Astington and Gopnik 1988; Perner, Baker, and Hutton 1994).

Operating parameters   Like her predecessors, the young psychosocial interpreter continues to operate situatedly from the perspective of her current motivational and cognitive stance. It makes sense. Infants and young children are credited with an underdeveloped memory for facts, particularly facts of interpretation. At the same time, the use of attention, emotion, and feeling as evidence for mental sharing necessarily restricts one to ongoing interactions.

Symptoms   Here is one but very important symptom of psychosocial interpretation.

• *Protodeclarative communication* Young children communicate experiences and emotions with others, comment on an object or situation as a topic of interest, concern, fear, or fun, and thus publicly ascertain and measure the value (fun, disappointment) of a shared experience (Baron-Cohen 1993a; Hobson 1994; Mundy, Sigman, and Kasari 1993). Such forms of communication by mental sharing are a precursor of and rehearsal for linguistic communication.

Given the pivotal role of the psychosocial moment in shaping human interpretation, a preliminary point must be stressed before turning to the conditions that selected for it. The distinctions between psychobehavioral and psychosocial interpretation in general, and between joint-attention behavior and joint-attention sharing in particular, are not standard in the literature. Yet I think they are suggested by the data. The latter distinction is usually thought to hold between forms of *communication*—protoimperative and protodeclarative, respectively. Since primate communication depends on interpretation, I think that the communicational distinction is one of *symptoms* rather than accomplishments. Joint attention is established by an interpretive skill, whatever its further use. Directing the joint-attention skill to action and the world, as in joint-attention behavior, or to experiences, as in joint-attention sharing, requires *distinct* skills resulting in distinct accomplishments, *before* impacting communication one way or another. Yet, as we will see shortly, in the order of selection, it was probably the communicational use that may have pressured most for these skills.

Conditions for selection The case for the selection of early psychosocial interpretation is bound to be complex and apt to be made from several perspectives. Here is one. As a phase of development, situated psychosocial interpretation enables infants and young children to do well and at the same time prepares the ground for future developments. The dual role is admirably exemplified by the topic-comment format. This format, managed by means of emotion and attention in the early phases, resurfaces as a standard format for imparting or exchanging information in linguistic communication. The same relation can be found between the early category of mental take and its successor, that of attitude. And so on.

Another perspective is synchronic. The young interpreter must handle current challenges. Many, perhaps most, are epistemic and have to do with education and enculturation. Given how adult culture works, children must learn plenty of things from adults, with speed and motivation. Whether it concerns language or social practices or public patterns of gestures and actions, the learning must be precise and focused. The information exchanged during learning must be monitored in small doses by both interpreter as learner and educator as subject, so that changes and corrections may be effected as the process goes on. Both partners need feedback by appropriate signals at each important juncture, whence the importance of expressions of emotions and affect on both sides, a form of "signal-dependent affective communication ... as a principal mode of inter-individual coordination" (Hobson 1993b, 213; also 1994). Evolution can be expected to have installed an appropriate package of emotive and affective tools around the interpretive skill involved in joint-attention sharing. A clear instance of the fine choreography in which joint-attention sharing relies on emotive and affective feedbacks at each incremental step of the process is language learning. Learning new words in contexts of ostensive pointing and adult instruction requires children to attend to how adults relate to objects and events, where their attention goes, and how behavior correlates with the focus of attention and the objects or events attended to. Not only linguistic communication but also the learning and execution of simple tasks under adult supervision require some of the same abilities (Tomasello, Kruger, and Ratner 1993).

On some readings of the evidence (Hobson 1993b, 1994), joint-attention and mental sharing evolved separately from, and possibly independently of, joint-attention behavior and psychobehavioral skills in general. This is what best motivates the distinction between psychobehavioral and psychosocial interpretation. The distinction may have architectural import. The interpretation of agency and of single and joint attention-to-goal patterns are primate-wide (Premack and Dasser 1991) and likely handled by distinct modules (Baron-Cohen and Ring 1994, Baron-Cohen 1995b). Autistic children have no problem interpreting agency and attention-to-goal patterns and in general interpreting psychobehaviorally but are impaired in their psychosocial aptitudes for sharing information, emotions, and affects. Since their impairment appears to be organic (Frith 1989, Volkmar and Klin 1993), the psychosocial skills for joint-attention sharing may draw on distinct modular architectures.

Finally, whatever happened to cognition? The massive underinterpretation of the subject's cognition in all forms of situated interpretation has been amply documented observationally, experimentally, and in the analysis of child speech (Bartsch and Wellman 1995, Perner 1991, Wellman 1990). This phenomenon raises interesting issues. The interpretation of cognition lags systematically behind that of conation and emotion, probably for good evolutionary reasons. Contrary to mainstream views in philosophy and cognitive science (encapsulated in the incantational slogan *belief*-desire psychology), the interpretation of cognition is less important evolutionarily than that of goals, emotions, and motivations. As one follows the evolutionary turns, one notes that cognition is worth interpreting *when* and *to the extent that* the interpretation of goals, motivations, and emotions so requires. That extent is still minimal (gaze and attention monitoring, attention sharing) at the teleological and psychobehavioral turns. Not only does the interpretation of conation drive the evolution of the interpretation of cognition in general, but also, at least in the early stages (including even the metarepresentational), it does so *in order to* facilitate the interpretation of conation. Gaze monitoring (in natural teleology) and attention monitoring (in psychobehavioral interpretation) and attention sharing (in early psychosocial interpretation) are all focused on *goal* identification rather than on the subject's access to the world. No matter how you look at it, the goals run the cognitive show not only in the evolution of cognition itself (Bogdan 1994) but also in that of its interpretation. To paraphrase the old lady who told Bertrand Russell that the earth rests on elephants and nicely preempted his unstated but obvious question (Don't you worry, dear! It's elephants all the way down!), one can say that in biological, cognitive, and now interpretational affairs, it's teleology all the way down.

So it appears not to be in the evolutionary interest of the situated interpreter to interpret cognition to any considerable extent. The investment is not worth making. Why? Or more cumbersomely asked, how can the ape or child interpreter get away with interpreting so little cognition, so minimally, given that she is so intricately linked to her subjects in all walks of life and that the information the subject has about the world is bound to make a causal difference to what the subject does, which in turn is bound to make a causal difference to what the interpreter does? (Got that?) It looks as though the subject's cognition might afford an effective strategy for the interpreter, and yet evolution does not care. Again, why?

I can only speculate. An interpreter, limited to the here-and-now of current stimulation and motivation is apt to embody two evolutionary assumptions. I call them *reality assumptions*. One is that the subject *also* lives in the here-and-now of *his* current stimulation and motivation. The other is that when interpreter and subject interact here and now, they *share* a world. The assumptions entail that interpreter and subject perceive and operate in the *same* world. As a result, the world pretty much tells the interpreter *what* the subject cognizes. Reality assumptions are also used to figure out what the subject knows or wants (Davidson 1984; Mitchell 1994; Perner 1988, 1991; Wellman 1990, chapter 3). Once installed by evolution, the reality assumptions provide situated interpreters with a simple and economical way of assimilating the subject's cognition to theirs. As a result, the interpreter is under no pressure to separate the *origin* of a cognitive experience (seeing, in particular) from the experience itself. It is this separation, forced upon the interpreter at the next evolutionary turn, that brings the subject's cognitive relation to the world and its distinct relata (origins, causes, targets) into the focus of interpretation.

As long as reality stays put, so to speak, and is shared perceptually, as in situated interpretation, selection would favor the reality assumptions. (This is an instance of a wider policy where evolution relies on the world to do as much informational work as possible, thus sparing cognitive complications in the organism [Bogdan 1994].) It is only when reality is in flux and no longer sensorily present to both interpreter and subject that the pressure mounts for recognizing cognitive relations and their relata. This happens later in human ontogeny, mostly at the metarepresentational turn, and apparently never in prehuman primates. This is why the recognition of belief and inference are such late and exclusively human acquisitions.

Looking ahead   If the hypothesis of distinct architectures for psychosocial skills, and particularly for joint-attention and mental sharing, is sound, then we have grounded the bifurcation of the psychobehavioral and psychosocial interpretation in facts about biological endowment. At the same time, we should be ready to entertain the possibility (evoked by Hobson 1994, 78–79) that psychosocial skills may exploit or build on psychobehavioral antecedents, in the following way. Whereas the perception of full-fledged *attitudes* (complex desires, beliefs, intentions) is a uniquely psychosocial achievement that revolves around sharing information and experiences, the interpretive perception of the *aboutness* or *content* of these attitudes may build on psychobehavioral accomplishments, such as the recognition of goals, agency, gaze, or attention-to-goal patterns. That is to say, determining *that one desires* (the *attitude*) may be a uniquely human achievement grounded in psychosocial skills, but determining *what one desires* (the *content*) may have psychobehavioral roots.

To look ahead, the genetic grounding of distinct psychosocial skills, such as joint-attention sharing, and the fact that such skills are exercised so early in human ontogeny, prior to the full mastery of language, invite two further speculations. The more ambitious is that the psychosocial line in the evolution of human interpretation is *prelinguistic*, whatever its later benefits for linguistic communication. If so, then the reconstructional properties seen in adult interpretation may originate in prelinguistic skills and owe nothing of substance (as opposed to form and expression) to the mastery of a language, as is often believed. This may also be true of discursive and deliberate thinking. The parsing of information in mental sharing, which underlies a good deal of social learning, cooperation, and communication, may format the way in which people organize and formulate their public language-based thinking. Construed as sharing of information and experience, the roots of reconstructive interpretation are thus prior to, independent of, and probably contributory to, the discursive form of linguistic communication and language-based thinking. That would mean that interpreters engage in such forms of communication and thinking *because*, as interpreters, they are *already* primed to share information and experience, and not the other way around. The narrower speculation is that reconstruction has its prelinguistic seeds in mental, and specifically joint-attention, sharing, and, like its metarepresentational precursor, is selected for sharing information and experiences. This happens when joint-attention behavior can no longer do the job, because the contexts of sharing are no longer limited to spatiotemporal immediacy. These speculations will be amplified in chapters 6 and 7.

In brief Such, then, is the evolutionary picture of situated interpretation as an instinctive practice. There are three key forms: natural teleology, psychobehavioral interpretation, and early psychosocial interpretation. As separate fragments, they may all be present in young human infants. Lower primates are natural teleologists, while chimpanzees and perhaps other great apes also have use of some psychobehavioral skills. Each form was distinguished in terms of dimensions (accomplishments, operating parameters, and symptoms) that correlate nonaccidentally with selective pressures of the epistemic, communal, and political sort in the appropriate contexts of evolution. This information can now be put to use to approximate what situated interpretation is up to, by way of goals and tasks. That is the business of the next chapter.

Chapter 5

Practical Design

This part of the book has two aims. One is to show that situated interpretation has evolved by natural selection. That was done in the last three chapters. The other aim is to use the insights derived from the patterns of correlations between the forces of selection and the dimensions they bring about to get a sense of the design of situated interpretation. This is the brief of the present chapter. The most salient evolutionary insight is that interpretation is *practical* in two senses: it operates as a practice and has practical aims. It operates as a practice in that it conceives of and handles subject-world relations and a subject's attributes and behaviors in terms of effective strategies of involvement, and it has practical aims because it picks up those subject-world relations and attributes that afford such effective strategies.

The notion of practical interpretation goes against the current consensus. The best expression of this consensus is the idea that interpreting is like scientific theorizing, only so much more naive. I disagree, and in section 1, I suggest instead that interpreting is more like experimenting. In section 2, I gather evolutionary support for this reading of interpretation. So grounded, the argument takes off in section 3, where I explicate the design of interpretation in terms of goal settings. The latter is a construct that links selective forces for interpretation with its job design, thus providing the needed conceptual bridge on which evolutionary materiel can be ferried to help with the design analysis. The notion of goal setting captures key explanatory joints of the environment where interpretation was selected as a battery of effective strategies. This is what confers practicality on interpretation. Section 4 provides some background for the general notion of situated and procedural cognition. Sections 5 and 6 examine the situatedness and procedurality of early interpretation and its categorization policies. As the complexity of situated interpretation grows, evolution may favor simplification tactics that yield more effective but economical categorizations. These tactics concern the manner in which procedures are coded and their access routes. This is the topic of section 7.

1 Experiment, Not Theory

Spectatorial options The major accounts competing for explaining situated interpretation are behaviorism, strong modularism (MoM), and theory of mind (ToM). They all take a *spectatorial* view of interpretation, portraying the subject as a remote object of observation and prediction. For behaviorism, the interpreter is an inveterate learner who puts two and two together—that is, stimuli, behaviors, and states of the world—and comes up with the right solutions. Enough has been said about and against behaviorism (mostly in chapter 2, section 5) to not warrant any further discussion. That leaves MoM and ToM. There are significant differences between them, pertaining to how much is innate and in what form and also to which phylogenetic and ontogenetic stages they explain better. The focus now is on features they share in their spectatorial stance on interpretation.

One such feature can be called *theorism.*[1] ToM, understandably, excels at theorism. It may have found its source of inspiration in philosophical views, functionalism in particular, according to which interpretation anticipates scientific theorizing in being a network of theoretical constructs linked in lawlike generalizations that use (but go beyond) the behavioral evidence to explain and predict. This is how intentional realists (Fodor 1981, 1987; Lewis 1983; Pylyshyn 1984) came to regard interpretation as a true though naive psychology of mind and eliminativists (Churchland 1989, Stich 1983) as a false one. Many, perhaps most, ToM theorists follow this philosophical lead and take an almost literal view of interpretation as theory construction and application and its development as theory change or data-driven revision of concepts and generalizations (Astington and Gopnik 1991; Gopnik 1993; Gopnik and Wellman 1994; Meltzoff and Gopnik 1993; Wellman 1990; Whiten 1993, 1994), and at least one ToM theorist sees a "deep continuity between folk psychology and scientific psychology" (Gopnik 1996, 181).

MoM theorists do not buy the theory-change argument and take the view that interpretive knowledge is not descriptive or largely explicit, as the ToM accounts have it, but rather procedural, innate, and modular.

Yet MoM too can be read as buying into the spectatorial line of theoretical constructs and generalizations used for prediction and explanation; the difference is that the constructs and generalizations and their use are implicit in the program, built into its instructions and database, the way grammar is. Saying that ToM and MoM buy into theorism is not yet saying what the interpretive theory, explicit or implicit, is *about*. It could be about many things. Yet the mind stands out as the target of interpretation. So say the philosophers, so suggests ordinary language, so is the psychological evidence read. So it must be the mind. This is the second feature that ToM and MoM share. I call it *mentalism*. This is the notion that interpretation systematically picks out, mostly from external signs, types of mental states that are causally efficacious in the subject's mentation and behavior. On this view, mental types such as desires and beliefs are more like electrons and forces in theoretical physics, hidden entities that cause. I return to this analogy in a moment.

Another feature associated with MoM but particularly with ToM can be called *explanatorism*. This is the notion that interpretation is essentially in the business of explanation and prediction, just as theoretical science is, only so much more spontaneously and naively. The ToM-type mix of theorism, mentalism, and explanatorism is clearly articulated by Gopnik and Wellman: "We will argue that (1) the child's understanding involves general constructs about the mind that go beyond any direct evidence. (2) These constructs feature prominently in explanation. (3) The constructs allow children to make predictions about behavior in a wide variety of circumstances, including predictions about behavior they have never actually experienced and incorrect predictions. (4) Finally, these constructs lead to distinctive interpretations of the evidence" (1994, 267).

To sum up, MoM, ToM, and their variants, like their realist and eliminativist cousins in philosophy, regard interpretation through the glasses of a philosophy of science that sees theories as positing constructs for causal or functional entities and generalizations for laws, and employing both to explain and predict facts. This is a philosophy of *theoretical* science. The targets of interpretation are assimilated to the protons or genes or other theoretical posits of science, with their laws. I think that this is the wrong analogy for interpretation and that this is not suggested by evolution, as I read it.

The doer's view My reading of evolution is exactly the opposite. It recommends that interpretation be understood in terms of *experiment* rather than theory. (I say experiment, not observation, for the latter would invite behaviorist learning, and this is verboten.) The knowledge of psychological attributes is better viewed as analogous to experimental strategies rather than theoretical posits. For simplicity, I focus now on the putative link between attributes in interpretation and theoretical posits in science, and neglect (but criticize later) the alleged theorylike organization of interpretive knowledge: the explanatory and predictive use of this knowledge and changes in it modeled on conceptual revision in science. So my claim now is solely against attributes being treated in interpretation as theoretical entities are in science, and therefore as real and knowable along theoretical lines.

For the philosophy of mind I need, I go to a dissident position, that of Ian Hacking, whose iconoclastic primer on philosophy of science (1983) echoes several healthy marxist and pragmatist themes: that practice dominates theory, that acting precedes and constrains representing, and that successfully intervening in the order of nature is evidence of knowledge and test of reality. Hacking finds even Popper echoing these themes when writing (uncharacteristically) that "the entities which we conjecture to be real should be able to exert a causal effect upon the *prima facie* real things; that is, upon material things of an ordinary size: that we can explain changes in the ordinary material world of things by the causal effects of entities conjectured to be real," and then comments that "Popper points in the right direction. Reality has to do with causation and our notions of reality are formed from our abilities to change the world" (1983, 146).

Hacking notes further that "the experimenter cheerfully regards neutral bosons as merely hypothetical entities, while electrons are real. What is the difference? There are an enormous number of ways in which to make instruments that rely on the causal properties of electrons in order to produce desired effects." If you wonder what this has got to do with interpretation, please, read on, mentally substituting 'evolution designing an interpretive device' for 'the experimenter designing an apparatus', and 'attention' or 'simple desire' for '*electron*'. Hacking continues, "We spend a lot of time building prototypes that don't work. We get rid of innumerable bugs. Often we have to give up and try another approach. Debugging is not a matter of theoretically explaining or predicting what is going wrong. It is partly a matter of getting rid of 'noise' in the apparatus.... The instrument must be able to isolate, physically, the properties of the entities that we wish to use, and damp down all the other effects that might get in our way." And now the conclusion in the author's grave italics: "*We are completely convinced of the reality of electrons when we regularly set out to build—and often enough succeed in building—new kinds of device that use various well-understood causal properties of electrons to interfere in other more hypothetical parts of nature*" (Hacking 1983, 265).

Hacking's analysis of electron experimentation provides an apt analogy for my position. Interpretation evolved to cope with social behavior and socially relevant mentation (especially conation) in environments crisscrossed by communal, epistemic, and political fields of selective forces. Its success at prediction, training, manipulation, and coordination (achievements that best measure its adaptedness) must be explained in these evolutionary terms. The interpreting mind has a grip on the interpreted mind not because it chanced upon the right representation or prototheory of the latter but because evolution designed interpretive tools able to isolate the *relational* (not intrinsic) properties of subjects, properties *used causally* by the interpreter to engage and, if necessary, interfere in other (often hypothetical or future) patterns of social interaction, to paraphrase Hacking. No wonder that the relational properties first engaged by early interpretation are behavioral and conative and take the form of goals, gaze, attention, and simple desires. These properties are exploited informationally and manipulated behaviorally by early interpreters, as the evidence surveyed earlier documents. It is natural, then, that such properties should become the first candidates for attribute recognition.

Like the philosophy of theoretical science that focuses on the physicist who contemplates mysterious bosons, the ToM and MoM positions regard the interpreter as a distant and passive spectator who maps the subject's mental causation with the help of theoretical posits, such as desires and beliefs, that causally explain and predict his actions. This, I argue, is not how and why the interpreter develops and deploys her knowledge of attributes. She is more like an experimenter with electrons than a theorist about bosons. Her angle on causation is not mental or intrasubjective but intersubjective. An attribute, for her, is a "mental electron" (if you like) that can be interfered with or used to interfere with something else, rather than a hidden "mental boson" posited to organize the data and thus afford explanations and predictions.

Despite its popularity in psychological circles, theoretical science does not look like the right analogy for interpretation, nor do theoretical posits look like the right analogs for psychological attributes. For good reason.

As Hacking notes elsewhere, "Long-lived theoretical entities which do not end up being manipulated commonly turn out to have been wonderful mistakes" (1982, 73). Contrary to eliminativism, the successful endurance of interpretation points to its practical, not theoretical, proclivities. Experiment and its targets are thus much better candidates for the analogies. The experiment analogy makes evolutionary sense and comports well with the empirical evidence and theoretical insights about interpretation. So I argue in the next section.

2 Selected for Involvement

We come to a juncture where the evolutionary investments made in earlier chapters begin to bring dividends. Looking back at the evolutionary record, with an eye now sensitized to the practicality of interpretation, one cannot fail to note two striking facts. One is that the communal, epistemic, and political interactions that selected for interpretation were rife with engagement, intervention, and reaction, mostly by way of information, in coordinating actions, tutoring, or competing for something. The other fact is that each revolution in interpretation occurred at phylogenetic and ontogenetic junctures where the old interpretive means no longer managed to secure an active informational engagement of the subject and, when needed, an intervention in his affairs or a reaction to his initiatives. For economy, I call the mix of effective engagement of the subject, intervention in his affairs, and reaction to what he is up to or does *practical involvement*. It may be effected physically, through behavior, or informationally; in either case, it has *intersubjective* causal impact. Practical involvement was not the only evolutionary stimulus for interpretation, but it was the most consequential. Recall, for example, that the recognition of simple desire superseded that of basic goals when the subject's planning conation could no longer be predicted and dealt with by merely triangulating environment, gaze, and bodily posture. Likewise, it appears, the recognition of belief emerges when the child interpreter can no longer influence or take advantage of the information flow in the here and now; the recognition of intention imposes itself when the target of involvement shifts from immediate desire to longer-term planning; and so on.

Equally symptomatic of the selection of interpretation for reasons of practical involvement are two other points. One is that key advances in interpretation, such as the recognition of belief, were *accelerated* by increased opportunities to interact with or manipulate subjects and slowed down by lack of such opportunities. The other point is that primate cultures always train and even speed up the development of interpretive skills in deliberate contexts of practical involvement such as teasing, play, or games like hide-and-seek. These contexts offer well-structured and well-guided opportunities for fine-tuning strategies of involvement and for practicing with the informational and behavioral affordances of the new skills. Teasing is a particularly revealing example. It refines the abilities for causal intervention and prefigures the recognition of those psychological attributes that afford such intervention. As Dunn describes it, "In teasing children attempt to annoy, disturb, upset or amuse others. The interest of such actions lies in the understanding that they reflect what will upset, annoy or amuse a particular person, and our observations showed that teasing the sibling and teasing the mother had developed into highly precise and differentiated strategies by 24 months" (Dunn 1991, 53; see also Reddy 1991). The invariants of what upsets, annoys, or amuses become guides to, and may even scaffold, the attribute recognition that affords practical involvement.

Pretence is another good example. From early childhood pretence appears as a training ground for planning, counterfactual reasoning, intentional communication, and interpretation (Leslie 1991, Harris 1993). One's pretend actions can be viewed as a sort of causal play with reality under different mental descriptions, which is what all these mental exploits require. Understanding pretence in others rests on interpretation. Shared pretence in particular resembles joint-attention sharing and ostensive communication by generating fine-grained interactions between what one does verbally or behaviorally, how the other responds, how one responds in turn, and so on. To this extent, shared pretence can facilitate the use of interpretation in communication and other forms of interaction.

What I find interesting about teasing and pretence is that, like joint-attention sharing, they seem to anticipate in the *behavioral* domain (where the situated action is) the linguistic parsing of information around points of interest by way of plots unfolding in the topic-comment format (which is where the most of the later unsituated action will be). In so doing, these forms of deliberate and finely choreographed interaction may scaffold and refine psychosocial interpretation. For example, the topic-comment format they encourage is apt to locate the joints where the interlocutor's attitudes can be engaged and influenced along the informational lines of an unfolding narration. Like teasing, shared pretence, and play, but more effectively than them, linguistic communication draws on knowledge of attributes and can actively inculcate and control them in an interlocutor. Indeed, the knowledge of psychological attributes may have first evolved in contexts of inculcation and control. I speculate but not wildly.

In general, my argument is that an attribute type, psychobehavioral and psychosocial, is categorized in terms that reflect the interpreter's knowledge of how she would engage the subject behaviorally or informationally and how the latter would respond to what the interpreter has done or said. In situated interpretation, this knowledge may be modularized and proceduralized as instructions; in unsituated interpretation, it takes the conceptual form of explicit rules whose utilization can be flexible and open-ended. In either case, the knowledge is *practical* because it sponsors an understanding of attributes as effective strategies of causal involvement. To return to the analogy with experiment, this means that the attributes are more like "mental electrons" to be inculcated, controlled, or changed, rather than like "mental bosons" to be contemplated from afar. Inducing and altering an attribute in others by way of information is the practical test and proof of interpretive knowledge. Having previewed the argument and recalled its evolutionary credentials, let me begin to unpack it.

3   Goal Setting for Interpretation

This section links the selectionist analysis of the previous three chapters with the job of interpretation to be sketched later. The link emerges from an examination of the environment where interpretive skills were selected *in terms revealing their adaptedness*. The latter confirms that interpretation is a competence apart with evolutionary roots and, by identifying what the skills are good at, validates its practical nature.

Environment of selection   I have assumed so far that the forces of selection arise from and operate in an appropriate environment. Having taken a liberal view of selection as a durable fixer of traits, I treated the environment of selection either as ancestral or as successive versions that maintained the selected traits. Cued by Bowlby's notion of "an environment of evolutionary adaptedness" (1982, chapter 3), I view the *environment of selection for interpretation* as a space of practical interference between the interpreter's goals and the subject's.[2] The idea behind this notion is fairly simple.

Interpretation was selected as a cognitive instrumentality that factors the subject's goals into those of the interpreter. I call the latter *private goals*. The interface between the interpreter's goals and those of the subject forces the interpreter to come up with *social* or *subject-regarding goals*. The interpreter has to deal with the latter in order to satisfy her private goals. This is the reason for evolving interpretive skills as effective strategies for coping with the subject-world relations. The relation between private and social goals in turn calls for *interpretation goals*. The last reflect the fact that the interpreter must know certain things about the subject's relations to the world in order to do something about them (social goals) and thus satisfy her private goals. An environment where interpretive skills were selected in terms of this trilateral interface of goals is a *goal setting for interpretation*.

To illustrate, suppose that organism *A* (interpreter) has a private goal (say resting). It interferes with the goal of another organism *S* (subject), which is to eat *A*. Those *A*-type organisms will be selected who manage to form the social or *S*-regarding goal of avoiding the nasty type *S* by countering their inimical behavior, say by threat or deception. The latter goal in turn selects for interpretation, specifically, for interpretation goals such as desire identification and behavior prediction. Those *A*-type organisms are selected who form and reach such interpretation goals. The environment that selected for such accomplishments is a goal setting *of a certain kind*, say of behavior manipulation by behavior prediction and desire identification. There could be as many kinds of goal settings for interpretation as there are interpretation goals and tasks to achieve them, and hence as many skills.

The notion of goal setting for interpretation has several virtues that clarify the job of interpretation. First, it has the merit of constraining selection by structuring the action of its forces and thus capturing the fine-grain sense in which interpretive skills are adaptations. The rough idea is this. No goal can be secured without steps being taken or *tasks* being executed. The satisfaction of goals selects for skills to perform such tasks. Tasks are configurations (arrangements, sequences) of states of affairs that an interpreter's cognition can do business with; they are realizable, finite, and can be parsed into further subtasks. Evolution likes this sort of structure. A second virtue is that a goal setting formats an environmental context along perceptual and behavioral coordinates that trigger a specific strategy of interpretation. It takes an instance of a goal-setting type to indicate that (and explain why) an organism resorts to a particular strategy of interpretation.

Third, a goal setting manifests and motivates in evolutionary terms the fact that interpretive steps are selected as *effective strategies* to do something about the subject's goals and behaviors when the latter interfere with those of the interpreter. Interpretation begins as a cognitive instrumentality with practical import. Behavior manipulation or any other sort of causal intervention in the subject's affairs, with the aim of furthering the interpreter's goals, constitutes a sort of *practical envelope* within which effective strategies of prediction and action evolve; among these strategies, interpretive skills are most prominent. The goals and tasks of interpretation come to reflect the interventionist coordinates of the practical envelope in which they are evolutionarily configured. All this is important, so let me amplify.

Task adaptation   The goal-and-task combination at the heart of what is selected in a goal setting for interpretation characterizes the *design of the job* of interpretation, that is, what interpretation was selected to do. Here is how this proposition fits into a selectionist analysis. An adaptation is a trait selected for being *good at* something, which now means being good at performing a task. A competence is an adaptation if selected to handle a task, relative to a goal. To put it more formally, building on Sober's definition, I say that a competence is *an adaptation for a specific task, relative to a goal*, in a population, if and only if the competence became prevalent in the population because there was selection for the competence in an environment bearing the marks of a goal setting for interpretation and its selective advantage resulted from the fact that the competence helped perform the task and thus satisfy the goal (Sober 1984a, 208; also Sober 1993a, 84; West-Eberhard 1992, 13).

A goal setting is the historical locus of selection for the interpretation goals and tasks that characterize skills as adaptations. It follows that the skills kick into action whenever the interpreter finds herself in a goal setting and registers it as the right instance. The features of the setting are picked up perceptually, and this pick up launches the programs selected to handle the goals and tasks typical for that sort of setting. As a result, the interpreter's cognition enters the interpretation mode. Schematically, the picture is as follows:

(5.1)   *The flow of interpretation*

a. *Goal setting*: interpreter values survival (private goal), enemy in sight →
interpreter is primed to avoid enemy (social goal) → to decide which
avoidance action to take, interpreter must establish what enemy is up to
(interpretation goal) →

b. *Interpretation goal*: to determine the enemy's goal (interpretation
goal), the interpreter must execute some interpretation tasks →

c. *Specific interpretation tasks*: e.g., identify the enemy's behavior or goal
from gaze and/or bodily posture: *if* [data about gaze and/or posture are
such and so], *then* [expect goal in that direction] →

d. *Response*: *so* [interpreter acts appropriately: informationally or
physically]

Schema (5.1) can be regarded as a sort of global input-output mapping.
Its input is the registration of a specific goal setting and the activation of
an effective strategy to handle the subject by positing a subject-regarding
goal that can be reached by way of an interpretation goal. The mapping is
actually effected at steps (b) and (c), where the interpretation goal is formulated and the right tasks executed. These steps explain the sense in
which the goals and tasks specify the design of the job of interpretation.
The output of the mapping is the interpreter's response to the evolutio-
narily-shaped demands of the goal setting. That response and its benefits
are the evolutionary reason why interpretation evolved in the first place;
specifically, particular types of responses and their fitness-enhancing benefits ultimately determine which interpretive skills get installed.

The job design   So grounded in a selectionist analysis, the goals and tasks
provide a handle on the programs that make up the interpretive competence, for the former indicate what the latter must be doing. The goals
specify the destination, as it were, and the tasks the steps taken to reach it.
This is the *job profile* of interpretation. Whenever I talk of the design of
interpretation, I have in mind the design of its job, not of its programs
(the more usual meaning).[3]

I am aware that this angle of analysis may be too abstract. Never mind.
Besides my professional bias, I invoke in its defense (as I did in chapter 3)
its recognized value in the study of grammar, vision, and other cognitive
aptitudes, and its ability to link evolutionary theory with a top-down
analysis of the design of a competence—a connection needed for my

current argument. For I suggested (in chapter 3) that, unlike vision or grammar, the job of interpretation is not transparent without appeal to how evolution shaped it. The implication is that the classical ICM method (information task → competence → mechanism) must be embedded in an account of the evolutionary envelope of the competence. This envelope is now portrayed as the goal setting where the job of interpretation was designed by natural selection. The joint *evolutionary ICM method* of analysis thus has the following form:

(5.2)   *The evolutionary ICM method*
Selective pressures = goal setting for interpretation → goals → tasks → competence (programs) → functional mechanisms[4]

My strategy is to follow this scheme in both directions, the speculative downstream and the empirical upstream, in order to bring them in reflective equilibrium. I am heartened to note that this policy is shared by some psychologists and that those who take an evolutionary view (Baron-Cohen 1995b, Cheney and Seyfarth 1990, some authors in Byrne and Whiten 1988, Mitchell 1994, Povinelli 1996) adjust evolutionary speculations about selective forces to guesses about the interpretation goals and tasks warranted by the behavioral data. What I am *not* doing, however, is to presuppose that task descriptions provide more than liberal or modest constraints on the executing programs.

Having outlined the finer print of the evolutionary shapers of interpretation as a practice of involvement, I turn next to the question of how these shapers work on situated interpretation. To speculate on that intelligibly, I must first say a few words about situated cognition, of which situated interpretation is a particular form.

4   Situated Cognition

Situated interpretation organizes its tasks in the procedural form of conditional and domain-situated instructions. This is the hypothesis I develop in the rest of this chapter. The argument goes from the general (situated cognition) to the particular (interpretation). I begin in this section with a few serviceable generalities about situated cognition. This background is needed for understanding my points about situated interpretation. Then in the next section I suggest reasons why early interpretation is situated, propose the specific format of its tasks, and examine the evidence.

Information by if/then Any cognizing organism samples correlations in the flow of information conditionally and under assumptions (Barwise and Perry 1983; Bogdan 1988a, 1994; Dretske 1981, 1986; Lloyd 1989). Information is useful to the extent that a state of the world, which the organism registers, informs about another state—present, past, or future, under some law or local constraint. To get the information it needs, an organism conditionally samples the flow because the information is neither obtainable nor useful all at once. Given how the world is (in flux), how organisms live in it (busily, in motion, changing their goals and behaviors), what they access (poor, fragmented inputs), and how their senses work (by picking up only some aspects of the input), all that organisms can do is sample fragments of the states correlated with each other under constraints. The sampling can be represented as having a conditional format: *if* a current condition is such and such, *then* expect, predict, retrodict, or fear that a future, past, or current condition will be, was, or is such and such. No organism is cognitively adapted unless it so treats information. Yet the sampling cannot be done without a further important trick.

Assumptions If an organism expects or predicts rain upon seeing dark clouds and hearing the thunder, it must do so by having the knowledge that dark clouds and thunder correlate with rain, most of the time. This knowledge is either explicit or assumed. It is *explicit* when the brain contains data structures about (or systematically covarying with) the correlation in question (that rain follows dark clouds and thunder most of the time). In humans, we find not only explicit concepts (of darkness, clouds, rain) systematically covarying with the physical phenomena in question; we also find explicit beliefs that dark clouds and thunder are followed by rain. In other species (great apes, perhaps), the same knowledge could be encoded in images, with some index of regular association. This knowledge would also be explicit, though differently encoded. By contrast, if we find that a brain systematically codes for rain, thunder, and clouds (via concepts, images, or specific sensory states) but *not* for their correlations, and yet the brain has knowledge of the correlations, then this knowledge is not explicit. It is implicit or by assumptions.

This is a contrast drawn but not yet explained. Although not intuitive, the notion of assumption is legitimate, often used, and rather well understood in biology and cognitive science (Clark 1989, Marr 1982, Vogel 1988; also Bogdan 1994). In mobile organisms, the programs for walking, for example, assume the solidity of the ground. The design of the programs evolved to comply with the solidity of the ground. The visual processing of information is possible under assumptions about the world (the existence of bounded surfaces, reflectance of light off such surfaces, and so on) and interaction with it (e.g., that a structure in ambient light correlates with distal features). Vision computes the information-carrying correlations among distal features, light input, and retinal patterns under such assumptions. Visual design evolved to reflect these assumptions.[5]

It is not my aim here to explicate how assumptions are built into programs and mechanisms. One would think of the usual bargain—genes propose and natural selection disposes—through which biological functions are inserted into the grid of nature with beneficial effects on the genetic lineage. It suffices to say that assumptions are not explicit encodings. The visual cortex contains no data structure about the fact that light bounces off surfaces; the cortex acts "as if" it knows this truth implicitly. Its sequence of operations on the input data shows that evolution has molded its design around that truth, just as other biological functions have been molded by evolution around various laws of nature.[6]

The metaphor of evolution molding the design of a skill in a way that assumes ecological regularities and laws of nature is central to two hypotheses of this work. One is that interpretation evolved in an arms race against socially utilized conation, and later cognition, in environments rife with communal, epistemic, and political forces of selection. A good deal of this evolutionary escalation is reflected in assumptions, *not* in the procedures and data structures that exploit them. The other hypothesis concerns the predictive and explanatory success of interpretation, which is the main reason why interpretation is taken so seriously by so many people as a guide to, and a prototheory of, the mind. Interpretation (that reasoning goes) must know something about the mind to be successful in its job. Well, yes, it must, but in a special sense of 'know' that (I now argue) is captured mostly by assumptions and built into the design of interpretive skills. This is the same sense in which vision "knows" something about light bouncing off surfaces and how the bouncing reveals properties of surfaces. Vision and interpretation evolved in ways that assume certain truths in their domains and exploit them by certain procedures, and these two facts account for the success of the procedures. It takes a long and ultimate look at the evolutionary conditions in which interpretation tracks the subject's conation and later cognition to uncover the assumptions and procedures that secure its success at manipulation, prediction, training, and coordination of behavior, among the chief achievements that measure its adaptedness.

Systematic tracking   Yet assumptions can do only so much for interpretation. The latter needs a finer-tuned grip on the world. An aspect of the world cannot be causally affected, influenced, or otherwise used to accomplish something, in a nonaccidental manner and in a variety of situations, unless specialized programs are able to spot and reliably reidentify the aspect in question. I call this ability *systematic tracking*. Situated interpreters so track gaze, attention, and bodily posture, and through them goals or simple desires. Systematic tracking includes, but goes beyond, what is explicitly represented. Representations are explicit data structures that covary systematically with a target, say in virtue of their parts covarying systematically with parts or aspects of the target. This is how visual images or sentences covary with their targets, though in different formats. This is *explicit aboutness*, which is one form of systematic tracking. There are also *implicit* forms that track targets systematically but without explicitly representing their properties.

Here are some examples pertinent to interpretation. Eye recognition is explicit. Many species recognize and react to eyes and eyelike patterns (Povinelli and Eddy 1996, Ristau 1991). The recognition results in data structures matched against some appropriate template in the knowledge base. Gaze recognition is more complex, being partly explicit, partly implicit. It may require explicit eye recognition but it also needs (at least) three more pick-up tasks, namely, identifying the line of regard, following its direction, identifying its target. These are distinct tasks that implicitly provide systematic tracking. Eyes are pretty alike across species and conspecifics and remain configurationally stable across contexts; their explicit recognition, quick and standardized, makes evolutionary sense. But line of regard, its direction, and its target are variable across situations and depend on sundry parameters, such as prior behavior, bodily posture, expectations, or environmental layout. A flexible battery of instructions operating as implicit but systematic trackers do better than a large set of explicit templates.[7]

The distinctions between assumptions and systematic tracking and then, within the latter, between its explicit and implicit forms, are crucial to my argument because they chart more precisely the patterns in which interpretation engages the mind. The systematic trackers engage those subject-world relations and their external relata that are targets of involvement by being of practical interest and subject to causal influence. The assumptions go for pervasive and gross conditions underlying and enabling systematic tracking. A distinguished subclass of such conditions consists of the subject's mental and behavioral dispositions. This, I conclude in chapter 9, section 2, is as specific but indirect a knowledge of mind as interpretation is likely to get. In the same look-ahead spirit, note also the evolutionary norm that emerges from this discussion. Systematic trackers, explicit or implicit, are apt to be selected whenever fine-grained patterns must be recognized with some specificity across a variety of circumstances of vital interest, something that assumptions cannot do. In simple cognition, of which situated interpretation is a form, implicit trackers can do this job more efficiently than a few explicit (analog) templates. Hence the next topic.

Instructions   I adapt an example from Cummins 1986 (see also Bogdan 1994, 87–88). Suppose I give you instructions how to reach my home from where you are: straight on street x, left on y, go three blocks, right on z, stop at the third house on your left; that is your destination. The instructions to reach my home do not encode data structures that covary systematically with (represent) properties of the destination, my house. There is no explicit *semantic* relation between the data structures and the house. The information represented is not about the house. My instructions tell you how to reach the house without telling you anything explicit about the house. Being sentences in English, my instructions have semantic values and represent conditions connected with the destination (street, left, straight, etc). Yet the sentences are not about the destination. It is this possibility that is realized in situated interpretation but even more radically. Here is why.

The discussion so far allowed that rules be encoded explicitly, although the information about their object (destination) was not explicit. If explicitly encoded, the rules would be stored as text in memory. With appropriate access, the organism could have explicit knowledge of the rules and deduce certain things from the form of the rules. (For example, from the instruction 'left on y' one could deduce 'not right on y' by knowing words and logic.) Interpretation could be like this but is not likely to, at least not when situated. More likely, its rules are fully proceduralized. This is how genetic programs work. Their rules can be regarded as having the conditional form *if* [condition x], *then* [do y]. For example, the command to a cell could be, *if* [chemical gradient z is registered], *then* [split in two right there].[8] This is a *condition/action* form representing a rule fully proceduralized. Following Cummins 1986, I call it an *instruction*. An instruction does not describe anything; it is not explicit; it simply initiates and controls a process, including the activation of another instruction.

The full proceduralization of rules as instructions complies with the modular and innate character of situated interpretation. Data structures explicitly encoding rules raise the question of origin and formation. Think of explicit knowledge as a text (formulas in some code) and of procedural knowledge as expertise (a way of doing things). We can understand how evolution installs an expertise by playing with the dispositions of and links among functional mechanisms. It is harder to understand how evolution imprints texts in memory, however liberally we construe the notion of text (images, shape or sound structures, whatever). How could a text be imprinted? And how would the brain know when to consult it? Perhaps by consulting another text? A text is more apt to originate in learning. For reasons already examined, learning is not a viable option in situated interpretation. But learning can install instructions. Thus when organisms are conditioned to react to stimuli, a conditional rule is installed by learning, but the rule is not encoded anywhere; grafted on dispositions to associate events, the rule takes the form of an instruction.

What remains literally *explicit* in instructed cognition is the input registration and some items in its knowledge base (on which more in section 6 below). The cell registers a chemical gradient by forming a configuration (data structure) that covaries systematically with some state of affairs and conveys information to the genetic instructions. Similarly, the interpretive cortex registers an eye and activates a gaze-recognition instruction that in turn activates a goal-searching instruction. In such cases, the sensory input is matched against some control feature that can range from a recognition pattern to a sensory threshold. As explicit as the sensory registration and the control feature may be, they are not *about* the targets of cognition, unless the latter is extremely primitive (Bogdan 1994, chapter 4). Interpretation surely is not that primitive. So *if* situated interpretation is instruction-based, nothing in its procedural know-how (aside from the input registration and control features) would explicitly encode data about anything of interpretational significance in its domain, least of all about mental states or architectures in the subject's head.

Domain situatedness Procedural knowledge, based on instructions, is *domain-implicit* (Cummins 1986, 119–120). The idea is this. Suppose that some procedural knowledge works in a domain. Its implicitness resides in the fact that the knowledge is operative without being explicitly encoded in data structures that covary with aspects of the domain. (Having been told how to get to my house, you possess implicit knowledge about its location; the knowledge is implicit in the instructions that govern your behavior.) At the same time, to paraphrase Cummins, procedural knowledge is as much in the instructions as in the domain itself; to this extent, the knowledge is *domain-dependent* for its application. There is nothing in the knowledge that allows an inference from its instructions to the outcome of their execution; the outcome can be reached only by *actually* executing the instructions in the domain. (You can't infer the location of my house from my geographical instructions; you have to actually follow the latter in the territory I choose; in another territory, the same instructions will get you to another destination or no destination at all.) Given the domain (the layout of the territory), the instructions contain the knowledge needed to achieve the outcome (arrive at the destination). It is the assumptions associated with procedural cognition and the design of the procedures that make the cognition domain-implicit and effective because domain-dependent. Of procedural knowledge that is both domain-implicit and domain-dependent, I say that it is *domain-situated*.

Early interpretation is domain-situated. This is the technical sense in which it is situated. Let me anticipate what this entails, so that the readers will know what they bought so far. *If* interpretation were instruction-based, then it would be domain-implicit and domain-dependent. The domain implicitness means that its instructions are not explicit data structures about targets of interpretation, nor do the instructions generate such structures. Explicitly encoded are (say) the subject's eye or his bodily posture, but the object of interpretation, not so encoded, could be the subject's goal or some attitude or a future behavior. The subject's goal is implicit in how his gaze relates to the world around, and his gaze implicit in eye recognition and the direction of regard.

Domain dependency means that the objects of interpretation are reached because of a fit between procedural knowledge and a user-friendly domain. The fit itself is not explicitly encoded anywhere but is assumed in the format of the knowledge. If the interpreter's goal is to identify the subject's goal, then a task-executing instruction could be to follow the direction of gaze until a solid thing is met. This is how situated interpreters, apes and children, seem to do it (Povinelli and Eddy 1996). As in the geographical analogy, if the domain does not "cooperate" (there is no solid thing in sight or whatever), there is no way of applying the instructions and no way of knowing, just by examining them, what the instructions were supposed to track. The lay of the domain, assumed in the evolution of the design of the competence, holds the key to its successful application.

Situated interpretation is designed to operate here and now. It satisfies both domain implicitness and domain dependency because it is constantly immersed perceptually in its domain and uses the domain to interpret. The evolutionary challenge that would radically transform this style of interpretation emerges when the here and now must be transcended; at that point perceptual immersion in the domain no longer works, and domain situatedness must be abandoned. Notice that the more domain-situated a form of cognition, the more instruction-based is the format of its tasks. And the more embedded a form of cognition is in the here and now, in the passing perceptual show and in immediate action, the more domain-situated it is. Instinctive cognition exemplifies these connections. Early interpretation is instinctive. In situated contexts that selected for interpretive reflexes, human adults are as situated and instinctive as early interpreters; they'd better be. Even when a situation is not actually perceived but merely imagined (a perceptually deferred or projected situation, if you like), the situated interpreter still deploys instructions apt to engage a perceptual domain.[9]

The joys of procedurality   In addition to saving one's life, what would interpretation gain from being procedural in general and instruction-based in particular? One benefit is *modularity*. Instructions are best executed by modular programs. Conversely, if there are independent reasons to think that situated interpretation is modular (as there seem to be), then one can expect it to be instruction-based. Another benefit is that instructions are good at (and hence likely adaptations for) *mapping real-time transitions* by specifying that if some conditions obtain, then some changes will take place. Without such procedures, an organism would have to rely on storing, retrieving and processing too many often disconnected episodes, which is the cumbersome alternative of declarative knowledge and explicit learning, cumbersome at least at early evolutionary stages. "For efficient operation in a changing environment, a system is much better off if it has the capacity to use [procedures] for quick generation of expectations" (Holland et al. 1986, 15). This is precisely what situated interpretation needs.

A third benefit is that procedural tasks can be executed *in parallel* and even in *competition* in a fast changing and uncertain environment, again typical of interpretation, much better than can text units of declarative knowledge. Finally, and importantly, conditional procedures have the *inherent flexibility* to get modified and extended, plugged, nested into or connected with other procedures to face new transitions and changes in the environment. Rules can do all of this on a quick and ad hoc basis; instructions need more time and sweat either by limited learning or by slow evolution. Yet the resulting benefits are multiple. Learning itself becomes more efficient and focused, as it builds around existing mappings of correlations and transitions, as opposed to random co-occurrence of separate features (Anderson 1983, Holland et al. 1986).

In principle, then, interpretation has good evolutionary reasons to be procedural, and situated interpretation to be run by instructions. But at what level of processing and in what format? The first answer, argued for in chapter 3, is categorization. Situated interpretation is mostly *behavioral categorization* (Bogdan 1989b, 1994, 88–92; Gomez 1996). Its tasks are to discriminate and classify sensory inputs and map them directly into behaviors. This is typical of sensorimotor cognition, which is where the second answer comes in. Situated interpretation *is* a form of sensorimotor cognition, particularly in its early phylogenetic and ontogenetic stages. What this means is explored next.

5 Tightly Instructed Interpretation

To say that early interpretation operates as sensorimotor cognition and employs instruction-based effective strategies amounts to saying, not very misleadingly, that to interpret an attribute or disposition of a subject is to have an effective strategy of doing something about it and the behaviors it sponsors. For example, to recognize a simple desire is to be able to cause, influence, or exploit the mind-world relation it indicates and the actions it anticipates. In this section I map out the theoretical and empirical background of this hypothesis; in the next I provide a schematic analysis and illustrations of the hypothesis.

Interpretation as sensorimotor practice Perhaps the most potent argument for early interpretation being instruction-based and domain-situated is that, as a form of simple cognition, it is *sensorimotor*. Sensorimotor cognition is known to be fully procedural, situated, and run by behavioral categories (Gomez 1990a). As part of it, so is early interpretation. There are several ways to reach this conclusion. One points to phylogenetic and ontogenetic coincidences: the dominance of the sensorimotor in cognition coincides with that of situatedness in interpretation. The coincidence is firmed up by the observation that crucial features of sensorimotor cognition, such as effective strategies of causal intervention, also show up in situated interpretation. There is also a parallelism of functions: both situated interpretation and sensorimotor cognition are deeply into causal interaction with and manipulation of conspecifics and physical objects, respectively. Both ways of looking at the link between sensorimotor cognition and situated interpretation permeate the remainder of this chapter. But I would like to begin with a third theme.

There is some evidence and insightful speculation that evolution may have shaped situated interpretation around sensorimotor cognition or tapped the latter for interpretive work. Recall that modularity nativism construes interpretation as having evolved its own sensorimotor modules, while starting-state nativism sees available sensorimotor skills as tapped for interpretive jobs. In either case, the result is procedural interpretation by effective strategies that operate situatedly. The MoM view finds three modules—ID or intentionality detector, EDD or eye-direction detector, and SAM or the shared attention detector—that develop before ToMM or the theory-of-mind module (Baron-Cohen and Ring 1994; Leslie 1991, 1994; Leslie and Roth 1993). The first three modules are in the sensorimotor business at an age (between birth and the second year) when infant cognition is mostly sensorimotor. (At least the first two modules, ID and EDD, are also shared by other higher primates.) It comes as no surprise, then, that such interpretive devices were under pressure to assist sensorimotor cognition and share its procedural and situated operation. ToMM, the attitude-recognition module, is supposed to kick into action sometime during the second year, on the basis of SAM inputs (Baron-Cohen 1995b).

It is at this ontogenetic juncture that starting-state nativism makes its alternative move. Two proponents of this view (Meltzoff and Gopnik 1993) suggest that existing sensorimotor skills are tapped for interpretive duties. The idea is that the interpreter's motor plans (and later more calculative plans) may be mapped into the behaviors of the subject, thus giving rise to the category of simple desire (and later, possibly, to that of intention). Meltzoff and Gopnik think that an infant's bodily movements and postures, monitored internally by proprioception, are treated as equivalent to the bodily movements and postures seen in others. Such imitation has many benefits, so it is no wonder that it is practiced since birth. It not only allows infants to treat others as similar to themselves but also helps them hone new skills, such as object manipulation, instruction, and communication. Imitation is viewed as proof of, and training ground for, cross-modal capacity for projection. The projection maps the perceived behavior of a subject into the interpreter's bodily impressions of internal states (such as pains and feelings) and of motor plans and (later) intentions. The latter act as a frame of reference and classification for attitudes imputed to subjects. This proposal reinforces the notion that situated attitudes are categorized as causally effective strategies. Motor plans *are* effective strategies of action. So if a subject's simple desires are projected from motor plans, one would expect the projection to preserve the property of motor plans to be effective strategies for action. On this account, a situated interpreter would recognize simple desires *in terms of* how she would act according to her motor plans.

The frame of reference provided by sensorimotor projections is instruction-based, not theorylike, and tightly constrained, not open-ended. Even though the interpretive projection is not managed by a proprietary module, it is still managed by other modules, such as those for motor planning and behavioral execution.[10] The mechanisms running the procedural tasks of imitation and more generally of assimilation of a subject's behavioral patterns to one's motor plans are not yet known. Reporting on earlier work by Meltzoff and collaborators, Meltzoff and Gopnik speculate about a "primitive supramodal body scheme that allows the infant to unify acts-as-seen and acts-as-felt into a common framework" (1993, 342–343).[11]

In sum, whether one adopts MoM nativism or the ToM version of projection from motor plans, one gets procedurality and situatedness for early interpretation, and one gets it whether the modules are interpretive or not. In the former case, the procedurality is dedicated to interpretation tasks; in the latter, it follows by projection from instructions that govern motor plans. In either case, it is the procedurality of effective strategies. Being sensorimotor, the effective strategies can only operate in a situated manner. This is the line I want to develop now, and it brings us to the other theoretical ways of tying situated interpretation to sensorimotor cognition.

Causal intervention   In general, sensory abilities map changes in the environment as they affect behavior. Sensory discriminations and behavioral categorizations evolve in forms that make such mappings effective. An organism knows how to behave when the outside conditions sensed are of a certain sort, and it knows how to modify its behavior when the conditions change. Primates are known to have evolved a new sensorimotor ability: they *do* things with their bodily implements in a *causally organized way* selected to produce definite results; they not only behave in the world or respond to it but also *act* on it. This matters to situated interpretation because it evolved not merely in contexts of behavior but (for epistemic, communal, and political reasons) also in contexts of *doing things to get specific results*. This, in my current vocabulary, is action.

Since Piaget, sensorimotor cognition geared to action has been associated with a causal and practical understanding of the physical and social world. As Gomez put it, a *practical* understanding "is not based upon the mere detection of contingencies among stimuli. It involves a focus upon the *causal* links that mediate contingencies and the ability to *manipulate* them" (1991, 203; my italics). Such manipulation is critical to a sensorimotor cognition capable of recognizing and manipulating causal relations. The reason is as old as Hume. As long as *perception alone* is involved, the fact that B-type phenomena regularly follow A-type phenomena can be construed as no more than constant conjunction. It could be learned by association, or it could be a Gestalt extracted by a specialized module. One way or another, the constant conjunction shapes the organism's expectation that B whenever A. The expectation can also guide behavior: do A whenever you want B. Given that most species behave but do not act (in the sense of this section), getting used to, taking advantage of, or influencing the behavior of, other organisms need not require interpretation; stumbling upon the right associations will do.

Given the evolutionary pressures on them, this is not good enough for primates. Think of the apes who have the planning intelligence not only to do A in order to get B but to do so in a variety of contexts, many new and unfamiliar; they can also produce conditions of type A in order to get outcomes of sort C, which are similar to B solely with respect to their goals; and they may plan intermediate conditions F, G, and H, which will get them from A to C. We reach now a critical point that was lucidly formulated by Gomez (1990a, 415): unlike an association of two events, a causal relation between them not only can be focused on and manipulated but *can be analyzed into its overt elements* in order to achieve a goal. This is the idea at the heart of the notion of a categorization parser as an effective strategy of practical involvement. Although already used, this notion is now ready for further elaboration.

Effective strategies   Instead of passively relying on observed associations between antecedent and consequent events, cognitive strategies are *effective* because they pick up features of antecedent conditions that, when causally produced by action or communication, deliver the desired outcomes in various contexts, some familiar, some not. This is not to say that the organism capable of effective strategies discovers causation in nature or forms an explicit idea of cause. It is the other way around. It takes an effective strategy to organize procedurally a causal relation between a condition and an outcome. So viewed, the causality of an effective strategy is an artifact of action.[12] An organism is primed to treat the domain of its action causally. It is the organism's insertion in the world—through action, communication, or other forms of intervention—that shapes the organism's sense of causation. This is why the organism's knowledge of causation is practical in intent and procedural in form.

The causal grasp afforded by effective strategies and their practical employment in interpretation is not the familiar one according to which an interpreter knows that the psychological attributes recognized in a subject cause his other attributes and his actions. That is *intrasubjective* or mental causation, concerned with what happens inside the subject and is responsible for his behavior. I am now talking of *intersubjective* causation: causation among interpreter, subject, and the world. Whatever understanding an interpreter (as interpreter) has of intrasubjective causation is going to be parasitic on her knowledge of intersubjective causation. The reason is this. To expect an attribute recognized in the subject to cause action mentally or intrasubjectively, the interpreter must *first* be able to individuate the attribute itself. This ability is shaped by evolution in order to form and deploy effective strategies that causally affect the subject and his world; attribute recognition is *in terms of* such strategies. It is this evolutionarily *antecedent* story of intersubjective categorization that is unfolding right now.

Interpretation provides effective strategies of intersubjective causation by means of information. Looking back at (5.1), in section 3 above, one notices that the perception of an instance of a goal setting for interpretation activates a strategy that posits an interpretation goal to be met by executing certain tasks. What makes this strategy effective as interpretation is that its operational core 〈perception + goal positing + task execution〉 allows an interpreter to engage in appropriate action (the response part) toward a subject and a shared world. The action is part— the most important part from the viewpoint of natural selection—of the design of the strategy.

Let us pause for a minute and note two far-reaching implications of this story. One is that if interpretation is about anything, it is first and foremost about *intersubjective* causation, not intrasubjective or mental causation, as varieties of mentalism advocate. If and when interpreters come to know anything about minds, it is through the prism of their knowledge of intersubjective causation. The other implication is that interpretation from inside, or simulation on, one's own motor plans is also practical and geared to what the self does to and in the world. Whatever the simulator would know about the subject is bound to derive from her practical knowledge of self-to-world causation.

Practical manipulation: tools   As intimated already, the effective strategies of interpretation require not just causal intervention but manipulation. The analogy between interpretation and tool use is more than apt and often comes close to literalness (Bogdan 1991a, 175; Gomez 1990a, 1991). A tool user can treat the domain of tool use thus: when an action with the tool is initiated according to some instructions, the user can expect an outcome in virtue of the action so instructed and in patterns shaped by the action. The idea that the interpreter treats the subject as a tool need not be construed in an exploitive sense, although such a sense was seen to be important evolutionarily. More basic, however, is the sense that tools are *good at something*. To this extent, tools are adaptive *extensions* of cognitive and motor adaptations present in the tool user. To use such an extension adaptively, a tool user must know what a tool is good at. This is procedural knowledge relative to goals pursued. What I know about cars is defined by my utilitarian goal of transportation; a car freak, moved by passion and aesthetics, though no mechanic, would know more; a mechanic still more; and so on.

So it is in interpretation. A tool is an affordance kit; so is the subject under interpretation. The insight about tool use that I find relevant to interpretation is that tools are known in terms of their *practical affordances*, that is, of what they allow one to do. A tool user is adapted with respect to a tool when she knows what effective strategies the tool affords, relative to her goals. A natural teleologist views her subject as a reactor to certain events; her goals require no more; her knowledge of the subject's behavioral reactions tracks what the subject is good at doing when causally prompted by some event. The psychobehavioral interpreter remains interested in the subject's behavioral responses but is pressured to be sensitive also to the subject's conative life; there are new things the subject is good at, such as simple planning, and the interpreter must become good at handling the new tool with its new affordances. Both types of interpreters treat their subjects as social tools, but they treat them almost physically because of their exclusive sensorimotor take on the world (Cheney and Seyfarth 1990, chapter 7). This take manifests a practical grasp of conspecifics as actors and reactors to causal influences. Deception, the telling sign of primate interpretation, is within the power of sensorimotor intelligence (Chevalier-Skolnikoff 1988, Gomez 1990a). But there are other equally telling signs.

Gomez (1991) has tested an elaborate case of primate interpretation that nicely weaves together sensorimotor cognition, social problem solving, and the interpretational use of social tools. His experiment shows how interpretation enables a gorilla to use others as tools in solving a problem. Since the knowledge involved in tool use and problem solving is procedural, quite likely so is the interpretation that operates as part of that knowledge. The experiment has a gorilla needing to open a door by reaching a latch that is high up. She tries three solutions. One is to bring a box on which to climb, the second to get a human to open the latch by pushing him to do so, the third to get the human to do the same through visual protoimperative communication (looking at the latch, then at the human, then again at the latch, and so on). This problem-solving setting must be new to the gorilla, which is why past experience is not much help. Gomez's experiment also shows how early interpretation manipulates causal relations in settings displaying procedural similarity among the behavioral and interpretive solutions to the same problem. Or so I propose to read it. The action on the box and on the human involve similar effective strategies, although one is physical and the other informational and interpretation-based. The solutions involving the human subject (treated first mechanically and then communicationally) differ with respect to how the subject is treated (object versus agent), which of his properties are causally engaged (physical versus mental), and how they are engaged (mechanically versus informationally). Before attending to a crucial difference, I will first stress procedural similarities because they point to causal manipulation. The critical difference will be in what is being manipulated.

Similarities first. Both solutions have the same overall causal direction, which can be phrased as 'interact with tool to get tool to effect action bringing about desired effect', and both share fine-grained sequences of actions deployed to bring about the solutions by instantiating the required causal structure. I stress this procedural similarity because I read the experiment in an evolutionary light. Imagine that way back, selective forces pressured social apes to treat conspecifics as tools in contexts of vital interaction. Imagine that the first move was to treat each other as physical tools, in the spirit of the first human-based solution in Gomez's experiment. The move did not work, or not always, or not efficiently. Some apes evolved new skills, which worked with information instead of physical causation, and managed to insert them in their sensorimotor cognition. The rest is history. Projected back into the evolution of interpretation, the problem was therefore one of *substitution*: how to treat conspecifics as tools and intervene effectively in their affairs in order to serve one's goals by informational rather than physical means? It was a problem of action at a distance, if you like, as opposed to proximal physical impact. Providing effective strategies of intersubjective causation at a distance by means of information in epistemic, communal, and political interactions was *the* evolutionary problem to which interpretation was *the* solution. Action at a distance by means of information was not only more suitable to communal, epistemic, and political primate life than proximate physical action; it was also more efficient. Yet action at a distance by means of information required a new take on the subject as tool and his causal manipulation. Thus the critical difference.

In the mechanical scenario, the gorilla acts physically on the tool according to (what may be called) a *causal push* pattern. It may appear that she does the same with information in the communicational scenario (the naive cognitivist and mentalist assumptions). Yet this is not how I read the facts. The gorilla targets an external state of affairs (the door and the latch) as part of her goal, and communicates about it and her relation to it, after which she checks the trainer's gaze in relation to her goal, then in relation to her posture and her gaze toward the latch. It is in *this* pattern that the gorilla causally manipulates her subject's relations to the world. I would call it a *pull pattern*. Using interpretive resources, the gorilla might be read as choreographing a mutually intelligible communicational pattern through which she attempts to co-opt and coordinate the subject's goal and information access with her own. If the subject is pulled into the right pattern, interpretation and communication are effective and success-ful. The *inter*subjective causal effort, through interpretation and commu-nication, is to pull the subject into the right pattern.

Efficacy and success   The ontological reason why interpretation works and is effective in the pull pattern, rather than the push pattern, is that it was selected for, and designed to operate in, *goal settings* animated by interacting *agents*. To treat the subject as goal-directed is to view his be-havior as driven by, and pulled toward, external opportunities (whatever his internal machinations). To be effective, the toollike manipulation of the subject must therefore be aligned to the external and teleological coordinates of the goal settings of social interaction. The causal push of information that affects the subject and affords practical involvements follows those coordinates if it is to be effective. The gorilla knows that a human is an agent and that the way to causally manipulate an agent is to affect his goals, objects of attention, and mental relations to them. This is intersubjective and externally targeted manipulation.

What knowledge of subjects does such involvement require? The tool analogy helps again in general terms. Tools matter *relationally*, not intrinsically, because their practical affordances consist in relations to the world they act on. The user need not know the internal intricacies of a tool, as long as she has a practical grasp of what it affords (dispositions) and how the affordances are realized in action. (Reading the manual for tool use is enough, as long as the tool works. Think of natural and later cultural selection as installing such procedural manuals in primate inter-preters.) The relational properties of tools are recognized, categorized, and utilized *only to the extent that* they afford effective strategies of uti-lization. Evolution is a miser: it tends to install as economical or super-ficial a knowledge of tools or minds as it can get away with. In the case of interpretation, this knowledge is embodied in its procedural categories and skills.

Behaviorism versus mentalism: the wrong contrast   My reading of Gomez's experiment and of other instances of situated interpretation may be wrong, but this matters less than the practicalist line I advocate on evolutionary grounds. The familiar objection in a case like the gorilla in Gomez's experiment is that she simply learns some observable correlations, as behaviorism predicts (Heyes 1993). In developing this objection, Whiten (1996) makes explicit reference to Krebs and Dawkins's (1984) account of the "interpreting dog" examined in chapter 4, section 3. On that account, interpretation reduces to associative learning and exploitation of statistical correlations. I argued at that time that this is not interpretation, even of the simplest sort (natural teleology), because it fails to meet the conditions of communal, epistemic, and (complex) political selection. Ape interpretation reflects these conditions of selection in that it is practical knowledge, and in particular it reflects them in what the gorilla does in the experiment. I have argued a few pages ago that the practical and causal knowledge that scaffolds sensorimotor cognition and its interpretational form cannot be reduced to behaviorist associations. So, whether my reading of Gomez's experiment is right or not, it remains true that the gorilla has practical interests, which she pursues as a causal manipulator and tool user, and that this sensorimotor stance animates her interpretation. It is this practical aspect that I care about.

The trouble is that the practicalist truth is obscured by what many authors view as an exclusive and exhaustive opposition between behaviorism and mentalism (Premack and Woodruff 1978; Whiten and Byrne 1988a, 1988c, 1991; Whiten 1993, 1994, 1996). The opposition ensures that if a form or strategy of interpretation is seen not to pick out mental-state types, then it must be about behavior, acquired through learning, based on statistical correlations, and hence not genuine. I don't buy this opposition, because I think that situated interpretation has targets other than the mental, is not spectatorial, not theoretical, yet is a genuine competence, innate, domain-specific, and fully procedural. The behaviorism/mentalism opposition has the bad implication of making life easy for behaviorism or behaviorism-inspired skepticism by making it hard, if not impossible, to prove that a situated interpretive category or strategy is about a mental state. But this is the wrong contrast, if construed monopolistically. Practical situated knowledge, in interpretation as in other forms of sensorimotor cognition, is an alternative that fits neither behaviorism (because it is innate, domain-specific, procedural) nor mentalism (because it is not about mental states and does not track mental causation). The next section provides some concrete models of this alternative. And *pace* Whiten and other mentalists, the section following it suggests that even higher-level procedural schemes need not be construed as "intervening variables" that represent mental states.

6 Situated Parsers

The point of the previous sections can be summarized in the following syllogism: to be adaptive, action requires effective strategies; interpretation evolved as part of, or linked to, sensorimotor cognition to serve action; it can do so only by evolving effective strategies for action; these strategies call for behavioral categories of an interpretive sort; the categories in turn ensure the recognition of relations and attributes in terms commensurate with their function as effective strategies of practical involvement. This syllogism is at the heart of my notion of situated interpretation. I argued so far that interpretation is a procedural and situated practice of involvement; these properties must therefore be reflected in the format of its tasks. This is to say that natural selection has designed the tasks to identify and track those joints and interjoint links and sequences that afford effective involvement. The categories that map the subject's relations to the world evolved to execute such tasks, just as the categories of physical object and tool evolved to handle tasks that pick up properties and relations affording effective strategies of action in their domains. Such is the argument of this section. First I need to place my argument in my overall story and specify its range.

Envelopes To find its proper location, consider three explanatory envelopes: (a) an *evolutionary envelope*, which explains how, upon detecting an instance of a goal setting, an organism's cognition enters the interpretation mode, (b) a *practical envelope*, which explaine how, to pursue her goals in such a setting, the interpreter posits a subject-regarding goal, and (c) an *involvement envelope*, which explains why and how satisfying a subject-regarding goal requires effective strategies of interpretation. Once activated, the strategies cause an informational or behavioral response by the interpreter. It is this last envelope that is being examined now.

Situated relations We have reached a point where the analysis requires a distinction, sidelined so far, between how early and advanced interpretation construe the subject's rapport with the world. It is a distinction between situated relations (in teleological and psychobehavioral interpretation) and situated or unsituated attitudes (in psychosocial interpretation). Here the evolutionary investments made earlier again pay dividends. One such investment concerned the dimensions of interpretation sampled in chapter 4. They come in handy to characterize situated relations: a subject-world relation (whatever its specific type) is *situated* if its interpretation is domain-situated, complies with the operating parameters, and is manifested in the dimensions identified in chapter 4.

Another investment concerns the pressures that selected for the dimensions reflected in situated relations. These pressures can reveal the practical *formats* in which the categories of situated relations are deployed. If one knows why some dimensions of interpretation evolved (under what selective pressures) and in what environments of selection (goal settings), then one can approximate what the skills involved were good at achieving (as adaptations) through the practical involvements they generate. One can thus examine the epistemic, communal, or political contexts in which situated skills are formed; derive the frequent patterns of tasks they execute; and on this basis formulate hypotheses about the design of the skills. Not being too empirically minded, I will not go so far but will try instead to convey the spirit of the proposal with some suggestions based on the evidence surveyed in chapter 4.

Categorization parsers   What follows is a sketch of an analysis. It is abstract and schematic—close to how computational psychologists and AI theorists look at cognition (Anderson 1983, Holland et al. 1986) and specifically at interpretation (Shultz 1988, 1991). The emphasis (as always) will be on the format of the tasks of situated interpretation, not its programming, let alone its neural coding. The core idea is a logical composite of elements already planted throughout this chapter and the last, and derived from the psychological literature cited along the way. It can be summarized as follows. As a causal tool manipulator based on sensorimotor cognition, situated interpretation is an adaptation because it categorizes its domain of subject-world relations in formats affording effective strategies of causal involvement. This means classifying, segmenting, sequencing, and combining the subject's relations to, and actions on, the world into units and interunits links that afford effective opportunities for causal involvement. This, I take it, is what Gomez (1990a, 414) characterizes as "analyzing the causal chain into its overt elements" subject to practical involvement. Looking at the naturalist and experimental data on epistemic, communal and political interactions, one can see that practical involvement may take such forms as alteration of, influence on, or reaction to, behavior and also opportunities for control of behavior by fine-tuned expectations, predictions and feedback. I will call the behavioral and (later) conceptual category employed in interpretation for the tasks just outlined the *categorization parser*. There is ample evolutionary reason for such a cognitive ability. The epistemic, communal, and political commerce among primates was shown (a chapter ago) to require fine-grained and well-structured discriminations and classifications of the subject's mind-action-world relations if practical involvements are to be effective and successful. This was particularly obvious in communication, joint-attention behavior, self-regulation, joint-attention sharing, and adult tutoring (Bruner 1983; Gomez 1991; Hobson 1994; Povinelli, ongoing research; Rogoff 1990; Tomasello, Kruger, and Ratner 1993. I borrow the term 'parser' from Povinelli and note that our discussions about, and his reports on, his current experimental work were very helpful in clarifying the fine print of the parsings effected by interpretive categorization).

The general idea of procedural algorithms that would inhabit categorization parsers is not so far-fetched and seems to be congenial to some MoM and ToM researchers (Baron-Cohen 1995b; Baron-Cohen and Ring 1994; Gomez 1990a, 1991; Leslie 1994; Povinelli 1996; Shultz 1988, 1991; Whiten and Byrne 1988c; Whiten 1993, 1994). This idea is not far-fetched particularly when procedural algorithms are viewed as part of sensorimotor cognition. Research on the latter has looked for procedural algorithms in charge of motor behaviors (Jeannerod 1994). A pertinent analogy, already evoked in this chapter, is tool manipulation. Tool use has been long viewed as an evolutionary springboard for primate intelligence.[13] What is important for our discussion is that tool manipulation suggests hierarchical complexity and combinatorial generativity (Chevalier-Skolnikoff 1988, Gomez 1990b, Greenfield 1991), which are two important properties of situated (and unsituated) interpretation. As work on advanced motor behavior shows, rules with such properties can be fully proceduralized as instructions (in the sense of section 4 above). This is also good news for situated interpretation. Equally encouraging in this analogy is that the formatting and segmenting made possible by hierarchical complexity and combinatoriality can be explained evolutionarily by the well-structured engagement, intervention, and incremental interception they afford, whether in handling tools, units of communication, or units of interpretation. In short, tool manipulation is an effective strategy, as is linguistic communication, and for reasons similar to those for which interpretation is an effective strategy: they all afford causal involvement in their domains. And as the discussion earlier in this chapter suggests, natural teleology and psychobehavioral interpretation may actually have been closer to the procedural spirit of *physical* tool manipulation, even when information replaced physical action.

I turn now to some specifics. Unpacking the notion of categorization parser, I propose that for each type of situated relation there is a type of parser made of conditional instructions organized in sequences called *routes* connecting *joints* that afford effective practical involvement. The joints specify the points where causal pressure of an informational or behavioral sort is either generated or can be applied; the routes indicate the casual paths from one joint to another. The categorization parsers constitute the (procedural) *knowledge base* of the interpretation competence. The set of instructions accessible to a particular parser is called its *category list*. A parser can have one or more lists, some more basic than others. Some parsers are almost always *subordinate* because their job is to identify only the components of a (superordinate) situated relation. By analogy with grammar and tool manipulation, one can speculate that categorization in early interpretation is organized in hierarchical form— from global parsings at the top to more specific parsings downstream (Greenfield 1991, Shultz 1991). On this analogy, the topmost unit of categorization is a *superordinate* subject-world relation, whereas the identification of a subject as agent and of his relation to the world are subordinate. Think of the agency and gaze parsers as subordinate: they characterize minimal situated relations, for example, agency and visual contact, respectively.

The category lists associated with each parser contain *core instructions* and may also contain *derived and explicit data lists*, perhaps in imagistic or linguistic or some other data-structural form. The data lists are built by experience around core instructions and form the (explicit) *database* of a parser. The interpreter may learn, for example, that a facial expression associated with a bodily posture indicates something resembling doubt or hesitation, a feature not necessarily selected as an innate recognition pattern. Derived data lists become more important in conceptual and language-based interpretation. One last detail. The outputs of categorization parsers can be fed into further parsers or utilization algorithms that guide behavior (the practical involvement part).

Time now for illustration and elaboration. The situated parsers sampled below are extracted and adapted mostly from the psychological literature. I am aware of the empirical difficulty of verifying them, but I am encouraged by the fact that some investigators not only look at the matter in somewhat similar terms (Shultz 1988, 1991) but construct their experiments accordingly (Gomez 1991; Gomez, Sarria, and Tamarit 1993; Povinelli, personal communication on current work). The idea I find worth defending is not whether a particular categorization parser turns out to be empirically real and testable, but rather that its work be intelligible in terms of effective causal involvements and motivated in evolutionary terms.

Crude agency   Crude agency is a basic subject-world relation handled in situated interpretation. The interpreter is assumed to know how to identify objects, movements, and their causes. This is naive physics, itself an innate competence (Carey and Spelke 1994). Leslie (1994) talks of a "theory-of-body module" that identifies the mechanical properties of bodies. It does so in two stages: first by finding stable three-dimensional objects and then by finding the sources of energy responsible for their motions. It is at this second stage that *mechanical* agency is represented procedurally. This is not yet goal directedness because the relation of agency-to-goal is not represented in the tasks; only mere agency is. The categorization of crude or mechanical agency amounts to a procedural representation of the fact that agents behave mechanically. Adapting Shultz's (1991) suggestion, I present here a few instructions for the parser that categorizes mechanical agency:

(5.3)   *Mechanical agency parser*
a. *If* [object moves and the movement has no external cause], *then* [object is agent], *so* [involvement]
b. *If* [object moves and its movement has an external cause], *then* [object is patient], *so* [involvement]
c. *If* [interpreter wants an object to move and the object is known to be a patient], *then* [the interpreter should cause the object to move directly], *so* [involvement]
d. *If* [interpreter wants an object to move and the object is agent], *then* [interpreter should communicate to the object to move itself], *so* [involvement]
e. Etc.

Suppose that this is a plausible category list for the crude agency parser. Inspired by the geographical example of section 4 above, I suggested that we think of its tasks (a) through (d) as routes that charts opportunities for involvement. A route was said to link joints where engagement, intervention, or reaction are possible and feasible. An object in motion is a joint, and so is its external cause. They afford involvement. Thus, knowing that a moving object is a patient allows interference with its external cause to stop or deflect the movement; this would not be the case if the interpreter knew that the moving object were an agent.

Gaze   Given its centrality, gaze monitoring is paradigmatic of situated interpretation and its practical format. Gaze recognition translates into three types of tasks: explicit recognition of eyes; procedural identification of the line of regard; procedural tracking of the line of regard; and if a link between direction of regard and goal is entered, a fourth task is the procedural identification of the goal as the end point of the line of regard. The earlier geographical analogy again comes in handy. Think of the tasks as articulating the main stages in the interpreter's trip from E (eyes) to G (goal). In the geographical trip, one can get to D only by locating and recognizing A, then going left to B, then left again to C, and finally right to D. Likewise in interpretation, if an interpreter wants to get from E to G, she must first pass through LR (line of regard) and then follow DR (direction of regard) until G is located. In both cases the starting point (the eyes in interpretation, location A in the geographical trip) requires explicit recognition, the rest being done procedurally by following instructions. And just as the geographical instructions tell the traveler to [recognize A], then [go left to B], etc., so the interpretive instructions can be paraphrased as [find and recognize the eye], after which [identify the line of regard], then [follow the line of regard], then [other things being equal, the first solid thing encountered is the subject's goal].

Such instructions evolved to track systematically key joints of the gaze-to-goal relation. My suspicion is that each joint and route are so tracked not only because their sequencing allows an efficient determination of goals from regard but also because each joint and route, or combination thereof, afford involvement. The latter claim is bolder than the former. The regard-goal link could have been sufficient for selection (since beneficial) but not necessary. Other links, such as those between bodily posture and goal or between direction of movement and goal, could have been as effective. Yet all interpreting species place a high premium on gaze. The difference in value, I think, is that the gaze-to-goal relation, unlike other candidates, can be more reliably read and causally manipulated. Even more importantly, the gaze-to-goal relation has a compositional structure that affords effective strategies of incremental and fine-tuned involvement, which the other candidates do not. The fine texture of the epistemic, communal, and political interactions among situated interpreters suggests that the proposed articulation of the gaze-to-goal relation may be no evolutionary accident.

The gaze-to-goal relation turns out to be as valuable practically as its parts. In the geographical example, routes and joints offer so many occasions for involvement. If one wants to check on how well the traveler is doing, one can follow him from joint to joint along a route; if one wants to prevent the traveler from reaching his destination or an interim joint, one can remove a joint before the traveler gets there. This is more effective, more economical, and quicker than attempting a more ambitious deception, which is more likely to go wrong or be detected. So with gaze. Specific routes yield fine-grained information, specific joints along a route allow fine-grained involvement. To see this point, consider one category list in the gaze parser. The arrow stands for the flow of information tracked conditionally from one joint to another along a route. (This is an alternative rendition of the *if/then/so* instructions.) The list samples several routes affording involvements.

(5.4) *Gaze parser*

a. Eyes open → alertness and propensity for behavior → involvement

b. Eyes open + line of regard → interest and its general direction → involvement

c. eyes open + line of regard tracked → goal to be identified or the direction of a behavior to be initiated or something happening somewhere → involvement

d. eyes open + line of regard tracked + the target of the line of regard identified → specific goal → involvement

Each route has its informational value in a context and hence affords specific occasions and forms of involvement. Consider route (a). Closing a subject's eyes, as a mother does with her child, slows down or extinguishes his alertness or propensity for behavior. The same is true of (b). Merely obstructing one's line of regard, as apes are known to do often, effectively prevents one from seeing something or diminishes one's interest in something. The latter effect can also be obtained by switching one's line of regard in another direction, as in the following anecdote. Whiten and Byrne (1988c, 237) report that a young baboon, threatened by a few adult males, distracts their attention by looking intently into the distance; his pursuers forget about chasing him and look in the same direction, giving him time to vanish. This clever ploy exploits the interpretive expectation that line of regard connects with something of interest. Baboons may know more about the overall gaze relation, but its line-of-regard segment suffices for the deception.

I have stressed so far the information-gathering virtues of gaze monitoring. They are not the only reasons for which gaze was selected. Linked to other subject-world relations, gaze has further practical uses. Because of its internal composition (various routes), the gaze parser can lock into other situated relations to avail herself of further involvements. Consider a well-known experiment in which one-year-old infants are placed in front of an apparent brusque drop in the surface they crawl on. Facing them are a toy they want and mother looking on. Noticing the "visual cliff," the infants looked immediately at the mother's face. A happy face encouraged most of them to cross over; a fearful face stopped all infants from crossing; an angry face made most retreat (Hobson 1993b, chapter 3, reporting on work by Sorce and colleagues). The infant interpreter not only recognizes joints of the gaze relation, specifically, the eyes and direction of regard, but reads the mother's emotion *at these joints* and reacts accordingly. For the sake of contrast, imagine a young interpreter parsing the gaze-to-goal relation more extensively: the child looks at the mother; the mother looks frightened in a certain direction; the child follows her line of regard, determines the object of her worry, and then reacts one way or another. There are more things the child can do with the information from the mother in the second case than in the first case. If we add to this picture the fact that in the experiment cited infants show signs of psychosocial interpretation, such as social referencing, recognizing and sharing attitudes, and protodeclarative communication, we get a sense of the already powerful "gaze grammar" that can be recruited to engage at different joints various attributes imputed to the subject.

Developmental research shows that at each new stage in infancy the interpreter picks up new joints and routes in the gaze relation and finds new uses for them. For example, around 12 months infants begin to understand manual pointing associated with gaze; as they sharpen their understanding of the target of gaze, infants come to pick out the target of pointing. This combination seems responsible for a good deal of information and attitude sharing, and may enable the infant to grasp the referential function of language (Hobson 1993b, Butterworth 1991). For a more complex example, let us put gaze and mechanical agency together. This combination yields recognition of goal directedness or full agency. With this in mind, let us look back again at Gomez's experiment (described in the previous section) with the gorilla who wants a human to open the door for her. The first two of the gorilla's solutions clearly rely on executing patient-relevant tasks (b) and (c) in the agency parser, (5.3). I surmise that the third solution recognizes the human as an agent, substitutes informational push for physical push as a causal effector in (5.3.d), and possibly plugs an "activist" (i.e., attention inducing and guiding) reading of the gaze parser, (5.4.d), into the communication slot of the agency parser, (5.3.d). This "activist" reading may be the novel solution to the gorilla's practical problem of opening the door.

As seen in the earlier anecdote of an ape distracting the attention of others, apes seem to exploit, in various patterns, the routes and joints of the gaze relation. There is debate as to how many routes and joints they access and how much that access reveals about their interpretive grasp of mental or even behavioral dispositions (Povinelli and Eddy 1996). No matter how this debate is settled, I think Gomez's experiment illustrates the gorilla's ability to parse the gaze relation in some way, say by looking at the human's eyes, then looking at the latch, then repeatedly alternating between the two while waiting for the human to act. This parsing yields practical effects, such as checking whether the human attends to the gorilla's action and goal, and helping with the goal.

Crude desiring   The interpretation of agency and gaze are normally part of larger enterprises. Consider natural teleology, for a moment. It revolves around basic goals. Its categorization of basic goals might be done by parsers like the following:

(5.5)   *Basic goal parser*
a. *If* [intense gaze], *then* [expect pursuit of basic goal], *so* [involvement]
b. *If* [line of regard is in a direction], *then* [track line of regard and expect basic goal in that direction], *so* [involvement]
c. *If* [line of regard reaches an end point], *then* [other things being equal, that could be the basic goal], *so* [involvement]
d. Deception aside, *if* [gaze follows a direction], *then* [expect it to guide behavior in that direction], *so* [involvement]
e. And so on

The natural teleologist also knows how basic goals link up with behavior. Call this the goal-behavior parser, although one should not exclude a learned data linkage between specific goals and specific behaviors.

(5.6)   *Goal-behavior parser*
a. *If* [basic goals], *then* [expect aggressive behavior], *so* [involvement]
b. *If* [metabolic or sexual goals are active], *then* [expect them to dominate other pursuits], *unless* [outranked by other basic goals, such as defense or protection of offspring], *so* [involvement]
c. Other things being equal, *if* [basic goal is blocked], *then* [expect subject to continue to act], *so* [involvement]
d. *If* [subject displays fatigue or boredom], *then* [expect pursuit of basic goal to be weakened or even terminated], *so* [involvement]
e. And so on

The procedural knowledge represented in the parsers above can be deployed in different context-sensitive articulations. For example, the interpreter may combine her knowledge of intense gaze, line of regard, and its connection with a basic goal, and as a result look intently in the direction of a coming danger, knowing and expecting that her suitor would rank danger higher than courting her. Or if the interpreter wants to deter a subject from pursuing a goal, she can use her knowledge of (5.6.d) and induce fatigue or boredom. And so on. This sort of knowledge survives in more advanced interpretation. Interpreters may know that agents often manifest emotions in the pursuit and satisfaction of their desires. This knowledge also affords practical involvement. The interpreter may know that the subject is disposed to be happy (grins and nods exuberantly) when goal is achieved, morose when not. Such knowledge translates into such practical instructions as the following: *if* [interpreter helps with the subject's goal], *then* [subject gets happy], *so* [involvement], and *if* [interpreter interferes with the subject's goal], *then* [subject gets unhappy], *so* [involvement]. To be effective, the instructions are plugged into the right readings of gaze, posture, and other signs of goal pursuit and emotions. If the interpreter has further plans for the subject, she may plug the instructions into other instructions recommending (say) that *if* [you want reliable cooperation from the subject], *then* [as often as possible help him get his goals when accompanied by positive emotional expression], *so* [involvement].

The naturalist and experimental literature on apes and children is full of such examples. I trust the pattern I am after is getting clearer: the procedural categorizations sampled here parse situated relations along routes and at joints affording practical involvement, which is why (I think) they were selected in the first place.

7   Code and Access

Almost every categorization parser of the sort sampled above can contain
large numbers of lists, each with its many instructions. These numbers
increase as evolution pushes interpretation to further complexity. Beyond
natural teleology, interpreters of all phylogenetic and ontogenetic stripes
face combinatorial explosion, and hence computational and memory
overload. So the question is how they cope with this challenge. It is mostly
a question of *coding* and *accessing* the knowledge formatted in parsers,
their lists of instructions, and their associated databases. The answer is
simplification. I begin by stepping back in order to take the evolutionary
measure of this cognitive gambit. Simplification too turns out to be driven
by practical constraints. I conclude with a few words about why procedural simplification is neither behaviorism nor mentalism and why phenomenological access and procedural interpretation can enjoy a fruitful
symbiosis.

Why simplification?   In the order of evolution, psychobehavioral interpretation is probably the first to feel increased pressures for simplification.
Chimpanzees are crafty social planners. The trouble is, their intelligence
is conative, interpretation is cognitive, and primate cognition manages to
lag behind conation. True, the great apes have a mighty memory for faces
and social situations. But even if it could store enough about a subject,
such memory would not outmaneuver a crafty planner. Add to this the
fact that there are plenty of subjects in one's group, and if one changes
groups often, as chimpanzees are prone to, one meets new challenges with
no memories to help.
   All this could be a processing nightmare. Can it be managed with the
tools surveyed earlier plus some learning tricks? Not likely. The old tools
may no longer help when at least two developments come together. One is
an increase in the complexity of tracking the subject's nonbasic conation.
The other, typical of complex social life, is remembering vast amounts of
data about the subjects' broad and durable character traits and their specific propensities to act. This is not just memory for faces, ranking order,
past incidents, and the like—that is, the sort of memory noted earlier for
not helping much with the interpretation of a crafty planner. The question
now is of memory about what a subject may do, as a matter of individual
propensity, when the context is of one sort and his behavior of another
sort, or when somebody else is present, or when a quarrel just took place,

or the like. If there are many subjects worth worrying or caring about in one's group, as is usually the case, this may be a lot to remember. This memory problem is not about facts (situated interpreters do not remember facts) but about how to represent and store memories of individual propensities through clusters of instructions in category lists.

The two developments require some solution. I propose to proceed by reflective equilibrium and first consider the matter speculatively, on the evolutionary drawing board, as it were, and then examine a few cases, find some theoretical and empirical support, and extract some implications.

Summaries The solution I speculate about is a sort of shortcut across the lists associated with a category. I call it a *summary* and construe it as a second-order task that reorganizes and simplifies a vast array of first-order tasks described by specific lists of routes and joints. How is this done? By what sort of coding policy? One way would be to index, label, or symbolize in some form (images or other sensory signs) frequently encountered patterns of instructions in frequently used category lists. This could nail down a good number of recurrent patterns. For example, a type of stimulus in a given type of goal setting may be taken to anticipate a specific form of planning by the subject; any time the stimulus is displayed, interpretation takes that shortcut across relevant segments in the right category lists. In time the interpreter may evolve a strategy of indexing or labeling such networks of transition-mapping instructions by means of sensory registrations or in some other fashion.

Another way would be for the interpreter to find an internal experience—a sensation, image, or emotion—to summarize and label what a subject is up to specifically or prone to generally. Although not directed at the planning tricks of the subject but at his character, this policy could help considerably with anticipating planning and other things besides. If realizable, such a simplification policy could solve both the coding and access problem. It simplifies the coding of various category lists, and it simplifies and speeds up access to the right instructions.

Does such a simplification policy make *rational* sense? I think so. Consider Macintosh software. Its user-friendly iconography does not burden one with learning and remembering the extensive procedural knowledge needed to operate it. The summaries evolved in situated interpretation may be functionally like icons on the Mac's visual menu. Clicking the icons activates procedures the user may not know about or not know consciously at the time. Likewise, the use of summaries triggers programs

whose tasks are to track complex patterns of conditions. In the phenomenological economy, sensations like pain or hunger have this coding and
access role; they signal bodily conditions that have causes and effects to be
handled in certain ways. It would be surprising if in interpretation and
other domains, evolution had not taken advantage of an external iconography or an internal phenomenology to regiment and simplify the
operation of bodies of procedural knowledge and activate them directly
and speedily when the occasion arises. (For all we know, the phenomenology of pains and feelings may have evolved for these very reasons.)

The summarization policy can then be viewed as a three-steps procedure. Think of chess. A player perceives a board configuration as an instance of a variant or strategy that summarizes a network of moves and
countermoves. Her perception of the board configuration (1) accesses (2)
a summary representation of (3) a complex array of moves—a three-step
process. In the Mac analogy, we have (1) an icon, whose clicking (2)
activates a macro or compacting function, providing a shortcut for (3)
a complex array of lower-level procedures. Something close, I guess, may
have occurred in the evolution of interpretive tricks, of which summarization is a notable and potent example.

Does the simplification policy make *biological* sense? The answer is
again positive. There is a general tendency of life forms to handle complexity economically. Starting from the notion that the hierarchical
organization of the information encoded by biological systems reflects
the evolutionary necessity of controling bioprocesses, Dawkins (1976b)
showed the evolutionary benefit of having high-level units of information
or clusters of such units act as summaries of lower-level data and guide
the activity and outputs of a variety of lower-level branching hierarchies.
This biological point has psychological significance for interpretation.
This is how two primate psychologists relate Dawkins's thesis to interpretive summaries: "In the primate mind ... representations of the behavior of another individual at the lower levels of a hierarchical analysis
might be summarized at a higher level in what amounts to mentalistic
terms. Thus, for example, it might be useful for one primate's mind to be
able to summarize the available information about a second individual at
the level of whether or not that second individual intends to chase a first
individual, or a third party. If it is this property of the second individual
that is the best guide as to how the first individual should act, then it
makes functional sense that the brain of the first should code the situation
in this way" (Whiten and Byrne 1988b, 62). Aside from the mentalist
twist, to which I return below, I think this is the right reading.

Does the simplification policy make *psychological* sense? Again, yes. Let me make the case first in intuitive terms and in a less controversial area, that of character traits, and then draw parallels and implications for less intuitive and more controversial areas, such as attitudes.

The ape who likes One evolutionary story of simplification might have unfolded as follows. I adapt it from an example of Ristau's (1986, 167–168). Ape C, the interpreter, watches ape A often sitting near ape B, huddled next to B, carrying B's infant, grinning happily when B is around, getting excited—the usual story. Suppose their social life is such that A's attitude to B matters to C. Instead of storing and (when necessary) recalling all these and other relevant facts and the contexts in which they occur, wouldn't it be easier for C to recategorize A's relation to B in a *summary* fashion as (to phrase it in our way) *friendly, cooperative*, and *helpful*? This would be a *first-order* summary of a variety of lower-level instructions in several category lists. The contexts in which A displays relations now coded and accessed as *friendly* or *helpful* are bound to vary extensively, even when the contexts center statistically on B more than on other apes. So it would makes sense for C to *resummarize* the first-order summaries even more compactly as A *likes* B. The new *second-order* summary allows C to predict and do something about relations and behaviors not previously exhibited by either A or B and not necessarily predictable or practically manageable in terms of first-order summaries. For instance, if D attacked B, the interpreter C could anticipate that since A likes B, A would help B and C would not have to intervene. And so on.

Thus reprogrammed, the interpreting ape C can now take the perception of a happy grin or of getting excited or of huddling next to someone as external signals (icons) that activate (provide access to) the second-order summary *like*, which in turn activates the first-order summaries *friendly, cooperative*, and so on. The latter, recall, are shortcuts of various separate instructions, as routes in different category lists, and generate appropriate expectations, predictions, and practical measures of involvement. Imagine now that C herself, the interpreter, comes to *like* somebody E according to the script outlined so far: E is *friendly, cooperative*, and *helpful*, which means so many other lower-level relations to C. Like any sentimental ape, C gets certain feelings when E is around. As phenomenological icons, the feelings (like the sensory signals considered earlier) may represent the second-order summary *like* and, when necessary in a context, access the first-order summaries, and then the relevant category lists and their constitutive routes and nodes of intervention, and finally trigger the appropriate predictions and practical measures. This line of analysis has several implications for the practical profile of interpretation. One concerns the practical bent of simplification, another its access to phenomenology.

The practicality of simplification   Many psychologists of interpretation might agree with my account of simplification, up to a point. Like Whiten and Byrne, they may be tempted to read summaries such as personality traits, situated relations, or propositional attitudes as "intervening variables" between sensory registrations and behaviors that pick out types of mental states (Byrne and Whiten 1991; Ristau 1986; Wellman 1990, chapters 4 and 8; Whiten 1993, 1994, 1996). This can be read in a weak mentalist (taxonomical) sense, in which the "variables" organize input-output stimuli in manageable patterns, or in a strong mentalist (postulational) sense, in which the "variables" pick out mental types with internal structure and causal potency derived from that structure (Samet 1993).[14]

Much as I applaud this line on simplification, I deplore its theorism and mentalism, weak or strong. My account of first-order character summaries, such as *friendly* or *cooperative*, is that they link and simplify portions of categorization parsers, relative to certain classes of goals and contexts of interaction. Like the constituent parsers, they assume dispositions whose input-output patterns are explicitly or implicitly classified, sequenced, and tracked in terms of opportunities for practical and hence intersubjective involvement. There is nothing in this interpretive policy of categorization that points to a homogeneous type of mental state or process in the subject. One might be tempted to fit the disposition assumed under that mental type, but that is not going to work. If we take away the input-output patterns, understood practically in terms of strategies of involvement, the assumed disposition is as propertyless for the interpreter as Locke's substance, a "I-do-not-know-what" sort of what. In interpretation the assumed disposition is like a peg on which to hang patterns of correlations that (in my account) secure strategies of intersubjective involvement. The practical patterns are implicit in the categorization parsers.

As a result, being interpreted as *friendly* or *helpful* cannot capture a mental type, if by 'mental type' one means (strongly) an intrinsic and homogeneous structural or functional property of cognition, conation, or character that is causally potent in virtue of its internal structure or function. Mental types, so construed, is what cognitive science, but not interpretation, is after. Resummarizing *friendly* and *cooperative* in terms of a higher-order summary such as *likeable* does not change the picture. Being *likeable* is not an intrinsic, homogeneous, and causally potent mental type either. Nor are higher-level summaries economic representations of input-output correlations. Their job is to be procedural simplifiers relative to patterns of practical interest to the interpreter. Both their basis (categorization parsers) and their practical identity prevent such simplifiers from being mere (weak) mentalist taxonomizers.

The case of the ape who *likes* also suggests that the interpretive categories of character traits are as practical as those of situated relations examined in earlier sections, and for the same evolutionary reasons. As a homework exercise, the reader can look back at the story of the ape who *likes* and construct appropriate parsers for *friendliness* or *helpfulness*, on the model of the earlier ones like the *goal-behavior parser*, (5.6), or others. Like the latter, the former would contain lists of instructions that identify routes linking joints affording practical involvement. The *friendliness* parser could include, for example, an instruction to the effect that *if* [the subject gets excited in the interpreter's presence and grins happily], *then* [expect cooperation or positive neutrality in case of conflict], *so* [involvement]. A combination of parsers, like those for *friendliness* and *helpfulness*, would allow a finer-grained structure of affordances of practical involvements and may be subsumed under a higher-order category such as *liking* or *alliance*.

The phenomenology of access   Philosophers have long debated the nature of psychological attributes in general and of attitudes in particular. One influential line of thought (going back to Plato but perhaps best articulated by empiricists such as Locke and Hume) takes the interpretation of attitudes either to consist in, or else be systematically associated with, perceptual or introspective vivid impressions, feelings, and other phenomenological indices measuring degrees of confidence or strength of reaction or readiness for action or something similar. This is not mere philosophical fancy; it is also robust ordinary observation. People often represent and talk about their attitudes in phenomenological terms.[15] Belief construed as a degree of felt certainty or hope construed as a feeling of physiological élan are commonplace. As with character traits, the phenomenology of situated relations and attitudes may well turn out to be a matter of *access* to summaries of categorization parsers.

How plausible is this suggestion? For one thing, we have a naive grasp of attributes that combines a phenomenological profile with procedural knowledge of its environmental causes and behavioral effects. I read this as complementarity of function. By providing access to the right attribute file—first, to a higher-order summary, if any, and then through the latter to lower-level clusters of parsers with instructions or rules, as the case may be—the phenomenological profile individuates the attribute *type*. It tells us that "there is 'something it is like' to have ... attitudes, just as much as there is 'something it is like' to see red" (Goldman 1993, 24) or to feel friendly toward someone or the like. I mention Goldman's work because, in arguing persuasively for a "phenomenological model" based on introspective recognition of the qualitative features of attributes, it opposes a functionalist, and by implication proceduralist, account of interpretation. I don't see the implication, or at least am not convinced by Goldman that there is one. Goldman's work is too intricate and sophisticated to be tackled here.[16] The point I want to raise now is that there need be no incompatibility between phenomenology and procedural interpretation, and no need for one to replace the other. Phenomenology can provide immediate and clever access to the knowledge base of procedural interpretation. This may not be its only role, but it is surely one apt to serve the simplification policies discussed in this section.

The foregoing was a proximate line of speculation. One can also look at the matter in an evolutionary spirit. Suppose that there are good evolutionary reasons for a phenomenology of pains, which accesses and guides defense and behavioral reactions, and for a phenomenology of feelings and images, which accesses and guides the attribution of character traits. I see no reason why a similar gambit would not work in the recognition of situated relations and even in the attribution of unsituated attitudes. In all these cases, the phenomenology may have evolved first as a response to complexity problems as well as control and reliability constraints. This function is compatible with other uses of phenomenology, as for example, self-regulation in the case of feelings or visual problem solving in the case of images. In interpretation, phenomenological indices are easy and quick to access, correlate reliably with the procedural files they activate, and economize time and processing effort. This is reason enough for selecting a role for phenomenology in interpretation. Yet again, the resulting units of phenomenological access need not be about the interpreter's mental architectures or their representational outputs, anymore than they are about the subject's.

Chapter 6
The Big Little Step

The metarepresentational turn in interpretation is investigated and discussed feverishly in philosophy and psychology. For good reasons. Not only does it bring aboard remarkable new skills—the attributions of crucial propositional attitudes such as desire, belief, and intention—but in so doing, it begins to free psychosocial interpretation from its situatedness, thus opening entirely new avenues of development and utilization. The dimensions of this critical rupture in interpretation and the evolutionary reasons for them are explored in section 1. Taking its cues from the relations between these dimensions and selective pressures, section 2 looks at the design of the new attitudinal categorizations and finds it as practical, in terms of effective strategies of involvement, as could be evolutionarily expected.

Despite its undeniable importance, the metarepresentational turn is not an evolutionary cul-de-sac, as most philosophers and psychologists tend to think. New evolution-sponsored developments are in store. The next two chapters show in what sense and why. To prepare the ground for that, section 3 punctures the alleged finality of the metarepresentational turn by arguing (a) that it is mostly an apprenticeship phase interpolated in the ampler ontogenesis of psychosocial interpretation started in infancy; (b) that the psychosocial agenda, not fully consummated at the metarepresentational turn, is visible in later developments; and finally, (c) that during the metarepresentational turn, the young interpreter is still not that good, in several key respects, as she will become several years thence.

1 Awakening to Representation

A word about representation   The notion of representation is much too generous. So we need some distinctions to single out what matters to interpretation at this evolutionary turn. First of all, the mind is intrinsically representational in that it computes data structures according to rules designed to map proximal stimuli into distal arrangements. This is the sense in which vision, language, and interpretation are representational as a matter of cognitive processing. Second, at the metarepresentational turn, interpreters become sensitive to some representational aspects of the subject's mental life. It does not follow that interpretive concepts are *about* the subject's representations (as specific data structures) or representational processes. These are mentalist entailments I argue against throughout this essay. My position is that the sensitivity of interpretation to representational mentation translates into dimensions indicating that the new skills track representing-revealing parameters of the subject's *relations* to the world. This is the sense I attach to *metarepresentation*. I will often use the noun 'representing' to mark that interpretive metarepresentation is about representing relations, not data structures. Having the skills to track such parameters entails neither an explicit notion of metarepresentation nor the use of the notion or the word 'representation' in interpretive thoughts or linguistic reports.

Metarepresentation   According to most data, the ability to recognize complex desires, beliefs, and intentions that children develop around three or four years of age shows systematic sensitivity to how the subject represents the world. The interpreter begins to appreciate the intrusion of the subject's representational mind into the network of subject-world relations she tracks. By six, most clues to the subject's representings seem to be fully recognized (Forguson and Gopnik 1988, 237), among them, that people can have different goals relative to their experience, memory, or current perception; that they can have the same goal but construe and pursue it differently relative to the same differentiating factors; that they project their goals and the situations in which the goals could be satisfied in the future; that people change their goal policies or their views as a result of differentiating factors, such as new data or how others react; that people may fail to satisfy their goals by misdirecting their desires; and so on.

Accomplishments   These recognitions are sampled in the following list of accomplishments (Forguson and Gopnik 1988; Perner 1991, chapter 9). Since attitudes, more than other attributes, are metarepresented, I confine my discussion to them.[1]

• *Opacity*   Early psychosocial interpretation construed the subject's attitudes in external terms, transparently, as situations desired or perceived. Metarepresentational interpretation can model the subject's relation to the world in terms of how the subject represents the world, whence its ability to capture diversity of attitudes from subject to subject, and also change of mind and misrepresentation.

• *Diversity in mentation and action*   The interpreter realizes that different people can desire and believe and hence behave differently with the same things and in the same situations; or that some desire or believe things and situations that others do not; or that some desire or believe or act better or more accurately or more realistically or more successfully than others.

• *Perspectivality*   The realization of diversity entails the realization that desires and beliefs can be perspectival or dependent on a point of view. This happens first in the visual mode and is later extended to other modes of experience, such as memory, learning, and so on.

• *Misrepresentation*   The interpreter realizes that the subject's desires and beliefs may fail to match his targets, and thus can be unfulfilled or misdirected or false by assigning properties that their targets lack.

• *Appearance/reality*   Another realization is that because of position, access, or available information, the subject may take things and situations to have properties different from how they really are.

• *Futures*   The interpreter sees the subject as having desires and beliefs oriented toward the future and about things and events that do not exist. The psychobehavioral interpreter could do this, transparently, only with situations simply desired, that is, situations desired as actual in the future (Perner 1991). The metarepresentational interpreter can relate the subject to situations that are desired or believed to happen in the future *in the form* in which they are conceived by the subject.

• *Hypotheticals*   The interpreter realizes that the subject may relate to things and situations merely imagined by him as possible or likely.

• *Change of mind*   The interpreter comes to understand that the subject may change his attitudes to the same things and situations.

• *Internal connections*   The interpreter becomes aware that desires, emotions, and beliefs are influenced and shaped by association with memories, perceptions, preferences, imaginings, and other experiences.

Operating parameters   I limit myself to one crucial parameter:

• *Spatiotemporal expansion*   The interpreter is no longer confined to the here and now of ongoing perception and immediate behavioral response.

Her interpretation ceases to be situated. The interpreter can see the subject evolving in his own space-time frame, here or elsewhere; present, past, or future; real or imagined.

Why interpret representation?   What is it about the child's life after three or four (or even before, on some dissenting views) that explains the turn to metarepresentation? One would assume that earlier forces of selection continue to operate, but in an increasingly linguistic and unsituated environment. There are also important evolutionary novelties, many of them continuing to operate at the next turn.

On the *epistemic* side, this is a period when, having mastered the basics of vocabulary and grammar, children turn increasingly to language use or *speech acting*. The literal meaning of sentences does not capture use. Children learn various features of speech acts, locutionary and illocutionary, as a preparation for discursive and narrative speech (Bruner 1990, Slobin 1990). They also learn that what one says reflects not only the world described or projected (literal semantics) but also how much the speaker knows about it, how he represents what he knows, and what implications (behavioral, emotional) are conveyed by how the speaker formulates his speech. Grasping the complexities of speech acts is required for gathering and imparting social information and for new forms of learning, instructed and collaborative.

Unlike imitative learning (handled by situated interpretation), *instructed learning* requires that "children learn about the adult's understanding of a task and how that compares with their own understanding. As the adult regulates the child's performance, usually through intentional speech acts that occur at critical decision-making junctures, the child tries to understand that regulation from the adult's point of view, that is, to enter into an intersubjective understanding of the task" (Tomasello, Kruger, and Ratner 1993, 499). Understanding the adult's point of view requires awareness of his representings. According to the authors just cited, taking the adult perspective also serves another epistemic function emerging at this stage and requiring metarepresentation, and that is *self-regulation*. Children reenact or mentally rehearse adult instructions in regulating their behavior in situations similar to those of active instructions; they use speech acts to monitor themselves and engage in dialogue with themselves; and they mimic what others would say, in regulating their behaviors relative to how others would respond.

On the *communal* and *political* side, a significant break with the past also takes place at this stage. The interpreter is no longer confined (mostly) to parental and sibling relations. She goes out in the social world. As a result, her access to resources and attention depend increasingly on her behavior toward strangers and their behavior toward her. These are platitudes backed by naturalist and experimental data. Young children with siblings are said to be better interpreters than those without. Those with siblings appear to acknowledge false belief in others sooner than those without siblings (Perner, Ruffman, and Leekam 1994). This, presumably, is a rehearsal for things to come outside the family.

Siblings have more opportunities than unrelated children to see each other frequently as competing for the same goal. As a result, noticing any *differentiating* factor, such as access to different information (beliefs) or different ways of desiring a goal (complex desires) or different ways of going about satisfying it (intentions), becomes beneficial if not indispensable for one's goal policies. The pressure for spotting and exploiting such differentiating features outside the family also heats up. The process is bound to continue and intensify as the child enters new and competitive social arrangements (kindergarten, school, sport teams). It must dawn on her that people are more complicated and even more devious than they seemed from the family perspective. There is more teasing, pretence, and make believe than before; lies compete with, and tend to displace, the good old-fashioned behavioral deception; and so on (Dunn 1988, 1991; LaFreniere 1991; Leekam 1991).

In case the young interpreter did not get the message by natural exposure to the new facts of life, *cultural practices*, mostly in the form of games and initiations, make sure that she does. Hide-and-seek games, for example, are widespread across cultures and practiced intensely by children five years old and older (but not younger!) and consist in preventing others from gaining informational access to the location of oneself or of a critical object. It is speculated that the widespread use of this game may be explained by its role in teasing out the skills involved in belief detection and assessment of epistemic success or failure, all bound up with meta-representing (Leekam 1991; Wimmer, Hogrefe, Sodian 1988, 190).

Play, various games, and forms of social posturing become a training ground that provides natural or deliberate pressures for enhanced interpretation, as a prelude for forming the wherewithal needed for an accelerated social education and enculturation. As children grow out of early psychosocial interpretation, parents take more time to explain the new ways of the social world, and evaluate what is going on around them, and particularly the various mishaps ("Beaten up by the bigger bully, eh?"

"Cheated by a smartie?" "Snubbed by a friend?") that occur more frequently and are more consequential than earlier. This is a deliberate *initiation* into the explanatory and evaluative *language of interpretation* and presages the later turn toward reconstruction, often by way of narration. Children whose parents talk a good deal about mental states develop false-belief explanations earlier than those whose parents do not (Dunn et al., 1991).

The *use of language* generally is a major breakthrough in the maturation of interpretation. Linguistic behavior takes center stage in expressing the mental life of subjects, both in honest and deceptive ways. After four, there is an increased awareness of lying and its consequences, and of language-based pretence. It is in the sociopolitical interest of the maturing child to master and, when necessary, counter these techniques. It is also in her interest to differentiate between jokes and lies, honest mistakes and intentional falsehoods, teasing and calculated deception, and so forth. This cannot be done without an interpretive grasp of the linguistic expression of representation-based mentation.[2] Language becomes an index to mental events that are informative to the young interpreter. The arrangement of words and intonation become as important as direct expressions of emotion or behavior in revealing what the subject is up to and how it affects the interpreter. What the subject says (or doesn't) can assist or encumber interpretation but, in either case, it frames it much more tightly than before.

A comparative look at the forces and climate of selection and the accomplishments selected for should reaffirm two basic tenets of my analysis. One is that interpretation becomes sensitive to representing relations because the information yielded by them is now parsed in patterns reflecting practically engageable aspects. Mere sensitivity to representings is not enough to account for an evolutionary upheaval in interpretation. The interpreter cares not just for information but for information to act on in pursuit of her goals. Every big item on the evolutionary menu cries for effective strategies of one sort or another. Thus, for example, understanding the representational underpinnings of language use is essential to conversation, and conversation is a causal give and take in which the participants not only exchange information and size each other up but influence each other's attitudes to the world. Similarly, instructed learning is a causal give and take in which the learner has to parse the information from the teacher, act on it, and send information back to the teacher for evaluation and adjustment. This causal pattern gets even clearer in communal and political interactions. Nothing reflects better the conjunction of the two factors—a new parsing of the information interpreted and the causally effective strategies it affords—than the much discussed categories of belief and intention.

2 New Attitudes

It is not yet clear how the categories of attitudes emerge ontogenetically or when. Nor is it clear whether all these categories are subserved by distinct and specialized modules, or only some are, or none. What is somewhat clearer is that some categories are more basic than others, and to this extent bear more directly the marks of evolution. I am thinking in particular of the basic categories of desire, belief, and intention. They appear to enjoy a relatively tight ontogenetic schedule, and to this degree look like adaptive responses to definite pressures, with variations in the pressures echoed by changes in the ontogenetic schedule. Also supporting this conjecture is the fact that the metarepresentational turn, during which these categories are mastered, is itself a formative period subject to developmental strictures, and hence under the more direct watch of evolution. If this conjecture is on the mark, then the categories of basic attitudes might well have *initially* had the practical format of effective strategies of involvement. The parsers suggested below are based on this assumption.

Other categories of attitudes are likely to be derived from basic ones. Those of hope, disappointment, or regret are just a few in a long list. Philosophers have proposed accounts of how combinations of basic attitudes, particularly desire and belief, might structure derived attitudes (Gordon 1987, Green 1991). It is an open question whether this picture is the right one psychologically. The actual ontogenetic derivation is apt to be a complex affair brought about mostly by cultural and linguistic training. The brief of this chapter does not extend that far. The focus here is on the practical design of basic attitudes and its evolutionary rationale, with illustrations about belief and intention.

Given this focus, my analysis does not depend on whether a basic attitude category is modular (MoM) or formed by exposure to evidence (ToM). Nor is the timing of the category formation important. Also kept at bay is the question of whether the knowledge of attitudes becomes available following the internal clock of the competence (some MoM positions) or the maturation of other cognitive capabilities (the performance line taken by Fodor [1992] and Leslie and German [1995]). No matter how these issues are settled, I think the categories themselves are shaped by ontogenetic pressures of the sort just sampled, and as a result are formatted practically.

What does matter to my analysis is that the interpretation of attitudes evolves solely within the *psychosocial* matrix. The category of attitude builds on the categories of mental take and mental sharing but also inherits from earlier evolutionary phases the recognition of the directedness of an attitude to an aspect of the world and the means-ends (hence practical) format in which subjects are viewed (Bruner 1983, chapter 2, 1990; Hobson 1993b, chapters 6 and 7, 1994). What probably happens during the metarepresentational turn is that these components are integrated, harmonized, and adjusted to the unsituatedness of interpretation and the representational parameters of the subject's relations to the world.

Belief   Belief interpretation has become a polemical danger zone in the recent psychological literature. I will stay clear of it, try only to make a case for the practical design of the belief category, and examine some further reasons for evolving it. I will sketch two belief parsers. I happen to think that the interpreter possesses no general and abstract category of belief. At best, such a category would be a common denominator averaging over available parsers. (Ask the interpreter in the street what belief is and the odds are she will answer in terms of some parser or other enriched with some cultural habits. More on this in chapter 8, section 2.) Consider the following parser:

(6.1)   *Belief-action parser*
a. *Given* [a desire], *if* [subject has past or current informational access to a situation], *then* [this can cause the subject to act], *so* [involvement]
b. *If* [different subjects have different informational access to a situation] *but* [subjects have similar desires], *then* [subjects can act differently], *so* [involvement]
c. *If* [different subjects had different past access to information] *but* [subjects currently have similar desires and perceptions], *then* [subjects can act differently], *so* [involvement]
d. *If* [a subject had information about a situation], *then* [the subject can be surprised by new information about it and delay his action], *so* [involvement]
e. And so on

This is just one category list in the parser, itself incomplete. It construes belief as the informational access that causes a subject to act or not to act when linked to desires and other attributes. For another example, consider a belief-emotion parser and one of its lists, which enables an interpreter to know belief is connected with emotion.

(6.2)   *Belief-emotion parser*
a. *If* [the information the subject has always acted on is contradicted], *then* [subject shows agitation or unhappiness], *so* [involvement]
b. *If* [information the subject has always acted on is confirmed], *then* [the subject shows contentment], *so* [involvement]
c. And so on

There are many other belief parsers, each with several category lists, but these two examples should suffice for making the points I am after. The first concerns the practical format of the parsers. Look at (6.1). The interpreter who knows (a) or (b) can anticipate and promote or, to the contrary, preempt the subject's action by manipulating his information access; she who knows (d) can delay his action by producing new and unexpected information. As for (6.2), if the interpreter wants to upset the subject, contradicting him is a good option; confirming his beliefs is a good way of keeping him happy and cooperative; and so on. I think this is part of the practical basis on which children build up their understanding of belief. Psychological evidence and commonsense observation favor the notion that children do not explicitly learn the truths expressed in such parsers, at least not those belonging to core instructions, such as (6.1) and (6.2).

The second point concerns the evolutionary ambiance in which the practical format of the belief parsers is selected. Belief is an attitude; the categories of attitudes are psychosocial creatures selected to handle mental sharing by recognizing and getting involved in the mental take of subjects. This fact bears on how interpreters come to isolate routes like (a), (b), and (c) in the parsers above and segment them at appropriate joints. The argument about mental take and sharing (chapter 4, section 5) was that these achievements were first possible, and then retained as effective strategies, because interpreter and subject shared topics of mutual concern and (keeping the topics fixed) could react to and get feedback about the factors that differed (i.e., comments), such as judgments, attitudes, the world itself. Thus it is when children want the same thing (a shared topic) and know that they do (through verbal comments or expressions of emotion) that they are pressured to recognize how the other's informational access, past or present, can make a behavioral difference—as seen, for example, in route (b) of (6.1).

As an important aid to this practical reading, I recall the suggestion most responsible for the intense study of the ontogenesis of belief interpretation, that of Dennett (1978b). I construe it as being about the practical design of the belief category. Here it is, slightly reformulated in terms of the interpreter doing something because she thinks the subject *believes* something:

(6.3)   *Dennett's proposal*
a. Interpreter thinks that the subject believes that *p*
b. Interpreter thinks that the subject desires that *q*
c. Interpreter infers from his thoughts in (a) and (b) that the subject will therefore do *x*
d. Anticipating his doing *x*, interpreter does *y*
e. Because she thinks that if subject does *x*, then unless she does *y*, she won't get something she wants or will get something she wants to avoid

I construe this proposal in terms of the notion of goal setting as an evolutionary shaper of interpretive skills. My reading of (6.3) is that clause (a) is true because (b) through (e) hold together, evolutionarily speaking. That is to say, the interpreter's goals interact with those of the subject and hence with his actions; *doing something* about the latter is a rationale for the ability to recognize his beliefs and provides a proper domain where the ability is formed and exercised. So I wholeheartedly agree with Chandler that "one should avoid ascribing theories of mind not only to those who systematically fail to *use* beliefs about the beliefs of others, but also to those who cannot *employ* another mistaken person's wrong beliefs as *subgoals in their own planning strategies*" (1988, 395; my emphases). The recognition of belief would not be selected and contextually prompted unless it occurs in a goal setting for interpretation. I also read Dennett's proposal as specifically stressing, in step (e), a pattern of engagement between the interpreter's action and the subject's, a pattern normally generated by competitive or cooperative interactions. These are all practical factors at work in the ontogenesis of belief interpretation.

As a matter of intellectual history, the irony is that psychologists have followed Dennett's insight (1978b; see also 1987, chapter 7) in setting up experiments to spot the category of (false) belief in apes and children without following his advice about the practical contexts where the category is normally formed and applied. Whether this omission has to do with the logic of experimentation (a point considered by Dennett) or is encouraged by a theoretical and spectatorial stance favored by most students of interpretation, I do not know, but the loss has been critical, to my mind.[3]

Intention   Recognizing intention is recognizing that plans satisfy goals by integrating desires and beliefs and thus mediating between the latter and ensuing actions. The category of intention draws on, but does not reduce to, that of representing desire, despite the fact that the distinction is not easily captured by observation or experiment (Perner 1991, chapter 9). The recognition of intention arrives late, around four or five, for evolutionary reasons discussed earlier in the chapter. The contexts that best reveal the child's understanding of intention are connected with *action*. No evolutionary surprise here. The following is a basic parser that may have been selected in a context of action:

(6.4)   *Intention-action parser*

a. *If* [the subject acts to meet a goal] and [the target of his action is a goal], because [the subject shows neither surprise nor contentment about the consequences of the action], *then* [expect the subject to have planned the action], *so* [involvement]

b. *If* [the subject acts to satisfy a goal] and [the target of his action is not the goal], because [the subject is surprised or disappointed by the consequences of his action], *then* [the subject did not plan the action], *so* [involvement]

c. *If* [the subject shows a desire for a goal] but [given new evidence, the subject overrules that desire], *then* [expect the subject to replan his action toword the goal or change the goal or abandon the whole thing], *so* [involvement]

d. *If* [the subject is observed to closely monitor an action and its outcome] and [in addition, to try to control the action and its outcome], *then* [expect planning], *so* [involvement]

e. And so on

This again is just one parser, with one category list assembled from the experimental literature (chiefly Astington 1991, Astington and Gopnik 1991, Poulin-Dubois and Shultz 1988, Shultz 1991, Wellman 1990). The parser and the list are basic enough to substantiate the point about their practical design. The psychosocial texture of practical concerns leads children to decipher the routes and joints sampled in (6.4), which track how subjects plan their actions and react to the outcomes. From the political stance of the interpreter, for example, it is clear that knowledge of a route like (d) is rewarded because it affords the tactic of interfering with the subject's close monitoring in order to thwart or damage his planning.

An alternative epistemic stance might involve a form of instruction in which the interpreter is (say) trained for a type of mental and (later) behavioral problem solving by imitating how the tutor monitors himself while doing something or by internalizing rules of self-regulation. One can expect parsers and routes selected for several evolutionary reasons, and therefore employable in several types of contexts of interpretation, to dominate in virtue of their economy and versatility. Politically, again, route (c) could have initially been selected because it affords the outcomes predicted in its consequent (e.g., changing goals or plans).

Why belief?   Important dissent aside (on which more later), the recognition of belief, signaling an increased and subtler awareness of the subject's representational cognition, is thought to emerge around three or four.[4] The question is why. To answer this question, we need to consider first the *environment* of selection. Here I found the psychological literature less helpful, although the authors who stress the psychosocial character of child interpretation provide important clues. It would be surprising (by making interpretation too easy) if the child discovers, simply by looking at others, that they misrepresent or cognize the same situation differently. Yet this spectatorial and passive stance on belief, so dear to philosophers, is implicit also in many psychological studies. It does not make much sense. If looking at others facing situations were enough, why haven't apes evolved belief recognition? What is the incentive for the human child to recognize belief later rather than sooner—or, occasionally, sooner rather than later? And what makes that recognition effective?

I think the psychosocial matrix of active and practically motivated mental sharing provides a clue. Given that the chief ontogenetic pressures operate in contexts of intense interpersonal interaction and that the meta-representational turn evolves out of the psychosocial, it is natural that the environments of selection and stimulation for belief interpretation *already* contain psychosocial constraints, such as mental sharing and topic-comment format, among others. So it is plausible to expect the formative stages of belief recognition to share these constraints. The logistics of belief recognition requires a psychosocial matrix of active interaction. How would one ever begin to recognize that someone else has a different perspective on, or is mistaken about, something unless that something is cognitively shared? And how would the interpreter know that a subject's judgment or her own is mistaken about something unless she is shown what the right judgment about that something is? But how could she be shown *that* unless she already knows how to relate to someone else's judgments on shared topics? Could one recognize that another has a different perspective on something or is mistaken about something if that something is *not* kept fixed and shared, as topic, while different judgments (comments) are made about it? The answers to these questions point to the wider psychosocial surround that scaffolds the maturation of belief interpretation.

Trained in the recognition of different emotions, feelings and later desires, attention toward a shared topic, the psychosocial interpreter has the basis, when the time is ripe, to extend that recognition to new kinds of comments and the attitudes they reflect. In an active, imagined, or routinized way, the recognition of belief and of the standards of correctness that allow such recognition requires a relation to a shared topic and, simultaneously, a relation to someone else's stance on and possible judgments about that topic (Hobson 1994, 107–108). This triadic relation must be one of active and practical interference, as a give-and-take of information, experiences, and comments in epistemic, political, and communal contexts of interaction. Thus, for example, epistemically the triadic relation could involve a tutor, with a recognized authority to impose a mutual topic and standards of correctness. Instructed learning, problem solving, and even self-regulation work only if the child can remember how the instructor related to a certain task in the past and what he said about the relation at that time. ("Did you see how I looked at the object?" is the information the child would remember later when reenacting the task execution.) Politically, the triadic relation can be imposed by a competitor whose actions force the interpreter to guess the topic and the standards of correctness.

This diagnosis of the rationale for belief interpretation, combining practical involvement and its psychosocial surround, may also account for the reservations expressed by a number of dissident students of the phenomenon (Chandler 1988, Chandler and Hala 1994, Lewis 1994, Mitchell 1994). One suggestion is that the standard false-belief experiments lack practical import and the right psychosocial texture, and as a result fail to elicit the right knowledge; when these two factors are in place, the ability to interpret (false) belief is manifested earlier than three to four years of age. This suggestion gets support from the fact (already noted) that children politically exposed to situations of manipulation and deception interpret false belief earlier than those unexposed.

Nevertheless, the political facts may also explain why (false) belief interpretation does not normally show up very early in childhood. Except for premature intrasibling rivalry or other unusual pressures, children before three to four are oblivious to deception, lies, and other nasty tricks that typically range beyond a world shared here and now; whatever manipulation and deception young children engage in can be done in the present by the strategies afforded by the epistemology of situated interpretation. This relative innocence comes to an end when children become aware of, and must develop effective strategies to respond to, the new adversarial games of social life played on a much larger space-time scale. (A lie told yesterday may have repercussions tomorrow or later.)

These considerations point to an additional, critical set of pressures for belief interpretation having to do with the newly unsituated domain of interpretation. These pressures can be clustered around three major dimensions: (a) the representational specificity of cognitive relations, (b) the reidentification of such relations across time and situations and relative to topics other than current one, and (c) the realization that the relations are affected by how the subject registers or remembers the world or desires it to be now, in the future, or in the past. These dimensions can no longer be managed with an informational access confined to a world perceptually shared, where the specificity of topics and comments was triangulated from the interpreter's perception and current behavioral and environmental signs of the subject's goals.

Belief interpretation does not make much evolutionary sense for situated interpretation. This is partly why apes and very young children do not seem to need it. (Apes, in addition, could not have evolved it for lack of psychosocial skills.) Situated interpretation does not travel in time. Its practitioners do not remember or anticipate the subject's cognitive relations to situations, nor even their own. There is no need to, evolutionarily speaking. Astington and Gopnik (1988, 201) note that when the present alone matters, data about one's own earlier misrepresentations, even if conceptualized and stored, would not have much utility. The interpreter's current visual experience of x or her noticing that a subject has current visual contact with x suffice to manifest her or his knowledge of x. In either case, there seem to be no need, and hence no pressure, to factor in the *origin* of one's experience or of the subject's visual contact, and so no possible mismatch can be identified between the origin and one's experience or another's visual contact (Chandler and Hala 1994; Wellman 1990; Wimmer, Hogrefe, Sodian 1988).[5]

Language use, of course, has a decisive role in the belief revolution. It not only brings a representational specificity unmatched by perception but also reidentifies objects and situations across time and space, as often and as finely as needed, with an inexhaustible ability to select some properties and discard others. With respect to past or future, real or possible, situations, words can be worth a thousand pictures, as far as interpretation is concerned. For the interpreter, language can makes the difference among deception, lie, and accidental mistake, between something happening here and now and a report about what happened to the subject in the past and elsewhere, between the subject's seeing something now and coming to think something because of what he is told he will see ten minutes from now. That's a big difference. Harris (1996) notes that after treating subjects mostly as planful agents, three-year-olds begin to treat them also as epistemic interlocutors, and this also calls for belief recognition. Three is the age when children acquire conversational proficiency. The connection is not accidental. Neither apes nor very young children converse well, if at all. Conversation transcends perceptual immediacy and assumptions about reality and forces new interpretive policies. Also telling is the fact that conversation requires full possession of psychosocial skills of interpretation, which is what apes, very young children, and autistic children do not have; they are also the ones that do not recognize belief well, if at all.

Why intention? Having risked a few selectionist speculations about belief, I will push my luck a notch further and venture a few about intention as well. As an interpretive category, intention is different from the representing desire, on which it builds. For the interpreter, a subject desires when he has a goal; he desires representationally when the desire has dimensions such as perspectivality or opacity; but the subject intends when he also has a plan to satisfy his goal. Chimps were said to plan (simply) and to interpret planning. Is this an interpretation of intention? Not likely. For one thing, the latter requires interpreting representation-based attitudes, and chimpanzees do not do that. Also, the planning they interpret is a sequence of simple desires, some basic, some not, probably arranged in some alternative patterns. By contrast, the interpretation of intention requires a sense not only of how desires represent goals but also of how the subject plans the action that would satisfy the intention. Even if apes plan their actions under some representation, it is not obvious and not documented that they interpret that planning.

Children are said to understand intention at around four or five. Until then they see actions as caused at most by desires and beliefs; thereafter they see intention as causally mediating between desires and actions (Astington 1991; Astington and Gopnik 1991; Poulin-Dubois and Shultz 1988; Wellman 1990, chapter 10). Why do children interpret intention at around four or five? Why would a plan for action become visible and open to interpretation, and why would such be needed, in addition to the interpreting of desire, as the representation of a goal? Epistemically and communally, the age of four or five marks a passage to more regimented forms of work, social cooperation, and education, and this means increased practical and moral accountability not only for what is being done but also for how the action is conceived and planned. Both life and deliberate instruction teach older children about the cost-benefit analysis of what they plan to do, with appropriate rewards and punishments. For this gambit to work, an understanding of intention is very useful. Also, at this time education and enculturation take a longer-term view (doing something now in order to do something else later and reap the full benefits still later), so that not only the motivation and rationalization of what is being taught but also the ability to intervene in the process, to modify and correct, depend on identifying and handling a distinct plan-capturing attitude. Like other key attitudes, intention is selected for affording effective strategies.

The same is true of self-regulation. Older children are taught by parents and school and by an increasingly complex social life to reflect on, evaluate, and often change their desires and their plans for action. Exercising freedom of will and self-control requires interpretation, in the form of reflection and mental impact on one's volition, and this in turn requires an understanding of intention (Perner 1991, chapter 9). There is also increased pressure to justify to others how one went about figuring out and preparing a course of action. Politically, in an environment in which deferred and future actions are more frequent, both current and future plans become objects of scrutiny, influence, and manipulation. One can influence and manipulate a subject's desires to one's advantage by making the subject's plans easy or hard to execute, or by describing them to him in such terms.

Another important pressure emanates from the use of language as the main avenue to information and manipulation. Language use is bound to generate plenty of false statements. In school, at play, and in other normal interactions, the child is better off if able to distinguish among falsities due to mistake, lying, or joking, and able to respond accordingly. The distinguishing factor is that of intention. A mistake lacks intention, whereas a lie or joke is intention-driven, though in different ways (Leekam 1991). Grades of deception or ill will are also judged on the basis of the complexity and timing of intentions. And so on.

The view from autism   A persuasive case for the systematic links between the selective pressures in midchildhood and the evolving adjustment to representing mentation is provided by autism. Autistic people play an important role in the evolutionary story of interpretation because, being interpretively abnormal, they provides a good control group against which to test proximate and ultimate hypotheses about normal interpretation. The autistic connection fits into my argument at two critical evolutionary turns: psychosocial in general and metarepresentational in particular. I begin with the latter.

Research on autism shows a strong causal link between the interpretive deficits of autistic children and their social and communicational failures. The inability of these children to develop skills that capture representational features of their subjects' relations to the world dramatically harms their social and communicational performances (Baron-Cohen, Leslie, and Frith 1985; Frith 1989; and the articles collected in Baron-Cohen, Tager-Flusberg, and Cohen 1993). I read these harmful effects of interpretation upon social and communicational behavior as indicating that the requirements of communal and political life placed clear and strong selective pressures on metarepresentational interpretation.

Yet the autistic failure to handle metarepresentation originates in the more basic and earlier failure to handle joint-attention sharing and thus to graduate to full psychosocial interpretation. As a result, autistic people lack the interpretive wherewithal to grasp and use the practical affordance of the social and cultural information conveyed by other people (Loveland 1991, 1993). One can reasonably conjecture, then, that the interpretive grip on representation is *first* selected in epistemic, communal, and political contexts where *sharing* and *influencing the sharing* of information and experiences is vital. Let me review some of the evidence backing up this conjecture.

Autistic children are models of social virtue; they do not cheat, lie, pretend, or deceive.[6] They can engage in simple sabotage by thwarting other people's simple plans, but (apparently) not in complex sabotage or lying that would involve other people's intricate, intention-based plans. Yet the data are ambiguous; it may turn out that autistic children understand deception as behavioral manipulation and not as intent to mislead (Sodian and Frith 1993). Autistic children are remote socially, locked in their own privacy, hard to engage in a group activity, hard to instruct, converse with, or amuse with stories, gossip, or play. Their social life is fairly minimal.[7] By now we have a sense of how many interpretive skills must be missing or impaired in order for these communal, epistemic, and political failures to be possible and so systematic. Rigorous observation and experiment confirm the diagnosis. By failing to engage in joint-attention sharing, autistic children do not fully understand the intentions and beliefs of others. Generally, they fail many metarepresentationality tests in interpretation.

At the same time, the interpretive deficits of autists cohabit with, and are occasionally compensated by, normal and even advanced intellectual abilities in other areas. Autistic children show normal mastery of language and concepts, and they operate well in various intellectual domains. Not surprisingly, if we acknowledge the modularity of human cognition, this shows that the selective pressures for interpretation must have diverged from those for other cognitive abilities, such as concept formation, language, and specialized forms of reasoning. Having concepts, dressed in linguistic forms and processed logically, does not yield the interpretation of one's beliefs and intentions. Very importantly, the difference between interpretation and conceptual, linguistic cognition is further confirmed by data showing that autistic individuals understand the representing relation in the *semantic* sense in which words, sentences, or images have meaning and reference but not in the full *interpretational* sense of somebody mentally representing something. That is, autistic persons easily identify concepts, images, and sentences, and understand that and what they represent, but fail to understand and attribute beliefs and intentions. Two consequences follow from this important difference.

One is that the interpreter does not construe the representationality of beliefs and intentions as she construes semantically the representationality of concepts, sentences, and images. As a result, the interpretational notion of representing cannot be the *same* as the semantic notion of representing involved in understanding words, sentences, and images. (This conclusion should make scores of philosophers of mind and language trepidate with irritation—They'd better!) The other consequence is that the difference between understanding the representing relation semantically and understanding it interpretationally may originate in *distinct* paths of cognitive development. It may be that autistic children understand everything there is to understand about representing in a semantic sense but cannot graft the semantic understanding onto the interpretation of attitudes because of psychosocial deficits. Semantic understanding develops as part of language acquisition (perhaps as a distinct, modular, and brain-localized path), whereas the interpretational understanding first evolved in the area of information and experience sharing (equally distinct and at least initially modular), where autistic individuals are at their worst from the very beginning.

Autism thus appears to confirm the modular and innate basis of psychosocial interpretation. This competence operates from infancy, particularly in the domain of affect and emotion, and then extends to the sharing of information. The result could be either SAM (the shared-attention mechanism) or a precursor (Baron-Cohen 1995a, 1995b). Autistic children fail to manifest the workings of SAM and are known to be deficient in using and perceiving affect and emotion in others. Their deficits seem largely organic and innate and perhaps modular. Blind children have an intact SAM rerouted by touch (Baron-Cohen 1995b, 66–69). This excludes the possibility that autism is a deficit in the ability to access and use a competence rather than in the competence itself (as noted here in chapter 3, section 4).

To sum up, then, autism impressively confirms that the interpretation of attitudes is selected as an innately routed avenue to socialization and enculturation. A breakdown in the routing prevents the autistic child from recognizing an attitude, and therefore *its* representationality, and results in interpretive handicaps leading up to social impairment and eventually decreased fitness. This chain of effects vindicates the insight that even at relatively complex levels, interpretation is still within the reach of natural selection.

3   Beyond Metarepresentation

Against the zeitgeist   Before I show why the metarepresentational turn looks transitional, I need to place the issue in a larger perspective. I do so because at this juncture in our evolutionary journey we are apt to confront a powerful and resourceful zeitgeist in philosophy and psychology alike. It is a motley of biases, not easy to pin down and summarize. For my purposes, two arguments can be discerned: one about the mind, the other about interpretation. I simplify the former as holding that the mind is essentially a *representer*, that is, a semantic device governed by formal programs—in the human case, by logical and grammatical programs. So the interpreter of the mind must *end up* (evolutionarily speaking) as a representer of a representer, hence as a *metarepresenter*, in a naive cognitivist sense. It thus becomes almost analytically true that interpretation evolves into a naive cognitivist conception of metarepresentation. This is so because, in the eye of the interpreter, the subject is part of the reality she represents, a part that itself happens to represent. Or so we are told.

The other zeitgeist argument can also be simplified as holding that human interpretation consists in attributions of propositional attitudes, basically, perception, desire, belief, and intention; the skills for these attributions mature and are fully exercised during the metarepresentational turn; so the evolution of interpretation must *terminate* at that turn. Further developments, if any, must be variations on metarepresentational themes. Such variations concern performance rather than competence, and are therefore epiphenomenal, more like speech-acting in contrast to grammatical or semantic competence.

Lots of things are wrong with this zeitgeist view, so many in fact that I do not know where to begin.[8] For my purposes, the comparison with speech-acting comes in handy. To simplify a little, think of grammar, logic, and basic semantics as characterizing programs whose job is representation in a cognitive-scientific sense, that is, whose job is to encode and process data structures whose internal configurations covary with specific aspects of the world. If linguistic communication were merely exchanging representations by encoding and decoding them, with a literal interest in the formal structure and semantic content of the representations, then one would expect communicators to possess only logical, grammatical, and semantic programs, plus appropriate encoders and decoders.

But that is not what happened, thank God, or evolution. Zeitgeist aside, we *all* know that. Not only do we know from daily life that linguistic communication contains a huge and healthy dose of pragmatics that extends from exchanges of new and old information to removal of uncertainty, fixation of indexicals, metaphor, interrogatives, imperatives, metaphors, jokes, and so much more that cannot be captured by appeal to logical, grammatical, and semantic abilities. We also know from theory that the latter do not and cannot handle the pragmatics of language. If we were just linguistic representers, we would not have a capacity for pragmatics.

Actually we don't, retorts the zeitgeister. This brings us to the crux of the matter: is the pragmatics of language a competence or a family of performances? The zeitgeist, of course, opts for the latter. To think otherwise, it holds, is to think that we have, say, poetry programs because some of us write poetry. Usage need not point to specialized programs. I agree, and said so in chapter 3, which is why (when it comes to interpretation) my argument is not about usage but about competence. But my point about the pragmatics of language is not about poetry but about real linguistic universals of a pragmatic sort, such as topic-comment and metaphor. These pragmatic universals suggest distinct skills.

I am willing to push the analogy to language even further in a direction that matters to interpretation. The understanding of linguistic representation requires inferential programs that work pragmatically (Sperber and Wilson 1986). This is a matter of linguistic competence. There are good reasons to think that this pragmatic competence has an evolutionary rationale linked to interpretation, since (among other things) it requires figuring out the communicative stance and intent of the other. Infants probe such communicative stances and intentions before coming to terms with logic, grammar or basic semantics (Bruner 1983 and the literature on early joint attention, recently sampled in Moore and Dunham 1995). So much, then, for the ontogenetic "epiphenomenalism" of pragmatics.

The foregoing suggests another stab at the zeitgeist. I will phrase it bluntly, without nuances, to get the point across. If infants communicate pragmatically before doing so formally and even semantically, that can mean at least two things, both important from an evolutionary stance. One is that the pragmatic surround may contribute, if it is not essential, to the maturation of formal and semantic skills. This is an ontogenetic role for pragmatic competence. The other thing is that, more basically and lastingly, the pragmatic surround may define the overall evolutionary agenda for the development and use of language capabilities. This need not mean, for example, that the grammatical competence was selected for assisting or enhancing communication, although it could mean that, too. The implication, rather, is that the maturation of grammatical competence, like that of semantic competence, is an *interim* chapter in a larger ontogenetic saga of language acquisition, a saga whose key coordinates are pragmatic.

Knowledge of grammar is in place by four, but this does not end the child's initiation into language. There are other skills to be mastered, some tentatively at work since infancy. Moreover, grammatical and conceptual skills themselves must be woven into a larger mental fabric. This fabric is mostly pragmatic, as it pertains (among other things) to communicating and thinking. As one can see by considering the basic skills that animate it, thinking itself *is* pragmatic goal scripting rather than mere production and utilization of representations in virtue of their formal and semantic properties. (So I argued elsewhere in battling the psychosemantic face of the same zeitgeist [Bogdan 1986c, 1987, 1989a, 1993b, 1994]. I am glad to note that the evolutionary data support my preevolutionary arguments).

What does this linguistic detour presage for interpretation? Three hypotheses with polemical bite. One is that interpretation is more like the pragmatics, rather than the semantics or grammar, of a language. Another is that, like the mastery of grammar, the mastery of the metarepresentational categories of desire, belief, and intention is an interim chapter in a larger ontogenetic saga whose key coordinates, set up in infancy, are psychosocial, and hence pragmatic in that sense. The third is that even if the interpretation of desire, belief, and intention—key acquisitions at this turn—were exclusively metarepresentational (a view that does not go unchallenged in the literature), it does not follow that interpretation evolved simply to represent a subject's representings, anymore than that language or thinking evolved simply to make representings possible in the first place.[9] So, duly warned against indulgence of the zeitgeist and warmed up to the alternative, let us begin the laborious case for a further, reconstructional turn by arguing for the limited and transient scope of its predecessor.

The transience of metarepresentation   An important clue to the new evolutionary turn is the incompleteness of its predecessor. Despite its impressive acquisitions, the metarepresentational turn seems at best a bridge to something else. There are several reasons for thinking so. First and crucial is the clear and compelling ontogenetic fact that the mental development of the child *continues* to unfold much after the metarepresentational turn in ways that directly affect—indeed, redesign—interpretive skills. This is the story of the next two chapters. This argument should give pause and food for thought to those (a majority, it would seem) who think that adult interpretation is essentially metarepresentational. The child's interpretive skills evolve dramatically, not just cumulatively, before and after age four, and continue to do so for many more years. Interpretation ends up being a *thinking* person's interpretation, and this is simply not yet the case at the metarepresentational turn.

Second, the interpreter's grip of the representing thrust of the subject's attitudes takes a long time to firm up (several years), is incremental (with stages for desire, then belief, later intention, still later inference), arduous (intense and time consuming), and and actively induced and closely monitored socially (through games, linguistic instruction, story-telling exercises, and other forms of parental training). It has, in other words, all the marks of a serious apprenticeship *for* something else, a building-up process.

Third, another clue to ephemerality of the metarepresentational turn is the fact that key reconstructive skills are nurtured since infancy in the form of mental sharing, joint attention, inner dialogue, and so on, and recalibrated at the metarepresentational turn.

Fourth, even casual observation shows that there is something incomplete and immature about interpretation during the metarepresentational turn. Compared with adults, children at this turn just aren't that good at interpretation (and many other things, for that matter), which is precisely the point. As in their thinking and discourse, during the metarepresentational turn children interpret in small and brief bursts, choppily, without much continuity and linkage, without evolving plots. In fact, their interpretation barely escapes the situatedness of preceding versions. True, metarepresenters can project attitudes across space and time, beyond the current perception, but they do it in fairly simple and disconnected thrusts, like arrows in the dark; they don't weave these projections into a larger matrix where more of the subject can be mapped and mapped more coherently. True, metarepresenters develop new powerful procedures and learn key words and standardized phrases of interpretation, but they are still far from a continuous and coherent interpretive practice and discourse.

Again, the analogy with language is not fortuitous. During the same long period, children develop and master many linguistic techniques and yet are still far from the fluent discourse that will be theirs a few years down the road. And without fluent, integrated discourse, there is no genuine adult interpretation. What underlies fluent discourse is the explicit conceptual navigation and the reflective loops typical of mature thinking.

Neither discourse nor thinking are fully in place and operative during the metarepresentational turn, yet both are vital to mature interpretation.

In sum, the metarepresentational turn appears as a distinct, important, but interim phase when interpretation begins to transcend perceptual and behavioral immediacy, and thus the situatedness of attitudes. Yet metarepresentational interpretation remains limited and impoverished for a while for lack of further mental resources and lack of social and cultural opportunities to interpret. That changes at the next evolutionary turn.

PART III
Reflective Practice

The very shape of our lives ... is understandable to ourselves and to others only by virtue of cultural systems of interpretation. But culture is also constitutive of mind. By virtue of this actualization in culture, meaning achieves a form that is public and communal rather than private and autistic.

Jerome Bruner

Chapter 7

Time for Thought and Culture

Advanced interpretation is as hard to fathom as is thinking, with which it is closely interwoven because the two likely coevolved. Far from frontally confronting either topic or their possible and so fruitful collusion, I will follow the much narrower path of an evolutionary puzzle that promises to shed important light on human interpretation. Here are the key pieces of the puzzle. One familiar piece, noted in section 1, is the *mental revolution* that continues apace after the metarepresentational turn. It is marked by the mastery of concepts and the creative deployments they afford in inference, planning, deliberation, and imagination—all forms of think-ing. In interpretation the major effect of the mental revolution is release from situatedness and immediate behavioral practicality. The subject, occasionally present but so often perceptually absent, becomes a target of mental reconstruction. This exercise tends to be regimented, socially well coordinated, and generally effective and successful. How come?

Intentional realists in philosophy and ToM theorists in psychology have a ready answer. It is because interpreters have a naive but adequate theory of mind; the theory constrains and regulates the interpreter's thinking about the subject's mental states; the adequacy of the theory accounts for its success. Since I do not buy that, I must look elsewhere for an answer. This is where the second piece of the puzzle comes in. I call it *cultural coercion* and discuss it in section 2. Whereas the mental revolu-tion occurs inside the interpreter's head, its successful regimentation on behalf of interpretation originates externally in the way evolutionary pressures, acting through social institutions and public practices, recon-figure the domain of interpretation. The interpreter's mental radar is trained to look for arrangements of facts and regularities that yield effec-tive interpretations. This is when you will hear (a lot, I fear) about scripts and canons as cultural norms that align the mental revolution to the public ways of understanding social roles and psychological attributes. Culture thus coerces interpretation in two important senses: it redesigns its skills and shapes a new understanding of attributes; at the same time, it coerces the interpretation of the contents of attitudes, and of the causes or effects of other attributes, by making them intelligible in terms of shared institutions, norms, and ritualized modes of behavior. The first (redesign) sense will be the major focus of this chapter and a good part of the next. The second (content) sense will figure prominently in the second half of the next chapter.

This is all nice speculation, you would surely say, but can it work psychologically? How does the interpretive radar get to track the cultural signposts of mental attributes? Is there evidence of such deliberate priming? Enter the third piece of the puzzle, in section 3. Intriguingly, there is something that children do not fully master until adolescence, that is crucial to interpretation, and that they are assiduously and constantly trained in throughout childhood. It is *narration*. I do not argue nor believe (as some theorists do) that interpretation is narration or has narrative form or narrative aims. What I find psychologically interesting about narration, and argue for, is that as a pedagogical tool, it redesigns interpretation by sensitizing it to the cultural signposts to be tracked and factored into its operation. The concluding section 4 pits key dimensions of reconstruction against their most likely ontogenetic shapers. As with prior forms of interpretation, my methodological line is to look at what evolution does *to* interpretation in order to understand changes *in* the design of interpretation. The former story is told in this chapter, the latter in the next.

1 The Mental Revolution

To see why thinking-based interpretation is a mental revolution, let us step back for a moment. The tasks of early interpretation were said to be fully proceduralized in the sense that its instructions are domain-implicit and domain-dependent, or in short domain-situated.[1] The situatedness of interpretation was manifest in its total perceptual immersion in the here and now of interaction with subjects. Its success depended on that immersion. Being domain-dependent in fixed ways, the instructions could handle only those domains that instantiated versions or variations of ancestral environments of selection. Even when the domains varied in novel and unselected ways, apparently leading to new accomplishments, as in the case of human-reared and enculturated apes, the situatedness of the interpretation remained unaffected, though not its specific coordinates. Also symptomatic of situated interpretation are its immediate behavioral involvements. The responses are directly interventionist or reactive and normally effected in a continuous space-time frame coextensive with the actual domain of interpretation. So much for the past. The situatedness of early interpretation is undermined during the meta-representational turn and exploded during the mental upheaval leading to the reconstructional turn. What emerges is a quite different way of doing interpretation.

Thanks to thinking   Jerry Fodor once said that thinking is figuring out how the information in a database bears on one's current problem. To do that, the figuring must involve explicit data structures that are currently active because they represent aspects currently relevant to the problem or goal at hand, and the processing must be done under rules sensitive to the explicitness of current representations and the current problem or goal. This, for my purposes, is as good a bird's eye view of thinking as any (Fodor 1983; Holland et al. 1986, chapter 1; also Bogdan 1994, chapter 7). I assume that thinking engages several modalities, such as planning, deliberating, and imagining.

Insofar as interpretation goes, the key change fostered by the mental revolution is the replacement of instructions, as domain-situated behavioral categories, with inference-affording and domain-unsituated concepts. Think of concepts (quite informally) as *rules* mapping the explicit representation of a property into that of another. If, for example, a sensory representation reveals intense barking and four agitated legs under the gate, then the concept of dog is activated and representations of other properties are projected, depending on the context. Concepts themselves need not be explicit representations (of the rules involved) and most aren't. The defining condition is that they operate on such representations, but they can and also do operate on other concepts, as rules operate over rules.

Since one stores lots of properties about lots of things and situations, the work of a concept can be likened to that of a *navigation rule*: it allows flexible and precise navigation through the wide web of stored knowledge of properties of things and situations, linking only those properties, at that level of detail, that fit a particular problem or goal situation. If you ask me why I find cats irresistible (a specific and legitimate query), I remind you (with trembling voice) that they have four lovely short legs and two small, triangular, twistable ears, are invitingly furry, can stare ahead fixedly and opaquely for minutes on end for no good reason, hesitate cogitatively in doorways, are generally quiet but quite opinionated (I better stop now!). I have used the label 'cat' to activate a rule that links some properties that bear on your question. My conceptual cat net is much vaster (as you can well imagine). But I know where to stop (or almost), which is as important in thinking as knowing where to start. Concept and context conspire to cut a relevant path through the appropriate net.

What thinking brings to interpretation, and other domains as well, is not just flexibility, specificity, and creativity but, more basically, freedom from fixed patterns of dependence on and involvement in perceptual and behavioral domains. The result is unsituatedness. This in turn signals a radical break with the evolutionary past. The grip of natural selection on interpretation is dramatically weakened. In thinking-based interpretation, no ancestral goal settings need be replicated (although some may), and no forces of natural selection need be responsible for how the reconstructive skills shape up (although some may). Some theorists talk of the role of thinking in weakening the grip of natural selection as "evolution mentalized." This metaphor signals an evolutionary development whereby a high-powered and plastic brain acquires the ability to play in real time the natural selection game, as it were, by reproducing on its own, and fast, the very slow process of the evolving genome. The advantages, quite obvious, are aptly summarized in the Popperian comment that to think is to let beliefs die in one's stead. The brain can rehearse and respond quickly to the selective forces acting on it by choosing the functional structures that guide behavior adaptively in a context (Bonner 1980, chapter 3; Dennett 1969, 49, 52, 1991a, chapter 7; also Bogdan 1994, 119–121).

Mentalized evolution, open-ended thinking, unemployment of natural selection, and a possible "demodularization" of interpretation may be seen as marking an end to the evolution of interpretation, and hence to a selectionist analysis. Neither the available accounts of these phenomena nor the developmental facts warrant this conclusion. I briefly survey the former next and turn to the latter in sections 2 and 4 below.

Revolutionary options   I examine three options about how interpretation might be affected by the mental revolution. One upholds the modularity of interpretation, another proposes demodularization, and a third brings in other resources to do interpretive work. All options converge in accounting for the integration of information. In earlier forms of interpretation, modularity meant informational autarchy. In ape interpretation one module (e.g., the gaze-to-goal parser) knows that gaze in a direction means interest or a goal, and another (the posture-to-behavioral-disposition module) knows that a certain posture means aggression. Yet, it seems, the ape interpreter would not put the information together, either by connecting the modular outputs or by centralizing them in a single data space. That changes during the mental revolution, although the new format is much debated and not yet fully understood.

According to one account, the modularity of categorization in general and of interpretation in particular survive the mental revolution. Such is the message of Dan Sperber's (1994) notion of *concepts as modules*. Concepts can be domain-specific, have their databases (the definitional information they draw upon), operate autonomously (by working solely on data structures where the concept in question or a component of it occurs), be intrinsically innate or copied from innate concepts, and receive inputs from perceptual modules or other concepts in ways that integrate data without abandoning the informational autarchy of each contributor. The fact that the use of concepts in thinking allows an open-ended integration of data along many inferential routes does not speak against a modular architecture of concepts. Although modular, computers can engage in open-ended and flexible integration of data. So can conceptual systems. The integration trick lies in the functional links among processing nodes (concepts), not in the manner in which the processing is done at the nodes. Modularity characterizes the manner of processing at a node, not what is done to its inputs and outputs up and down the network of nodes. Modular concepts can be used very flexibly.

There is a further twist to Sperber's story. Not only does interpretation stay modular yet flexibly deployable (thus reconciling MoM and ToM positions) but, with its metarepresentational acquisitions, it provides the mind with the metaskills that allow the formation of concepts about concepts and of representations that accept or evaluate other representations—the whole thinking spiel. Guided mostly by culture, this development may yield new interpretive skills of a reconstructional sort. By scaffolding metathinking, interpretation "bootstraps" itself from a narrow metarepresentational basis into wide-ranging reconstruction. Or so I would look at Sperber's proposal.

A second option is Annette Karmiloff-Smith's (1992) account of the developmental process through which major segments of modular cognition, including interpretation, turn unmodular. She calls the process *representational redescription*. Its function is to have the information implicit in a cognitive system progressively made explicit as data structures to that system, thus bringing the information under conscious control. Domain-specificity remains, but other parameters of modularity go. If confirmed, Karmiloff-Smith's account could explain the ontogenetic transition from modular to reflective interpretation. Even strong modularists like Leslie (1991, 1994), Baron-Cohen (1995b, 1993c) and Baron-Cohen and Ring (1994) talk of a theory-of-mind module that could (in the words of Baron-Cohen and Ring) "organize mental state knowledge into a useful and coherent theory of action, such that it becomes both explanatory and predictive" (1994, 188). I read this as possibly allowing an integration of modular knowledge of basic attitudes with new interpretive experiences, perhaps along the route suggested by Karmiloff-Smith. I read in the same way, but in the other direction, the admission by Gopnik and Wellman (1994) that a ToM interpretation could take off from a modular basis.

Finally, there are views that construe the mental revolution as making noninterpretive resources available to interpretation as a sort of ad hoc exaptation (an old structure given a new function). Simulation is one much discussed example, to be explored in the next chapter. The interpreter is construed as using her practical-reasoning programs, possibly modular, to figure out what the subject is up to, when his concrete situation is factored in. As a possible variant, interpretation by projection or imagination could also qualify as using preexisting mental resources.

All these options seem to pose the following challenge to selectionism. Whether interpretive resources are functionally dedicated to interpretation (Sperber, Karmiloff-Smith) or to something else (simulation, imagination), their *utilization* seems to have little to do with evolution. The argument is that practical-reasoning programs or imagination skills or even modular concepts may have evolved for their own reasons, but this has nothing to do with their subsequent interpretational usage. That usage need not have been selected for any particular reason or constrained by anything of evolutionary ancestry or import. Thus concludes the antiselectionist argument.

Appearance is not good enough in this business. Nothing in the accounts considered rules out a novel but still *evolutionary* shaping of interpretation. These are accounts of how interpretation turns unsituated and flexible, not of how its work is redesigned and why. Either account is compatible with new forces of cultural selection redesigning interpretation. It is significant that the process of representational redescription might be slow in the interpretive domain (Freeman 1994, although Karmiloff-Smith [1992, 134–137] seems to confine this to the metarepresentational turn), and so is training in the use of imagination and possibly simulation. Such slowness would coincide with the formative period I assign to the cultural redesign of reconstruction. In short, the fact that interpretation becomes flexible, open-ended, and even demodularized is compatable with its core categories being modular and naturally selected and with its derived categories and their standard patterns of use being practically minded and shaped by selective pressures other than natural ones. This is shown next.

2 Cultural Coercion

If the mental revolution provides the means, it takes a cultural revolution to provide most of the opportunities for, as well as restraints on and guidance on, how the means are to be used in interpretation. If the mental revolution liberates child interpretation from perceptual and behavioral situatedness, the cultural revolution trains it to play adult games, and to this extent it can be as coercive as natural selection, though on a different scale. The cultural regimentation of interpretation is done mostly by scripts and canons, and results in fairly standardized interpretive schemes. This, in a nutshell, is the idea.

When social roles and psychological attributes (traits, emotions, attitudes, feelings) are interpreted in a situation, the interpreter applies a *cultural parser*, or several, in terms of one or more scripts that organize the role- or attribute-manifesting situation according to what is canonical in its type. A *cultural parser*, as a new sort of categorizer, is a sequence of rules that govern an interpretation. A *script* organizes role- or attribute-manifesting situations by identifying their type, their canonical constraints and their affordances for practical involvement. Finally, *canons* are standards of normalcy or accepted frequency or normativity of role and attribute manifestations assumed in interpretation.

Before unpacking all this, let me stress a point of evolutionary continuity. For epistemic, communal, and political reasons, nature scripts and canonizes behaviors and social interactions, as objects of interpretation, as much as culture does. What is different, and still not fully understood, in culture is the form, the scale, and the work of the enterprise, not its rationale or its effects on interpretation. I stress this point to alert the reader allergic to script and canon talk that nothing new or weird is being smuggled in. Your favorite ape was as much scripted by nature to recognize and counter deception in its canonical forms as is the child scripted culturally by games and tutoring to recognize and exploit false belief and pretence. The new terminology only simplifies the analysis in cultural terms. Speaking of terms, this chapter talks mostly of scripts organizing situations to reveal roles and attributes with their canonical manifestations and affordances. These are *role-* and *attribute-relevant* scripts and canons. In the second half of the next chapter I will also talk about *content-relevant* scripts and canons. Scripted situations that reveal canonical features of medical doctorhood or boldness or shyness are of the first sort, while those that manifest canonical behaviors in restaurants or the doctor's office are of the second sort. Although most situations of social interactions exemplify both sorts, the interpreter extracts and utilizes different data from them. This clarified, let us proceed.

Cultural parsers and schemes   The notion of cultural parser is that of a categorization parser formed through culture. Cultural parsers format *types* of role- or attribute-manifesting situations in terms suited for involvement. Compiled or stored in memory and cued by specific triggers, sensory or memorized, cultural parsers unfold when they meet the right situation. The unfolding is not unproblematic. Parsers are rarely applied individually or in totality. Normally, a situation of interpretation requires the joint application of several parsers (desire, belief, etc.) by selecting those sequences of rules that fit the context. This requires context-sensitive *schematization.* The notion of scheme is intended to capture the pattern of rule deployment that fits a context according to the relevant scripts and canons.

Like any abstract algorithm, a parser or scheme does not contain a recipe for either acquisition or application. The interpreter acquires a parser or scheme (the acquisition condition) and also knows when and how to apply it (the application condition). An apt analogy is that of scientific explanation. Think of a parser as being like the formula of a law of nature. Acquisition is about finding the formula; application about getting it to work in explanation. To apply the formula to a particular case, one needs to specify the contextual parameters of the case. This specification is not part of the formula but is added as another (context-specifying) premise, after which the explanation can go through.

In simpler forms of interpretation, natural selection shapes not only the categorization parsers but also the recognition of the application conditions. In human interpretation the acquisition and application of cultural parsers diverge. Even if innate and active very early, these parsers do not come off simply and on their own. It takes ample psychosocial interaction, tutoring, and games (hence culture) to form them. Their application is no longer sensorily and rigidly cued; at best, the sensory cues are part of complex triggering conditions. As a result, knowing when and how to interpret calls for more cognitive sweat. This is where cultural scripts enter the picture.

Scripting As an opening move, imagine the following story. Recall (from chapter 5, section 5) that a mechanical agency parser has such instructions as (a) *if* [object moves and the movement has no external cause], *then* [object is agent], *so* [involvement], and (b) *if* [object moves and its movement has an external cause], *then* [object is patient], *so* [(no) involvement]. The application of these (innate) instructions is cued perceptually. But let us assume, not unreasonably, that ape life is not always that simple. Imagine a group of imaginative chimps, say the bonobos. Suppose some small and vulnerable bonobos develop the habit of getting a friend out of trouble with a big alpha male by having the friend pretend body rigidity, as in death (think of Jerry Lewis as a bonobo), after which he is carried or pulled like a physical object out of the alpha's view. The pranksters assume, of course, that the alpha male will be cued perceptually to apply instruction (b) of his mechanical agency parser and just not bother. Imagine, finally, that the imaginative bonobos repeat the trick as often as they can, teach others, improve different moves, and make it standardized, efficient, and part of the education of any powerless bonobo.

This is an instance of scripting as a cultural accomplishment. Imagine also that such a script replaces other scripts or other natural defense habits because it is more successful in securing the well-being and eventual reproductive success of its users. Then we can say that the script was *culturally selected* for its adaptive value. The final part of the script, enculturation by careful education and game initiation, is truer of humans than apes. The point of this fantasy example is this. A script can install a parser or can extract and schematize sequences of rules from several parsers in patterns that define a type of situation, its measure of canon-icality, and its practical affordances.[2] The scripted patterns are associated with no single perceptual clue and hence cannot be revealed by simple conditioning.

Cognition is awash in scripts. Naive physics is based on scripts about how to behave around solid objects, what to expect from liquids in con-tainers or on surfaces, and the like. Physical scripts install parsers and schematizations and handle their application. For example, children are known to have physical parsers for object recognition. Such a parser contains instructions indicating that something is an object when it dis-plays such properties as unity, boundaries, persistence across space and time, and so on. A physical script tells the child how to deal with objects (thus recognized) in certain types of situations of behavioral interest.[3]

Scripts were said to be of the acquisition or application sort. In simpler forms of interpretation the two sorts may coincide because the conditions of acquisition, reflecting the ancestral environment of selection, are the only ones recognized (cued in) in any ongoing application. (That is what makes interpretation simple.) Yet even then, new schemes can be installed by old scripts. This would be transfer of scripts across domains. Recall Gomez's (1991) gorilla who tried to treat a human agent as a physical tool (chapter 5, section 5). On that occasion the gorilla may have been trans-ferring a mechanical script to schematize a social situation. That failed and an interpretive scheme close to the mechanical one may have replaced it.

Early human interpretation, still simple and rather rigid, teems with acquisition scripts that also handle applications. Adults script for children various classes of role- and attribute-manifesting situations that require specific schematizations. Remember this one? The child looks at an object, then at her mother, then repeats the alternance, eliciting mother's smile, and, watched by the mother, finally reaches out to the object. The script appeals to instructions from a joint-attention parser and from a gaze-to-goal parser, combines them and installs the result as a new scheme, perhaps a new parser. Conceivably, another script could have started in the same way but ended up in a different scheme, by having mother hand the object to the child. In either case, the script brings a type of role- and attribute-manifesting situation under one or several parsers that afford a practical benefit (getting an object with the help and under the protection of mother). These are variations on a get-an-object script.

Games are potent script installers. Hide-and-seek games were shown to be vital in installing interpretive schemes for false-belief recognition. Bruner has carefully and extensively studied how certain games format and routinize mental skills. For example, he has shown how the peekaboo game, based on successive appearance and disappearance of an object or person, scripts a structured format for distributing attention over an ordered sequence of events while interacting with another person (1983, chapter 3). In so doing, the game helps to install more specific scripts of interpretation and communication. In particular, the game scripts the topic-comment format essential to human communication and thinking. The topic-comment script in turn appears to be essential to scripting the reference relation in language. Children learn how and to what words refer in the joint-attention scripts of the sort noted a paragraph ago (child and mother exchanging looks about a shared object), on which a topic-comment script may be later superimposed (Bruner 1983, chapter 4; Hobson 1993b, chapter 7).[4] Scripting has a combinatorial and generative potency, not yet fully understood, that allows novel and flexible schematizations of experience, from interpretive to linguistic schematizations. Later in this chapter we will see how narrative scripts install reconstruction skills and their specific strategies of schematization.

There is a problem, though. Psychosocial interpretation is mentally creative and culture-driven, which is why, in its adult forms, it cannot possibly keep the acquisition and application conditions forever fused or even comparable. Acquisition scripts do not normally show up in later applications of the skills and schemes they helped fix. Adults (or most of them, anyway) don't need mother anymore to fetch objects or refer to things, don't reenact hide-and-seek situations to recognize false belief or induce it in somebody, don't need peekaboo games to talk and think in topic-comment formats, and don't always need narrations to make attributions. So the problem is this. If acquisition does not show up in application (as it does in situated interpretation), how is unsituated interpretation regulated? Subtly and indirectly yet firmly, through the growing recognition of what is normative or canonical in most situations of interpretation.

Canonizing   Scripts *canonize* the design of interpretation. They tell an interpreter when a role- or attribute-manifesting situation is normal, when it isn't, and often by how much and particularly in what respects it is or isn't. Scripts not only induce but also measure *canonicality* and deviance from it. I take *canonicality* to mean what is normal, regular, or frequent in nature and also what is expected or normative in culture.[5] However, the narrower canonicality that matters in this chapter concerns not any sort of situation molded by culture but specifically those that exhibit interpretable roles and attributes. Whatever their origins, canons regularize interpretation and supply it with shared standards that play a crucial role in prediction and explanation. Here is a rough proposal about the main canons at work in reconstruction. If it sounds familiar, it should, for such is the nature of canonicality.

I begin with *cognitive* canons that reflect constraints on cognitive processing, such as relevance of information, usefulness to goals and action, amount of processing effort relative to outcome, interest, and the condition of the organism. These operational canons have a hand in the formatting and public representation of interpretation. Gricean maxims, for example, can be viewed as translating cognitive constraints on information processing into cultural canons of conversation. The reason one often thinks and says that a subject desires that p or believes that q is not that one knows what is going on inside the subject's head, nor does one's formulation capture all there is about the subject's desires and beliefs; the reason for these standard formulas has to do as much with guessing what the subject is up to, given the interpreter's concerns, as with Gricean maxims of relevance or economy.

Other types of canons, *inherited* ones, reflect prior evolutionary programming. They mix operational canons with features of the proper domain that normally trigger standard responses. At each evolutionary turn earlier retained acquisitions may act as inherited canons. They spontaneously organize interpretation by activating its basic parsers. We cannot help but see agents as moved by desires and beliefs, because we are scripted by natural selection to see all organisms as goal-directed and affected by ongoing information. Likewise, many situations require that an adult interpreter only establish simple agency or a gaze-to-goal relation or raw perceptual belief, as children and apes would. Despite having subtler resources, the adult interpreter settles spontaneously for what is canonical in a simpler form of interpretation. Whenever the context allows it, the interpreter is prone to schematize a situation according to inherited canons before bringing in the more potent but more cumbersome artillery of advanced interpretation. There are also *congruence* canons—some natural, others cultural—that normalize interpretation. They capture relations of fit, from means-ends fit to logical fit. The interpreter is primed by nature and then culture to expect desires to fit goals, emotions to fit other attitudes, beliefs to fit each other, and so on. Departures from either sort of congruence typically launch a reconstruction.

Finally, with some trepidation, I group under the label *cultural norms* a vast assortment of canons that "portray how things normally are or ought to be done in a society.... In every culture we take for granted that people behave in a manner appropriate to the setting in which they find themselves" (Bruner 1990, 48). The cultural norms constrain and organize forms of individual agency and social behavior. The norms are acquired by means of cultural scripts and widely shared experiences. The latter define and canonize what it is to be bold or aggressive or, toward the more cultural end of the spectrum, polite, scrupulous, or boring.[6] (Specific examples will be given in the next chapter.) Interpretation stays minimal as long as people conform to cultural norms. As Bruner writes, "When people behave in accordance with Barker's principle of situatedness or with Grice's maxims of conversational exchange, we do not ask *why*: the behavior is simply taken for granted as in need of no further explanation. Because it is ordinary, it is experienced as canonical and therefore as self-explanatory" (1990, 48).

An initiation into canonicality is inevitably an initiation into what is deviant because noncanonical; it may also be an initiation into acceptable or intelligible departures from canons. One surmises from psychological work, such as that of Bruner (1983) and Tomasello and collaborators (1993), that a sense of intelligible and manageable deviance is built into the pedagogical and cultural scripting of norms. Thus games of initiation into interpretation or language acquisition allow for many variations.[7] One assumes that such variations teach the child what is a benign deviation from the norm and what is not, what (very deviant) departures require reinterpretation and what departures do not. One also assumes that whenever the variations are not manageable by standard scripts, because they depart too much from norms, remedial scripts step in or else make room for further reconstruction.

Implicit work   It is essential to see that the scripting and canonizing of cultural parsers is mostly implicit. True, scripting done by imitation, instruction, games, or narration (the main avenues) relies on explicit coding of elements in the domain. Imitation does depend on visual perception; instruction and games begin with and are guided by utterances or gestures about what to do and how; and stories, of course, explicitly tell things. Nevertheless, the initiation into scripts and norms need *not* explicitly represent either the patterns that bring instructions or rules together in a parser or the conditions in which the parser is applied. This is critical for understanding the implicitness of any form of practical knowledge, including interpretation.

How else but implicitly, through scripting, could a child be introduced to word reference? For there is no language (and little else) in place to describe the referring, on the assumption that this is possible. When mother scripts the child's word reference by means of joint-attention sharing and vocalization, she does not thereby provide him with an explicit representation of what is scripted. Having the skill (rather than the concept) of reference is not having an explicit representation of what it is to refer. Or consider naive physics. It may seem that naive physics contains knowledge of explicit laws, admittedly superficial, about the behavior of midsized objects. Yet because of behavioral involvement, it is more likely that children grow up assimilating a vast family of physical scripts as canonical conduits for action. The scripts schematize experiences of and actions toward physical objects and, in so doing, implicitly introduce the child to many physical regularities that can, but need not, be teased out later by reflection, linguistic redescription, and explicit comparisons with other bodies of knowledge. It is these latter exploits that give the impression that what children naively and spontaneously know about physical phenomena takes the form of explicit laws. The impression is an illusion of formulation, not a fact about the procedural knowledge involved.

I think the same is true of the "laws of interpretation" or "intentional laws," as they are sometimes called. Even if mature discourse and explicit reflection on how people interpret would reveal the presence of such "laws" behind patterns of related scripts, it does not follow that knowledge of the "laws" is wired in, let alone that it is explicitly represented in a database and consulted in explanation or prediction. As in the physical case, I think appeal to such "laws" is an illusion of conceptual redescription and linguistic formulation, rather than a built-in feature of the practice of interpretation. This is a promissory note to be redeemed as the argument unfolds in this chapter and the next.

3   Narrative Redesign

How does cultural coercion get a grip on the interpreting mind at the time when both it and the interpreted mind undergo a dramatic cognitive redesign? How, in general, does interpretation get aligned to the explicit and reflective mentation of late childhood and the surrounding culture in which she is gradually absorbed? One answer, crucial though not the only one, points to narration.

The dog that didn't bark: narrative clues   One thing that children do not do well until the onset of adolescence is narration. Very young children don't narrate at all. Few three-year-olds tell coherent stories, while most ten-year-olds do. The former tend to tell stories as if they describe a picture or scene, then another, and so on, serially pointing at discrete events in broken succession. No wonder. They are barely out of situated interpretation, still tied to the passing perceptual show.[8] The ten-year-olds, on the other hand, tell stories by chaining and nesting events into more continuous narrations; they can differentiate reported from reporting speech and thus can "anchor speech within speech"—a key facility in normal narration (Hickman 1987). Yet their stories remain stereotyped, still showing signs of apprenticeship; ten-year-olds are not yet capable of creative and improvised reconstruction (Slobin 1990). It turns out that ten-year-olds are not yet full narrative interpreters, either. They tell stories about others. But these are "mechanical" stories, such as 'He did that, and then went there, etc.'—not good *interpretive* stories.

What has narration got to do with interpretation? Lots, it appears. Let me first turn to the symptomatic links and then move deeper. One such link is obvious. Adult interpretation is mostly narrative as a matter of *performance*. Most stories that most adults tell most of the time are deliberately interpretive or shot through with interpretation. (Narration without interpretation is not much fun, and judging from the popularity of gossip, the converse is not far behind.) This is one reason why the expertise in story comprehension and story telling must be mastered for interpretations to be publicly formulated and shared. Not much disagreement here, I trust. Now for a deeper link. It appears that even seven-year-olds have not yet fully mastered the ability to tell stories in which the attribution of mental states is central (Leondar 1977; for a somewhat dissenting view, see Astington 1990). In sum, if by ten, *much after* the metarepresentational turn, children are still struggling to get their *general* skills for narration in place, and continue to struggle for several more years (Bruner and Feldman 1993; Feldman et al. 1994) *and* if by seven they still have specific troubles with *interpretive* narration, then there may be some noncoincidental links between these ontogenetic limitations, and these links may bear on interpretation. This is a working hypothesis worth examining.

As an amateur evolutionist, the explanation I fancy is that narration has a hand in redesigning the *competence* for interpretation at the reconstructional turn. Like instruction and sundry games, the initiation into narration nurtures reconstruction along as evolutionary midwife and training ground. The skills of reconstruction must operate, like the rest of mentation, thinkingly and hence explicitly and reflectively, free of the constraints of current perception and space-time immediacy. It is no accident that narration helps these skills along such new mental routes. Narration is, adaptationally speaking, good at doing that. To see better what narration does for reconstruction and to avoid unnecessary confusion, an important distinction is in order.

Protonarration versus narration   While allowing narration a critical role in the ontogenetic design of reconstructive interpretation, I do not take the latter to *be* narration. The identity does not follow from the (performance) fact that reconstruction is often expressed narratively or from the (evolutionary) conjecture that narration installs reconstructive skills. Interpretive attributions and explanations need not be narrative, and many aren't, and even most inquisitive reconstructions may fail to be narrative. Narration is a critical episode in the evolution of interpretation, a helping hand. Some students of interpretation (Bruner 1983, 1990; Bruner and Feldman 1993; Carrithers 1991; Lewis 1994) talk explicitly of *narrative* interpretation. Bruner thinks of "narrativized folk psychology" as "organization of experience" along two key coordinates—schematization of experience and affect regulation (1990, 55–56)—and rightly notes that "narrative structure is inherent in the praxis of social interaction before it achieves linguistic expression" (1990, 77). Lewis (1994) makes the point that most psychological experiments that test the presence of an interpretive ability, particularly the recognition of false belief, lack the narrative surround that children naturally associate with interpretation; as a result, the experiments distort the children's performances and misrepresent their abilities.

Bruner's work on scripting and canonizing and his narrative view of interpretation (and language acquisition), like Lewis's specific concern with the narrative underpinnings of attitude recognition, invite a distinction that serves me well in what follows. It separates *protonarration* from *narration*. The latter is the familiar story-telling expertise that children master late, after the metarepresentational turn. The former seems to be a narrower and more specialized skill, exercised since infancy in connection with joint-attention and mental sharing. As a skill, protonarration parses information in terms of topic, comment, and plot, and organizes sequences of data in terms of such parsings.

It may look as though this distinction does not amount to much (isn't narration a complex extension of protonarration?) but in fact it does. First, protonarration is prelinguistic and may scaffold the acquisition of language and the shaping of thinking. Narration, on the other hand, is the fruit of language. Second, protonarration is procedural, implicit, and in line with infant cognition, whereas narration is explicit, descriptive, and in line with advanced cognition. Third, children are good protonarrators since infancy but poor narrators until much later.[9] This is also connected with the fact that infants and young children, living in the present, have poor, if any, memory for interpretive accomplishments. Older children remember their attitudes and those of others and in larger numbers. Protonarration neither presupposes nor improves memory, whereas narration does.

The conclusion I draw is that protonarration is necessary but not sufficient for narration. A difference is made not only by language and thinking but also by the redrawing of the domain of interpretation. Even when enriched with plotlike stories, protonarration remains *situated*; it is as much narration as one may need and get, evolutionarily speaking, when one is confined to the here and now of current perception and action. In contrast, narration soars across space and time, and possible worlds to boot. It is unsituated narration, then, not protonarration, that makes a difference in redesigning interpretation as reconstruction. Protonarration made a tremendous difference in the early design of psychosocial interpretation, probably in the design of language use and thinking, and by implication, in the design of narration itself—no small accomplishments, these.

Narration for interpretation   What exactly does narration do *for* the design of reconstruction? Quite a few things, it turns out. Narration scripts plenty of cultural parsers, schemes, and canons in the child's database, as games did on a smaller scale at earlier stages. The standard stories of one's culture, from legends to proverbs, teem with cultural scripts and canons. The tribe and family add their contributions, as do friends, teachers, and others who matter in education. My interest in these cultural items is that they script one's interpretive understanding of social roles, psychological attributes, and behavioral patterns exhibited in a variety of recognizable types of situations. This initiation operates on the design of interpretation.

The accumulation of cultural scripts poses a cognitive challenge: memory. How to store and retrieve so many scripts and norms not procedurally built into the interpretive equipment, as they were in situated interpretation? It turns out that narration again provides an answer. Human cultures organize and store their collective representations as stories. Before writing, their transmission relied solely on individual memory and oral tradition. The results—in the forms of legends, myths, poems, and proverbs—have been impressive and passed the test of cultural selection. Recent work backs the ancestral insight. Memories organized and stored in narrative form do much better than those that aren't (Mandler 1984; see also Bruner 1990, chapter 2). This is also true of individual representations about subjects. Interpreters keep records of many subjects met over long periods of time. How does memory handle the overload and frame the right economical data to be fed into a current interpretation? Mostly by storing data about the subject's roles and attributes in the form of representative narrations. (Just introspect for a minute and see for yourself.) Not surprisingly, autistic individuals have problems with protonarration, which is why they have access to a very impoverished psychosocial interpretation to begin with, and they also show major deficiencies in linguistic narration and reconstruction (Bruner and Feldman 1993, Loveland and Tunali 1993, Tager-Flusberg 1993).

More important from an evolutionary angle, narration does a job of synthesis by aligning thesis and antithesis (to put it à la Hegel). The thesis is that a mental revolution frees interpretation from its situatedness and to that extent from the direct touch of natural selection. That freedom becomes a potential source of individuality, even idiosyncrasy, which interpretation must handle and control. The antithesis is that cultural coercion acts as the new "selectional" cop on the evolutionary beat. The synthesis, worked out mostly by narration and other installation gambits, aligns the mental revolution to cultural scripts and canons, as a sort of normalization.

I think this normalizing alignment works along several routes. One is the formation and organization of *attribute nets* around psychological attributes in each major class, such as character traits and attitudes. Thus I will talk (in the next chapter) of character and epistemic nets. Possibly through representational redescription or other strategies for making the implicit explicit and also through scripting, each net is organized around core attributes inherited from earlier forms of interpretation (e.g., fear in the emotion net and desire in the attitude net), and is populated at less central locations by a variety of derived attributes (e.g., disappointment in the emotion net and expectation in the attitude net). Narration is good at teaching the child the lay of the net and at defining intuitively some of the derived attributes to be weaved around the core ones. Another route, also well mapped by narration during the education of the young interpreter, is that of engaging attribute nets in the right order, given the demands of the situation. Reconstruction, I also argue in the next chapter, operates according to *rules of engagement*, which ensure respect for scripts and canons, and thus maximize public coordination in interpretation and minimize the need for improvisation.

A third route is the *disciplining of imagination*. This has to do with projecting subjects in situations of interpretation across time and space as well as actual and possible worlds. Narration again is good at doing this by providing early examples and standards and also by nurturing the young imagination along such lines. Relatedly, narration also disciplines the imagination into factoring into interpretation many actually or potentially interacting agents who must be treated alternately as subjects and interpreters. A fourth route leads to *dramatic reconstruction*, as opposed to well-scripted and canonical reconstruction. Narration is not only good at installing this skill but literally takes over its use when norms are violated. Not only does narration install reconstruction skills (the theme so far); it also provides resources for and guidance to the application of the skills when scripts and canons are not obvious or are absent.

One suggestion is that dramatic reconstruction takes the form of a *plot* characterized by "a canonical steady state, followed by some precipitating event, followed by a restoration, followed by a coda in which the game is proclaimed to be over"—meaning restoration of canonicality or explanation of departures from it (Bruner and Feldman 1993, 272). Familiar examples are witnessing people quarreling or somebody suddenly gesturing vigorously in a direction or hearing a startling piece of gossip or being surprised by one's uncanonical attitude or action or the like. On such occasions people shift interpretive gears and reframe a prior canonical and probably minimal interpretation in dramatic plotlike, narrative terms. All these are no small accomplishments and should not be taken for granted just because adult interpreters do it so naturally, flexibly, quickly, and efficiently. The fact that they so interpret confirms that the skills are well oiled and deployed spontaneously.

To sum up, the result of these developments is that reconstruction is served by skills that navigate specialized nets, such as those for social roles or traits or beliefs, mostly under cultural guidance. What I like about the net-navigation metaphor (like the Mac analogy used in chapter 5) is that the interpreter can be primed by natural selection or culture to use a program, and to do so in adequate pursuit of her goals, without having more than a working acquaintance with the program, without the knowledge embodied in the program being about the innards of the subject's mind, and without that knowledge being explicitly represented in the interpreter's head.

4 Dimensions with Reasons

It is time now to turn to our favorite methodological game, dimensions of interpretation versus the forces shaping them, as a basis for extracting insights about the design of reconstruction—a task to be undertaken in the next chapter. I begin with a historical preface. In the ontogenetic scheme of psychosocial interpretation, reconstruction may have been the real game all along. There are signs of it in infancy. The give-and-take of mental sharing and joint attention, the rudiments of inner dialogue, and the plotlike structure of early communication can be seen as building blocks of adult interpretation. So viewed, the first third of life looks like a gradual initiation into reconstruction, a process that picks up speed in late childhood and adolescence and shows signs of development even later (Bruner 1983, 1986, 1990; Bruner and Feldman 1993; Carrithers 1991; Loveland and Tunali 1993; Tager-Flusberg 1993).

Key dimensions A leitmotif of the next chapter will be the contrast between the iceberg of reconstruction and the tip of concise representations of its outputs in the form of attributions or explanations. I mention this to anticipate that I depart from the philosophical and (to a lesser extent) psychological fashion by focusing on the iceberg, where the real work is done and where the evolutionary pressures are felt and reflected the strongest. Although little has been said so far about the dimensions of reconstruction, most of them have already been identified, illustrated, even discussed at some length. So I will be brief and sample those that have plausible evolutionary credentials and design-illuminating value.

• *Interpretive narrativity*   This was noted to be a late childhood accomplishment. It is a distinct capacity with a well sequenced ontogenetic schedule. An apt characterization has it that interpretive narrativity is "a capacity to cognize not merely relations between oneself and another, but many-sided human interactions carried out over a considerable period.... [It] consists not merely in telling stories but in understanding complex nets of deeds and attitudes.... Human beings perceive any current action within a large temporal envelope, and within that envelope they perceive any given action, not as a response to immediate circumstances, or current mental state of an interlocutor or of oneself, but as part of an unfolding story" (Carrithers 1991, 310). Although adults do not have to narrate in order to interpret, for the numerous and evolutionarily significant types of cases cited by Carrithers there is always a narrative surround that can be activated or imagined by the capacity to interpret narratively. This is its importance. Relative to such a surround, the snappy attributions appear almost as conclusions of long inductive reconstructions, on which more in the next chapter.

• *Interpretive improvisation*   Adult interpretation recognizes attributes in diverse and often novel and forms of agency, communication, education, cooperation, play, competition, and conflict. Although the mental revolution and the help of narration were crucial in installing and running interpretive improvisation, this skill does not reduce to assembling an interpretive story; it can also improvise story-free explanations and rationalizations and handle departures from scripts or stereotypical situations.

• *Inferential recovery of attributes*   Unlike simpler forms of interpretation, reconstruction retrieves roles and attributes that bear no direct and univocal relation to behavioral manifestations or states of the world. Traits or attitudes are rarely attributed, in a shared context of interpersonal interaction, solely on the basis of behavioral or linguistic data. A variety of other data are used to fill in the gaps through various inferential strategies: inductive, analogical, simulational, imaginative.

• *Mental utilization*   In earlier forms of interpretation, the categorizations of attributes and actions were fed directly into the interpreter's goal scripts and behavioral routines. The same categorizations now find mental utilization in reasoning, planning, deciding, and imagining.

The next and last two dimensions are perhaps best viewed as a contrasting tandem:

• *Individualization* This dimension is not easy to pin down. Nevertheless, it is worth the effort, and even a rough approximation will do, for it and its companion dimension say a good deal about reconstruction. Individualized interpretation is the ability to zoom in as specifically as needed on a unique combination of attributes displayed by a person in general or in rare contexts of behavior. (The qualifiers 'specifically,' 'unique', and 'rare' are relative to the interpreter's experience.) Why would this be an unusual accomplishment? Because it wasn't possible before, not as a systematic policy. Individualization relies on the other dimensions just listed, and these are all new. The evolutionary perspective may help sharpen the idea. Although apes and very young children recognize and relate (socially, emotionally) to many conspecifics as unique individuals (parents, relatives, friends, enemies), they don't seem to *interpret* these others in terms of possibly unique combinations of attributes. Early interpretation is standardized along the ancestral lines set by the environments of selection for the skills involved. Situated interpreters do not remember facts and attitudes to facts, which is required in order to retain sequences of attitudes over time. Also, situated interpreters, particularly the apes, likely use interpretive modules that cannot integrate their data in a unique psychological profile.

• *Normalization* Reconstruction reflects the tension between mind and culture—one being a source of individuality, the other of conformity. (I sense this theme in Bruner 1990, particularly chapter 2.) The mind-driven individuality of the subject is a challenge to interpretation, but culture steps in to provide a normalization grid, in terms of publicly intelligible and context-appropriate standards, as well as measures of deviations from them. After a long and arduous maturation under cultural supervision, the interpreter comes to recognize the subject's individuality by plotting his individuality coordinates over this normalization grid.

Pressures for reconstruction However drastically redesigned by culture, advanced interpretation still responds to the perennial (hence precultural) pressures that brought interpretation into existence: pressures epistemic, communal, and political. In situated interpretation, these pressures acted directly, with genetic impact. In unsituated interpretation, filtered by culture, the same pressures are indirect, exercised through socialized learning, and no longer expressed genetically. This development reflects a critical fact: unlike its predecessors, reconstruction has few if any innate skills of its own. Culture responds to the pressures we are about to sample by fashioning out of available resources and ontogenetically prior inter-

pretive modules the new skills needed for reconstruction, and it starts all
over again with each new generation.

Epistemic pressures   Gathering and imparting information, mostly by
linguistic communication, continue to be the chief epistemic pressures on
interpretation. Adult communication about people operates in a topic-
comment format, typically revolving around a plot of complex agency.
That calls for interpretation, twice. Interpretation is first needed to *access*
a plot or more by following the topic-comment formats for long stretches
and through recursive loops of shared information (about what the interpreter knows about what the interlocutor knows and expects, and so on);
interpretation is also needed to *make out* the plot itself. As a control
group, autistic individuals fail on both counts (Bruner and Feldman 1993,
Tager-Flusberg 1993). Communication also becomes the main avenue to
the psychological attributes of others. Adults talk about their attributes
and express them in speech often more than in behavior. Recovery of
attributes from the flow of communication requires the reconstructive
skills that narration was instrumental in installing.

We know from experience that imposing a plot or story as a gestalt on
daily experiences is a natural and often therapeutic thing to do: it helps
organize scattered data into a meaningful and interpretable whole. Two-
year-olds begin to do this on their own by way of inner monologues
(Bruner 1990, Lucariello 1990). This exercise has several parameters
whose full interpretive value is cashed later at the reconstructional turn:
self-generated reconstructions train the child to recognize what is canonical (in various senses) and what is not, how departures from canons can
lead to conflicts and how conflicts can be solved, how justifications
are provided and how a return to canonicality is effected (Bruner and
Feldman 1993).

There is further epistemic pressure from new forms of socially regimented *learning*; these forms of learning too point to narration-installed
reconstructions. Adults teach older children by means of narrative communication, and do so more fluidly and naturally and less emphatically
and choppily than with younger children. School-age children also learn
things together: they work on and solve common problems, imagine various activities and play together, discuss public issues among themselves.
This is *collaborative learning*, as opposed to imitative or instructed learning, which is adult-dependent (Tomasello, Kruger, and Ratner 1993).
Notice that all forms of regimented learning are powerful installers of
cultural scripts and canons, including standardized ways of interpreting

people. One feature of collaborative learning is that the participants must take different perspectives on, and have different data about, a given subject matter. Not only does one need to recognize perspectival diversity (a metarepresentational acquisition); one also needs to perform a fine-tuned sequential integration of data and perspectives. This integration calls for new skills. As a control group, autistic children show an inability to engage in collaborative learning, and indeed, they do poorly even in instructed learning. Reporting on these results, Tomasello, Kruger, and Ratner (1993, section 3) estimate that what the autistic children lack is the ability to converse with teachers and to internalize such a dialogue for self-control and self-monitoring. Again, those would be reconstructive skills.

This brings in still another epistemic pressure, one that has communal and political import. It is *self-regulation*. Instructed learning was shown (chapter 4, section 5) to lead to self-regulation by internalizing adult instructions and reproducing them, often in a dialogical manner, in similar situations. Later on, in collaborative learning and other social inter-actions, children go beyond the alternating dialogue and mimicking of adult input and recreate in a recursive and integrated fashion the partner's or interlocutor's attitudes and actions toward the interpreter, the latter's responses, and so on. This recursive dialogue with the self requires interpretation. Not surprisingly, this form of dialogue begins to show up in the child's mental life no earlier than six to seven years of age, which is when the turn to reconstruction is seriously under way (Tomasello, Kruger, and Ratner 1993, section 2.3).

Communal and political pressures   Many of these pressures grow out of those active at the metarepresentational turn. The younger child must graduate to metarepresentational interpretation because the individuals she interacts with have a representational mind *and* this is reflected in their relations to, and behaviors in, the social and political environment shared with the interpreter. Likewise, the older child entering adolescence must graduate to reconstruction because she interacts with minds that engage in and talk about social plots, collaborate in and plan joint efforts, and the like *and* all of this gets reflected in relations shared with the interpreter. This is the larger picture. From closer by, one discerns more specific pressures.

One of them has to do with the adult complexity of *social exchanges* in the form of "prestations and deferred counter-prestations" (Carrithers 1989, 203). This is not something new in political species. The form, however, is new in human societies, and this makes an evolutionary difference. In other primate species, social exchanges may be simple tits for tats. This is how altruism among nonkin works. Adult human life is full of such reciprocations, from barter and money exchanges to services and counterservices in various walks of life and under different forms. The sheer number of such reciprocations would not require reconstruction. The latter becomes indispensable when the perception and execution of social exchanges are filtered culturally through a maze of activities and attitudes in which there are no canonically unique, hence obvious, commensurate reciprocations and no clear standards of measurement. How does one reward the boss who increased one's salary? Is a smile in the corridor or a lunch invitation appropriate and, if so, commensurate with the increase? How does a student reward a good teacher? How does one reward the intellectual opponent who unexpectedly came to one's defense? One has to think about, calculate, plot, and take into account character, other people's sensitivities, cultural norms, and so much more. In short, one must interpret reconstructively. Adult social life has this texture, and nothing less will do as interpretation. Again, autistic individuals miss this game entirely (Sacks 1994).

Another set of pressures for interpretation by reconstruction has to do with the *rationalization* and *justification* of actions and relations to others. The roots of these interpretive exploits could be traced back to the peacemaking strategies of earlier primates. Frans de Waal (1989) has presented and illustrated a variety of such strategies, usually connected with tolerance and reconciliation. Precisely because primate societies are so highly communal and political, the sources of divergence of interest and outright conflict are bound to be numerous. Social cohesion, on which these species depend so heavily, is therefore under constant and often dangerous pressure. It makes sense to speculate that evolution might have come up with peacemaking mechanisms (such as grooming, calming gestures, eye contact and avoidance) for communal and political quarrels and violent encounters.

Human children enter social contexts where misunderstanding and conflict are permanent fixtures by the time they move outside the family and into the world of the village, town, kindergarten, and later school. This is when they awake to metarepresentational interpretation while fast assimilating the rudiments of its successor reconstruction. At earlier stages the conflicts with siblings and other kids are explained and rationalized as a peacemaking exercise by parents and other adults almost in a form of instructed learning. Family politics calls for some reconstructive deftness in interpretation. "The child's task when conflict arises is to balance her own desires against her commitment to others in the family. And she learns very soon that action is not enough to achieve this end. Telling the right story, putting her actions and goals in a legitimate light, is just as important. Getting what you want very often means getting the right story.... A 'right' story is one that connects your version through mitigation with the canonical version" (Bruner 1990, 86). The child's efforts at rationalizing others or herself in terms of canons pick up after five and become more efficient and versatile as the child grows into an accomplished reconstructive interpreter. Peacemaking too depends on telling the right story about you to somebody who sees conflict in what you did or thought and, in the opposite direction, on getting the right story about somebody else whose actions look inimical to you.

In a word The mental revolution liberates, culture coerces by scripting and canonizing, and narration mediates between the two by channeling the forces of the former into the patterns of the latter. Subject to a plethora of evolutionary pressures, these interfacing developments conspire to redesign the interpretive skills that categorize and effectively engage attributes and social roles unsituatedly and hence reconstructively. In the opening quotation to this part of the book, Bruner writes that "culture is ... constitutive of mind" (1990, 33). I take this to mean two things. The first is that culture scripts, canonizes, and normalizes the way an interpreter construes the interpreted mind in terms of roles and attributes and what they relate to in the world.

The other thing is this. In social interaction and communication the participants are simultaneously interpreters and subjects. Their social thinking and communication are therefore shot through with interpretation. Interpretation is also active in private thinking involving self-regulation, metatalk and evaluation, dialogue with the self, and the like. So one gets the further sense that in a large number of contexts, culture aligns minds with each other with respect to how they think and what they think about, and this makes minds interpretively visible and intelligible to each other. Nevertheless, such intermental coordination owes little to a deeper psychological (i.e., naively cognitivist) understanding of minds and quite a lot to the common grid that culture has trained human minds to recognize and use by plotting and tracking attributes and actions.

Chapter 8

Reconstruction

There is one crucial fact about the design of adult interpretation, made plain and intelligible by evolution yet largely invisible to mainstream analyses, particularly in philosophy. It is the contrast between the laborious underground work of reconstruction and its snappy public summaries—the iceberg versus its tip. An exclusive tip perspective can mislead one about the design of reconstruction and misrepresent the nature of its knowledge. Interpretation shares the iceberg-tip relation, and the reasons for it, with other cognitive capacities, such as linguistic communication, mental imagery, and memory recall. This distinguished company matters to my argument. In each of these domains, the realization that thinking animates its form of processing has led researchers to reconsider the nature of the enterprise. In each of these domains it took bold and speculative theorizing, unimpressed by the phenomenology of the tip, to fathom the tasks handled deep inside the information-processing iceberg. I think the same is true of reconstructive interpretation.

Against this background theme, this chapter argues for the practical design of reconstruction as a reflective enterprise: spontaneous and mostly unconscious, evolved in response to the challenges posed by the mental and cultural upheavals of later childhood. Although as practical as its predecessors, reconstruction departs dramatically from them. For obvious reasons, situated interpretation put the highest premium on perceived situations and immediate behavioral reaction. Being unsituated, reconstruction puts a higher premium on understanding others in past, future, possible, and counterfactual situations as preconditions of involvement. Involvement need not materialize as either verbal or behavioral performance, and often doesn't, although this is what reconstruction was designed for as a competence.

The guiding hypothesis of the chapter, outlined in section 1 and unpacked in the rest of the chapter, is that reconstruction is done in three successive steps, each with its goals and tasks: (a) recovery of roles and attributes in terms of recognizable norms (scripts, canons, shared experiences), (b) alignment of recovery outputs with involvement-affording patterns, and (c) formatting the alignment outputs for functions played in the interpreter's mentation and action. Recovery is discussed in section 2, alignment in section 3, and content formatting in section 4. Assisted by this conceptual framework, the concluding sections examine two hotly debated areas of reconstruction: explanation and simulation. Rebelling against the influential view that interpreters explain by positing mental causes and their laws as reasons, section 5 finds interpretive explanation to be a cultural product designed to appeal to cultural norms for reasons and to check out roles and attributes in order to establish conformity to or deviance from the norms. Section 6 estimates that simulation has decent evolutionary chances, when construed narrowly and modestly as a planning-based predictor, but not when construed widely and ambitiously as an installer of interpretive concepts and skills.

1 The Hypothesis

That one ends up making a specific attribution of a propositional attitude does not mean that in the flowchart of interpretation one *begins* with such an attribution. Even when, as a matter of performance, one appears to snap one's fingers when making an attribution, it still does not follow that one's interpretive equipment had evolved to do just that. Performances need not reveal competence or explain its rationale. Attributions would not be possible unless other interpretive moves are made first. This is what this chapter endeavors to prove. Here is a preview of its guiding hypothesis.

Reconstruction comes in functional stages. The first is *recovery* and results in the recognition of roles (mostly epistemic, social, or political) and psychological attributes on the basis of situational, behavioral, and verbal data relative to scripts, canons, and shared experiences. This is done by accessing and linking up appropriate categorization parsers. I call them *cultural parsers*, to emphasize their installment history and their rationale. A cultural parser specifies the sorts of situations, causes, actions, postures, and effects associated culturally with a role or (usually nonbasic or derived) attribute. Such roles and attributes afford involvements of various cultural sorts, but only in principle. This is why recovery is only a starting point.

Although a cultural parser specifies a canonical matrix of opportunities of involvement, it needs further constraints in order to apply involvement to a specific *context* and thus yield context-specific involvements. In situated interpretation, the perceptual sharing of a context and its relation to (typically, an instantiation of) a normal goal setting provide such constraints. The constraints secure the parser's *alignment* to context. Unsituated interpretation needs new tricks. Its task is to align a role or attribute parser to the unsituated coordinates of a context of involvement. This requires selecting out of a cultural parser the portion (category list) relevant to a context. I call it *practical selection*. Here is an analogy. When one thinks of a house in a context, one thinks of it in contextual terms. A practical selection of the concept of house defines that appropriateness. If the context is buying a house, then the selection activates those properties at that level of detail that fit the context. If the context is renting a house, then a somewhat different selection takes over. And so on. Likewise, relative to a context, one can think of a role (e.g., father) or attribute (e.g., emotion) in terms of an appropriate selection (e.g., Father always remonstrates in this sort of context; this is why he shows anger).

Even when practically selected and tailored to a context, a cultural parser is still only half of the story, the contentless part, as it were. Roles and attributes are relational, with types of situations as their external relata, and parsers provide routes to involvement in such situations, properly contextualized. For this to be true, their practical selections must be related to those *practically salient* features of a situation that generate representations of affordances. This is information about a context that the interpreter can utilize in some way. Hence the notion of contexture. A *contexture* is to the information conveyed by a subject about a situation what a practical selection is to a role or attribute parser, namely, a practical contextualization promising specific affordances.

In situated interpretation a contexture and its practical affordances are out there in the world, shared in sensorimotor terms and constrained by common goal settings and familiar experiences. As conspecifics, interpreter and subject are designed and trained alike and live in the same world. Their goals are mutually transparent, most of the time, and can be read off behavioral and environmental clues present in the shared world. They both come to know quickly and reliably which items in a situation are practically salient and hence worth interpreting. The scripts created by evolution or experience help structure the interpreter's perception around points of practical salience. Unsituated interpretation is different. It does not usually benefit from such a simple and inexpensive solution as a perceptually shared and situated domain, with its contextures almost staring at the interpreter. The unsituated interpreter must supply the contextures mostly (though not only) from her cultural knowledge. This is where contexture-revealing scripts and other cultural guidelines come to the rescue.

There is one more hurdle to clear. A leitmotif of this essay has been that interpretation is selected to service the interpreter's interests, and this is reflected in its design. Reconstruction is no exception. The output of alignment, a practical selection tied to a contexture, must play its role in the interpreter's thinking and action. It must be formatted for that role. *Formatting for a role* is the third major goal of reconstruction. The outputs of recovery and alignment must be readied for further utilization. This is where the notion of *content* comes in. I will suggest that the main job of a content ascription is to format representations of contextures for playing suitable roles.

The entire hypothesis can be now summarized as follows:

(8.1) *Reconstruction goals and tasks*
Recovery: evidence → cultural parsers
Alignment: cultural parser → context of involvement by
a. practical selection: parser → its portion of contextual relevance, and
b. contexture: context → points of practical salience (affordances)
Formatting: contexture → role in the interpreter's mentation and action =
content ascription[1]

I begin with the first stage.

2 Rules of Engagement

The order of interpretation in general and of recovery in particular matters practically. It reveals the interpreter's priorities, as they were shaped by nature and culture. To get an evolutionary perspective on the phenomenon, let us retrogress for a moment and imagine an ape interpreter confronted with a subject. Given the texture of ape life, what relational properties of the subject would it be best to figure out first? The answer is loud and clear: *role*, in the form of sex, rank, and power. Suppose that the interpreter is a simple member of the group and the subject is an alpha male. The context of the encounter being normal, it is hard to tell what the subject will do. Which of his other relational properties would it be wisest to handle next? Character traits leap to mind. They are durable and hence likely to have a hand in whatever else the subject does. Being vain, irritable, or friendly can make all the behavioral difference in a variety of contexts, and so can emotional tendencies, basic goals, and other durable attributes, for the same reasons. Once these critical determinations are made, the interpreter can turn to more specific but episodic coordinates of the situation and fathom the subject's ongoing desires and beliefs. Given the interests of the interpreter, the stakes and costs involved, this gambit makes evolutionary sense.

It does so for humans as well. Their culture sees to it. Subjects wear many hats at the same time. They simultaneously occupy biological roles (sex, age, race, state of health), social roles (profession, status, wealth), political roles (power, influence), and epistemic roles (experts, informants, tutors, pupils), and in doing so they exhibit a vast assortment of durable attributes associated with roles and personality. Recall how child narratives and parental comments on the children's exploits first insist on roles and durable attitudes before engaging the episodic attitudes of the context. The pedagogical point is to train the child to parse interpretation in a certain order: by first retrieving scripts and canonical situations of some generality before attending to episodic particulars. In short, before the last stage of attribute reconstruction is reached—that of episodic desires, beliefs, and intentions—elaborate travail has already been done. This is why unsituated interpretation cannot reduce to a desire-belief psychology and also why the latter rarely, if ever, does all or even most of the work. Moreover, before the subject's episodic attitudes show up on the interpreter's radar, much has already been done to constrain the interpretation of the attitudes.

Roles first The evolutionary reasons for engaging roles first are neither new nor uniquely human. In any primate and possibly animal society, ascertaining biological or political roles first is crucial and, in most encounters, is more vital than attending to the short-lived vagaries of psychological attributes. This gambit is also more informative, more economical, and more apt to lead to useful stereotypes, generalizations, and hence predictions, because roles tend to be thoroughly scripted and canonized, certainly more so than attributes, and therefore are widely acknowledged and respected by the group. As a result, role interpretation opens up standard categorizations and links among attributes and generates quick and reliable expectations about the first layer of involvement opportunities. Take any role-revealing script (e.g., classroom or office work). Each party (who is simultaneously interpreter and subject) knows what the roles are and what is expected when they are played out. Any script-conforming action can be predicted or explained before appealing to attributes. (This fact will figure prominently in the account of interpretive explanation proposed in section 5 below.) Any role transaction —student-teacher, buyer-seller, doctor-patient—evokes the appropriate scripts and canons. This suffices to frame the public coordinates (educational, legal, medical) of interpretation. In this way role attributions provide the first interpretive understanding of a situation.

Role attributions also constrain and occasionally fix the *psychological* interpretations that follow. Interpreters are prone to associate roles with attributes or at least let roles influence attributions. Roles generate expectations and predictions about character and emotional propensities (slick, aggressive politicians or sales people; shy mathematicians; nerdish computer hackers; eccentric theoretical physicists—take your pick). Getting the roles in first is a clever ploy on the part of both Mother Nature and Father Culture. It simplifies, minimizes, and regulates the harder psychological part of reconstruction. It also increases the chances of success in interpretation, for in most situations roles are the most visible and matter more than other factors. The moral is that in the bush and in human culture, psychological reconstruction does not start from scratch, is not radical, and has much of the work already cut out for it.[2]

"But surely," one could say, "on the one hand, knowledge of roles is infused with psychological interpretation from the beginning, in which case the former cannot really ground and help the latter. On the other hand, many, perhaps most, psychological interpretations need not go through the role phase or other preparatory stages dictated by culture; most of the time interpreters focus solely on the psychological side." Let's go slowly here, OK? For starters, do not be so sure about the no-show for roles; hang on to hear about automatic pilot and default assumptions, for this is how roles are handled most of the time. As for the first observation, recall that cultural knowledge is installed gradually through tutoring, games, imitation, example, narration, and so on. At each stage, interpretation of attributes and roles is both presupposed and further shaped. (To the very young, mother is both roles and attributes.) Most competencies are built up in this gradual way. Whatever the installation history, the fact now under discussion involves no circularity: any normal adult knows roles (according to scripts, canons, and practical affordances) and knows what to expect from others playing roles without necessarily bringing in psychological interpretation.

Psychological order   Within the psychological domain there is also an order of engagement whereby some attribute nets are opened up and charted before others (Fiske and Taylor 1991). In the realm of the non-episodic, the recovery of traits or moods tends to kick in before that of feelings, emotions, and attitudes, and in the realm of the episodic, the recovery of feelings and emotions often before that of attitudes. These priorities again make cultural sense in the same way that the priority of roles over attributes did. Nonepisodic character traits, emotional profiles, or other durable attitudes are more persistent and pervasive in what the subject says or does, and hence more consequential, than episodic emotions or attitudes. The categorizations of the former pack more information more economically, and trigger more standard associations, than those of the latter. So it is easier and quicker to stereotype the subject in terms of character or mood than in terms of desires and beliefs. Episodically, the subject's feelings and emotions may have a quicker and stronger impact on his actions, and by implication on the interpreter's goals, than his attitudes.

As work on attribution has shown, the combination of role and character is potent, attractive, economical, and for these reasons is apt to overemphasize canonical arrangements and broad psychological dispositions and disregard data on context and episodic attitudes, which may happen to be more explanatory. This is the notorious fundamental attribution error. It is known from the work of Tversky and Kahneman (1974) that people misjudge probabilities by favoring canonical links among psychological attributes and social and cultural roles (e.g., shyness and asociality links up with being a scientist or computer hacker) at the expense of contextual judgments of frequency and probability base. At times, in a reversal of priorities, the psychological standardization can be so strong as to go against and even cancel out other general parameters, such as social or political role (Fiske and Taylor 1991, 67–73; Nisbett and Ross 1980, 120–122).

Automatic pilot   Interpreters are people of habit—or primates of habit, I should say, because the propensity is universal among interpreters.

The habits embrace both what is interpreted and how. In situated interpretation, natural selection is a strict and tight-fisted installer of habits. Unsituated interpretation is also habit-prone, but the selective leash is longer and looser. In directing interpretation to proceed in descending order of generality, from role to persistent attributes to episodic attitudes, the rules of engagement favor the habitual and the general over the unusual and the particular. This is true of both situated and unsituated interpretation. In the former, the episodic parameters are fixed in the perceptual here and now shared by interpreter and subject; in the latter, the fixation of episodic parameters requires considerable cognitive effort, which is an evolutionary stimulus for reconstruction. Yet clearly such effort is a matter of last resort. The advanced interpreter prefers to handle things canonically in terms of scripted roles and durable attributes. She would decanonize her interpretation, and attend to episodic and uncommon desires and beliefs, only under pressure. It takes some precipitating event to generate a dramatic plot that calls for decanonization and sustained attention to deviant particulars (Bruner 1990, chapter 2). Even then the interpreter's tendency is to return to equilibrium by recanonizing the plot in terms of further scripts or regularities. This ploy confirms the suspicion that episodic attitudes are not a priority, even during reconstruction. It is almost as if the interpretation of episodic attitudes is destined (and possibly designed) to pick up the slack left by roles and durable attributes.

This goes to show that a good deal of interpretation is done on automatic pilot. If the situation is perceived as well scripted, then there is no need for further reconstruction. The same is true when the situation is canonical by evolutionary inheritance, in which case ancestral skills take over. (For all primate interpreters, someone's eyes looking intently in a direction is a perceptual signal of a potential goal or some other item of high interest.) Equally on automatic pilot is the routine perception of various sorts of roles. The fact that in familiar activities and surroundings, interpreters are not explicitly aware of roles and the underlying scripts and canons does not mean that their expertise was not designed to register them and filed them as canonical, well scripted, not worth a bother.

The automatic pilot works mostly by default assumptions and expectations about what is canonical, well scripted, durable, hence familiar, and it is designed to stop at that level of categorization unless more specific and deviant information shows up and calls for elaborate reconstruction (Holland et al. 1986, chapter 1). Mindful of the balance between costs and benefits, both nature and culture opt for what is easily and quickly accessible and processable before succumbing to the laborious retrieval of details and exceptions—a policy reminiscent of prototypical categorizations (Rosch 1977). The rule of thumb in reconstruction thus seems to be 'Schematize according to scripts and canons whenever possible and reconstruct particulars only when necessary'. Reconstruction operates on a need-to-know basis. When the stakes are high and the costs of being wrong equally high, because of increased responsibility, accountability, or risk, interpreters abandon scripted schematizations, resist tempting biases in attribution, and pay more attention to the particulars of the case and of the subject (Fiske and Taylor 1991, 156–160). It is at this point that the navigation skills needed for reconstruction become useful and potent.

3   Practical Attributions

Inside the net   Having speculated about the order in which role and attribute nets are recovered, let us now peek inside a net or two to see how the recovery is being done and how, as part of the next alignment business, practical selections are made. From now on it will be attribute nets that hold center stage. Think of such a net as a conceptual space organized around a core. The space is conceptual because it is mapped by concepts encoded and deployed as rules over representations (chapter 7, section 1). The core contains basic attributes, treated as psychologically canonical in that they are tracked automatically by reflex parsers inherited from earlier evolutionary turns. There is little if any reconstruction needed to determine that somebody is angry or sad or in pain or has formed a perceptual belief by seeing something. Thus in the emotion net, basic attributes would be anger or sadness; in the perception net, gaze or behavioral posture; in the epistemic net, perceptual belief. Imagine also that around the core there is a widely distributed array of attributes, some clustered together, some more isolated. Most attributes outside the core derive their interpretable identity from cultural scripts and are tracked by learned skills. The further an attribute is from the core, the less canonical, and therefore less amenable to reflex categorizations. Elaborate recovery then takes over.

The attributes distributed over a net can be viewed as partitioned along axes defining distinct regions according to some pervasive feature or contrast. For example, emotions may be divided into factive (fury) and epistemic (fear) or positive (delight) and negative (annoyance), and character traits into antisocial (deceitful) and social (honest) or active (domineering) and passive (shy), and so on. Most attributes are packed between several axes. For example, the modesty trait will be nearby the passive, good, and social axes, whereas vanity sits opposite, cornered by the bad, antisocial, and (somewhat) active axes (Morton 1980, 21). Distance from an axis would measure the kinds and degrees of canonicality shared by an attribute (thus domineering is closer to the active axis than vain, but vain is closer to the bad axis than domineering). The recovery of a derived attribute first locates its position relative to the core and the relevant axes: the further from the core of the net and its various axes, the more open-ended its conceptual links. Vain is further from the core than friendly and more distant from the bad axis than friendly is from the good axis. Hence there is more freedom in conceptualizing vain than friendly or irritable (Morton 1980, chapters 1 and 6). There was no natural selection for recognizing being vain or boring, for there is no unity of sensory input or behavioral expression that would reveal such traits, and so there is no sensorimotor recipe for such reflex recognition.

Following the rules of engagement, I began with the character and emotion nets, whose navigation allows the interpreter to map situational data into possible actions. The same general picture is true of the epistemic nets, whose navigation maps subject-world information relations. Seeing, knowing, believing, and remembering are interpretive concepts of the epistemic sort. They operate along such axes as modality (perceptual, memory), time (present, past, future), and reliability (accidental, justified, incorrigible). Each axis further constrains the mapping. Thus modality identifies type of information contact—external contact, as in vision or hearing, or internal contact, as in memory recall or inference—and thus the causal routes involved. In the eye of the interpreter, information transactions along such coordinates place the subject in an *epistemic condition*, such as seeing a scene or believing a rumor. For an interpreter, an epistemic condition consists of an attitude and a content.

An epistemic attitude is recovered along such axes as modality, time, and reliability. Thus, seeing is construed as a (very reliable) type of information relation in the perceptual mode, and believing as a type of relation that, like knowing, can, but need not, be modality-neutral and, unlike knowing, is fallible. Epistemic attitudes inform about the world according to the subject. Different attitude attributions provide different informational guidance. If I interpret Max as having *seen* my cat chasing a fly, I come to know several things conceptually associated with seeing: a state of the world some time ago, according to Max's registration of it; Max's causal contact with the world in a sensory modality; a cognitive state of his (an image); and some of its possible consequences (what Max might think and say, how he will react, and so on); and finally, conative, cognitive, and behavioral states of my cat. But if I interpret Max as *believing* that he saw my cat chasing a fly, then the reconstruction changes course, for belief is a different sort of guide, working from different rules, and so is the information it yields: it is more tentative, less reliable, more influenced by other psychological attributes of Max and the data he has.

This is recovery along the modality and reliability coordinates. There is also temporal-net navigation guided by epistemic attitudes. The point is not that nets are mapped in time (trivially true) but that nets are mapped *in order to* track conditions in time across causal routes. The guidance to such mapping can be present-looking, forward-looking or backward-looking (Barwise and Perry 1983, 227–228, 243–245; Stalnaker 1984, 14). When I interpret Max as seeing the cat playing with a book, I am informed about a current situation and, by means of a seeing-belief rule, I anticipate that Max will form a belief to this effect, which thus opens a belief net, where a belief-action rule predicts that Max might also say or do something about the event he saw. The attributions of seeing and belief guide my temporal-net navigation, and so do the attributions of other attitudes, epistemic and nonepistemic, each with its guidance rules.

There is also a lot to be said about how epistemic attitudes guide mapping along the reliability axis. A vast epistemological literature, spawned by philosophical behaviorism and ordinary-language analysis, has addressed this issue with verve, imagination, and plenty of examples.[3] There is no need to go into details, though. With exegetical modesty, I summarize its theses (relevant to my analysis) as follows. Epistemic talk signals the speaker's stance on the reliability of the information; this stance in turn guides interpretation with respect to the epistemic credentials and values of the information imparted. For example, knowledge versus belief indicates and measures the reliability of the causal route through which the information was acquired; knowledge indicates the impossibility or improbability of error or doubt as well as the futility of further search, whereas belief gives a reasonable chance to either of these options.

There is psychological evidence that during the metarepresentational turn and after, children become cognizant of these dimensions of guidance nested in the notions of epistemic attitudes. Perner (1991, chapter 7) notes that the young child first understands knowledge within a theory of behavior, where successful action is the key indicator of knowledge, and later becomes aware that a properly caused mental representation and access to sufficient and reliable information are also necessary for knowledge. These criteria for knowledge—successful action, proper causation, and sufficient and reliable access—cannot be guides to the subject's mental architecture or specific representations, for there is nothing in the criteria to pick up architectural features of, or specific representations in, the mind. They are guides to how the subject's epistemic condition informs the interpreter about some aspect of interest.

Practical categories   Having looked from on high at the overall dynamics of recovery, let us move closer to the fine print of the concepts that do the work, and show how, in line with their predecessors, they too were designed to provide affordances for practical involvement. I begin with character traits and then consider epistemic attitudes.

For the sake of a tightly guided illustration, imagine the following party scene. "*A*: Oh dear, *C* is *so* boring. *B*: How do you mean? *A*: Blah, blah, blah. *B*: I see, poor you. That *is* boring." The blah-blah story is a piece of recovery by net navigation. (The fact that the reader can easily fill in the blah-blah slots makes my point.) *A* walks *B* across the character net they naturally and culturally share to make her point and validate the concept applied to the unfortunate *C*. Far from probing the innards of *C*'s mind (if any), interpreter *A* projects her schematizations on the public space of the character net and plots her moves according to shared rules. *Boring* being a derived attribute, far from the core of the character net, its rules are a cultural product. When *A* tells *B* about boring *C* by walking *B* across the character net and pinning down the specific linkups that single out *C*'s character profile, *A* actually projects *C*'s conditions and actions on various attribute-relevant scripts and canonical situations that both *A* and *B* are familiar with. For what *A* is saying in effect is, "When *X* would say or act like this in that type of situation, one would think of *X* such and such; and when *X* would say or act like that in another type of situation, one would think of *X* so and so, and so on. Well, *C* is the sort of *X* about whom one would think this and that, which amounts to being boring."

A can tell such a story, and *B* can understand it (and so can poor *C*, if consulted), because they share a cultural parser (as a sort of cultural definition) of the attribute in question. A particular interpretation selects the practical selection that is relevant and sufficient in the context. The story told by A to B above is an instance of a practical selection sufficient in the context to nail down C's boring character. The cultural parser that defines an attribute can be thought of a set of practical selections. Interpreters may, but need not, advert explicitly to cultural parsers or their constituent selections. Yet this is how they are scripted to think about attributes. Practical selections are almost always in the background of an attribution. It is as though the appropriate programs scan the domain of a cultural parser, pick out practical selections that fit a situation, reach a verdict, and compact it into a concise attribution.

To put the picture in evolutionary motion, recall the ape who likes and her *friendly* parser (chapter 5, section 7). For the interpreting ape C, subject A was interpreted as friendly to another B when several conditions were met. For example, if B showed up, A would get excited, grin happily, or groom B with unusual care; if B carried a baby, A would come up and stroke the baby or bring it some fruit; and so on. These conditions are captured by instructions in C's interpretive machinery and were selected for affording practical involvement. They constitute a practical selection for the category *friendly*. There are, of course, major differences between early and advanced interpretation. The former is compiled. Its only explicit data structures are perceptual and concern the antecedent and consequent of an instruction, such as *if* [A smiles when seeing B], *then* [A grins happily]. The correlations between these events and their subsumption under *friendly* are assumed in a rigid and reflex manner.[4]

Being conceptual, human knowledge is run by rules that link up across one or more nets with many other rules. Eventually, all the rules range over data structures of various sorts (symbolic, perceptual, imagistic, whatever). This fact is conducive to extensive and flexible net navigation. It is enough for the human interpreter to hear or read that A is friendly to B to know that this *means* (by explicit activation of other concepts) being cooperative toward B, smiling in her presence, cooking for her, reading to her from *The Economist*, finding out what she likes, and much more. The latter eventualities mean (activate) other concepts, and so on down the net. Another contrast is plain. Situated interpretation is steeped in the immediacy of perception and action and is not open to cognitive inspection and revision. That is not true of reconstruction. If I knows that A is friendly to B, I can imagine all sorts of situations in which that would please C or offend D; I can also make calculations about my actions, get further insights into A's preferences and B's tastes, and so on.

These differences notwithstanding, the category *friendly* is as practical-minded in reconstruction as it was in situated interpretation. It still means being cooperative, helpful, sympathetic, and so on. The latter traits in turn connect with dispositions, postures, and actions of a subject that afford specific types of involvements. Ask the person in the street what friendliness means, and she is likely to respond in terms of practical selections incorporating scripted types of human postures and inter-actions. It is mostly through the latter that children learn what friend-liness means. Proverbs about friendliness and many other attributes are practical; in memorable and concise forms, proverbs have an uncanny way of capturing how culture discerns and canonizes the affordances of various attributes.

On the basis of the argument about basic attitudes (chapter 6, section 2), I speculate that durable attitudes fit the same pattern as traits and emotional tendencies in that they are individuated in terms of practical selections belonging to a cultural parser. For intuitive reference, consider the following parallel:

The trait version   *A*: "*X* has been so friendly to me lately, dear. He did this and that, and was cooperative when I was around, and smiled when-ever I said something but didn't when *C* spoke, and didn't mind when I messed up things, and came to help when I needed it, and [blah, blah, blah]." *B*: "Right you are. This is what I call *friendly to you*."

The belief version   *A*: "*X* said such and so, and was startled when I told him [blah, blah], and even went out of his way to find out whether [blah, blah], and so on." *B*: "You are right, dear. This is what I call *believing that p*."

What *B* calls 'friendly to one' and 'believing that *p*' are synoptic char-acterizations that evoke familiar attribute-revealing scripts sampled by *A*'s descriptions; they are practical selections from cultural parsers of friendliness and belief, respectively. To make these two practical selec-tions as parallel as possible, suppose that in both cases the attributes have a relation to a target: friendliness to somebody, belief about something. (Although traits are not intentional, for they do not represent, they can be relational.) In either case, the cultural parser informs about normal pat-terns of behavior and delineates possible opportunities for involvement toward the subject, whereas the specific practical selection makes these patterns and opportunities pertinent to the context.

The action connection   Most attributes are interpreted in the light of their impact on action and, through action, on the world and on the interpreter. Not surprisingly, then, the interpretation of actions is as practical-minded as that of the attributes responsible for them. The interpretation of action appeals minimally to bodily movements and weaves around them a variable and flexible network of schematizations that convey relevant information and afford different involvements. This is familiar yet worth stressing at this point.

Actions are individuated with a practical eye to various interests, such as information about their causes and effects, assigning responsibility, justifying, explaining. This is a theme much discussed in philosophy of action (Davidson 1980). Here are some well-known examples. One flips the switch, turns on the light, illuminates the room, and alerts a prowler; one moves the finger, pulls the trigger, fires the bullet, hits the tree; one presses the pedal, stops the car, obeys the red-light rule, pleases a watching grandmother. Same bodily movements, different action descriptions, with different practical selections, which pick up different causal networks across time and inform about different more or less distant causes and effects. In philosophy of action such navigation is known as the "accordion effect," and it shows how far on the action net a bodily event can be stretched out by redescription (practical selection), and along which routes, depending on what the attribution aims to accomplish. The interpretation of action is not about bodily movements as such but about reconceptualizing and placing them in patterns that are intelligible, informative, and useful to the interpreter. Replace 'bodily movements' with 'mental condition', also construed minimally, and the same characterization applies to roles and attributes. The congruity between the interpretive conceptualization of action and that of attributes is not fortuitous, as we see next.

Public semantics   The practicality of recovery and alignment go hand in hand with their public semantics. This goes against the widespread but misguided view that interpretation is about mental states. Interpretation tracks *relations*, whether to behavior (in the case of traits or feelings) or to the world (attitudes), not to entities in the head. In each case the tracking keeps an eye on how the external relata (behavior, the world) affect the interpreter. Such relations are individuated *externally*, in terms of their observable or publicly shared relata. The interest of the interpreter is in how the subject-world relation yields information about opportunities to do things in the world. In situated interpretation the behaviors observed and the world perceptually shared gave public clues to psychological attributes. This gambit no longer suffices in unsituated interpretation. One may venture that, as an evolutionary substitute, the public domain of reconstruction is built into its semantics. How this is done is a matter of debate, but some areas of consensus have begun to emerge. I outline them in general terms, drop a few names, and let the reader's fingers do the walking.

Jon Barwise and John Perry (1983) have made a good and elaborate case for the notion of "indirect classification" of mental relations by public facts, specifically "the exploitation of patterns and constraints to classify one situation [mental] with another [public]. The constraints allow the latter to contain information about the former. An attitude report is [an] example of indirect classification. The situation described by the embedded sentence [content sentence] classifies the agent's cognitive situation by exploiting constraints of Folk Psychology. The attitude verb used (SEE, KNOW, BELIEVE, etc.) signals which constraints are relevant" (Barwise and Perry 1983, 225–227; my square-bracket interpolations).

The patterns and constraints used in indirect classification need not be concrete and causal, as in situated interpretation, but can also be abstract, as Barwise and Perry (1983, 227) suggest in an analogy with chess: "the physical situation right there on the board can be used to get at various aspects of the cognitive situation of the two players—it can be used to represent their mental and emotional situations." To go one step further, I think that the representation of mental relations is only a guide to representing some further condition of the world that interests the interpreter. This is one reason why attributes and actions are parsed and formulated in the same terms: to ensure a smooth conceptual traffic between them. Further philosophical references fortify this diagnosis.

Philosophical behaviorism—construed as a doctrine about interpretation, not about the mind—argued that people translate mental notions into perception and action talk when speaking and thinking of others. Gilbert Ryle's still authoritative account (1949) is full of such arguments and examples. He portrays attributes as dispositional notions that function as "inference tickets" licensing the transition from perceived facts about the environment to other such facts or actions. In a different vein, Wittgenstein (1953) argued that the rules for employing the interpretive language are public and any design for private use would be unintelligible. Morton (1980) notes that children begin by understanding character and mood in terms of patterns of behavior ("Angry people curse and kick and move abruptly; sad people move slowly, don't notice much and cry") and that mature interpreters also tend to project a subject's characteristic actions into a feature of their personality. I quote at some length: "We describe people as clumsy, hasty, meticulous, abrupt, and use these labels to justify our explanations of actions that are not themselves clumsy, hasty, meticulous, or abrupt. What one is saying in describing a person as abrupt is roughly, 'think of an action performed abruptly, imagine what it takes to act that way, and now keep this imagined state in mind while thinking what one might do in the following situation....' With the right characteristics of action to project, and the right unobtrusiveness at insinuating them beyond their area of literal application, the trick works. We get some increase in understanding of what people are likely to do and what their motives may be" (Morton 1980, 156). Morton also remarks that the same public projection in terms of actions works in the interpretation of practical reasoning, motivation, and deliberation ("In effect, one describes deliberation as covert action") and concludes that with such action-to-attribute or action-to-motivation projections the interpreter ends up "construing the mind as a nested system of fields of action" (1980, 156). Couldn't have said it better!

The public semantics of facts and actions classifies the subject's roles and attributes as relations to the world, and only indirectly and minimally as components of his mental condition, because the aim of interpretation is to have the information about the world bounce on the subject and then back on the world, thus telling the interpreter what the subject is up to next or how the world was before or will be later. The subject's mind is mapped to the extent that it allows such back-and-forth bouncing of information. If the aim were detailed knowledge of the subject's mind, as mentalism has it, then interpretation would have been designed quite differently.[5] In situated interpretation such information traffic was policed by the strictures of the ancestral goal settings, the basic goals of the participants, and the perceptual dimensions of a shared situation. In unsituated interpretation, these constraints rarely suffice. So culture takes over and the interpreter has to defer to its strictures to make sense of the information traffic. This is why interpreters think of roles and attributes in terms of actions *and* think of the latter in terms of situation types that fit natural and cultural patterns of involvement. Below is an apt analogy that puts these things together and remains a memorable frame of reference for the argument developed in this chapter.

Summing up: the chess analogy   If one knows the rules of chess and the scripts of expert play, one understands not only a current position on the board but also how it came about and what it may lead to. One also understands chesswise the mental conditions of the players by treating them as bridges from a past or current board configuration to a future or possible configuration in terms of the scripts and strategies followed. Thus a player thinks chesswise of the mind of another player *in terms of* board configurations and their affordances.

As in chess, so in interpretation. In its situated form, the game was played in the here and now, publicly, and in the open, on a board perceptually accessible to everybody. In unsituated interpretation, the game can also be played on a mental board, like the chess player who mentally rehearses her moves and those of the opponent. In either case, the mental board provides a semantics for the subject's (or opponent's) mental conditions that is as public and practical as that provided by the physical board. In the early stages of unsituated interpretation, as in the early stages of chess playing, the game is played tentatively and awkwardly, by following rules mechanically and inflexibly (as in metarepresentational interpretation). Mastery of the game is to a large extent enculturation into scripts, canons, and shared experiences. In chess, this translates into the ability to see board configurations not so much as individual pieces located here and there in ad hoc patterns but rather as instances of canonical patterns and well-scripted openings, attacks, or defenses, or as intelligible departures from them. Analogously, the experienced interpreter perceives the key configurations of the situations of interpretation not as individual properties or behaviors but rather as instances of canonical cases and well-scripted opportunities for involvement, or as manageable departures from them.[6]

Chess strategies resemble cultural scripts in providing matrices of affordances for moves or involvements in the respective domains. The matrices are mentally represented by strategies in chess and by cultural parsers in interpretation. Board configurations resemble interpreter-subject configurations; in terms of the scripts and strategies they evidence, the configurations approximate other configurations via estimates of the player's or interpreter's mental relations to them. A particular context of the game or of interpretation generates a practical selection in the relevant strategy or script-reflecting parser; that practical selection constitutes an estimate of the player's or interpreter's mental relation to the context. In either case, the points of practical salience, which would motivate the moves to be made, form a contexture. How the mental representation of the practical selection and of the contexture come to play its role in the interpreter's thinking and action is the (hard) topic I turn to next.

4 The Manufacture of Content

As Stephen Stich observed, "There is no preexisting notion of a content-entity to be found in folk psychology. Talk of there being some thing which is 'the content' of a belief is a theorist's term of art, often used though rarely explained" (1983, 59). The quest for explanation is still on. The analysis I will only sketch here concerns the practicality of content ascription within the larger envelope of attitude attribution. In line with the issues raised earlier in this chapter, the question I address is, Why so much mental work to get the information of interest (contexture) and then package it in a tiny and neat content formula?

The outline of the answer is not meant to prefigure a theory of content but, more modestly, to show that content ascription is as practical-minded as attitude attribution. I begin with a warning about language, survey a few salient properties of content that point to the practical nature of its job, then venture a guess as to what that job might be, and conclude with a diagnosis of content compression. Methodologically, I think of a content ascription as a job to be done, by way of tasks to be carried out, instead of as an entity, state, or relation to be individuated, which is the standard but often unhelpful strategy.

Not just language   Philosophers are transfixed by the linguistic cloth of the content formula, the ubiquitous 'that' clause affixed to an attitude attribution (believes that p, expects that q, and the like). Yet a content ascription need not be linguistic or take the form of a 'that' clause. As far back as the evolutionary eye can see, primitive contents were ascribed whenever situated relations or attitudes were. Any ape recognizes gaze as a situated relation and recognizes its target as content. Language makes a mighty difference in representation and formatting but is not the source or shaper of content. Language also injects its type of meaning into content but this too is a contribution, not a constitution. The attributions of core attitudes (desire, belief, basic emotions) are effected by programs that have nothing to do with language; they parse content without dressing the output in linguistic cloth. It takes further training and enculturation to align such attribution skills to public language, and on particular occasions it takes thought to choose the right linguistic formula for content ascription.[7]

Since the hypothesis proposed below transcends language in its evolutionary sweep, it should not be judged by consulting intuitions about 'that' clauses in ordinary-language attributions, which is a standard philosophical gambit. To say, as many philosophers do, that it takes an analysis of 'that' clauses to pin down the nature of content is at best to venture an explication of its linguistic summary; whereas what I seek answers to is what is so summarized and why.[8] My quest begins with a few properties of content ascriptions that are symptomatic of their job. The hypothesis I explore attempts to account for these symptomatic properties in terms commensurate with the tasks of reconstruction analyzed so far.

Externality Philosophers have identified some properties of content ascriptions that point to their practicality and even to some of the specific tasks involved. One familiar argument is that, as in the case of linguistic meaning (Burge 1979, Putnam 1975), an ascription does not locate content in the head (Barwise and Perry 1983, Stich 1983). The idea is not that content ascriptions track mental relations rather than mental states or that external facts individuate such relations. This was shown earlier in this chapter. The claim here is stronger. Content ascriptions assume physical, social, and cultural facts and constraints that need not be reflected by the subject's mental condition *as* individuated in cognitive-scientific or introspective terms. As a result, changes in those facts and constraints, unmatched by changes in the subject's mental condition individuated scientifically or introspectively, *do* lead to changes in the contents ascribed, and conversely, changes in the subject's mental condition, under the said individuation policy, can be disregarded by the interpreter as long as they are not reflected in changes in external facts and public constraints.

This content-ascription policy, which wisely reflects the interpreter's preeminent interest in subject-world relations that bear on the interpreter's goals, indicates not only the (external) *terms* on which contents are individuated but also the flexible practicality of the *focus* of the ascription and therefore of the finer or coarser texture of the content assigned. Since content ascriptions play some role in the interpreter's mentation (prediction, explanation, imagination), this role determines the fine or coarse grain of the focus of the ascription. I argue in the next section that there is a good reason why interpretive explanations deal in contents that do not pick up mental conditions individuated cognitive-scientifically or introspectively. Contrary to current dogma, when so individuated, mental conditions are not explanatory; they generate the wrong equivalence classes. The same is true of prediction, justification, and communication.

By missing on the practicality of having its role define the terms and focus of a content ascription, the prevailing mentalist dogmas saddle interpretation with unrealistic and wrong-headed content-ascription policies. When the interpreter zooms on some details of the subject's mental condition, the move is still dictated by external interests, stakes, costs, and benefits and is still done in external terms. What changes is the focus of the ascription: there is a narrowing of the equivalence classes so as to approximate more closely the mental conditions compatible with the external individuators. These features of content ascription (external individuation and practical focus) are implicitly reflected in the linguistic and interpretive intuitions and practices cited by the advocates of the externality of content ascription but are not always properly understood.[9]

Holism Another familiar argument concerns the holism of attribution. The idea is that an interpreter checks (or makes assumptions about) a surround of attitudinized contents to individuate a particular content and assess its logical or epistemic credentials. I think this is right, but I read it somewhat differently. The check (or assumption) ranges not internally over the subject's mental states as specific representations but externally over a public semantic space on which the content ascription is projected and plotted. The measure of holism is given by what fits (and how) into the typologies of situations that afford content classifications. This external holism is then projected back onto the subject with the same pragmatic interest in checking whether he is within a reasonable range of accepted typologies. When I ascribe to you the belief (content) that Babeau is aggressive, I envision the scripts and canonical situations that characterize aggressiveness and would fit Babeau's behavior. I think you believe Babeau is aggressive because I check the symptoms of your belief against the public space provided by such scripts and canonical situations. (Babeau, by the way, is a bird. There is birdy aggressiveness—you'd better believe it!)

Versatility   This property is directly symptomatic of the laborious mental work behind a content ascription. It is also symptomatic of its practical bias. There are sundry familiar cases that point to the practical versatility of content ascription. I limit myself to a sample (but see Bogdan 1986d, 1991a, 1993a). The interpreter can vary the form of the content assigned with no variation in the subject's mental condition, or can keep the assigned content fixed despite such variation. (This is different from the Burge and Putnam gambit, evoked earlier, when the environment was varied while the mental condition was kept fixed.) The former option is exercised when the interpreter redescribes contents in various formats associated with the same cognitive modality or the same occurrent state. Thus the interpreter can establish that the subject saw the cat, or saw that it was a cat, or thought he saw a cat, or saw the cat approaching, or saw that the cat was approaching, and so on. The attribution redescribes perceptual content in terms of visual target, either as object (cat) or fact (that it approaches); it also redescribes perceptual content in a *de re* fashion (e.g., of a cat he saw that it was approaching; or of an object he saw that it is a cat) or in a *de dicto* fashion (e.g., he saw that a cat was approaching). These distinctions in content ascriptions do not correspond to differences in the subject's perception, let alone to differences in his visual architecture or its specific outputs (images).

The other option is exercised when the content ascribed stays put despite mental differences in the subject. An interpreter can represent a subject as perceiving that p and believing the same p despite the fact that (in cognitive-scientific or introspective terms) perceiving and believing are vastly different forms of processing with respect to format (images are analog, hence nonfactive; beliefs are factive and digital), degree of abstraction (images take in lots of detail; beliefs don't), and functional implications (beliefs interact inferentially with other beliefs and desires, images don't; beliefs often need linguistic encoding, images don't; and so on). Intuitively, the interpreter may know all this but not care. The same could be said about other combinations of attitudes, such as beliefs and desires. This picture does not change when an interpreter brings several subjects under the same content attribution. Interpreters often attribute the same type of belief or desire to different people in different places, doing different cognitive and behavioral things; such beliefs or desires are virtual in that they are entailed or suggested by a variety of mental states the subjects do not share (Dennett 1987, 56–57).

I take the externality, holism, and versatility of content to be among the chief symptoms of the practicality of ascription and its interest in how the subject's relations to the world, physical as well as cultural, can be charted for opportunities for useful information and involvement. Suppose that this is a plausible reading of the facts about content ascriptions. Why do content ascriptions operate this way? What is the point? As forewarned, I do not propose a theory of content ascription. The present sketch picks up themes that fit into this chapter's story about reconstruction. So, consistent with this modest agenda, I will venture a thought or two about what content ascription is for and then spend the remainder of the section outlining the reasons why content compression occurs and why, as a result, an ascribed content is not meant and not apt to represent a mental state of a subject.

The job: from contexture to function   I warn the reader (as I keep warning myself) that the hypothesis I am about to propose is not linguistically or introspectively intuitive and is prompted by the evolutionary argument of this chapter and by symptoms like those just surveyed. So here it is, as a starting point:

The job of a content ascription is to map information about a context of practical salience, or *contexture*, into a function that the information plays in the interpreter's thinking; the resulting representation reflects the constraints under which contextural information must be packaged (encoded, efficiently represented, and framed) in order to function in thinking.

In the flowchart of reconstruction, the contexture-to-function mapping is done by formatting tasks. Recall that an unsituated interpreter arrives at a contexture by recovering pertinent scripts and familiar situations that reveal points of interest and by aligning this schematized information to the coordinates of the context. For an intuitive reading of the plot, consider again the belief example of the previous section. B was given evidence in A's story not only about X's *believing* something but also about the kinds of situations revealing *what* was believed. The evidence allowed B to figure out contexture-revealing scripts and familiar situations that help nail down the right contents. In recreating a contexture-to-content mapping from a database containing cultural knowledge, B might have cogitated (not necessarily consciously) as follows: "If in a situation scripted as being of type *M*, *X* says such and so, and then in a situation close to those scripted as of type *N*, he is startled when *A* says such and such (and so on), then the guess is that *X* believes *that p.*"

It is worth speculating that the primitive and reflex content ascriptions of situated interpretation may proceed in the same spirit (though not in the same cognitive letter) by nailing down contextures in terms of canonical scripts and situations. If, for example, ape *A* has noticed a banana and has also noticed that ape *B* looks in the same direction and grins mischievously, then *A* will determine *what B* is likely to have noticed and likely to want, badly. This is a familiar script in the ape world. Likewise, when apes or humans interpret what others perceive, they map the contextual evidence into common representations of perceptual and sensorimotor routines. If the evidence points that way, I end up assigning to you the (compressed) perceptual content that the cat is on the table because, to begin with, my organization of the perceptual space into objects and relations is canonically similar to yours and the evidence points to the cat-table script of interest. The point, in short, is that contents are assigned in terms of a shared grid of typologies, whether psychologically canonical (as in perception or sensorimotor behavior), experientially canonical, or culturally canonical. It is in these terms that the interpreter categorizes the information conveyed by the subject. The question, then, is why and how this elaborate categorization ends up as snappy description.

Formatting for thinking   The short answer is that, given how we manage cognitive affairs generally and thinking in particular, without a summary of the output of prior processing that output cannot play its role at all or not efficiently. The longer answer goes as follows. Evolution tends to reward cognition for economical design and compression of information (an issue already taken up in chapter 5, section 7). In particular, reconstruction operates thinkingly, and thinking is designed to execute elaborate cognitive tasks (the iceberg theme) culminating in compact outputs (the tip theme). The same is true of other cognitive modalities animated by thinking: linguistic communication (Sperber and Wilson 1986), mental imagery (Kosslyn 1990, for a pictorial reading; Pylyshyn 1984, for a descriptive reading), and memory recall (Loftus 1980, for psychological evidence; Damasio 1994, for neurological evidence). Besides the evolutionary reasons for the summarization gambit, there are specific pressures generated by the roles that thoughts must play. These roles are bound to have a hand in formatting the thoughts. Images and memories are outputs that feed into reasoning or communication, which is why their format must fit their usage. The same is true of interpretations.

If thinking animates planning, communicating, and interpreting, then its outputs, thoughts, would be units *shared* across these modalities. A thought would be what is planned, communicated, and remembered; or interpreted, reasoned about, and communicated; or the like. This is how thoughts fit into the horizontal work of mentation; they are shaped into forms exchangeable across distinct processing areas. Vertical (or meta) work is also apt to shape thoughts. Thinking loops back on itself in various modalities. One forms thoughts about thoughts, is conscious of them, metarepresents them. In such loops one thinks to control one's planning or imagining, evaluate their outputs, comment on them, steer their flow. So, as a matter of *encoding*, the generic shape of a thought can be viewed as a common currency that various thinking-based modalities do business in and pass to each other.[10]

Yet there is more to the shape of thoughts than their encoding. Thoughts must also be represented efficiently and framed to play suitable roles. Here is an intuitive analogy. To communicate, one must know a language, such as French, and specifically its vocabulary and grammar. This is knowledge of how to encode meanings in French. Such knowledge does not yet determine what sentences to construct and how. Vocabulary and grammar allow a wide spectrum of options. A sentence can be as long and convoluted as time and memory permit. Economy, relevance, brevity, informativeness, truthfulness, and other (Gricean) strictures on *efficient representation* must be brought in. They are not part of the encoding knowledge. An utterance is not only an instance of encoding; it is also a unit of efficient representation. The strictures on efficiency are different from those of encoding, for they reflect functional constraints and cognitive limitations.

Likewise, it is not enough to view thoughts as encodings assembled under rules, as units of mentalese, if you like. They must also be represented so as to be functionally efficient. One such function can be inter-modality commerce; another metarepresentational ascent. There may be units of thought that traffic best from memory to attention, or from reasoning to speech centers, and others that best comment on and evaluate thoughts. As a result, whatever the actual surround and details of the thinking process in some modality, its output is compacted into a unit of representation that is efficient for a specific traffic route and role.

Yet efficient representation is not enough, either. In using a language, one also communicates something or understands what is communicated, which is more than efficiently representing meanings. People do things with words; they intend words to have effects, to play roles. This requires *framing* utterances for an effect or role. A speaker frames an efficient representation to convey a communicative intention. To do that, she chooses her words, puts them in some order, delineates a topic from comments, highlights some portions by emphasis or suitable constructions —the explicit part. She also enters assumptions about hearer and shared environments, and thus conveys implications by what she says and how she says it—the implicit part. Both explicit and implicit accomplishments are pragmatic contributions to framing. (At the receiving end, a hearer not only deciphers the meanings conveyed and rerepresents them efficiently but also has to get the frame of the utterance and read it right.) Whether linguistically expressed or not, a content ascribed is a thought pragmatically framed. My earlier discussion and illustration of the practical focus and versatility of content ascription revealed the pragmatic framing of content. My discussion of explanation in the next section will add further details.

Summing up   Encoding, efficiently representing, and framing are distinct sets of tasks constitutive of formatting thoughts and their linguistic expressions. If content is represented by a thought and expressed linguistically, it must be (a) encoded, in order to have cognitive reality, (b) efficiently represented, in order to comply with cognitive limitations and requirements for its employment and traffic across modalities, and (c) framed to play in the interpreter's mind and action a role consistent with the contextural aspects of practical interest as revealed by the subject's attitude. As an iceberg-to-tip policy, framing in particular links up with the below-the-surface work done at the prior stages of reconstruction: those of recovery and alignment. If the tasks of encoding and efficient representation reflect the pressures of economic compression and inter-modality traffic, those of framing pick up features that can play the roles intended by the interpreter. The flowchart of tasks would look as follows, with emphasis on the last leg, which is formatting:

Recovery → alignment → formatting =
a. *Encoding*: secures common representational format
b. *Efficient representation*: secures economy, relevance, brevity, informativeness, etc.

c. *Framing*: chooses pragmatic parameters (order, topic-comment, emphasis) for certain effects; makes relevant assumptions

Let me conclude by taking a wider view. This has been a barely serviceable sketch of an (evolving) analysis of content ascription in interpretation. As forewarned, the analysis is not about the meaning of ascription sentences. We can now see why a logical or semantic account of the formula '*S* desires (believes, thinks) that *p*' does not exhaust a content ascription and why it provides few clues to what underlies ascription policies. My analysis is about tasks, not necessarily linguistic, whose execution packages aspects of interest for further mental use. One such use is in interpretive explanation, the topic I address next. The most popular views on interpretive explanations are mentalist, for they take content ascriptions to reveal mental causes of behavior. My story of content does not support this line. A look at the scheme just diagrammed, and the account behind it, shows that a content ascription has little, if anything, to do with the architectural, processing, or representational details of the subject's mentation—the only serious candidates for mental causation. The account of interpretive explanation to be sketched next confirms this conclusion.

5   The Culture of Explanation

Interpretive explanation is a topic as much debated as misunderstood. My angle on it will be narrow and intent on firming up the evolutionary argument about reconstruction. My main claim is that interpretive explanation is an ontogenetic creature of culture designed to project a subject's roles, attributes, and actions on the grid of culture. This goes against the prevailing view in philosophy, which is that interpretive explanation (also called 'intentional') is *psychocausal* in the sense that it (a) places the weight of explanation on what is going on in the mind of the subject and (b) appeals to mental causes as reasons for his thinking and acting as he does. I join a small minority in rejecting this mentalist view. My critical fire is aimed specifically at *psychosemanticism*, the strongest version of psychocausalism, according to which mental states cause, and hence explain, in virtue of what they represent. I argue that psychosemanticism fails to jibe with ordinary practices and recommends (science-inspired) policies that do not serve the aim of interpretation. I then turn to an alternative proposal that places the explanatory weight on cultural norms and construes conformity to norms, via content ascriptions, in practical and external terms commensurate with the interests of the interpreter.

Psychosemanticism Anyone concerned with interpretive explanation feels the tension between the contribution of what is inside the subject's mind and what is outside it. Inside are the causal wheels that move mentation and behavior; outside, the destinations of, and most often the reasons for, the moves. Those who place the explanatory weight on the representation of what is inside the mind may be called *mentalists*; those who place it outside *externalists*. Most philosophers of interpretive explanation are mentalists. I am not. During the age of Cartesianism, the main reason for mentalism was a phenomenology-based metaphysics of mind. In this age of science and materialism, the main reason is mental causation. There is a psychocausal syllogism at the heart of mentalism that may be summarized as follows: only mental causes explain what an agent does; interpretation does that successfully, so it must premise mental causes and their laws in its explanations; since interpretation explains mostly in terms of attitudes to propositional contents, as reasons, it follows that mental causes = explanatory reasons = attitudes to contents. QED, more or less.

Given this popular syllogism, the only question is how to construe mental causes as explanatory reasons. There are different proposals on the philosophical market. They all assume that mental causes are internal structures at some level of scientific or metaphysical description but are ultimately brain states. The main choices are either brain-state types (type physicalism) or brain events (token physicalism) or functional-state types (functionalism). The position that makes the case for psychocausalism most cogently, by explaining how propositional attitudes cause, is *psychosemanticism*. On this conception, mental structures cause and hence explain in virtue of their semantic content or what they represent. Even if psychosemanticism were a sound metaphysical or cognitive-scientific doctrine (which I don't think it is), it misses what *interpretive* explanation is about. Or so I will argue.

There are differences among psychosemantic positions, depending on how they construe mental representation and on what weight, if any, they give to external factors in individuating what is represented and hence what is mentally causal and explanatory. I will not get into exegetical details because I do not buy the basic premise. I do not think that mental representations as internal causes are treated as explanatory reasons in interpretation. I find it even surprising and question-begging that psy-chosemanticists are unaware that what they prove metaphysically or cognitive-scientifically about mental causation, as a psychological phe-nomenon, might not be what interests the interpreter.[11]

The question that needs to be asked is, *Why psychology?* What does psychology do for interpretive explanation? The latter does not cite any physical, chemical, or neural underpinnings of attitudes to contents, that is, more basic internal structures. Why should it cite mental representa-tions? Why the psychology but not the anatomy, physics, or neuroscience of the content-encoding brain states? Because, we are told, psychology alone provides the right level of abstraction and explanatoriness. This, in turn, is because only mental representations have causal potency in virtue of their contents, and mental representations are in the domain of psychology. True, psychology is closer than physics, chemistry, or neuro-science to the information-processing level of mental causation that explains conation, cognition, and behavior, but this is a matter of *scien-tific* explanation. The question is why interpretation would need to oper-ate at *that* level to do *its* explanatory job. If the assumption already is that interpretation is a naive psychology whose job is to track an agent's mental representations and their causal impact on his actions, then, of course, the explanations must operate close to the domain and at the level of abstraction best poised for that sort of explanatory success. That not only begs the entire question of interpretive explanation but actually misrepresents its job and rationale.

Mental irrelevance   I begin my critical counterargument intuitively by appealing to ordinary explanatory practices, and then provide a rationale for these practices and for why psychosemanticism is wrong. Listen first to the ordinary voice of interpretation, in philosophical rendition: "From the fact that a man intends to press the button in front of him, it does not follow that he performs certain specific bodily movements. It only follows that with the movements he means to press the button. From the fact that a crowd demonstrates, it does not follow that its members will perform certain specific individual actions. It only follows that with the actions they perform are intended to be a demonstration" (von Wright 1971, 133). My paraphrase is that from the fact that a subject intends to press the button, it does not follow that he *is interpreted* to have specific mental representations about the button, pressing it or other relevant matters, anymore than he is interpreted to do specific behavioral or neural things, and from the fact that a crowd demonstrates, it does not follow that its members *are interpreted* to have specific mental representations about how to move their legs, what to say, what is around, and so on—even though in both cases mental representations are causally involved. (The crowd example is reminiscent of Dennett's point about a shared virtual belief attributed to a variety of persons in different cognitive and behavioral conditions; the attribution is indifferent to how the persons specifically represent what they do.)

The critical point (still made intuitively) is that for an interpreter, mental representations or other internal indices of attitudinized contents can be *too specific and variable*, and hence as explanatorily irrelevant as are bodily movements, neural events, or physical states. Psychosemanticism posits the *wrong level of abstraction* for interpretive explanation by failing to provide adequate stability and regularity and hence explanatoriness. There is a methodological rationale behind this failure. To be successful, any type of explanation, scientific or commonsense, must delineate the *right equivalence classes* in its domain. What counts as the right equivalence classes is dictated by the interests that guide the explanation and hence by what makes a relevant difference to those interests.

Think of it this way. (I follow the example and insightful analysis of Garfinkel 1981, chapter 1.) Suppose I want to know why a car accident happened. If I take the accident in *all* its particularity, then everything about it would count: the shape of the car's lights, the shirt of the driver, the color of his eyes, and so on. If any of these details had not been there, it would not have been that particular accident. Since no explanation can be so absurdly specific, the question is which differences from the particular accident count as irrelevant; surely, the shape of the lights and eye color could vary without making a relevant difference. The criterion of irrelevant difference defines the right equivalence classes and sustains the right counterfactuals (e.g., had it not been for that difference, the fact to be explained would not have occurred). The equivalence relations set up by the criterion of irrelevant difference classifies the phenomena to be explained and in so doing defines a measure of explanatory stability: the smaller and more numerous the equivalence classes, the less stable the resulting explanations. 'Reckless driving causes accidents in some form or another' is much more stable under changes of situational parameters (whether, of road condition or driver condition) than 'reckless driving and metaphysical daydreaming and lots of coffee and a violet shirt, etc.'

So the question is, What are the right or optimal equivalence classes for interpretive explanations? The shortest answer is culture. To translate this slogan into a tighter argument, while maintaining common ground and terminology with the views I oppose, I will pretend for a while that interpretive explanation is deductive-nomological and will organize my constructive argument around this pretension. I do not think that interpreters normally explain deductive-nomologically, not unless they have to or are in need of a Ph.D. or tenure, but I provide the supporting brief only at the end of this section.

Major reasons, minor contexts   To understand my proposal, I take as my comparative frame of reference scientific explanation of the deductive-nomological sort. This frame posits a law of nature or some other regularity as major premise and the contextual coordinates of the event to be explained as minor premise. The law specifies the reason why things generally are in a certain way; the contextual conditions bring an instance under the reason-giving law. Switch now to interpretation. The reason-giving pattern supplied by the major premise of an interpretive explanation, far from being a psychological generalization true of subjects (the mentalist hypothesis), is usually a social directive or habit, cultural institution or practice—in short, a *cultural norm*. This is to say that the interpreter does not locate the reason-giving norm in the subject and need not even take it to be explanatory in virtue of being mentally instantiated.

The minor premise specifies and even measures contextually the subject's relation to the norm, typically one of conformity, approximation, or deviance. This is what attitude attributions do, on the basis of evidence. This endeavor need not target the subject's mental causation either explicitly, through specific representations, or implicitly but systematically, through interpretive programs. Some internal causation is assumed, for any living being is programmed by natural selection to know that another being acts causally on its goals and information access. But that is not yet explanatory. The interpreter needs to identify *specific* reasons for thought and action. In doing so, she need not explicitly represent or systematically track the subject's mental causation; she needs only the right equivalence classes, and these are rarely construed in terms of mental causation. The intuitive examples noted earlier suggest that the specific probing of mental causation could be counterproductive.

This is the general direction of my argument. I will next amplify and illustrate its main joints. The logic of exposition, still committed to the deductive-nomological fiction, recommends beginning with the minor premise.

Look first for goals   Content ascription was said to make manifest a contexture, in terms of salient practical aspects, and to map it into categorizations or equivalence classes that respond to the interpreter's interest—now explanation. What are the salient practical aspects that generate those equivalence classes? Evolution is unambiguous about the first half of the answer: the subject's goals. The environment of selection for interpretive skills was said to be teleological (chapter 5, sections 2 and 3). Organisms are goal-directed and primed to recognize the goal directedness of others. The latter recognition was a launching pad for interpretation. It stands to evolutionary reason that the first thing an interpreter does is to check the agency and goals of a subject. Many students of interpretation agree with the primacy of goals but construe goals differently. The difference must be spelled out carefully, lest we lapse back into mentalism.

The difference is between a causal and internal view of goals (psychosemanticism) and a teleological and external view (adopted here). The former identifies goals with desires, construed as mental representations and therefore as causes of action in virtue of their semantic content. The latter view takes goals to be external states of affairs brought about by action under some mental initiative. It may not look like much of a difference, but that is misleading. To see why, consider an example of Davidson's (1980, 47–48). If one interprets Smith as setting the house on fire in order to collect the insurance, one explains Smith's action (in part) by noting one of its causes, which is his desire to collect the insurance (the other cause being Smith's belief that his action would lead to what is desired). This is the psychosemantic view. The teleological view has it that the interpreter explains Smith's action (in part) by noting its goal—collecting the insurance, an external state of affairs—but leaving it open at this stage *how* exactly the goal was represented by the subject as a specific desire.

The interpreter's construal of the goal may assume a mental condition of the subject (his desire) and may even assume it as a triggering cause of his action, but without specifying its actual structure. (To the same extent, the construal may be committed to some neural or even physical condition as the triggering cause without specifying their structures.) It is the goal that matters most, not the details of its representing desire or its underlying physiological need, if any. (Needs link up with goals at least as much as desires do, yet we explain them teleologically, without bothering about their physiological details.) In most walks of human life, goals explain in virtue of their place in various natural and cultural patterns. So there is a tight connection between placing explanatory weight on the latter and taking an externalist angle on goals. Before pressing on with this idea, I pause to put the argument in a larger perspective.

Teleology downgrades the role of mental causation in interpretation in two steps. In biological systems, causal routes implement functions. There are many causal ways of performing a function and many functional ways to achieve a goal (Bennett 1976, Bogdan 1994, Collins 1987). This is an objective fact about life that interpretation evolves to factor into its calculations. Pressured by evolution to measure costs against benefits, interpretation settles first for goals (externally construed) not only because they matter vitally but also because they are more visible, more widely shared, more practically salient, and thus easier and cheaper to figure out—in a word, more stable explanatorily or predictively—than their internal (mental, physiological, or physical) indices. Underlying mental functions and causes are harder to identify, involve greater cognitive expense, and most often offer no higher benefits. There is thus an objective reason why mental causation is irrelevant. The alternative would be expensive and not always predictive or explanatory, since it is irregular and unstable. Teleology is generally more stable than mental causation because it provides more reliable and regular equivalence classes relative to the interpreter's interests.

Yet, as anticipated, this is only half of the story. Goals do not explain, and are not intelligible, without being plugged into relevant patterns in nature and culture, just as the patterns themselves cannot begin to explain without first touching base with goals. The subject's goals are indices to what patterns are involved in a situation. So the next question is how the interpreter relates goals to the patterns that explain. Thus the second half of the story.

A quick return to roots: prediction versus explanation In situated interpretation most goals and actions taken to satisfy them fall under patterns specified by goal settings configured ancestrally ("situated norms," as it were). When the situated interpreter tracks the subject's goal and his access to a situation, she attempts to recognize an instance of a normlike goal setting that tells her what to expect and how to get involved. Most of the predictive work (italics and double arrow in the scheme below) is done by the goal setting and not by the conative and cognitive causes allegedly imputed to the subject. This idea can be schematized as follows:

(8.2)   *Situated prediction*
Goal setting type selected for [perception of goal-setting instance as instance of norm $\Rightarrow$ (estimate of [subject's goal + situation] $\rightarrow$ estimate of subject's access to situation $\rightarrow$ expectations or predictions of subject's actions)]

This scheme follows from the argument of chapter 5, particularly sections 2 and 3, and supplies a useful comparative prop for understanding unsituated explanation as follows. Except in cases of ancestrally selected norms, there are few cases of unsituated interpretation that would fit (8.2). There are many reasons for this: most instances of unsituated explanation are not perceptual; the behavioral and verbal data vastly underdetermine possible goals and forms of information access; the functional (including representational) and a fortiori causal (including neural) routes to goals and information multiply and vary dramatically, the latter exponentially in relation to the former.

Yet the most important difference, worth a minute of attention, is that explanation is not prediction. It may not look so from the stance of philosophy of science, a stance occupied by mentalism, theorism, and psychosemanticism, but (for the nth time) interpretation is not science. There are many reasons for explanation being so different from prediction, in interpretation. To begin with, explanation is not urgent phylogenetically and ontogenetically, certainly not as urgent as prediction. Apes and very young children don't explain and do not seem to mind not doing it. It is prediction that matters most, because it is immediately practical. As far as I can tell, explanation shows up late in human ontogeny, perhaps not before the metarepresentational turn. That is a time of intense enculturation, when the child has to justify, defend, excuse, advertise, and rationalize what she and others are doing. These are culturally induced and trained accomplishments. Prediction is natural, but explanation is cultural.

Further differences back up this diagnosis. Interpretive prediction is indexed temporally and spatially and has rather limited ranges in both directions. That squares with the limits of situated interpretation. This latter is tied to the present and the immediate future and to the surrounding space, and that is the usual range of its predictions and practical involvements. Explanation can be temporally and spatially extended or largely indifferent to either space or time. The unsituated interpreter must often track a subject and the information he conveys across vast space and time expanses, or across possible or counterfactual situations, in order to check conformity to canonical patterns. This is precisely what interpretive explanation is good at, as a cognitive adaptation, and why it evolved. In the time of culture, the explanation skill is of practical value precisely because many, if not most, affordances that subjects reveal and interpreters need to know about and exploit are visible and intelligible only according to the patterns revealed by cultural norms. Explanation is no less practical and practically motivated than prediction, but it has a different agenda. Given these differences between situated and unsituated interpretation, and between prediction and explanation in particular, what is the unsituated interpreter supposed to do?

Cherchez la norme   Fortunately, culture has supplanted and even bested nature by installing cultural norms that index and standardize types of goal settings as patterns for explanation and unsituated prediction. Under the fiction of explanation as deduction from laws, the proposal was that when an interpreter looks for reasons why a subject acted in some way or said something, she mentally scans (not always consciously) the known cultural landscape for signs of which norms might be operative as reasons in the case at hand (major premise). The other step (minor premise) is to establish whether the norm as reason relates to the subject. In doing this, the interpreter may, but need not, assume that the subject has an explicit representation or some other active (chemical, neural, introspective) cognizance of the norm. It suffices that the data show some interpretively intelligible relation to the norm. As a result, the reason embodied in the norm is linked to the subject and thus made explanatory of what he does. The fiction that interpretive explanation is of argument form allows a neat pedagogical demarcation of the two steps (major, minor premise) and of the tasks involved. This is a vast simplification, but it conveys the thrust of the proposal.

The interpreter may, but need not, have a *psychological* reading of the explanatory norm. In our example, in order to explain what Smith did, she need not mentally represent that people who want to collect insurance from their damaged houses and believe that setting them on fire will damage the house are likely to set them on fire. Nor, therefore, need her database contain lots of such psychological readings of cultural norms that step forward, neatly represented mentally and linguistically, as major premises in explanation. The contextual evidence can activate the norm [damaged house → collecting insurance] and her inferential powers can do the rest.

Let me roll this story in slower motion, with the help of a summarizing scheme and an example:

(8.3)   *Unsituated explanation*
Cultural-norm setting installs [recognition of the norm ⇒ (interpretation of [subject's goal type + situation type] → estimate of subject's desire and belief) → prediction, explanation)]

The interpreter is culturally primed to recognize a norm and use the contextual evidence to recognize a goal type and a content-revealing situation type. These recognitions *predate* the further recognition that the subject has that goal as a specific desire and has a specific belief about how to accomplish it. To reconsider Davidson's example, when one interprets Smith as setting the house on fire to collect the insurance, one first recognizes a goal type (collecting insurance) and a situation type (the house on fire) that instantiate a widely understood norm (that people collect insurance when their houses are destroyed). More exactly, one first recognizes the norm [house on fire → collecting insurance] and then "psychologizes" it by translating it into possible goal types and situation types for agents. In turn, the goal type and the scripted situation provide estimates of possible contents for Smith's attitudes. The interpreter then links instances of the goal and situation types with Smith by estimating his desires and beliefs, but not necessarily as specific mental structures. The desire attribution says that Smith has the goal in question (collecting insurance), and the belief attribution that his action (burning) fits the situation (the house on fire and damaged) without either of them informing about how Smith *specifically represented* (actual data structures about) the goal and the action-situation fit. Think also of second-hand information or gossip, where nothing may be said explicitly about a subject's mental condition, yet the texture of the report and the context allow a distant interpreter to estimate the subject's relation to norms and thus to explain or anticipate whatever could be the case.

Figuring out the subject's specific representations is a costlier, riskier, and hence relatively rarer endeavor, that is inductive fallible, elaborate, usually narrative, and undertaken only when normality is violated in novel or otherwise significant ways, when curiosity is intense, and when the stakes and costs of being wrong with the minimal strategy are high and the benefits of being right with a maximal mindreading strategy are commensurately ample. The costs and risks of the latter strategy are obvious on the Garfinkel-inspired analysis evoked earlier. As the interpreter moves away from cultural norms to more idiosyncratic arrangements, she loses the larger and stabler (since norm-bound) equivalence classes, because more differences and accidents now become relevant. The explanatory stability provided by culture is sacrificed for mental singularities. Yet clearly the inferential and narrative skills honed during the reconstructional turn are ready to help by enabling the interpreter to take this adventurous path in ways that were neither possible nor called for at earlier evolutionary turns.

Taking stock   Interpretation is successful not because it is committed to causally potent particulars of mental architecture or representations but because most often it ignores them on behalf of the external constraints of nature and culture, which are more explanatory as far as interpretation is concerned. When interpretation appears to "read minds," it does so from outside, in terms of public configurations defined by norms, goals, and information access as well as roles and attributes. As it progresses along this avenue toward mental particulars, interpretation has access to increasingly narrower and less stable equivalence classes. The process can be reviewed with the help of the serviceable chess analogy.

A player (the interpreter) explains what another player (the subject) does, or guesses what he might do, in terms of board configurations. The configurations approximate chess norms (standard moves, classical strategies). When the subject makes a move, the interpreter first looks up the relevant norm and thinks, "Aha, this is a Capablanca variant," then "psychologizes" the representation of the norm in general terms (i.e., goal and situation types) by thinking that anybody in that position, making that move, is likely to play the Capablanca variant, and finally, with or without further evidence and inference, estimates that the subject's desire and belief fit into that norm. The Capablanca variant is a stable explanatory norm with large equivalence classes for the possible specific contents attributable to the subject. If the subject plays the variant straight, there isn't much need to further "psychologize" his conformity to the variant. If the subject does something different, the interpreter is puzzled, quickly scans her mental chess manual, smiles back, "Aha, this is an Alekhin twist," proceeds to combine the two variants, and continues in the same style of explanation. But now there is more instability, since the equivalence classes get smaller and more accident-prone. Suppose, finally, that the subject's next move is normatively inexplicable—there is no known strategy or variant or intelligible improvisation on something familiar. "Oh holy zut," thinks the interpreter, "this guy thinks for himself. Trouble awaits." This is when interpretation goes in full psychological gear to narrow down specific contents that might be at work. I said contents, not their representing data structures that do psychocausal work in the subject's mind. Contents are still identified externally in (chessboardlike) terms of public facts and relations (though no longer known norms) in narrower and hence more singular equivalence classes, in an attempt to zoom in on specific desires and beliefs.

Is this progression from norm to specific content a sign of increasing "mindreading"? It depends how we construe the claim. For the interpreter, animal or human, situated or not, what the subject "has in mind" is intelligible in external terms of facts and norms. The interpreter's content ascriptions reveal equivalence classes in terms of cultural and physical board configurations, so to speak. So at all times the subject's mind is "read" from outside in terms of such contents. The difference is that when conformity to norms is sufficiently explanatory (i.e., when the subject plays a Capablanca variant or a restaurant script straight), the mind is "read" in terms of wide and stable equivalence classes, compatible with many sets of contents and, of course, many more sets of specific representations of contents. When no norm is in sight or for some reason a specific identification of content is needed, the "mindreading" gets focused on increasingly specific external configurations that yield much narrower and more unstable equivalence classes, compatible with fewer sets of contents and of actual representations of contents. In this (still external) sense, the interpreter's estimate comes closer to the content the subject may have had in mind but still without necessarily coming closer to its specific representation that was causally effective. All along the interpreter remains a reluctant "mindreader," for good evolutionary reasons. Interpretive explanation counts on this reluctance for its average success.

Pragmatics versus argument The fiction has done its job; the fiction must go. Neither (8.3) nor the account spun around it were meant to capture how interpreters *actually* spontaneously explain. The exercise was pedagogical and intended to convey the spirit of my proposal in close comparison with mentalism, particularly its psychosemantic versions. Although I do not have a concrete model of spontaneous interpretive explanation, I would like to conclude by gesturing toward some of the tasks involved.

I begin by noting that there are occasions when interpreters explain in argument form, even by deduction from explicit generalizations, but those tend to be formal, deliberate, ritualistic occasions of justification and rationalization. Even then the arguments tend to be contrived and shortened paraphrases of complex spontaneous travails. These paraphrasing policies are themselves creatures of culture. So, either in spontaneous or deliberate form, interpretive explanation is an artifact of culture, which recruits available resources and weaves them into domain-specialized skills. Yet contrary to the fiction indulged in so far, the resources tapped for spontaneous explanation are not those of explicit logical argument but rather those of spontaneous thinking, inductive and narrative, rather than formally deductive, skills. Spontaneous explaining is put in motion by curiosity, surprise, uncertainty, or a need to understand normwise. That makes it a *pragmatic* enterprise in daily life as in science (Garfinkel 1981, van Fraassen 1980).

The pragmatic models of the commonsense and scientific explanation suggest an *inductive* operation in terms (familiar from problem solving and decision making) of context, problem or question, relevant database, possible answers, measures of relevance and plausibility, and so on. These are not the argument terms of deductive-nomological explanation. The distinction is critical not only for the nature of explaining but also for what counts as a satisfactory and successful explanation. In general, an explanation is deemed *pragmatically* successful when it answers a question, removes an uncertainty, or finds an understandable pattern in *its* inductive terms; an explanation is deemed *formally* successful when its argument form is valid and its premises true or at least justified. In addition, an interpretive explanation is deemed *satisfactory* when (on my account) it locates the right norms or scripts or departures from them in the cultural space.

Two examples mark vividly and amusingly the distinction between formal and pragmatic explanation in interpretation. Carruthers's is first: "No adult ever says things like 'Daddy has gone to the shops because he wants food to eat tonight, believes that there is nothing suitable in the house, believes that the shops are the best place to get food, believes that now is a suitable time to go to the shops' and so on. One simply says

'Daddy has gone shopping to get supper.' Not even the endless why questions of a 2-year-old will lead one to articulate a generalization like 'When people want something, and believe that they can do something to get it, they tend (other things being equal) to do that thing' " (1992, 120).

Having been persecuted for years by countless philosophical discussions taking the line ridiculed here, I can only laugh, approvingly. After that, I read the example as follows. The child easily understands why Daddy went shopping to get supper. A goal, a script, a norm, and little else can do explanatory wonders. Scripts assume or point to norms. Some scripts might even have been drilled into the child's memory in explicit terms (e.g., people who want to eat generally shop, people who want to shop tend to transport themselves to the shops, etc.) or may be so formulated by her in the script activation. Nevertheless, these are not psychological laws and are not about people as subjects of interpretation. They are descriptions of ritualized patterns of doing things, matrices of action, to which people are expected to conform. The subject's specific desires and beliefs do not come into the picture at this stage, for scripts are about people and action settings generally. The subject's goal is determined from the available evidence (verbal, in the example) as an external opportunity for action.

The second lawlike paraphrase ("When people want something and believe, etc."), being an elemental law about everything alive, is a psychological canon that every being is cognizant of. The irony (in this context) is that by being so basic and ubiquitous, it does not explain much, if anything. No wonder that almost nobody (save philosophers) invokes it. Explaining a particular action requires much more, usually a cultural pattern. The first solemn paraphrase ("Daddy has gone to the shops because he wants ... and believes ... and believes ... and believes ... ") is a psychological rehash of something that an interpreter, including a very young one, would know from scripts and social routines, and know in nonpsychological terms. This psychological rehashing turns many cultural and other nonpsychological verities into alleged intentional laws. A simple deconstruction could expose the trick. (Oh, no! "Derrida rereading Fodor!"—big title in *Le Monde*. The cafés are buzzing with excitement. Cognitive science finally comes to the literature departments.)

Another well-worn example exhibits even better the inductive traits of explaining (Garfinkel 1981). When Willie Sutton was asked why he robbed banks, he said that that's where the money is. (Can't quarrel with that.) Sutton's answer activates and values several inductive parameters of

pragmatic explaining. (Jokes, puns, and proverbs do this too.) It delineates a topic and a comment—key features of socialized thinking, which
reconstruction is primed to recognize. The topic highlights assumptions
(people need money and robbing is one way of getting it—two very cultural arrangements) compatible with several courses and targets of action.
Sutton's comment faintly hints at an evaluation measure (for lots of
money, given the effort and risk, banks still have no rival). The explaining
needs no psychological laws; the required patterns are all out there, are all
public and cultural. I could ape Carruthers and give you an erudite psychological paraphrase, but let's leave that for entertainment with unsus-
pecting dinner guests.

Notice several things about this example. Once framed pragmatically,
the satisfactoriness of the explanation of why Sutton robs banks has to do
with his comment relative to the topic, and not with alleged psychological
laws imputed to him. This is because he injects the assumption that robbing is his way of earning a living, and the question then becomes what to
rob. With this move Sutton carves up the cultural space so as to narrow
down the class of applicable scripts and norms surveyed by the interpreter. His answer is surprising (at least to some) in his choice of class, but
almost *any* answer would have carved up the cultural space in some way
and selected some class of relevant scripts, norms, or shared routines.

Interpretive explanation is normally pragmatic. When it is so, it takes a
narrative form in which the operative norms are submerged and implicit
in plots and collateral descriptions (Lloyd 1989, chapter 8). Clues from
behavior, context, or what is said or previously known delineate the topic,
in the guise of assumed norms or canonical situations, and the explanatory interest focuses on which particular norm or situation was complied
with or deviated from, and how tightly or loosely. The psychological
paraphrases ascertain a subject's conformity to or deviance from norms
and canonical situations. The desire-belief estimates reflect the expectation that norms and canonical situations are followed by the subject, no
matter how in precise mental detail.

Cultural versus interpretive explanations   The presence of cultural norms
and their links to economic, legal, and political institutions and practices
require a distinction between purely cultural explanations and interpretive
explanations that appeal to cultural norms. So far my discussion has
focused on the latter sort. The former belong to social sciences and their
commonsense counterparts. I will tackle this distinction by reference to

Lynne Baker's stimulating and congenial book (1995). She examines (in chapter 4) a class of explanations that are causal, intentional but non-psychological, and cultural (in my sense). An explanation is said to be *intentional but nonpsychological* if it presupposes propositional attitudes but does not mention them explicitly. It may look like my notion of interpretive explanation, but I sense a narrow though important difference. My account, like Baker's, downgrades the psychological dimension in interpretive explanation. It allows for an explanation to causally track what happens to an agent, by plotting him against norms and institutions, without bringing in his mental life. The question is whether Baker's notion of explanation is always interpretive, as opposed to purely cultural. Here is what I have in mind.

Both cultural and interpretive explanations of what people do or what happens to them presuppose propositional attitudes (since people are treated as agents) without necessarily citing the attitudes explicitly. That does not yet make the two sorts of explanations equivalent. Here is Baker's example: Al's application for a gun permit was turned down because Al is a convicted felon. You guessed mine: Daddy went shopping to get supper. Both explanations presuppose attitudes without citing them, both appeal to cultural norms, and both can be read causally. The difference is that an interpretive explanation needs to establish the relation of a subject to a cultural norm or institution even when not citing attitudes. This, after all, is what reconstruction has evolved to do. A purely cultural explanation is under no such obligation. Establishing conformity brings in content and attitude ascription in interpretive explanations; this need not be so in purely cultural explanations. There is, for example, an implicit content ascription, in the form of an explicit goal specification (to get supper), in the Daddy example but none in the gun-permit example. It is the goal ascription embedded in a cultural norm that supplies an interpretive explanation. It may be argued that there is an implicit goal specification in the gun-permit example (Al wanted a gun permit, after all) but none, as far as I can tell, in Baker's other examples of cultural explanation (such as that Janet Reno began to be accompanied by Secret Service agents upon being nominated Attorney General). There is always some goal assumed in *any* cultural explanation that involves agents. The question is whether the assumption has anything to do with the explanation, and in lots of cases, including some contemplated by Baker, it doesn't.

Having said that, I am ready and glad to grant that many explanations that look interpretive are actually purely cultural, and thus a further step away from a subject's mind. This is particularly true of contexts where the agents are treated as faceless pawns caught in cultural games. Phrasing the problem this way highlights the business of interpretive reconstruction: to bring culture to bear on a *particular* subject whose relation to the world has practical significance for an interpreter. Purely cultural explanations, agent-oriented and tacitly relying on propositional attitudes as they may be, do not bring in this practical and particularizing perspective, and therefore need not activate the right skills.

6 If I Were You: Simulation

So far I have left untouched one question that has fired many recent debates: are interpretive skills intrinsically other-regarding (the MoM and ToM positions), or do they draw on one's own resources and possibly self-knowledge to interpret others (simulation)? This is a debate that has rapidly acquired a conceptual complexity that I cannot adequately cover and do justice to here. So I will limit myself to venturing some partial and tentative thoughts, enlightened by what has been argued so far in this essay.

The practical charms of simulation For convenience, I assume that the consensual construal of simulation is that one interprets others by using one's mental resources. Specifically, one feeds data about the relevant conditions of the subject into one's practical reasoning mechanism, runs it off-line, disconnected from its outputs, as it were, and takes its feigned output as the appropriate interpretation, typically in the form of a prediction of action or attribute (Gordon 1986, 1992a; Goldman 1989, 1993; Harris 1992; Morton 1980). I refer to this construal as the *consensual definition of narrow simulation* or simply as *narrow simulation* and to the surrounding doctrine as *narrow simulationism*. Later I identify a wide version of simulation. There are variations on the narrow theme—for example, does it involve introspection or imagination or other phenomenological tricks?—but I ignore them here.

Just from this simple abstract it appears that narrow simulationism could be friendly to a practical stance on interpretation. The simulator does not have to know the subject's mind or her own in order to interpret; she runs her conative and cognitive processes with pretend input and comes up with an interpretation—as simple and natural as that. There is, of course, an assumption of likeness of mind (which is why simulation works) but that is not what simulation represents and is not something the simulator explicitly knows. Narrow simulation also serves the practical interests of interpretation. By definition, the interpreter cannot help but look at the subject's goal situation as if it were hers; the practical salience of what is interpreted thus comes for free (Gordon 1992a, 15). Finally, despite unfortunate terminologies that often portray narrow simulation as directed at the mental states of a subject, one can coherently construe simulation as directed at the subject's relations to goals and aspects of the world.[12]

Evolutionary check up   Evolution might also smile on simulation as long as it is narrowly linked to planning skills. At first it may seem difficult to make sense of the idea that apes or infants simulate others. But that is because we are misled by the notion of simulating mental states. Narrow simulation applies solely to predictions of actions and attributes understood relationally and practically. This sort of simulation apes and young children can do, though probably not introspectively, imaginatively, or in some other high-grade phenomenological fashion. How do they do it? By making predictions on their planning board. Such a board, evolution suggests, they appear to have. Noted in chapter 4, section 5, was the fact that, possibly alone in the ape kingdom, chimpanzees plan (simply). This particular skill may have lots to do with interpretation. Young children also have the skill, although in the beginning its exercise may be less intense and less socially directed. Another clue is that young children and chimpanzees plan and interpret situatedly. So if they simulate to interpret, they do it either on-line, mixing simulation with current reactions, or off-line but solely with currently perceived data about a subject. These are distinct options, still hard to confirm empirically (Harris 1992). A further clue is that autistic children, known as poor interpreters, have problems with pretend play and turn out to be poor planners as well, particularly in social contexts (Harris 1993). How about advanced interpretation? Do the mental and cultural revolutions and the reconstructive skills they generate jibe with simulation? It would appear so. The planning skills of older children become sophisticated, far reaching, and socially oriented, and hence form an apt launching pad for complex counterfactual simulations. The narrative redesign trains children to use their imagination in interpreting others, a use that becomes endemic in adult life (a line pushed by Morton 1980 and Gordon 1992a).

In sum, evolutionary considerations allow that simulation could be an option if treated narrowly as a predictor and explainer of the subject's actions and attributes. It is an important but limited assignment. Viewed in this way, simulation would be an application procedure drawing on existing noninterpretive resources (planning, mostly). Narrowness of domain and reliance on preexisting machinery are features that make simulation attractive to many workers in the field.

This evolutionary estimate has some concrete ramifications. Two are particularly notable. One evolutionary scenario probes the developmental roots of simulation and in so doing, I think, firms up its narrow reading. The roots are in early imitation. Like other theorists, Meltzoff and Gopnik think that interpretation operates on a principle of like-mindedness but go further and propose specifically that "infants' primordial 'like me' experiences are based on their understanding of bodily movement patterns and postures. Infants monitor their own body movements by the internal sense of proprioception, and can detect cross-modal equivalents between those movements-as-felt and the movements they see performed by others" (1993, 336). Facial imitation is thought to be a critical clue to this way of looking at the ontogenesis of interpretation because it is the first instance when an infant connects how others look and behave to how she feels inside. The intriguing fact, of course, is that the facial imitator has no way of visually comparing her own face with the one she imitates (Meltzoff and Gopnik 1993, 337).

The implication is that children begin with facial imitation, then move to imitation of behavior, where they map externally perceived behavior onto a set of internal bodily impressions and finally onto motor intentions and plans (Meltzoff and Gopnik 1993, 339). Intentions and plans are key words in the evolutionary talk about interpretation and now simulation. Meltzoff and Gopnik think that the capacity to map one's internal sensations via motor plans onto the behaviors of others might form the "aboriginal basis for a simulation device" (1993, 340). With or without simulation, they think of motor intentions and plans as "midpoint between the physical and the mental." This is not an isolated line of reasoning. From a phylogenetic perspective, it appears that tool use requires foresight and planning, and these in turn "confer upon the individual the cognitive machinery for contemplating minds" (Mitchell 1994, 23) when the right social pressures set in. That individual could also be a tool-using chimpanzee (Whiten and Byrne 1991; Tomasello, Kruger, and Ratner 1993 and ensuing discussion; Tomasello 1995).

The other piece of evolutionary evidence in favor of narrow simulation also comes from imitation but this time concerns learning. Tomasello, Kruger, and Ratner (1993) argue that imitative learning, which is the first infant phase of cultural learning, reveals behavioral affordances of objects and communicative uses of symbols through actions and gestures. The authors speculate that imitative learning and perhaps its successors may involve simulation, but their account makes clear that the involvement is task-specific and the tasks are typically about how to plan and do things with objects and words. They insist that presumed child simulation cannot presuppose the child's understanding of her own mind and need not require a transfer of the interpreter's experience of mental activity to the subject (1993, 502). This line of approach in which simulation connects with specific tasks of motor activity and planning, whether freely undertaken or educationally closely supervised, would confirm how practical were the phylogenetic and ontogenetic springs and shapers of early interpretation. But the point now is to add evolutionary weight to the notion that simulation evolved from a narrowly defined basis.

Yet all is not well with simulation. Theoretical ambition wants simulation to be central to interpretation, and this is problematic.

Problems Some simulation theorists (Gordon 1986, 1992a, 1992b; Harris 1991) go beyond the narrow perimeter and claim that simulation also works as a prime *conceptualizer* of actions and attributes and actually *installs* interpretive concepts and skills. Is this wider hypothesis supported by evolution? Does it make practical sense? I think not.

The installment options are innateness or learning. The installment question is not about the simulation skills, most probably innate, but about the simulation-based *categorizations* of psychological attributes. And the question is not the recognition of a particular attribute in a context or the reliability of the particular recognition, as the debates often and somehow misleadingly suggest (Goldman 1993, Gordon 1995; but see also Bogdan 1995). These are questions of concept application, of its success conditions, and of the evidence for the application. The installment question concerns the very possession of the concept and its formative history. Before venturing an evolutionary estimate, here are the pluses and minuses of the installment options: in principle, innateness is more likely but less appealing to the wide simulation position, whereas learning is more promising but less likely. Not much of a choice. Here is why.

Suppose that the categories used in simulation are innate. One problem is that the phylogenetic and ontogenetic evidence surveyed in earlier chapters shows that relatively few basic categories are innate, and the key ones, such as gaze recognition, are hardly simulable, certainly not in terms of one's mental experiences (one does not see one's gaze). By analogy with facial imitation, there could be gaze imitation in terms of motor plans, as Meltzoff and Gopnik (1993) suggest, but that is not simulation; at best it could be a basis for simulation (just as facial imitation is not simulation but only a basis), and only a basis that keeps simulation task-specific and not a launching pad for interpretation. On the other hand, most human interpretation involves categories—for handling *complex* emotions, traits, and attitudes—that are not basic and not innate but installed culturally.

Another problem that creates lively dissension in the simulation camp is that for the innate option to work there must be a supply of innate interpretive concepts of one's mental self used by analogy or projection to figure out the other. The question that arises is how one would know how and when to apply the self concepts to the other. It may look simple, but it isn't. One reason is that the proposals I have seen talk of similarity of mental architecture plus awareness of one's mental states and of the contexts one faces (Harris 1991), yet neither factor (I argued) delivers interpretive concepts. Architectural like-mindedness helps only if one knows what to look for, which is precisely the issue at stake, whereas awareness of mental states may provide only the evidence or the application conditions for a concept, not the concept itself (Bogdan 1995).

Even if we assume that one can nail down the innate self concepts and does not mistake them for occurrent mental conditions, the proposal might still fail because one doesn't know whether the concepts are actually about the self or the other. This may look paradoxical, but it shouldn't, for several reasons. First, it is lively contested whether or not self interpretation derives from the interpretation of the other.[13] It may look as though simulation settles the issue by denying the derivation, but this is not so. Human simulation appears to enter the ontogenetic picture *late*. (Infants interpret minimally but do not appear to simulate. Their planning ability is still dormant.) It exploits innate concepts, just as it exploits innate planning or motor skills. The value of simulation is not in being about the self but in simplifying interpretive predictions (at least when compared with the ToM alternative) by tapping existing resources. Second, being innate and presumably installed by evolution, interpretive concepts do not have a primary target that is intuitively or a priori obvious. The primary target must be determined by informed theorizing and empirical data. Neither supports the idea that under the selective pressures discussed in this essay, self-knowledge is more advantageous than knowledge of the other. Narrow simulation may be advantageous and practical, but innate self concepts need not be. No contradiction here. Third, even if (for the sake of the argument) one grants the evolutionary value and priority of self concepts, it is still conceivable (horror of horrors, for the simulationist) that what these concepts disclose about the self comes in a naively theoretical form. As with other-regarding concepts, self concepts must afford inferences and generalizations. Their deployment is open-ended. I am not talking now of introspection or of running one's conative or cognitive processes on or off line; these tricks buy the nontheoreticality of prediction within narrow simulation but not of the concepts it employs.

So we seem to be back to square one or almost, as Gordon (1992b, 1995) recognizes. Hence his opting for *learning*. In principle, this is a more promising option because, unlike innateness, learning can allow a controlled determination of what the learned concepts are about. Alas, learning does not square with the evolutionary data about the innateness of basic interpretive categories in apes and young children; it does square with the cultural inculcation of advanced categories but that, again, comes so much later. Gordon has a proposal about how the child would learn to recognize attributes within a simulation matrix (called "ascent routines"), but it is too early to say whether the proposal has empirical bite. My provisional sense is that, if successful, the proposal might have something to say about how children establish the "mental location" of the subject's attributes—no little accomplishment, this—but little to say, as Gordon is aware, about the *conceptual* structure of attributes (their net navigation dimensions, in the lingo of earlier sections). I take it that the latter, even more than the former, is the real challenge for a theory of interpretation. No simulation account I know of has so far met the challenge.

To conclude, then, simulation is more plausible in a narrow than in a wide sense. Yet narrow simulation is a limited endeavor and unlikely to be the launching pad for interpretation. This is why simulation theory is less apt to be a *complete* alternative to other ambitious contenders, par-

ticularly of the MoM and ToM sort. This occasions a more general
thought. Like most outcomes of evolution, interpretation may be too
complex and too opportunistically improvised out of too many disparate
pieces across phylogeny and ontogeny—a genuine kludge, in other
words—for a single, unified, and monopolistic theory to be true of it. It
seems much more plausible that narrow (planning-based) simulation and
its distant cousin, imaginative projection, emerge in the midst of and
alongside other, older interpretive skills by taking advantage of newly
available resources. The either-or absolutism now pervading the debates
is more a sign of ambitious theorizing and polemical zest than of sensitivity to the lessons of evolution.

Chapter 9

Adding Up

By way of summation, section 1 recalls a few salient patterns in the evolution of interpretation. With this background in our short-term memory, section 2 attempts to dot two critical and related *i*'s: what makes interpretation successful, and what does it know about the mind that would explain its success? With these cards on the table, section 3 does something neglected so far, which is comparing this account with other philosophical views of interpretation. And then, with a few forward-looking thoughts in section 4, I am through.

1 Patterns

The changing grip of evolution   The forms of interpretation emerging first in phylogeny and ontogeny are those on which the action of natural selection is the strongest and its grip the firmest. The natural teleology of monkeys evolved as a basic utility indispensable to survival and reproduction, so it must have been a clear candidate for natural selection. The same is true of the psychobehavioral interpretation of apes, which emerged in intricate social worlds where power politics is vital. The grip of natural selection weakens in psychosocial interpretation, particularly because of the mental and cultural revolutions. Reflex interpretation thus gave way to reflective interpretation. Yet, despite appearances, culture does not allow much freedom for interpretation. By replacing genetic inheritance with social memory and natural constraints with cultural constraints, culture remains a potent pressure cooker in which interpretive skills are selected for and applied often as tightly as in precultural times, at least through the early phases of the reconstruction turn.

Architectural changes   The shifting grip of evolution may also explain an architectural pattern. In early forms, natural selection installed fixed architectures as cognitive instincts. This is what natural selection does in all walks of life. So if one establishes that situated interpretation is instinctive, one can plausibly infer to its natural selection. Given the tight ontogenetic schedule in its early phases, psychosocial interpretation probably begins by evolving or recruiting instinctive or modular skills. Later, under cultural pressure and guidance, interpretation seems to "demodularize" and go from reflex to reflection. Although the nature of this process is still unclear, its outcome means neither anarchy nor relativism. Cultural selection rewards conformity and intersubjective alignment. Although it is too early to tell, it appears that the means of acquiring and deploying the new culture-induced skills may be close to what the ToM and simulation views suggest.

Increased psychological quotient   The evolution of interpretation displays an increase in (what one may call, rather warily) the "psychological quotient" of interpretation. The less physiological or reflex the subject's mental life becomes, first in conation and emotion, then in cognition, and the more diverse and unsituated but still vital to the interpreter are the contexts in which this mental life is manifested, the more the interpreter must factor these differences into her skills and strategies. Such evolution was said to show the signs of an arms race, during which interpretation chases the mind it reads (to speak nonliterally) and the mind read complicates its inner writing to frustrate the reading, which raises the chase to a higher level, and so on. This arms race stimulates mind literacy. The driving force in the arms race is the subject's conation confronted with the interpreter's, as the notion of goal setting for interpretation made clear. Whatever the interpreter knows at each evolutionary phase about the design of the subject's mind is implicit in how her effective strategies of interpretation parse the subject-world relations—a parsing motivated primarily by pressures to figure out the subject's goals in the light of the interpreter's. It is only under the escalating pressures of the arms race that the higher mental faculties are implicitly factored into interpretive calculations.

Yet the metaphor of the arms race and the factoring-in patterns it reveals need not suggest *intellectual progress* in mind reading. On the contrary, it has been a leitmotif of this work that, aside from maturational adjustments, at each evolutionary turn interpretation responds to those features of the subject's mind and behavior that (a) impinge externally on the interpreter's goals and relations to the world and (b) can be causally and practically influenced. Natural teleology is mind-illiterate because there isn't much of a (conative) mind to read in the subject anyway, aside from a bunch of behavioral dispositions. The latter get interpreted not in virtue of what they are—or else all organisms would be interpreters—but in virtue of how the just identified parameters (a) and (b) respond to the epistemic, communal, and political forces that call for interpretation. The natural teleologist is as good a reader of conspecific minds as is the adult human interpreter. As Premack put it, "A species will not attribute to others states of mind that it does not instantiate itself. Hence, the only states of mind the chimpanzees may attribute—if it attributes any at all— may be simple ones—seeing, wanting, expecting" (1988, 175). Only human children may be temporarily at a disadvantage, being around minds more developed than theirs, which is one reason why the early psychosocial and metarepresentational phases are transient. The apparent mind literacy evolving in later forms of interpretation and the associated increase in the psychological quotient of interpretation reflect not only the fact that there are so many more mental dispositions to assume, and hence so many more types of behaviors and content-bound attributes to track systematically, but also the fact that there is explicit talk about what is interpreted.

Interpret to get involved   Another pervasive pattern is that interpretive skills individuate and segment subject-world relations into structures of practical involvement—a sign that interpretation evolved as an adaptation. The unmistakable and durable preeminence of the interpretation of conation and affect over cognition also hints that for long phylogenetic and ontogenetic stretches, selection favored the former as more adaptive in involvement, or that involvement was easier or more effective that way rather than the other way. The neglect of the subject's cognition may be explained by its minor epistemic, communal, and political value and also by the fact that in situated contexts, cognitive relations offer poor opportunities for involvement to justify specialized skills and the cost of running them.

Adaptation as alternation   Another robust sign of adaptation is the presence of alternate strategies, developmental or behavioral, responding to alternate environments. It is hard to see how this could be a biological fluke, particularly when many species are known to evolve and use such strategies in various walks of life. Children and adults alike prefer situated interpretation whenever possible and easy, and turn to unsituated interpretation only when necessary. In reconstruction, interpreters first settle for what is canonical before engaging in the more arduous calculation of what is deviant. This is not done just for cognitive economy; it also reflects expectations about the high frequency of situated environments or of unsituated but canonical contexts. Finally, the phylogenetic retention in human interpretation of ancestral primate skills, such as gaze tracking and instant recognition of fear and anger, intimates that those skills remain adaptations for universal and enduring types of situations. This brings us to the last pattern to be reviewed.

One or many? One evolutionary question is whether interpretation is more or less continuous across primates or uniquely human. The answer is up to science to give. My armchair reflection favors a common basis but different lines of evolution. The *common* evolutionary base is that all primate interpreters seem able to recognize and do something about the goals and behaviors of others in contexts of education, self-regulation, cooperation, and competition. Also common, as a result, is the practical nature of all forms of primate interpretation as effective strategies of involvement. This practicality is best reflected in the categorization abilities to parse the domain of interest at those joints and along those routes where causal involvement, whether behavioral or informational, is necessary and beneficial.

The differences, on the other hand, are many and often radical. The gap between the psychobehavioral interpretation of chimpanzees and psychosocial interpretation of humans appears wide and unbridgeable. The natural teleology of lower monkeys could also be quite different from its psychobehavioral successor in great apes. Nonhuman interpretation is situatedly anchored in goals, behaviors, and information access to a shared world, whereas human interpretation is in addition anchored in mentally shared experiences, emotions, and attitudes, whether situatedly or not. That is as deep a difference as it can be. There are also partial continuities, not only ontogenetic as those noted earlier, but also phylogenetic, and they too are made intelligible by evolution. Like apes and young children, adults often employ psychobehavioral interpretation in contexts, such as gaze tracking or identification of basic emotions, like anger or fear. Evolutionary theory explains why: these are contexts of ancestral adaptedness that put a high premium on speed, efficiency, economy of resources, and reliability. The implication, however, need not be that psychosocial skills evolved out of psychobehavioral skills or the latter out of those of natural teleology. Evolution along parallel tracks is as likely an option, if not likelier.

2 Minding Success?

Three capital questions preoccupy many students of interpretation, particularly philosophers: How to explain the success of interpretation? Is it due to knowledge of minds? If so, what sort of knowledge is that? The assumption behind these questions is that interpretation could not be successful unless it knows something about minds. The questions and the assumption are pertinent but must be approached carefully, with methodological rigor and respect for evolution.

The success question Interpretation began as an adaptation, hence it is good at doing something that had biological benefits, and therefore is successful in that sense. Interpretation worked and had been selected, naturally and then culturally. I suggested that what the adaptation consists in, what it-is-good-at, is to be a practice of involvement through effective strategies that engage subject-world relations in patterns that respond to communal, epistemic, and political pressures. Good as this answer may be, it points to a still deeper question. What exactly makes those strategies *effective* and thus the enterprise ultimately successful? This is where the subject's mind is expected to enter the picture as the *causal* fulcrum on which all else turns. The expectation is that knowledge of the causal fulcrum is necessary for interpretation, particularly if it is to take the practical posture (influencing, manipulating) I assign to it so essentially. In short, the success of interpretation must be minded and minded causally. This psychocausalism, in one form or another, is the prevailing opinion in psychology and philosophy.

I do not share it and have given reasons why. Before reviewing them, I want to stress their methodological spirit. The grip that interpretation may have on conspecific minds and on the factors that make it effective and successful depend critically on what interpretation is supposed to do, what it is good at as an adaptation. Interpretation has a job, and what enables it to do the job, and do it effectively, must follow from an account of the job with no strings attached, particularly no cognitivist, mentalist, intuitive, or a priori expectations. I have offered such an account, and what it suggests about the effectiveness of interpretation and its take on minds could be summed up as follows.

The effectiveness question The key is the notion of effective strategy (chapter 5, section 5). The causal effectiveness of an interpretive strategy is *inter*subjective (not intrasubjective, or mental) and targeted on the subject's relations to the world and their external relata, such as goals, objects of attention or gaze, behavior, and the like. The involvements these strategies afford range over this intersubjective domain. Whatever renders the strategies causally effective resides in features of that domain and *not* in the subject's mind. So if one asks why intersubjective strategies are causally effective, and hence selected, it must be because they best meet the epistemic, communal, and political pressures on species that interpret. Other strategies may have been attempted in the misty past, but their users did not live long enough to tell the story of their failure.

For mentalism, the effectiveness of interpretation lies elsewhere. It lies in the interpretation of the subject's mind as a causal fulcrum, in which case knowledge of mental causation is indispensable. Recall the example of the gorilla that tries to get a human to do something for her by mechanical means and then by communicational means. According to mentalism, the gorilla must have used the *same* causal push pattern on both occasions; on the second, she merely replaces physical force with information and physical states with mental states. So understood, the gorilla must have almost literally thrown information at the human subject, somehow knowledgeably mapped its causal progression through his mind, and then expected certain actions to ensue at the other end.

My reading was different. I took the gorilla to have targeted subject-world relations for causal manipulation according to a teleological or pull pattern. The effectiveness of interpretation requires causal involvement, but the causation is directed not at the subject's mind as a causal mediator but rather at what his mind is externally and intersubjectively directed at, namely goals, objects of attention, line of regard, information access, and other such. The causal involvement affects what the subject's mind is directed at, the external target. In situated interpretation, the involvement is in shared perceptually and behaviorally contexts of practical salience; in unsituated interpretation, in mostly culturally shared contexts of practical salience. The subject's mind is affected indirectly by causally influencing or manipulating the world to which it is related; equally indirect is the gathering of the information that the subject conveys. The knowledge of the subject's mind originates along the *same* indirect routes used for practical involvement in epistemic, communal, and political encounters. In interpretation, minds are read from outside in, in terms of their intentional objects, external contents, and behaviors. Not only contents but even psychological attributes are read in same indirect, outside-in way, under suitable assumptions. This answer to the effectiveness question and the external mind reading it suggests provide the framework in which to dot the *i* on the next and much debated notion.

Knowledge of minds: practical, procedural, and architecturally minimal
To get my point clearly across, let me first simplify and exaggerate, but not too much. Interpretation was said to succeed not because of any direct knowledge of minds but because of effective practical involvements under epistemic, political, and communal pressures. Whatever knowledge of minds there is, it is *indirect* in that it is embodied in the skills (programs, databases, and assumptions) apt for such *inter*subjective involvements. So construed, a human interpreter was said to know almost as much about the architectural nuts and bolts of the mind interpreted—its functional mechanisms, programs, hardware, and specific outputs—as do monkeys and chimps about those of the minds they interpret. For this simplified exaggeration to make any sense, the reader must respect the distinction urged from the very outset (chapter 1, section 1) among different stances on the mind: interpretational, folkloric, phenomenological, ideological, and scientific. With the (yet unclear) exception of the phenomenological stance, all but the first are uniquely human. If these other stances intrude into human interpretation, then of course humans have so much more information (and misinformation) about the mind than their evolutionary predecessors. But the intrusion is not helpful in understanding interpretation. So, let us pretend three things: there is no penetration from other stances; human interpretation is a basic competence mastered by any normal adolescent unaffected by folklore, ideology, or science; and phenomenological self-access does not do much interpretive work.[1] What, then, is the *interpretive* knowledge of the subject's mind?

My contention has been that at each evolutionary turn the interpreter's knowledge of the mind is practical, procedural and architecturally minimal.[2] This amounts to assumptions of behavioral and mental *dispositions*. Nature and culture program and train the interpreter to assume as much of the dispositional design of the interpreted mind as is required for intersubjective involvements in epistemic, political, and communal contexts. The notion of disposition assumed in interpretation must therefore be *relativized* to these evolutionary parameters, and they are all external to the mind. What is known about dispositions (as about mental representations) was said to be a sort of outside-in individuation that starts from external facts and constraints and zooms in on mental items to the extent motivated by, and in terms of, the practical interests of interpretation.

The practically motivated matrix of external facts and constraints fixes on dispositions because they seem to yield the stablest, most regular, and most reliable attributions and predictions as far as practical involvement is concerned. Recall the argument about cultural explanation (chapter 8, section 5). Its point was that the stablest and most regular equivalence classes recruited for explanation are external—norms and canonical situations—and a reading of specific mental items is undertaken only when necessary, but still from the outside, with greater risks of explanatory instability. It is easier to make this point about explanation, but the point is actually more fundamental and applies to all interpretive strategies, beginning with the simplest categorization parsers. They all evolve to classify their domains in terms of stable and regular equivalence classes whose ultimate and most effective criterion of relevance is practical involvement. The subject's dispositions are assumed because they seem most apt to contribute to this outcome. Other assumptions about the mind, either more superficial (mere correlations) or more inquisitive (specific architectures) would normally be either destabilizing or not commensurate with the costs, the benefits and interests of interpretation, or both.

One can argue to the same conclusion from a reverse-engineering stance. If an evolutionary engineer had to design an interpretive knowledge base so as to accord with the evolutionary strictures envisaged in this work, I think she would settle on assumptions of dispositions as a rational solution, just as nature and culture did. Interpreters are primed to read conspecific minds insofar as is required (in terms of domain and depth) by the contexts subject to selection and by the range of the effective strategies employed in those contexts. Adaptations—and interpretation is one— operate on a need-to-know basis. In the case of interpretation, the need (as spelled out in this essay) does not warrant more than a practical, procedural, and architecturally minimal knowledge of minds as packages of dispositions.[3]

3   Philosophical Tally

The reader may have noticed that aside from the main villains of the play (mentalism, theorism, psychosemanticism) and aside from junctures where exegesis was locally helpful, I have refrained from comparative scholarship in philosophy.[4] I wanted to keep the argument in tight evolutionary and practical focus. My focus is singular enough to put most of the philosophical options on the nonevolutionist and nonpractical side of the divide, and at different locations, thus making a scholarly journey through these options too extensive and convoluted. Yet, much as I thought I could get away with scholarly neglect, it is a fact of academic mentality that many people need a minimal exegetical guidance, with an 'ism' label to help, to make out a particular view. I bow reluctantly, and in the same look-back-in-review spirit, I venture some little maps that locate my position relative to alternatives in the field. I restrict my brief survey to a few landmarks.

The radicals I acknowledge first the pioneering and influential work of Quine (1960) and Davidson (1984). I would characterize it as 'transcendental' to the extent that it probes the intelligibility of interpretation in terms of behavioral and verbal data, relative to radical or absolute presuppositions and criteria needed to make sense of them. I had nothing transcendental to say about interpretation but welcome the search for deep-seated principles and constraints behind the proximate data. Notoriously, Quine, Davidson, and also Lewis (1983) have construed interpretation as *radical*. I take this construal to be a thought experiment in the service of their transcendental quest. Yet anyone who would give the radicalism of interpretation an *empirical* twist, as an approximation of the condition of the *real* interpreter, trades in fiction. Although never fully determinate and almost always inductive, interpretation is not empirically radical, is not exclusively based on sensory evidence or some thin principles of rationality, charity, or humanity, and actually is heavily constrained by evolution and culture to work in well-patterned ways and to be effective and indeed to succeed most of the time.

The practicalists Closer to home, I gladly acknowledge a broad and disunited family of fellow practicalists who see interpretation as a practice servicing individual and social interests. I see some early analysts of the ordinary language of interpretation (Austin 1961; Urmson 1952; Malcolm 1952; and particularly the later Wittgenstein 1953, 1969) among protopracticalists. Language aside, I add to the list some more substantive practicalists, such as Baker (1995), Clark (1989), Morton (1980), and Wilkes (1981, 1984). Baker's book in particular is quite systematic and allied to an incisive critique of mentalism. Yet these practicalist accounts (including mine in Bogdan 1988b and to a lesser extent 1991a) are not sufficiently grounded in evolution. Baker, for example, writes that "the explanatory power of beliefs derives from the fact that their role in our practices makes it possible to manipulate behavior by manipulating attitudes" (1995, 187). True, but we are not told why. Saying, as practicalists are prone to, that it is our successful cognitive and linguistic practices that ground the interpretive grasp of attitudes is stating a truth in need of *further* explanation and grounding. It is this further step that I have undertaken here. Without it, practicalism is a wiser and more realistic alternative to mentalisms and theorisms of various sorts but is not yet properly defended and explicated.

In and out   A distinction worth revisiting is that between internalism and externalism (Stich and Ravenscroft 1994). Atypically, it concerns not the target (the mind or behavior of another) but the *source* of interpretation. To mark the distinction, I will prefix the new isms with an *s*. According to *s-internalism*, interpretation is internal to the cognitive mind, part of its architecture, and takes the procedural or implicit form of instructions or rules or else the explicit form of an innate database or a combination of both. According to *s-externalism*, interpretation is merely a learned database containing culturally and explicitly inculcated platitudes and rules of thumb. My account accommodates both sources but at different evolutionary times and not exclusively. Interpretation is s-internalist and exclusively proceduralist for the first evolutionary (situated) turns, more in the MoM than ToM spirit. Later developments allow an s-externalist and culture-driven option, but one that must be understood narrowly and carefully. For what is cultural and explicit in reconstruction seems to be grafted onto earlier procedural skills and continues to comply with the practical thrust and domain of interpretation. The linguistic form of interpretive knowledge brings explicitness and may create the database into which culture pours the wisdom of its external contents. Yet the cultural platitudes and rules of thumb that express and guide adult interpretation are neither spectatorial nor about mental architecture or specific data structures.

The big isms   Last but definitely not least, I cannot conclude this short but inevitably slippery slalom among the sacred cows of interpretation without handwaiving at the big isms that have shaped the recent philosophy of interpretation. Despite a record of sustained attacks on *behavior-*

ism throughout this essay, I can hear (and have heard) the knock-down question, Aren't you a behaviorist if you insist that the proper domain of interpretation is (a) external to the mind (subject-world relations), (b) defined by practical and ultimately behavioral patterns, and (c) engaged mostly procedurally, (d) with only an implicit knowledge of dispositions? No, I am not, but it is too late (and we are all so tired) to rearticulate a comprehensive and convincing answer. So let me point to the key slots of the answer and the reader can fill them in as a bit of leisurely weekend homework.

For starters, note that the question may be misdirected. It should not be about *me*, for as a theorist I am not into the science of the mind or behavior. I analyze interpretation, as a distinct competence, and about *it* I am not a behaviorist, for I theorize about goals and tasks revealing innate and well-structured programs. The question should be about the interpreter. Am I using an evolutionary brush that paints *her* as a naive behaviorist? Is evolution so shaping her, perhaps according to strictures like Lloyd Morgan's maxim (don't interpret mental details unless absolutely necessary)?

These are good questions and have received much attention in the literature. Situated interpretation looks behaviorist, but I do not think it *is*, even at its simplest. It looks behaviorist because it maps subject-world relations mostly in terms of sensory inputs about states of the world, states of the subject, and his behaviors; it also looks so because the dispositions assumed are few, simple, and apparently identified in input-output terms. Let me begin to deconstruct this "behaviorist illusion" with the last point. The input-output terms that identify dispositions are not simply correlations learned about subjects. The input-output identification signals a pattern of practical involvement, most often as an instance of a goal setting for interpretation. Whatever looks behaviorist about this picture refers not to the subject but to how the interpreter engages the subject. Even the subject's dispositions are assumed *in terms* of intersubjective engagement. So if we need an 'ism' label for my evolutionary portrait of the situated interpreter, it had better be that of *congenital pragmatist*: pragmatist because the truth about the subject and his relations to the world is determined by the interpreter's practical involvements with the subject; congenital because this is not a mental option but an evolutionary diktat.

Despite accumulating complexities and entirely novel skills, I do not think this picture changes substantially in psychosocial and unsituated interpretation. What does change is the fact that, under the pressure of new practical interests and patterns of involvement, the new forms of interpretation evolve to assume, as well as to learn culturally about, more intricate mental dispositions, and also about more specific mental relata of content relations. Dramatic as these changes are, they still comply with the intersubjective coordinates and interests of interpretation and its practical take on minds. As for the interpreter's interests in external affairs and behavioral patterns, that seems to be what evolution asked for. So much, then, for behaviorism. Now on to other isms.

Philosophical interest in interpretation, mine included, has been stimulated in recent years by the trilateral opposition among three mighty isms: intentional realism, eliminativism, and instrumentalism. I have learned much from these positions, particularly the thinkers most closely associated with them, Jerry Fodor (1987), Paul Churchland (1989) and Steve Stich (1983), and Dan Dennett (1987), respectively. Their vigorously articulated positions pointed to dialectical openings for my own, which resulted in differences as well as appropriations. *Realism* and *eliminativism* share the mentalist assumption that interpretation is about the mind in a psychosemantic sense, and the theorist assumption that its knowledge is organized as a naive theory. Realism finds the theory true of its domain; eliminativism false. I argued against both the mentalist and theorist assumptions, on the ground that one fails to identify the domain of interpretation, the other its goals and tasks. Both realism and eliminativism go further and reify the targets of interpretive concepts into mental-state types or architectures. This metaphysical maneuver doesn't square with the practical lessons I drew from evolution.

Dennett's *instrumentalism* is a more complex and elusive position, yet one I find more congenial in many respects. I already noted its evolutionist spirit. Congenial too are the notions that interpretation is a craft rather than a theory and that interpretive categories, instead of being psychosemantic, actually track external patterns, which I analyze here in terms of practical involvements. There are also differences. I focus on one that plays a central part in Dennett's thinking. It is the relation between the study of interpretation and a scientific understanding of the mind. This points to an intriguing and tough problem, with which I want to conclude this essay.

Dennett has given one of the best known philosophical versions of the top-down method of thinking about the mind, already classical in cognitive science. His version presents the method in three levels—the intentional stance, the design stance, and the physical stance—and takes the first to be an abstract competence model of mental design and therefore a guide to a cognitive-scientific understanding of that design (Dennett 1987, chapter 3, especially 74–75). Dennett takes interpretation to be the pre-eminent intentional stance and by implication *also* a guide to cognitive science. Therein lies a problem. I do not think that interpretation provides a competence model for, and thus top-down guidance to, the design of the mind. Noam Chomsky or David Marr didn't need the help or guidance of interpretation to put forward their competence models of grammar or vision. Furthermore, the competence models in cognitive science are focused and specialized, typically geared to the production stages of cognition; about those competencies interpretation is ignorant and keeps mum, as it should (Bogdan 1985).

So I conclude that there are *two* readings of Dennett's notion of intentional stance: a competence-model reading and an interpretation reading. The former approximates the top-down method in cognitive science and thus provides guidance to a scientific understanding of the design of mental competencies but has little to do with interpretation. The latter has everything to do with interpretation but little if anything with understanding mind design. Yet I think another relation between interpretation and mind may be more promising. Hence the closing but forward-looking remarks below.

4 Looking Ahead

Human interpretation is best at figuring out what people think and do as a result. This happens also to be what cognitive science, from psychology to artificial intelligence, is worst at explaining. According to pessimists like Fodor (1983), this failure is essential and lasting: thinking is intrinsically opaque scientifically, since it operates according to rules that are unintelligible to psychology. Hence the irresistible attraction of interpretation for a realist like Fodor or an instrumentalist like Dennett (under the competence-model reading of the intentional stance). Interpretation shows the way by realist mapping or heuristic hints, and cognitive science then picks up the trail and chases the design of the thinking mind, as successfully as it did that of the modular (production) mind. I argued in a number of works (Bogdan 1985, 1988b, 1993a, 1994) that if the design of the thinking mind is thought of architecturally in *the same classical manner* as the design of vision or grammar are, then the prospects are not good. Because of its studied indifference to architectural design or specific representational outputs, interpretation has nothing useful to suggest about thinking architectures, construed classically.

Yet there is another way of looking at the matter. The argument of this essay points to a parallel between interpretation and thinking. Interpretation was said (in chapter 3) not be transparent to classical cognitive science, for some of the same reasons that thinking is not. Like interpretation, thinking is categorization and utilization. These were shown to be areas that are *first* intelligible in evolutionary terms. As with interpretation, the evolutionary approach to thinking might be well advised to begin with an outside-in projection, from patterns reflecting selective pressures to the goals and tasks and then the skills evolved to handle them. The parallel may even turn into partial convergence at those junctures where interpretation has either coevolved with, or is architecturally implicated in, thinking. In those cases, there is a good chance that the evolutionary analysis of interpretation may help elucidate the relevant design portions of thinking. The evolutionary record is fairly supportive. Interpretation is deeply involved in the evolution of the primate mind generally: sharpening its intelligence, escalating its communicational abilities, securing sign and linguistic reference, and scaffolding inferential routines. To this extent, then, interpretation is bound to open a window on the thinking mind. That, I surmise, may be a genuinely explanatory connection between interpretation and a scientific understanding of the mind.

Notes

Chapter 2

1. Sober argues that "to say that there is selection for a given property means that having that property *causes* success in survival and reproduction; to say that a given sort of object was selected is merely to say that the result of the selection process was to increase the representation of that kind of object. 'Selection of' pertains to the *effects* of a selection process, whereas 'selection for' describes its *causes*" (1984a, 100).

2. As Lewontin (1984) notes, the three defining conditions of natural selection make no reference to adaptation. This is why, in principle, one can be a selectionist though not an adaptationist. Similarly, since natural selection is only one of the mechanisms of evolution (although admittedly the most important), one can be an evolutionist without being a selectionist. To add to this panoply of possible positions, since there are several forms of selection, one could be a selectionist without being a natural selectionist. And further distinctions can be made within selectionism, depending on what level of selection one chooses: genic, organismic, group, cultural. Decidedly, evolutionism is no simple game.

3. There is considerable disagreement and some terminological anarchy in the evolutionary literature on these matters. Some writers count as adaptation only an ancestrally fixed trait; others take the more liberal line suggested in the text (compare Sober 1984a, chapter 6, with Sober 1993a, 84–86, and also with Burian 1992 and West-Eberhard 1992). Some writers even see natural selection as an ahistorical phenomenon (Endler 1992). Some like optimization models (Smith and Winterhalder 1992); others distrust them (Kitcher 1985, Lewontin 1984).

4. The target of selection must be distinguished from the unit or level of selection (genetic, organismic, group, cultural), as an individuative framework of the targets of selection. The latter is a much debated matter outside our purview.

5. I follow here some of the guidelines set by Pinker and Bloom (1990) in their selectionist analysis of grammar. There are, however, differences between grammar and interpretation. Grammar shows more complex design than interpretation but is much less directly involved in securing fitness-enhancing benefits. As argued later, interpretation has an ancestral layer of basic skills naturally selected and a more recent layer shaped by culture. That is not the case for grammar.

6. Although metaphorical, the notion of an arms race comes close to capturing the escalating game of adaptation. According to Dawkins, the notion can be employed "whenever we have progressive improvements in adaptations in one lineage, as an evolutionary response to progressive counter-improvements in an enemy lineage.... One lineage will tend to evolve adaptations to manipulate the behavior of another lineage, then the second lineage will evolve counter-adaptation" (1982, 61). (Lineages can describe species or functionally distinct classes of individuals, such as parents versus offspring.) Among the reasons for the selection of interpretation, politics is best at generating an arms race.

7. This is a point made by Pinker and Bloom about language, which I think is equally valid about interpretation. As they put it, "there is no law of biology that says that scientists are blessed with the good fortune of being able to find evolutionary antecedents to any modern structure in some other living species.... [Therefore] we must be prepared for the possible bad news that there just aren't any living creatures with homologues of human [interpretation], and let the chimp [interpretation] debate come down as it will" (1990, 726; my square-bracket interpolations). Povinelli (1993) makes similar points about interpretation.

8. Goal directedness is relative. A bee lacks independent goal directedness when dancing to indicate the location of food but may display it when it is on its own and (say) must avoid danger. At the same time, collective goal directedness may require interpretation if and when the goals and behaviors of autonomous agents must be coordinated in some fashion. (More on this matter in Bogdan 1994, chapter 2, section 4.)

9. Recall this observation: "Chimpanzees do remarkably little most of the time. They move slowly, eat grass, sleep for a long while, groom one another. On the other hand, when the chimpanzees do wake up and cause some social ripples, there is no way an observer can record with pencil and paper all that is going on" (de Waal 1989, 36). Humphrey confirms this diagnosis and adds that "the same is arguably true for natural man. Studies of contemporary Bushmen suggest that the life of hunting and gathering, typical of early man, was probably a remarkably easy one.... [He] seems to have established a *modus vivendi* in which, for a period of perhaps 10 million years, he could afford to be not only physically but intellectually lazy" (Humphrey 1988, 17). What a life! We shouldn't have gotten into agriculture, ever.

10. It could, of course, be the other way around. Calculative planning could have been selected in the communal or political arena first, thus calling for interpretation, and then be recruited for other uses, such as tool making. It is also possible that tool manufacture and use might differentiate humans from apes. Unlike apes, humans (most of them, anyway) are able to work, including to work with tools, and use this ability often. So reconfigured, the tool-making view may be about what distinguishes the planning intelligence of humans from that of apes, not about what selected for planning intelligence in the first place.

11. It has been a constant mistake in the history of thinking about cognition to take what is registered, peripherally or consciously, as defining the *domain* of

cognition and the *nature* of its programs. The worst version of this mistake shows up in the argument for solipsism or proximalism, which says roughly that if an organism is simple, it must be no more than a stimulus-response machine, because it reacts only to stimuli. In this case, the simplest of interpreters would be no more than a stimulus reactor, but then she would be even worse than a sensor of dependencies; she would be solely a stimulus sensor, and that's not interpretation. My answer to this argument is that of course this is not interpretation. The whole picture is wrong, to begin with. No organism, not even a bacterium, is merely a stimulus sensor (Bogdan 1994, chapter 4). No cognitive equipment would ever be naturally selected for such a silly function. Stimulus sensing is always a cog in an elaborate functional construction.

12. The pattern-revealing theory should be sharply distinguished from the methodological (observational, experimental) ability to tell whether the theory applies or not. Behaviorism either takes the methodological inability to locate the patterns identified by a theory as counting against the theory or else reduces patterns to their sensory sampling. Neither gambit is crucially effective, once we make the right distinctions.

Chapter 3

1. I do not take Fodor to succumb to such an assimilation, but I do not exclude that, for him, any utilization of input, in thinking or elsewhere, is bound to be nonmodular if its database is not proprietary and informationally isolated.

2. This ontogenetic fact could explain why the interpretive *concepts* of belief and intention are formed during the metarepresentational turn and become fully operative at the reconstructional turn. These are concepts needed mostly for inference and reconstruction, as opposed to the instruction-based categories of gaze, attention, or simple desire, whose utilization has immediate behavioral import.

3. The biological implementation of what the classical theory predicts must have been messy because of tinkering, diversions of materiel and functions, building new functions on old structures, and being constrained by available opportunities—well known symptoms of the healthy opportunism of evolution. (Clark 1989, chapter 4, provides a lucid and nuanced analysis of how this opportunism applies to cognition.) This obvious truth is often invoked against the biological version of the reverse-engineering argument. It misses the point. The opportunism of evolution concerns the *implementation* of a competence and not necessarily its goals and tasks. The latter reflect selective pressures, utility functions, and general constraints such as physical laws, local regularities, and other limitations on what it takes to do a job (Bogdan 1994, 61–63). I construe the tactic of reverse engineering in evolutionary biology to apply to goals and tasks, not to the concrete implementations of their executors. Dennett (1978a, chapter 7; 1995, chapters 8 and 9), and Dawkins (1986, 1995) have been forceful advocates of the reverse engineering tactic.

4. This, indeed, will be part of my argument about why evolution matters to understanding interpretation: because the latter is a categorization enterprise, and thus closer to the direct reach of natural selection.

5. "Although the functional significance of various systems is sometimes relatively straightforward (e.g., visual perception), in other cases it is not, and all too often the theories and evidence concerning the structure of Pleistocene selection pressures (which define functionality for humans) are completely unfamiliar to psychologists. Considerations drawn from evolutionary biology can be used to carve the world along 'natural' lines into functional subsets or adaptive problems, which can then be matched to the domain-specific mechanisms that evolved to solve them" (Tooby and Cosmides 1989, 32).

6. As far as I can tell, the naturalist literature on child interpretation does not look more evolutionary than its experimental counterpart. The neglect of evolution in the developmental literature is obvious in many areas. Here is a criticism that echoes mine: "At puberty radical morphological changes occur. Textbooks on adolescent development have, through the years, faithfully detailed these morphological changes but without acknowledging that these biological phenomena must necessarily possess identifiable adaptive functions.... Even the suggestion that some of the behavioral changes of adolescence might have an evolved basis virtually never appears in textbooks" (Weisfeld and Billings 1988, 207). When the proximate research acknowledges the need for evolutionary explanations, the acknowledgment is typically tepid, vague, and uncommitted genetically. Consider another criticism: "It is clear that humans evolved to be parental in some broad sense. Dispositions toward nurturing children are part of the human genotype in the same way that dispositions toward being sexual are. Yet most family researchers balk at going further than that. Apparently, they are willing to accept the idea that evolution selected humans to be generally parental, but are unwilling to acknowledge that evolution may well have selected parents to be discriminating in their parental nurturance. The conventional view is that evolution produced a general tendency toward nurturing children but that individual differences in parental behavior are attributable to environmental factors" (Smith 1988, 274). I say the same about the tepid and soft view of the ontogenesis of interpretation in humans: either its adaptive functions and their genetic basis are not seen at all in proximate research (the former criticism), or else they are seen vaguely as general dispositions without adaptive structure (the latter criticism).

7. Two distinguished students of the natural behavior of primates note that "under natural conditions it is extremely difficult to distinguish between actions that result from knowledge of other individuals' states of mind and actions that result from knowledge of other individuals' behavior. Investigations ... are easily confounded by possible audience effects, since it is difficult to present subjects with evidence of another animal's *knowledge* while simultaneously eliminating all visual or auditory evidence of the animal's physical *presence*" (Cheney and Seyfarth 1990, 230).

8. Could an interpretation selected mostly for communal and political reasons be an exclusively or largely intraspecific enterprise? This is a legitimate question. Here is a guess. Communal interpretation among apes revolves around, and was largely selected for, kin and group interactions. Such species-specific coordinates cannot be instantiated in contact with humans. Political interpretation among

(mostly nonkin) apes revolves around, and was largely selected for, sexual inter-action and competition as well as power games. Both are species-specific features unlikely to be instantiated in contact with humans. These are so many disin-centives, then, for apes to go in high interpretation gear when presented with some funnily concocted test.

9. Sodian and Frith refer here to the work of Chandler, Fritz, and Hala (1989). The factoring of motivation (typically communal and political) into the laboratory investigation of interpretation requires a good understanding and measurement of relevance, computational effort, and cost-benefit comparisons—parameters that often don't get the right values in the lab. Yet one wonders whether trying to get realistic values for these crucial parameters, so as to elicit the right skills, would not push experimentation inevitably toward replicas of natural habitats with a history of selection.

10. This, I take it, is Lewis's (1994) point about the artificiality of the false-belief test.

11. Knowledge and belief attributions show a consistent phylogenetic and onto-genetic delay, compared with goal and desire attributions. The former may be computationally harder and, having lesser immediate impact on the interpreter's goals than the latter, may require more motivation to be effected. The processing effort and problems associated with attributions of belief or inference could also be related to the need to transcend the spatial and temporal immediacy of an interpreter-subject interaction (on which more in chapters 6 and 7).

12. A researcher who studies children naturalistically observes, "The under-standing of others' intentions and psychological states is ... closely tied to the children's social and emotional relationships. Yet paradoxically the study of the development of children's understanding of other minds has been conducted pri-marily in settings divorced from children's familiar relationships or their 'real life' social behavior; ... it is from naturalistic observations that we are likely to gain insight on the contexts in which [the mind-reading] capabilities develop, and on the salient influences that affect their development" (Dunn 1991, 51–52). I take this criticism to say that the experimental settings may violate some of the en-abling conditions.

13. This conceivably being the case, one should contemplate another option, that of ad hoc solutions to problems posed by laboratory tests. Having naturally evolved a lively intelligence and ability to plan (because of selective pressures for interpretation in the wild), chimps may recruit these resources to solve, in an ad hoc and contextual manner (i.e., not a durable and genetically transmissible manner), the interpretational problems raised by the experiments. Moreover, autistic humans, lacking the proper (selected) resources of interpretation and social commerce, are believed to recruit other resources to solve, again locally and ad hoc, some of the problems raised by the context. In either case, the solutions would not reveal a proper (i.e., selected) competence.

14. Chomsky (1980, 51) gives the following example: "Imagine a person who knows English and suffers cerebral damage that does not affect the language

centers at all but prevents their use in speech, comprehension or ... even in thought. Suppose that the effects of the injury recede and with no further experience or exposure the person recovers the original capacity to use language. In the intervening period, he had no capacity to use English, even in thought, though the mental (ultimately physical) structures that underlie that capacity were undamaged. Did the person know English during the intervening period?" As with recovery from aphasia, also noted by Chomsky, the answer is yes: in language, as in interpretation, there are durable knowledge bases and programs operating on them (competencies) distinct from the abilities to activate and use them.

Chapter 4

1. The technical concept of assumption cannot be explicated in a rush (see chapter 5, section 4, for details). An analogy will do for now. The eye explicitly registers light patterns of various sorts, but the programs that compute the registrations operate under the assumption that such patterns systematically correlate with edges, corners, and surfaces, which in turn reveal distal three-dimensional objects. The visual system embodies such assumptions by treating what is (proximally) registered as signs of what is (distally) seen. Likewise, the interpretive system embodies assumptions about basic agency and other dispositions of subjects by treating what is (proximally) registered, namely, environmental and behavioral clues, as signs of what is (distally) interpreted, namely, goals, intentions, and beliefs, construed as subject-world relations.

2. If this proposal is plausible, then the method by which one establishes the work of a competence depends on whether the competence tracks goals and other relations of the subject implicitly and by assumptions, as I think natural teleology does, or systematically by specialized programs, as I think subsequent forms of interpretation do. Yet no such form, however sophisticated, systematically tracks or explicitly represents mental architectures or specific mental states, which is why interpretation cannot be said (strictly) to be *about* minds. This is why my use of interpretation as "psychology" is heuristic, just to keep in touch with prevailing terminologies.

3. As Perner (1991, 45) notes, his notion of a single updating model is close to Piaget's notion of a sensorimotor scheme. This makes early interpretation a manifestation of what Piaget (1936) called sensorimotor intelligence, with its practical understanding of its domain (Gomez 1991, 203). Both themes—the practicality of interpretation and the closeness of its early forms to sensorimotor schemes—are congenial to my account and will be pursued in some detail in chapter 5.

4. This is also why, in the long run, learning would not be an efficient and speedy strategy for gaze monitoring and why the presence of such an innate program for gaze monitoring would confirm the cognitive specialization of natural teleology and undermine attempts to reduce gaze watching to learning. Learning may adjust the program to specific features of an environment. For example, an adult ape brought to a zoo would have to adjust the gaze-following algorithm to the habits of the human caretakers, but this need not mean that the ape learns how to watch gaze or learns how to connect gaze with goals.

5. One also finds in the literature comparisons between autistic children and apes (gorillas in particular) reared by humans in captivity (Gomez, Sarria, and Tamarit 1993) and between autistic children and chimpanzees (Tomasello, Kruger, and Ratner 1993; Baron-Cohen 1993b). Captive apes are less apt to reveal the ancestral pressures we are looking for and more likely to reflect the constraints of their artificial education, not unlike present-day humans, as Danny Povinelli pointed out to me. Autistic children and chimpanzees, on the other hand, may straddle natural teleology and psychobehavioral interpretation at joints not yet well understood. For these reasons, I limit myself to the (admittedly unilateral) comparison between monkeys and autistic children.

6. For many species that attack with their teeth (or other visible implements), *showing* the weapons while *not* attacking must have been a fortuitous behavioral mutation with beneficial effects both inside and outside the species, and so must have been the realization that most of the time it works.

7. I do not think that any significant and escalating arms race involving interpretation results from the setting assumed in Krebs and Dawkins's example of the "interpreting" dogs. The "interpreting" dog *A* exploits the statistical regularities connecting dog *B*'s gaze and goal in predicting the latter and starting her deception. *A*'s own performance is subject to statistical regularities that *B* is going to penetrate and perhaps frustrate sooner or later. Yet, with all due respect, dogs do not seem to be more astute "interpretationally" than they were in the distant past. (Left to their own devices, most dogs still bark aimlessly, just to disturb the peace and quiet.)

8. Primate communication not only relies on interpretation but also benefits from it. As their communicative skills improve, interpreters gain access to more powerful sources of data about the subject, thus refining their expertise (Baldwin and Moses 1994) and allowing it to be put to further communal and political work.

9. Whatever selects for the specificity of information must select for a capacious memory of individual features. This must have an effect on interpretation. A capacious memory can be used by chimpanzees for recognizing distinct faces ("Oops, that was my mother-in-law, and I didn't grin!") and dispositions (this guy is friendly, might help in the future, while his grim-faced companion should be watched closely). De Waal reports on two visits with the baboons at the San Diego Zoo. The first, just introductory, took less than ten minutes. On the second visit, three days later, de Waal was immediately recognized in the crowd although he was wearing different clothes. As he notes, "this is all the more remarkable when we realize that these animals see 3 million faces per year" (1989, 194).

10. Dennett (1987, 275–276) speculates on another consequence of chimpanzee life that may lead to psychobehavioral interpretation. He notes that unlike monkeys, who are all the time together and share information constantly, chimpanzees (like orangutans) venture in and out of groups and therefore can be on their own a good deal of the time. This allows them to be in a position to know things that other chimpanzees don't, and perhaps to know this differentiating fact, which will induce them to maintain and exploit their additional knowledge. If confirmed, this would be a further opportunity to transcend natural teleology.

11. A recent report (in *The Economist*, November 20–26, 1993, 99–100) about Frank Sulloway's work on the effects of birth-order on personality further supports this hypothesis. "A family cannot be seen as a single environment. It has as many environments as members because each family member is interacting with a different set of individuals, and the nature of each relationship is different. Parents respond differently to different children. Siblings have to contend for parental attention. And dominance among siblings is often determined by size and age— and therefore by birth order." No wonder, then, that Sulloway's research finds a statistically consistent pattern of superior creativity in younger siblings and greater dogmatism in the eldest ones. No wonder, also, that because of these selective pressures operating inside families, "eldest children resemble each other more than they resemble their younger siblings. They tend to be bossier, more dominant, more aggressive, more controlling, more conforming, more conventional, more respectful of authority, more conscientious, more prone to jealousy and more vengeful. They are also worse losers, less open-minded, less agreeable, less likely to admit mistakes, and less likely to take risks that their younger siblings." (Hey, some of us are really misrepresented here. Should we sue or something?)

12. Different concepts have been proposed in the psychological literature in an attempt to capture this phenomenon. "Interpersonal relatedness" is one proposal, "primordial sharing" is another, and there are "formats of sharing" and "primary and secondary intersubjectivity" (Bruner 1983; Hobson 1993b, 1994; Trevarthen 1979).

13. It is worth noting that communication neither is nor requires mental sharing. Lots of species communicate, yet very few (the primates) communicate by interpreting each other, and only humans communicate by mental sharing. Most species communicate ritually by a prearranged semiotics of fixed patterns of behavioral signs and states of the world. The same is true of behavioral coordination and other forms of social commerce.

Chapter 5

1. There are two versions of theorism. The weaker one, taxonomical, envisages interpretation as an organizer of experience that retains similarities and disregards differences. This is more like concept formation and may be the version favored by behaviorism. The stronger version, postulational, is the one that most ToM theorists favor. It posits hidden entities with causal powers (Samet 1993).

2. The environment of selection can be defined more technically in terms of relative fitness of different genotypes across space and time (Brandon 1990, 1992). For our purposes, we need not go into these details.

3. As noted in chapter 3, section 1, an ultimate analysis of the job design is different from a proximate diagnosis of how the programs or skills work. The latter indicates *how* things are done, how problems are solved, how tasks are executed, and *when*, at what stage of phylogeny and ontogeny. The analysis of the job design comes theoretically earlier, being concerned with *what* is done (tasks) to achieve goals.

4. An approach that puts natural selection on the top of the classical ICM method has been articulated forcefully and insightfully by Leda Cosmides and John Tooby in a number of articles (Cosmides and Tooby 1987; Tooby and Cosmides 1990b, 1992) as a programmatic blueprint for evolutionary psychology. They do not focus on interpretation and do not construe selection in such blatant teleological terms, as I do, but I think their message is consistent with mine. I find in their methodological script a layer of constraints that comes close to the goal layer I am talking about and seems to have the same explanatory role. Their script talks of "recurrent environmental features relevant to [an] adaptive problem, including constraints and relationships that existed in the [ancestral] social, ecological, genetic, and physical situation.... These constitute the conditions in which the adaptive problem arose, and indicate the informational resources available to solve the problem" (Tooby and Cosmides 1989, 40). I see guidance to goals as describing systematically recurrent patterns that all cognitive adaptations, including interpretation, display in their information traffic with the world. These patterns in turn define the informational (specifically, interpretational) tasks that the organism's cognition must execute to guide behavior to its goals (Bogdan 1994, chapter 3).

5. Assumptions, as Vogel (1988) put it, are opportunities capitalized. The more such opportunities are capitalized, the more efficient and economic the job of the competence. Yet one has to be careful with the notion of assumption. If the analysis gives assumptions too much work to do, cognition becomes too easy, but if its tasks rely too heavily on explicit processing, cognition may look very difficult if not impossible. A version of this dilemma shows up in the relation between learning and innateness. Both visual and grammatical computations are thought to be too difficult to be learned, so most of the knowledge embodied in them is thought to be innate. We know too little about interpretation to estimate its processing complexity. Like vision, it may be simple in some species, sophisticated in others. Yet in all its forms, interpretation is so vital, so early on, that it would be unlikely to take off without plenty of innate assumptions.

6. Here is a nice example of how DNA assumes natural laws. "When the developing frog embryo turns itself inside out during gastrulation, it looks just like a viscous fluid, flowing in an entirely natural manner. Some of the 'information' required to make this process work may be specified by the laws of physics, not by DNA.... Why should nature waste effort by programming the shape of the organism into DNA if the laws of physics will produce it free of charge?" (Cohen and Stewart 1994, 81–82). The authors make a convincing argument that not all that an organism is and does needs to be encoded in its DNA. A good deal can be done by assumptions and variable adjustment to the context.

7. The distinction between explicit encoding and implicit but systematic tracking shows why *theory*-of-mind is a misnomer for situated interpretation. Most ToM advocates know this but I think the point is worth making anyway. Theories and their axioms are explicit data structures; procedures are not. Data structures are about something. The early interpreter's data structures, mostly perceptual, are at best about world scenes, bodily implements, and behaviors, not about the subject's

mind. By contrast, procedures can track intricate patterns, including some that implicitly reflect aspects of the subject's mind. This is also why situated interpretation cannot *explain* anything. Standardly construed (and ToM views call for standard philosophy of science), explanation is an explicit derivation from data structures. Situated interpretation cannot give such derivations. If prediction is thought of as isomorphic with explanation, as it usually is, then situated interpretation cannot predict, either. But it does, so these cannot be the right terms of analysis.

8. Consider, for example, how homeotic genes instruct the spatial development of an organism. When the genes are turned on by some input, they instruct the cell to move in a given direction, with the help of positional information about its location at a given time. That information comes in the form of material clues, such as chemical gradients, that the cell is primed to recognize and react to. When the position is determined, the cell reads a DNA segment like a map to get further instructions about what to do or where to go next.

9. This is a point forcefully made by Perner (1991). He talks of early interpreters as "situation theorists." I do not count them as "theorists" but I take their interpretation to be situated in a sense close to Perner's, whether the situatedness is perceptually actual or imagined. It is because their interpretation is situated that early interpreters cannot be "theorists" and cannot "conceptualize" or "explain" in any plausible sense. The latter achievements require mastery of propositional attitudes, and this requires unsituated interpretation. I also regard Wellman's "copy theory" operative in early human interpretation to reflect its domain situatedness (Wellman 1990).

10. Facial imitation is a telling example. It begins so early (infants as old as 32 hours display it) as to rule out any possibility of learning. Experiments reported by Meltzoff and Gopnik also ruled out mere arousal to the sight of a human face or a reflexive mimicry, as a "kind of Gibsonian 'resonance' in which perception of human acts somehow 'directly' leads to their motor production with no intervening mediation" (1993, 341). Also ruled out is the possibility infants make direct comparisons between their faces and those they imitate. The only alternative left is procedural ("functional rules," according to Meltzoff).

11. We are not told how this is supposed to work, but there are some neuro-scientific hints. For example, Jeannerod (1994, 189–190) speculates that during learning by imitation the pupil could form a motor image similar to that formed if he were actually preparing the action he is observing. He thinks the same neural formations are involved in both endeavors. Jeannerod also reports that work on monkeys has revealed the same neurons firing prior to and during specific actions by the animal *and* when the animal observes another performing the same action.

12. I borrow the notion of effective strategy and its link to causes from Nancy Cartwright. As she puts it, "There is a natural connection between causes and strategies ...; if one wants to obtain a goal, it is a good ... strategy to introduce a cause for that goal" (1983, 36). I think that this is what evolution did with advanced forms of sensorimotor cognition. The spirit of the notion of effective

strategy in interpretation is present in Dennett's influential paper 1978b. He writes that chimpanzees "use the concepts of belief and desire (or concepts importantly analogous) *in their own action governance*" (1978b, 569; my approving italics). Dennett goes on to propose how chimpanzees and young children could be tested for false belief (for which the paper was deservedly influential), a proposal that specifically incorporates this insight. I return to this matter in chapter 6, section 2.

13. Recently, tool manipulation has been linked to the evolution of grammar-based language (Greenfield 1991). That is not my angle here, but I note that Greenfield cites research indicating that the chimpanzees alone among nonhuman primates can use the same tool on different objects or two tools sequentially on a single object—an exploit comparable to that of young children. This suggests an instrumental intelligence in the form of basic algorithms of hierarchical complexity for tool use, as opposed to mere learning. It also suggests that the algorithms for tool use might have something in common with interpretation, in terms of hierarchical complexity and generativity, when a conspecific is treated as a social tool.

14. For example, Whiten (1993), who has written extensively on "intervening variables," stresses that the interpreter resorts to them as shortcuts that provide "unitary categorizations" of the subject's mental states and improve the economy of her predictions. This would be a weak mentalist position. But like other mentalists, Whiten seems to waver (1996, 287–288), as he well should, because a weak mentalism would have a hard time explaining the success of predictions without lapsing into either behaviorism, strong mentalism, or my kind of practicalism.

15. The *interpretive* phenomenology of attributes, as understood here, should not be confused with *philosophical* phenomenology, à la Husserl or Merleau-Ponty. The latter is an epistemologically motivated doctrine committed to a rigorous but nonempirical description of mental contents from introspective or behaviorally accessible data, respectively. Philosophical phenomenology has no interest in interpretive practices. In contrast, interpretive phenomenology is a naive form of access and individuation of attributes and their contents.

16. I said a few things on this issue in Bogdan 1995. Goldman's target is functionalism as "a theory-of-mind approach to the meaning of mental terms" (1993, 15). I think that neither functionalism, as a philosophical doctrine, nor a meaning analysis have much relevance to a proceduralist analysis of interpretation. Goldman admits that the proceduralism of theory of mind fails to meet the requirements of functionalism (1993, 26). Learning interpretational words is a later acquisition; moreover, the meanings learned need not capture the workings of interpretation.

Chapter 6

1. Many accomplishments are interdependent and appear to be part of a package (Astington and Gopnik 1988). This suggests that the interpretive grasp of representation emerges from many sources and cannot be tested in isolation. So it is not always clear what is tested. Is it an interpretive ability, or the child's understanding

of the language of the experimenter's instructions and of the experimental set-up itself, or her understanding of the interpretive vocabulary or of other words used? Or is this testing other faculties (memory, reasoning, verbalization) involved in the overall performance? Inevitably, then, the selective pressures and the skills they instill at this phase must be thought of in rather coarse-grained terms.

2. Apparently, children become capable of genuine language-based deception around 4 years of age (Perner 1991, 199), although Piaget noted that children distinguish lies intended to deceive from other falsehood such as jokes or exaggerations much later, at about 9 or 10 (Leekam 1991, 161).

3. It is worth noting that the omission of the practical envelope surrounding the ability to interpret feeds neglect of the evolutionary cauldron in which the interpretive skills were cooked up historically and also neglect of how evolution illuminates the design of interpretation. Conversely, neglect of evolution fuels a spectatorial and nonpractical view of interpretation. This mutual reinforcement of prejudices misses the truth that evolution rewards behaviors with tangible practical results by retaining the programs responsible for them.

4. I am not prejudging at this point whether belief recognition is a distinct interpretive skill, on a par with those for simple desire or gaze recognition, or the result of inference or reconstruction, particularly when it comes to false belief. Whatever is behind belief recognition, it seems to emerge only at some point in development.

5. It should be noted that remembering past events is different from remembering past misrepresentations. In the former case one simply reenacts an experience, which one cannot do in the latter case. To remember a past misrepresentation, one must enter the *interpretive* mode and remember one's cognitive *relation* to a past situation. To do this, one has to hold fixed and within mental view (as it were) the relation itself and the relata (belief and fact believed). That turns out not be an easy feat either for memory or current cognition.

6. Sodian and Frith (1993) report how relieved the parents are to see the first clumsy "lies" of their intellectually able autistic adolescents. They write, "One mother who was very concerned about her sixteen-year-old autistic son's behavior problems (attacking her physically, throwing food and furniture), was even more worried about his social naivety, characterizing him as 'too good, totally honest, and unable to lie.' She reported, for instance, that her son would stick to a given instruction such as 'go to bed at 10 p.m.' whether or not she was there to enforce it" (1993, 167). (Is morality ultimately autistic?)

7. One can even contemplate the possibility of "autistic" chimpanzees who fail to join in the political fun for lack of an appropriate interpretation kit. If chimpanzees have access to fragments of psychobehavioral interpretation, that could mean that their "autistic" colleagues might operate without such fragments, being restricted to natural teleology and the public life it affords. This is pure speculation, but one cannot exclude comparable interpretive deficits in apes.

8. But I have made some efforts in Bogdan 1988b, 1989a, 1991a, 1993b and took a more comprehensive view in Bogdan 1994.

9. Indeed, it may be that the temptation of the zeitgeist to see language and thinking as essentially represers (the psychosemantic temptation) have inspired the notion, popular in the mainstream philosophy and psychology of interpretation, that interpretation must be essentially metarepresentational. It is symptomatic in this regard that Perner's excellent book is entitled *Understanding the Representational Mind* (1991) and contains several methodological chapters concerned almost exclusively with logical and semantic analyses of the notion of representation and metarepresentation.

Chapter 7

1. The knowledge of the domain is contained in instructions and not in explicit data structures about the domain. This is domain implicitness. The knowledge is also contained in features of the domain that the instructions must necessarily engage in order to do their job. This is domain dependence.

2. A simpler notion of script was first proposed by Schank and Abelson (1975) in artificial intelligence and then extended to social psychology (Nisbett and Ross 1980) and interpretation (Fiske and Taylor 1991), among other applications.

3. In a number of works (e.g., 1987, chapter 1; 1991b), Dennett has drawn a parallel between folk physics and folk psychology as cognitive crafts that we grow up and master. I think this is right, and I propose scripting as a core (but not the only) strategy tapped by this expertise. Carey and Spelke (1994) review the psychological evidence pointing to the similarities between naive physics and interpretation in terms of procedurality, innateness, and domain specificity.

4. Scripting and canonizing experiences culturally begin in the early psychosocial phases when interpretation is both relied upon and shaped. The early instances give valuable clues as to how later scripting unfolds. Thus Bruner (1983, chapters 4 and 5) has carefully analyzed tightly scripted and interpretation-based initiation into reference, which he emphatically regards as the canonization of a practice (not the formation of an explicit concept). He notes that the referential script has two aims. One, semantic, is to get the child to recognize that vocalization stands for something mother and child visually share and that the vocalization is canonical—a step in becoming a "standard speaker of a language." The other aim is purely cultural and consists in imparting to the child the sense that "there is a canonical way of negotiating reference, as seen, for example, in little contests over the disambiguation of a referent" (Bruner 1983, 124–125). The same with requests. The child must master canonically acceptable ways of signaling intention, referring to what is requested, and the like. The scripting is done laboriously, mostly by mother, in a preselected and preformed manner. Despite small variations to sustain interest, the scripts are "kept easily recognizable and highly constrained ... and made as gamelike as necessary to restrict them to a set of permissible 'moves' that define the context.... Only with mastery of these prearranged contexts [through practice and ritualization] does the child or his mother begin to 'transfer' the game to a wider set of alternatives" (Bruner 1983, 130).

This is how canons are slowly brought into existence in two areas of cognition, referring and requesting, that rest on early psychosocial interpretation and further drive its development. Tomasello, Kruger, and Ratner (1993) review and discuss many examples of how adults carefully script various cognitive tasks for children as part of their cultural instruction and how children then become capable of carrying on on their own. In this process of script enculturation, children mature the mental wherewithal with which they will spontaneously parse physical and social situations of involvement. This is how culture becomes second nature.

5. Bruner notes that "folk psychology is invested in canonicality. It focuses upon the expectable and/or the usual in the human condition" (1990, 47–48). His is a liberal notion of commonsense psychology, perhaps coextensive with that of social cognition or knowledge, as a "system by which people organize their experience in, knowledge about, and transactions with the social world" (Bruner 1990, 35). This notion includes more than interpretation, as I view it, but must contain interpretation as a core competence. The influence of Bruner's discussion of canonicality can be seen throughout this section.

6. The cultural recognition of derived attributes raises the possibility that some may be variable cultural constructs. It may follow that one can exhibit and interpret such attributes only if one is raised in a specific culture or even subculture, as Carolyn Morillo pointed out to me. That is possible. My guess is that any culturally manufactured attribute (Christian forgiveness, quixoticism, chivalrous attitudes?) recombines core attributes with derived but culturally universal attributes, though often in unique mixtures.

7. Bruner talks of game formats that have a canonical "deep structure" and "realization rules" that manage various "surface" expressions: "The deep structure of peekaboo is the controlled disappearance and reappearance of an object or a person. The surface structure can be constructed by the use of screens or cloths or whatnot, by varying the time and action between disappearance and reappearance, by varying the constitutive utterance used, by varying who or what is caused to disappear, etc." (1983, 46).

8. Carrithers (1991, 307) notes that most experiments with children before and during the representational turn involve very brief sequences of actions, cut from the normal flow of time. Yet the unrealism of such experiments seems for once to match the short-lived span of children's interpretation. The children's inability to tell stories seems intimately connected with their inability to extend interpretation across space and time.

9. Lewis (1994) plausibly points out that young children before four can recognize false belief if the right narrative context is in place. However this point is if he means 'narrative' literally, instead of 'protonarrative', as I suggest. For, as we saw, young children are not good at narration. But if protonarration is intrinsic to psychosocial interpretation, then it should not surprise that, devoid of protonarrative content, an experiment may fail to ask the right questions and get the right answers about the interpretive prowess of the very young.

Chapter 8

1. Behavioristically inclined theories of interpretation, much influenced by Quine's, tend to go from available evidence to content ascription, thus bypassing the steps suggested by the hypothesis. No wonder, then, that interpretation looks more radical and indeterminate than it actually is. Yet, as pointed out in chapter 9, Quine's angle on the radicalism and indeterminacy of interpretation is motivated by a transcendental project that is different from mine.

2. Fiske and Taylor report that the "guiding principle behind people's relative use of schemas and data seems to be the needs of the particular interaction and the costs of being wrong. People interacting with other people enact specific social roles, within particular social settings, and these limit the information necessary and useful to the social perceiver.... For many interactions, our schematic expectancies will be sufficiently accurate, but sometimes the interaction requires a more detailed look at the other person due to the potential cost of being wrong. In either case, people's perceptions are typically functional and accurate enough for the purposes at hand.... There is various evidence supporting people's pragmatic approach to accuracy and their typically functional trade-offs between schemas and data" (1991, 155–156).

3. Several major works stand out: Austin's "Other Minds" (in his 1961); Wittgenstein 1953, 1969; also Malcolm 1952; Urmson 1952. For a collection of the period, see Griffiths 1967; for a recent and forceful revival of the tradition, see Collins 1987.

4. If the ape could talk and her talk could describe only her explicit representations, then the ape would not be able to access and describe friendliness other than in terms of its input and output conditions—a point rightly made by philosophical behaviorists. This is something to consider when examining the mentalist talk of young children who, on many accounts, interpret from instructions rather than concept-like rules (see Bartsch and Wellman 1995 for an extensive study of how children talk about the mind).

5. This is why, throughout this essay, I let hypotheses about the job of interpretation determine its design and domain. Interpretation could not do its job if it didn't conceptualize its attributions in terms of public semantics. I later take the same job-to-design stance on content ascription and interpretive explanation. This stance can also deconstruct misrepresentations of other cognitive enterprises. Decades ago, mixing epistemology with psychology, philosophers claimed that visual perception targets sense data rather than distal objects. If that were the case, then vision would have been designed differently, for it would have to compute and recover different properties of light. The same can be said about memory, concept-formation, and thinking.

6. See Gopnik 1993, 10–11; also Bogdan 1995, 391. Humphrey (1988) was the first to make a forceful analogy between chess and social cognition and interpretation; see also Baron-Cohen 1995b, chapter 2. Gary Kasparov makes the interesting observation that Deep Blue (the IBM chess player) he was playing against recently was scriptless in a human sense (did not perceive the loss of a

pawn as a "sacrifice"). So when he changed the order of a well-known opening, the computer calculated like mad without seeing Gasparov's move as a meaningless departure from a script, the way a human opponent would have done (*Time*, March 25, 1996).

7. Dennett (1978a, 303–309) made a distinction between nonlinguistic and spontaneous belief formation and language-based and deliberate opinion formation. In terms of this distinction, there is belieflike and opinionlike content ascription. Only the latter has the linguistic form of explicit 'that' clauses. This means that the interpreter spontaneously and nonlinguistically *believes* something about the subject's relation to the world, but on occasion the interpreter deliberately and linguistically *opines* about that relation and formulates the opinion accordingly.

8. There is another danger in the standard philosophical line, often deplored but seldom avoided. This is the view that the study of language-based interpretation is a study of the *meaning* of attitude sentences in general and content ascriptions in particular. On this view, a meaning analysis would reveal what the 'that' clauses are about and hence what content is. This is an armchair and a priori position that is attractive and reassuring to philosophers. (The meaning game, after all, is one they know best how to play.) But it is far too simple to be true. An apt and close parallel to what is interpreted, contentwise, is what is communicated. In either case the answer points to a complex equation rather than a neat formula. Just to get the point across, I would say (unexegetically) that what is communicated can be parsed into (a) what is said and (b) what is conversationally implicated, where (a) in turn can be parsed into (a.1) meaning and (a.2) indexical coordinates of the context, and (b) into (b.1) logical consequences and (b.2) implicit assumptions of various sorts (Recanati 1989, Sperber and Wilson 1986). The speakers evolve the skills to value all these parameters and summarize them in an utterance, the listeners to retrieve inferentially values of the hidden parameters from the utterance. Content ascription in interpretation works in the same spirit of hidden complexity.

9. The externality of content is a matter of interpretive ascription and not necessarily an intrinsic property of mental states. Proponents of content externalism, such as Burge (1979), do not always respect this distinction, as convincingly argued by Pierre Jacob (1987).

10. When philosophers propose to view content as the common denominator of what is thought, believed, or said, the entity they come up with most often is a *proposition*. The topic is an ugly Pandora's box that I do not intend to open. The curious and brave reader may want to take a look at Stich 1983 or Schiffer 1987. I will say only this. Propositions are at best the objects of 'that' clauses and index or summarize full-fledged contents. They may be thought of as the polished and tight-lipped ambassadors or public-relations representatives of contents rather than the real thing.

11. I am not belittling mental causation, a worthy metaphysical and psychological topic. The issue is not whether an agent acts causally on the basis of conative and cognitive states and of what these states represent; of course he does, although the picture is more complex than that (Bogdan 1987, 1994). The issue is whether the

interpreter attributes to him desires and beliefs construed as internal causes with specific semantic contents; I say she doesn't. My critique is about the internalist notion that interpretation has a conceptual grip on semantic causation and successfully explains in virtue of that grip. The fact that most debates about internalism versus externalism begin or end up with consequences for *psychological* explanation tells me that interpretation is not really the issue—unless interpretation is already assumed (but not shown) to be a sort of protopsychology.

12. I cannot help but repeat that the notion of interpreting mental *states* comes close to incoherence, whether it is done by simulation or otherwise. Interpretation is after *relations*, not internal states as structures of some sort. The notion, at least as old as Hobbes, that we simulate the mental states of others by projection from ours thus courts incoherence twice. What is the mental state in us? A content, a representation of it, an attitude, or a combination of the above? And what about the target state in the subject? What dimensions does the simulator zoom in on there? Are these distinctions known and respected by the simulator? When indulging in mental-state talk, serious simulation theorists may misspeak, yet fortunately they mean well.

13. Tomasello, Kruger, and Ratner (1993), for example, see no incompatibility between simulation as a possible interpretation strategy and the Vygotskian line that understanding of self follows and relies on the understanding of others.

Chapter 9

1. Something else must be pretended. My account has rejected the idea that interpretive programs, their databases, or their outputs systematically track, either implicitly or by explicit representation, dispositions, other architectural items (mental programs, functional mechanisms), or specific representations. Since aboutness is literally established in one of these ways, interpretation cannot be *about* minds (i.e., their designs or contents). The latter are known indirectly and by assumptions relative to what *is* systematically tracked, namely, subject-world relations.

2. In a recent paper (Bogdan 1993a) I made this point about human interpretation on philosophical grounds. I think the evolutionary stance backs it up.

3. This diagnosis is also borne out by the ubiquity of knowledge of dispositions in the biological world. *Any* organism in constant interaction with another evolves to assume the basic agency of the other and also the different dispositions the other constantly and vitally manifests. There is nothing special about interpretation on *this* score. Special are the types of dispositions known under the selective pressures that called for interpretation. But then, special will be the kinds of dispositions known by various species under the selective pressures that called for strategies of defense or hunting or symbiosis.

4. I have done a bit of it in other works (Bogdan 1983, 1985, 1988b, 1991a, 1993a, 1995). For good surveys of the philosophical work, see Fodor 1990, chapter 1; Dennett 1987, chapter 10; Stich 1983; Stich and Ravenscroft 1994. For psychology, see especially Perner 1991 and Wellman 1990.

References

Alexander, R. G. 1990. "Epigenetic Rules and Darwinian Algorithms." *Ethology and Sociobiology* 11:241–303.

Anderson, J. R. 1983. *The Architecture of Cognition*. Cambridge: Harvard University Press.

Astington, J. W. 1990. "Narrative and the Child's Theory of Mind." In B. K. Britton and A. D. Pellegrini (eds.), *Narrative Thought and Narrative Language*. Hillsdale, N.J.: Lawrence Erlbaum.

Astington, J. W. 1991. "Intention in the Child's Theory of Mind." In A. Whiten (ed.), *Natural Theories of Mind*. Oxford: Blackwell.

Astington, J. W., and Gopnik, A. 1988. "Knowing You've Changed Your Mind: Children's Understanding of Representational Change." In J. W. Astington, P. L. Harris, and D. R. Olson (eds.), *Developing Theories of Mind*. Cambridge: Cambridge University Press.

Astington, J. W., and Gopnik, A. 1991. "Developing Understanding of Desire and Intention." In A. Whiten (ed.) *Natural Theories of Mind*. Oxford: Blackwell.

Astington, J. W.; Harris, P. L.; and Olson, D. R. (eds.). 1988. *Developing Theories of Mind*. Cambridge: Cambridge University Press.

Austin, J. L. 1961. *Philosophical Papers*. Oxford: Oxford University Press.

Baker, L. R. 1995. *Explaining Attitudes*. Cambridge: Cambridge University Press.

Baldwin, D. A., and Moses, L. J. 1994. "Early Understanding of Referential Intent and Attentional Focus." In C. Lewis and P. Mitchell (eds.), *Children's Early Understanding of Mind: Origins and Development*. Hillsdale, N.J.: Lawrence Erlbaum.

Baron-Cohen, S. 1991. "Precursors to a Theory of Mind: Understanding Attention in Others." In A. Whiten (ed.), *Natural Theories of Mind*. Oxford: Blackwell.

Baron-Cohen, S. 1992. "How Monkeys Do Things with Words'." *Behavioral and Brain Sciences* 15:148–149.

Baron-Cohen, S. 1993a. "From Attention-Goal Psychology to Belief-Desire Psychology." In S. Baron-Cohen, H. Tager-Flusberg, and D. J. Cohen, (eds.), *Understanding Other Minds: Perspectives from Autism*. Oxford: Oxford University Press.

Baron-Cohen, S. 1993b. "Are Children with Autism Acultural?" *Behavioral and Brain Sciences* 16:512–513.

Baron-Cohen, S. 1993c. "The Concept of Intentionality: Invented or Innate? *Behavioral and Brain Sciences* 16:29–30.

Baron-Cohen, S. 1995a. "The Eye-Direction Detector and the Shared Attention Mechanism: Two Cases for Evolutionary Psychology." In C. Moore and P. J. Dunham (eds.), *Joint Attention*. Hillsdale, N.J.: Lawrence Erlbaum.

Baron-Cohen, S. 1995b. *Mindblindness*. Cambridge: MIT Press.

Baron-Cohen, S., and Cross, P. 1992. "Reading the Eyes: Evidence for the Role of Perception in the Development of a Theory of Mind." *Mind and Language* 7:172–186.

Baron-Cohen, S.; Leslie, A. M.; and Frith, U. 1985. "Does the Autistic Child Have a Theory of Mind?" *Cognition* 21:37–46.

Baron-Cohen, S., and Ring, H. 1994. "A Model of the Mindreading System." In C. Lewis and P. Mitchell (eds.), *Children's Early Understanding of Mind: Origins and Development*. Hillsdale, N.J.: Lawrence Erlbaum.

Baron-Cohen, S.; Tager-Flusberg, H.; and Cohen, D. J. (eds.) 1993. *Understanding Other Minds: Perspectives from Autism*. Oxford: Oxford University Press.

Bartsch, K., and Wellman, H. M. 1995. *Children Talk about the Mind*. Oxford: Oxford University Press.

Barwise, J., and Perry, J. 1983. *Situations and Attitudes*. Cambridge: MIT Press.

Beer, C. G. 1986. "The Evolution of Intelligence: Costs and Benefits." In R. J. Hoage and L. Goldman (eds.), *Animal Intelligence*. Washington: Smithonian Institution Press.

Bennett, J. 1976. *Linguistic Behavior*. Cambridge: Cambridge University Press.

Bennett, J. 1991a. "Analysis without Noise." In R. J. Bogdan (ed.), *Mind and Common Sense*. Cambridge: Cambridge University Press.

Bennett, J. 1991b. "How to Read Minds in Behavior." In A. Whiten (ed.), *Natural Theories of Mind*. Oxford: Blackwell.

Boesch, C. 1993. "Towards a New Image of Culture in Wild Chimpanzees?" *Behavioral and Brain Sciences* 16:514–515.

Bogdan, R. J. 1983. "Fodor's Representations." *Cognition and Brain Theory* 6:237–249.

Bogdan, R. J. 1985. "The Intentional Stance Reexamined." *Behavioral and Brain Sciences* 8:759–760.

Bogdan, R. J. (ed.). 1986a. *Belief*. Oxford: Oxford University Press.

Bogdan, R. J. 1986b. "The Importance of Belief." In R. J. Bogdan (ed.), *Belief*. Oxford: Oxford University Press.

Bogdan, R. J. 1986c. "The Manufacture of Belief." In R. J. Bogdan (ed.), *Belief*. Oxford: Oxford University Press.

Bogdan, R. J. 1986d. "The Objects of Perception." In R. J. Bogdan (ed.), *Roderick Chisholm*. Dordrecht: Reidel.

Bogdan, R. J. 1987. "Mind, Content, and Information." *Synthese* 70:205–227.

Bogdan, R. J. 1988a. "Information and Semantic Cognition." *Mind and Language* 3:81–122.

Bogdan, R. J. 1988b. "Mental Attitudes and Commonsense Psychology." *Noûs* 22:369–398.

Bogdan, R. J. 1989a. "Does Semantics Run the Psyche?" *Philosophy and Phenomenological Research* 49:687–700.

Bogdan, R. J. 1989b. "What Do We Need Concepts For?" *Mind and Language* 4:17–23.

Bogdan, R. J. 1991a. "Common Sense Naturalized." In R. J. Bogdan (ed.), *Mind and Common Sense*. Cambridge: Cambridge University Press.

Bogdan, R. J. 1991b. "The Folklore of the Mind." In R. J. Bogdan (ed.), *Mind and Common Sense*. Cambridge: Cambridge University Press.

Bogdan, R. J. 1993a. "The Architectural Nonchalance of Commonsense Psychology." *Mind and Language* 8:189–205.

Bogdan, R. J. 1993b. "The Pragmatic Psyche." *Philosophy and Phenomenological Research* 53:157–158.

Bogdan, R. J. 1994. *Grounds for Cognition*. Hillsdale, N.J.: Lawrence Erlbaum Associates.

Bogdan, R. J. 1995. "The Epistemological Illusion." *Behavioral and Brain Sciences* 18:390–391.

Bonner, J. T. 1980. *The Evolution of Culture in Animals*. Princeton: Princeton University Press.

Bonner, J. T. 1988. *The Evolution of Complexity*. Princeton: Princeton University Press.

Bowlby, J. 1982. *Attachement*. New York: Basic Books.

Braitenberg, V. 1984. *Vehicles*. Cambridge: MIT Press.

Brandon, R. N. 1990. *Adaptation and Environment*. Princeton: Princeton University Press.

Brandon, R. N. 1992. "Environment." In E. V. Keller and E. A. Llyod (eds.), *Keywords in Evolutionary Biology*. Cambridge: Harvard University Press.

Bremner, J. G. 1988. *Infancy*. Oxford: Blackwell.

Britton, B. K., and Pellegrini, A. D. (eds.). 1990. *Narrative Thought and Narrative Language*. Hillsdale, N.J.: Lawrence Erlbaum.

Bruner, J. 1983. *Child's Talk*. New York: Norton.

Bruner, J. 1986. *Actual Minds, Possible Worlds*. Cambridge: Harvard University Press.

Bruner, J. 1990. *Acts of Meaning*. Cambridge: Harvard University Press.

Bruner, J., and Feldman, C. 1993. "Theories of Mind and the Problem of Autism." In S. Baron-Cohen, H. Tager-Flusberg, and D. J. Cohen, (eds.), *Understanding Other Minds: Perspectives from Autism*. Oxford: Oxford University Press.

Burge, T. 1979. "Individualism and the Mental." In P. French, T. Uehling, and H. Wettstein (eds.), *Studies in Metaphysics*, Midwest Studies in Philosophy, no. 4. Minneapolis: University of Minnesota Press.

Burge, T. 1993. "Mind-Body Causation and Explanatory Power." In J. Heil and A. Mele (eds.), *Mental Causation*. Oxford: Oxford University Press.

Burian, R. M. 1992. "Adaptation: Historical Perspectives." In E. V. Keller and E. A. Llyod (eds.), *Keywords in Evolutionary Biology*. Cambridge: Harvard University Press.

Butterworth, G. 1991. "The Ontogeny and Phylogeny of Joint Visual Attention." In A. Whiten (ed.), *Natural Theories of Mind*. Oxford: Blackwell.

Butterworth, G. 1994. "Theories of Mind and Facts of Embodiment." In C. Lewis and P. Mitchell (eds.), *Children's Early Understanding of Mind: Origins and Development*. Hillsdale, N.J.: Lawrence Erlbaum.

Byrne, R., and Whiten, A. (eds.). 1988. *Machiavellian Intelligence*. Oxford: Oxford University Press.

Byrne, R., and Whiten, A. 1991. "Computation and Mind Reading in Primate Tactical Deception." In A. Whiten (ed.), *Natural Theories of Mind*. Oxford: Blackwell.

Carey, S. 1985. *Conceptual Change in Childhood*. Cambridge: MIT Press.

Carey, S., and Spelke, E. 1994. "Domain-Specific Knowledge and Conceptual Change." In L. A. Hirschfeld and S. A. Gelman (eds.), *Domain Specificity in Cognition and Culture*. Cambridge: Cambridge University Press.

Carrithers, M. 1989. "Sociality, Not Aggression, Is the Key Human Trait." In S. Howell and R. Wills (eds.), *Societies at Peace*. London: Routledge.

Carrithers, M. 1991. "Narrativity: Mindreading and Making Societies." In A. Whiten (ed.), *Natural Theories of Mind*. Oxford: Blackwell.

Carruthers, P. 1992. *Human Knowledge and Human Nature*. Oxford: Oxford University Press.

Carruthers, P., and Smith, P. K. (eds.). 1996. *Theories of Theories of Mind*. Cambridge: Cambridge University Press.

Cartwright, N. 1983. *How the Laws of Physics Lie*. Oxford: Oxford University Press.

Chandler, M. J. 1988. "Doubt and Developing Theories of Mind." In J. W. Astington, P. L. Harris, and D. R. Olson (eds.), *Developing Theories of Mind*. Cambridge: Cambridge University Press.

Chandler, M. J., and Boyes, M. 1982. "Social-Cognitive Development." In B. B. Wollman (ed.), *Handbook of Developmental Psychology*. Englewood Cliffs, N.J.: Prentice-Hall.

Chandler, M. J.; Fritz, A. S.; and Hala, S. 1989. "Small Scale Deceit." *Child Development* 60:1263–1277.

Chandler, M. J., and Hala, S. 1994. "The Role of Personal Involvement in the Assessment of Early False Belief Skills." In C. Lewis and P. Mitchell (eds.), *Children's Early Understanding of Mind: Origins and Development*. Hillsdale, N.J.: Lawrence Erlbaum.

Charlesworth, W. R. 1988. "Resources and Resource Acquisition during Ontogeny." In K. MacDonald (ed.), *Sociobiological Perspectives on Human Development*. New York: Springer-Verlag.

Cheney, D. L., and Seyfarth, R. M. 1990. *How Monkeys See the World*. Chicago: University of Chicago Press.

Cheney, D. L., and Seyfarth, R. M. 1992. "Characterizing the Mind of Another Species." *Behavioral and Brain Sciences* 15:172–178.

Chevalier-Skolnikoff, S. 1988. "Classification of Deceptive Behavior According to Levels of Cognitive Complexity." *Behavioral and Brain Sciences* 11:249–251.

Chisholm, J. S. 1988. "Toward a Developmental Evolutionary Ecology of Humans." In K. B. MacDonald (ed.), *Sociobiological Perspectives on Human Development*. New York: Springer-Verlag.

Chomsky, N. 1975. *Reflections on Language*. New York: Pantheon.

Chomsky, N. 1980. *Rules and Representations*. New York: Columbia University Press.

Churchland, P. M. 1989. *A Neurocomputational Perspective*. Cambridge: MIT Press.

Clark, A. 1989. *Microcognition*. Cambridge: MIT Press.

Clark, E., and Clark, H., 1977. *Psychology and Language*. New York: Harcourt Brace Jovanovich.

Clark, H. H. 1979. "Responding to Indirect Speech Acts." *Cognitive Psychology* 11:430–477.

Cohen, J., and Stewart, I. 1994. "Our Genes Aren't Us." *Discover* 15 (April): 78–84.

Collins, A. 1987. *The Nature of Mental Things*. Notre Dame, Ind.: University of Notre Dame Press.

Cosmides, L. 1989. "The Logic of Social Exchange: Has Natural Selection Shaped How Humans Reason?" *Cognition* 31:187–276.

Cosmides, L., and Tooby, J. 1987. "From Evolution to Behavior." In J. Dupré (ed.), *The Latest on the Best*. Cambridge: MIT Press.

Cummins, R. 1986. "Inexplicit Information." In M. Brand and R. M. Harnish (eds.), *The Representation of Knowledge and Belief*. Tucson: University of Arizona Press.

Damasio, A. R. 1994. *Descartes' Error*. New York: G. P. Putnam.

Davidson, D. 1980. *Essays on Actions and Events*. Oxford: Oxford University Press.

Davidson, D. 1984. *Inquiries into Truth and Interpretation*. Oxford: Oxford University Press.

Davidson, D. 1987. "Knowing One's Own Mind." *Proceedings and Addresses of the American Philosophical Association* 60:441–458. Reprinted in Q. Cassam (ed.), *Self-Knowledge*. Oxford: Oxford Univerity Press, 1994.

Davies, M., and Stone, T. (eds.). 1995. *Mental Simulation*. Oxford: Blackwell.

Dawkins, R. 1976a. *The Selfish Gene*. Oxford: Oxford University Press.

Dawkins, R. 1976b. "Hierarchical Organisation." In P. P. G. Bateson and J. R. Krebs (eds.), *Growing Points in Ethology*. Cambridge: Cambridge University Press.

Dawkins, R. 1982. *The Extended Phenotype*. Oxford: Oxford University Press.

Dawkins, R. 1986. *The Blind Watchmaker*. New York: Norton.

Dawkins, R. 1995. "God's Utility Function." *Scientific American* 273 (November): 80–85.

Dennett, D. 1969. *Content and Consciousness*. London: Routledge and Kegan Paul.

Dennett, D. 1978a. *Brainstorms*. Montgomery, Vt.: Bradford.

Dennett, D. 1978b. "Beliefs about Beliefs." *Behavioral and Brain Sciences* 4:568–570.

Dennett, D. 1987. *The Intentional Stance*. Cambridge: MIT Press.

Dennett, D. 1991a. *Consciousness Explained*. Boston: Little, Brown.

Dennett, D. 1991b. "Two Contrasts: Folk Craft versus Folk Science, and Belief versus Opinion." In J. Greenwood (ed.), *The Future of Folk Psychology*. Cambridge: Cambridge University Press.

Dennett, D. 1995. *Darwin's Dangerous Idea*. New York: Simon and Schuster.

De Waal, F. 1982. *Chimpanzee Politics*. Baltimore: Johns Hopkins University Press.

De Waal, F. 1989. *Peacemaking among Primates*. Cambridge: Harvard University Press.

Dretske, F. 1972. "Contrastive Statements." *Philosophical Review* 81:411–437.

Dretske, F. 1981. *Knowledge and the Flow of Information*. Cambridge: MIT Press.

Dretske, F. 1986. "Misrepresentation." In R. J. Bogdan (ed.), *Belief*. Oxford: Oxford University Press.

Dretske, F. 1988. "Explaining Behavior." Cambridge: MIT Press.

Dunbar, R. I. M. 1993. "Coevolution of Neocortical Size, Group Size, and Language in Humans." *Behavioral and Brain Sciences* 16:681–694.

Dunn, J. 1988. *The Beginnings of Social Understanding*. Oxford: Blackwell.

Dunn, J. 1991. "Understanding Others: Evidence from Naturalistic Studies of Children." In A. Whiten (ed.), *Natural Theories of Mind*. Oxford: Blackwell.

Dunn, J.; Brown, J.; Slomkowski, C.; Tesla, C.; and Youngblade, L. 1991. "Young Children's Understanding of Other People's Feelings and Beliefs." *Child Development* 62:1352–1366.

Endler, J. A. 1992. "Natural Selection: Current Usages." In E. V. Keller and E. A. Llyod (eds.), *Keywords in Evolutionary Biology*. Cambridge: Harvard University Press.

Fiske, S. T., and Taylor, S. E. 1991. *Social Cognition*. New York: McGraw-Hill.

Flavell, J. H. 1988. "The Development of Children's Knowledge about the Mind." In J. W. Astington, P. L. Harris, and D. R. Olson (eds.), *Developing Theories of Mind*. Cambridge: Cambridge University Press.

Fodor, J. A. 1981. *Representations*. Cambridge: MIT Press.

Fodor, J. A. 1983. *The Modularity of Mind*. Cambridge: MIT Press.

Fodor, J. A. 1987. *Psychosemantics*. Cambridge: MIT Press.

Fodor, J. A. 1990. *A Theory of Content*. Cambridge: MIT Press.

Fodor, J. A. 1992. "A Theory of the Child's Theory of Mind." *Cognition* 44:283–296.

Fodor, J. A. 1994. *The Elm and the Expert*. Cambridge: MIT Press.

Forguson, L., and Gopnik, A. 1988. "The Ontogeny of Common Sense." In J. W. Astington, P. L. Harris, and D. R. Olson (eds.), *Developing Theories of Mind*. Cambridge: Cambridge University Press.

Frazier, L. 1990. "Seeing Language Evolution in the Eye." *Behavioral and Brain Sciences* 13:731–732.

Freeman, N. H. 1994. "Redescription of Intentionality." *Behavioral and Brain Sciences* 17:717–718.

Frith, U. 1989. *Autism*. Oxford: Blackwell.

Frye, D., and Moore, C. (eds.). 1991. *Children's Theories of Mind*. Hillsdale: Lawrence Erlbaum.

Gallup, G. G. 1970. "Chimpanzee: Self-Recognition." *Science* 167:86–87.

Garfinkel, A. 1981. *Forms of Explanation*. New Haven: Yale University Press.

Goldman, A. 1993. "The Psychology of Folk Psychology." *Behavioral and Brain Sciences* 16:15–28.

Gomez, J. C. 1990a. "Primate Tactical Deception and Sensorimotor Social Intelligence." *Behavioral and Brain Sciences* 13:414–415.

Gomez, J. C. 1990b. "Causal Links, Contingencies, and the Comparative Psychology of Intelligence." *Behavioral and Brain Sciences* 13:392.

Gomez, J. C. 1991. "Visual Behavior as a Window for Reading the Mind of Others in Primates." In A. Whiten (ed.), *Natural Theories of Mind*. Oxford: Blackwell.

Gomez, J. C. 1996. "Non-human Primate Theories of Mind." In P. Carruthers and P. K. Smith (eds.), *Theories of Theories of Mind*. Cambridge: Cambridge University Press.

Gomez, J. C.; Sarria, E.; and Tamarit, J. 1993. "The Comparative Study of Early Communication and Theories of Mind: Ontogeny, Phylogeny, and Pathology." In S. Baron-Cohen, H. Tager-Flusberg, and D. J. Cohen, (eds.), *Understanding Other Minds: Perspectives from Autism*. Oxford: Oxford University Press.

Gopnik, A. 1993. "How We Know Our Minds." *Behavioral and Brain Sciences* 16:1–14.

Gopnik, A. 1996. "Theories and Modules." In P. Carruthers and P. K. Smith (eds.), *Theories of Theories of Mind*. Cambridge: Cambridge University Press.

Gopnik, A., and Astington, J. W. 1988. "Children's Understanding of Representational Change and Its Relation to the Understanding of False Belief and the Appearance-Reality Distinction." *Child Development* 59:26–37.

Gopnik, A.; Slaughter, V.; and Meltzoff, A. 1994. "Changing Your Views: How Understanding Visual Perception Can Lead to a New Theory of the Mind." In C. Lewis and P. Mitchell (eds.), *Children's Early Understanding of Mind: Origins and Development*. Hillsdale, N.J.: Lawrence Erlbaum.

Gopnik, A., and Wellman, H. M. 1992. "Why the Child's Theory of Mind Really Is a Theory." *Mind and Language* 7:145–171.

Gopnik, A., and Wellman, H. M. 1994. "The Theory Theory." In L. A. Hirschfeld and S. A. Gelman (eds.), *Domain Specificity in Cognition and Culture*. Cambridge: Cambridge University Press.

Gordon, R. M. 1986. "Folk Psychology as Simulation." *Mind and Language* 1:158–171.

Gordon, R. M. 1987. *The Structure of Emotions*. Cambridge: Cambridge University Press.

Gordon, R. M. 1992a. "The Simulation Theory." *Mind and Language* 7:11–34.

Gordon, R. M. 1992b. "Reply to Stich and Nichols." *Mind and Language* 7:87–97.

Gordon, R. M. 1995. "Simulation without Introspection or Inference from Me to You." In M. Davies and T. Stone (eds.), *Mental Simulation*. Oxford: Blackwell.

Graham, G. 1987. "The Origins of Folk Psychology." *Inquiry* 30:357–379.

Green, O. H., 1991. *The Emotions*. Dordrecht: Kluwer.

Greenfield, P. 1991. "Language, Tools, and Brain: The Ontogeny and Phylogeny of Hierarchically Organized Behavior." *Behavioral and Brain Sciences* 14:531–551.

Greenwood, J. D. (ed.). 1991. *The Future of Folk Psychology*. Cambridge: Cambridge University Press.

Gregory, R. L. (ed.), 1987. *The Oxford Companion to the Mind*. Oxford: Oxford University Press.

Griffiths, A. P. (ed.). 1967. *Knowledge and Belief.* Oxford: Oxford University Press.

Hacking, I. 1982. "Experimentation and Scientific Realism." *Philosophical Topics* 13:71–87.

Hacking, I. 1983. *Representing and Intervening.* Cambridge: Cambridge University Press.

Happé, F., and Frith, U. 1992. "How Autistics See the World." *Behavioral and Brain Sciences* 15:159–160.

Harris, P. 1991. "The Work of Imagination." In A. Whiten (ed.), *Natural Theories of Mind.* Oxford: Blackwell.

Harris, P. 1992. "From Simulation to Folk Psychology." *Mind and Language* 7:120–144.

Harris, P. 1993. "Pretending and Planning." In S. Baron-Cohen, H. Tager-Flusberg, and D. J. Cohen, (eds.), *Understanding Other Minds: Perspectives from Autism.* Oxford: Oxford University Press.

Harris, P. 1994. "Thinking by Children and Scientists: False Analogies and Neglected Similarities." In L. A. Hirschfeld and S. A. Gelman (eds.), *Domain Specificity in Cognition and Culture.* Cambridge: Cambridge University Press.

Harris, P. 1996. "Desires, Beliefs, and Language." In P. Carruthers and P. K. Smith (eds.), *Theories of Theories of Mind.* Cambridge: Cambridge University Press.

Hastord, A. H.; Schneider, D. J.; and Polefka, J. 1970. *Person Perception.* Reading, Mass.: Addison-Wesley.

Heider, F. 1958. *The Psychology of Interpersonal Relations.* New York: Wiley.

Heil, J., and Mele, A. (eds.). 1993. *Mental Causation.* Oxford: Oxford University Press.

Heyes, C. M. 1993. "Anecdotes, Training, Trapping, and Triangulating: Do Animals Attribute Mental States?" *Animal Behavior* 47:177–188.

Hickman, M. 1987. "The Pragmatics of Reference in Child Language." In M. Hickman (ed.), *Social and Functional Approaches to Language and Thought.* Orlando: Academic Press.

Hildreth, E. C., and Ullman, S. 1989. "The Computational Study of Vision." In M. Posner (ed.), *Foundations of Cognitive Science.* Cambridge: MIT Press.

Hobson, R. P. 1993a. "Understanding Persons: The Role of Affect." In S. Baron-Cohen, H. Tager-Flusberg, and D. J. Cohen, (eds.), *Understanding Other Minds: Perspectives from Autism.* Oxford: Oxford University Press.

Hobson, R. P. 1993b. *Autism and the Development of Mind.* Hillsdale, N.J.: Lawrence Erlbaum.

Hobson, R. P. 1994. "Perceiving Attitudes, Conceiving Minds." In C. Lewis and P. Mitchell (eds.), *Children's Early Understanding of Mind: Origins and Development.* Hillsdale, N.J.: Lawrence Erlbaum.

Holland, J. H.; Holyoak, K. J.; Nisbett, R. E.; and Thagard, P. R. 1986. *Induction*. Cambridge: MIT Press.

Humphrey, N. K. 1988. "The Social Function of the Intellect." In J. Byrne and A. Whiten (eds.), *Machiavellian Intelligence*. Oxford: Oxford University Press.

Jacob, P. 1987. "Thoughts and Belief Ascription." *Mind and Language* 2:301–325.

Jaynes, J. 1976. *The Origin of Consciousness in the Breakdown of the Bicameral Mind*. Boston: Houghton Mifflin.

Jeannerod, M. 1994. "The Representing Brain: Neural Correlates of Motor Intention and Imagery." *Behavioral and Brain Sciences* 17:187–201.

Johnson, C. N. 1988. "Theory of Mind and the Structure of Conscious Experience." In J. W. Astington, P. L. Harris, and D. R. Olson (eds.), *Developing Theories of Mind*. Cambridge: Cambridge University Press.

Jolly, A. 1988a. "Lemur Social Behavior and Primate Intelligence." In J. Byrne and A. Whiten (eds.), *Machiavellian Intelligence*. Oxford: Oxford University Press.

Jolly, A. 1988b. "The Evolution of Purpose." In J. Byrne and A. Whiten (eds.), *Machiavellian Intelligence*. Oxford: Oxford University Press.

Karmiloff-Smith, A. 1992. *Beyond Modularity*. Cambridge: MIT Press.

Keil, F. C. 1989. *Concepts, Kinds, and Cognitive Development*. Cambridge: MIT Press.

Keller, E. V., and Llyod, E. A. (eds.). 1992. *Keywords in Evolutionary Biology*. Cambridge: Harvard University Press.

Kelley, H. H. 1973. "The Process of Causal Attribution." *American Psychologist* 28:107–128.

Kitcher, P. 1985. *Vaulting Ambition*. Cambridge: MIT Press.

Kosslyn, S. M. 1990. "Mental Imagery." In D. N. Osherson, S. M. Kosslyn, and J. M. Hollerbach (eds.), *Visual Cognition and Action*. Cambridge: MIT Press.

Krebs, J. R., and Dawkins, R. 1984. "Animal Signals: Mind-Reading and Manipulation." In J. R. Krebs and N. B. Davies (eds.), *Behavioral Ecology: An Evolutionary Approach*. Oxford: Blackwell.

LaFreniere, P. 1991. "The Ontogeny of Tactical Deception in Humans." In A. Whiten (ed.), *Natural Theories of Mind*. Oxford: Blackwell.

Leekam, S. R. 1991. "Jokes and Lies: Children's Understanding of Intentional Falsehood." In A. Whiten (ed.), *Natural Theories of Mind*. Oxford: Blackwell.

Leondar, B. 1977. "Hatching Plots: Genesis of Storymaking." In D. Perkins and B. Leondar (eds.), *The Arts and Cognition*. Baltimore: Johns Hopkins University Press.

Leslie, A. M. 1988. "Some Implications of Pretense for Mechanisms Underlying the Child's Theory of Mind." In J. W. Astington, P. L. Harris, and D. R. Olson (eds.), *Developing Theories of Mind*. Cambridge: Cambridge University Press.

Leslie, A. M. 1991. "The Theory of Mind Impairment in Autism." In A. Whiten (ed.), *Natural Theories of Mind*. Oxford: Blackwell.

Leslie, A. M. 1994. "ToMM, ToBy, and Agency." In L. Hirschfeld and S. A. Gelman (eds.), *Mapping the Mind*. Cambridge: Cambridge University Press.

Leslie, A. M., and German, T. P. 1995. "Knowledge and Ability in Theory of Mind." In M. Davies and T. Stone (eds.), *Mental Simulation*. Oxford: Blackwell.

Leslie, A. M., and Roth, D. 1993. "What Autism Teaches Us about Meta-representation." In S. Baron-Cohen, H. Tager-Flusberg, and D. J. Cohen, (eds.), *Understanding Other Minds: Perspectives from Autism*. Oxford: Oxford University Press.

Levin, M. 1984. "Why We Believe in Other Minds." *Philosophy and Phenomenological Research* 44:343–359.

Lewis, C. 1994. "Episodes, Events, and Narratives in the Child's Understanding of Mind." In C. Lewis and P. Mitchell (eds.), *Children's Early Understanding of Mind: Origins and Development*. Hillsdale, N.J.: Lawrence Erlbaum Associates.

Lewis, C., and Mitchell, P. (eds.). 1994. *Children's Early Understanding of Mind: Origins and Development*. Hillsdale, N.J.: Lawrence Erlbaum Associates.

Lewis, D. 1983. *Philosophical Papers*, vol. 1. Oxford: Oxford University Press.

Lewontin, R. 1984. "Adaptation." In E. Sober (ed.), *Conceptual Issues in Evolutionary Biology*. Cambridge: MIT Press.

Lewontin, R. 1990. "The Evolution of Cognition." In D. N. Oshersohn and E. E. Smith (eds.), *Thinking*. Cambridge: MIT Press.

Lloyd, D. 1989. *Simple Minds*. Cambridge: MIT Press.

Loar, B. 1981. *Mind and Meaning*. Cambridge: Cambridge University Press.

Loftus, E. 1980. *Memory*. Reading, Mass.: Addison-Wesley.

Loveland, K. A. 1991. "Social Affordance and Interaction, II." *Ecological Psychology* 3:99–119.

Loveland, K. A. 1993. "Autism, Affordances, and the Self." In U. Neisser (ed.), *The Perceived Self*. Cambridge: Cambridge University Press.

Loveland, K. A., and Tunali, B. 1993. "Narrative Language in Autism and the Theory of Mind Hypothesis." In S. Baron-Cohen, H. Tager-Flusberg, and D. J. Cohen, (eds.), *Understanding Other Minds: Perspectives from Autism*. Oxford: Oxford University Press.

Lucariello, J. 1990. "Canonicality and Consciousness in Child Narrative." In B. K. Britton and A. D. Pellegrini (eds.), *Narrative Thought and Narrative Language*. Hillsdale, N.J.: Lawrence Erlbaum.

Lyon, T. D. 1993. Unpublished doctoral dissertation, Stanford University.

MacDonald, K. (ed.). 1988. *Sociobiological Perspectives on Human Development*. New York: Springer-Verlag.

MacPhail, E. M. 1987. "The Comparative Psychology of Intelligence." *Behavioral and Brain Sciences* 10:645–656.

Malcolm, N. 1952. "Knowledge and Belief." *Mind* 51:178–189.

Mandler, J. 1984. *Stories, Scripts, and Scenes*. Hillsdale, N.J.: Lawrence Erlbaum.

Marr, D. 1982. *Vision*. San Francisco: Freeman.

McGinn, C. 1982. "The Structure of Content." In A. Woodfield (ed.), *Thought and Object*. Oxford: Oxford University Press.

Meltzoff, A., and Gopnik, A. 1993. "The Role of Imitation in Understanding Persons and Developing a Theory of Mind." In S. Baron-Cohen, H. Tager-Flusberg, and D. J. Cohen, (eds.), *Understanding Other Minds: Perspectives from Autism*. Oxford: Oxford University Press.

Mitchell, P. 1994. "Realism and Early Conception of Mind." In C. Lewis and P. Mitchell (eds.), *Children's Early Understanding of Mind: Origins and Development*. Hillsdale, N.J.: Lawrence Erlbaum Associates.

Moore, C., and Dunham, P. J. (eds.). 1995. *Joint Attention*. Hillsdale, N.J.: Lawrence Erlbaum.

Morton, A. 1980. *Frames of Mind*. Oxford: Oxford University Press.

Morton, A. 1991. "The Inevitability of Folk Psychology." In R. J. Bogdan (ed.), *Mind and Common Sense*. Cambridge: Cambridge University Press.

Mundy, P.; Sigman, M.; and Kasari, C. 1993. "The Theory of Mind and Joint Attention Deficits in Autism." In S. Baron-Cohen, H. Tager-Flusberg, and D. J. Cohen, (eds.), *Understanding Other Minds: Perspectives from Autism*. Oxford: Oxford University Press.

Newell, A. 1982. "The Knowledge Level." *Artificial Intelligence* 18:87–172.

Nisbett, R., and Ross, L. 1980. *Human Inference*. Englewood Cliffs, N.J.: Prentice-Hall.

Peacocke, C. (ed.). 1994. *Objectivity, Simulation, and the Unity of Consciousness*. Oxford: Oxford University Press.

Perner, J. 1988. "Developing Semantics for a Theory of Mind." In J. W. Astington, P. L. Harris, and D. R. Olson (eds.), *Developing Theories of Mind*. Cambridge: Cambridge University Press.

Perner, J. 1991. *Understanding the Representational Mind*. Cambridge: MIT Press.

Perner, J. 1993. "The Theory of Mind Deficit in Autism." In S. Baron-Cohen, H. Tager-Flusberg, and D. J. Cohen, (eds.), *Understanding Other Minds: Perspectives from Autism*. Oxford: Oxford University Press.

Perner, J. 1994. "The Neccessity and Impossibility of Simulation." In C. Peacocke (ed.), *Objectivity, Simulation, and the Unity of Consciousness*. Oxford: Oxford University Press.

Perner, J.; Baker, S.; and Hutton, D. 1994. "Prelief." In C. Lewis and P. Mitchell (eds.), *Children's Early Understanding of Mind: Origins and Development*. Hillsdale, N.J.: Lawrence Erlbaum Associates.

Perner, J.; Ruffman, T.; and Leekam, S. R. 1994. "Theory of Mind Is Contagious: You Catch It from Your Sibs." *Child Development* 65:1228–1238.

Piaget, J. 1936. *La Naissance de l'intelligence chez l'enfant.* Neuchatel: Delachaux et Niestlée.

Piattelli-Palmarini, M. 1989. "Evolution, Selection, and Cognition." *Cognition* 31:1–44.

Pinker, S., and Bloom, P. 1990. "Natural Language and Natural Selection." *Behavioral and Brain Sciences* 13:707–726.

Poulin-Dubois, D., and Shultz, T. 1988. "The Development of the Understanding of Human Behavior." In J. W. Astington, P. L. Harris, and D. R. Olson (eds.), *Developing Theories of Mind.* Cambridge: Cambridge University Press.

Povinelli, D. J. 1993. "Reconstructing the Evolution of Mind." *American Psychologist* 48:493–509.

Povinelli, D. J. 1996. "Chimpanzee Theory of Mind?" In P. Carruthers and P. K. Smith (eds.), *Theories of Theories of Mind.* Cambridge: Cambridge University Press.

Povinelli, D. J., and Eddy, T. J. 1996. *What Young Chimpanzees Know about Seeing.* Monographs of the Society for Research in Child Development. Chicago: Society for Research in Child Development.

Povinelli, D. J.; Nelson, K. E.; and Boysen S. T. 1990. "Inferences about Guessing and Knowing by Chimpanzees." *Journal of Comparative Psychology* 104:203–210.

Premack, D. 1988. "'Does the Chimpanzee Have a Theory of Mind?' Revisited." In R. Byrne and A. Whiten (eds.), *Machiavellian Intelligence.* Oxford: Oxford University Press.

Premack, D. 1990. "Do Infants Have a Theory of Self-Propelled Objects?" *Cognition* 36:1–16.

Premack, D., and Dasser, V. 1991. "Perceptual Origins and Conceptual Evidence for Theory of Mind in Apes and Children." In A. Whiten (ed.), *Natural Theories of Mind.* Oxford: Blackwell.

Premack, D., and Woodruff, G. 1978. "Does the Chimpanzee Have a Theory of Mind'?" *Behavioral and Brain Sciences* 4:515–526.

Putnam, H. 1975. "The Meaning of Meaning'." In K. Gunderson (ed.), *Language, Mind, and Knowledge*, Minnesota Studies in the Philosophy of Science, no. 7. Minneapolis: University of Minnesota Press.

Pylyshyn, Z. 1984. *Computation and Cognition.* Cambridge: MIT Press.

Pylyshyn, Z. 1989. "Computing in Cognitive Science." In M. Posner (ed.), *Foundations of Cognitive Science.* Cambridge: MIT Press.

Quine, W. V. O. 1960. *Word and Object.* Cambridge: MIT Press.

Recanati, F. 1989. "The Pragmatics of What Is Said." *Mind and Language* 4:295–329.

Reddy, V. 1991. "Playing with Others' Expectations: Teasing and Mucking About in the First Year." In A. Whiten (ed.), *Natural Theories of Mind.* Oxford: Blackwell.

Ristau, C. A. 1986. "Do Animals Think?" In R. J. Hoage and L. Goldman (eds.), *Animal Intelligence*. Washington: Smithonian Institution Press.

Ristau, C. A. 1991. "Before Mindreading: Attention, Purposes, and Deception in Birds?" In A. Whiten (ed.), *Natural Theories of Mind*. Oxford: Blackwell.

Rogoff, B. 1990. *Apprenticeship in Thinking*. Oxford: Oxford University Press.

Rosch, E. 1977. "Classfication of Real-World Objects." In P. N. Johnson-Laird and P. C. Wason (eds.), *Thinking*. Cambridge: Cambridge University Press.

Rutter, M., and Bailey, A. 1993. "Thinking and Relationships: Mind and Brain." In S. Baron-Cohen, H. Tager-Flusberg, and D. J. Cohen, (eds.), *Understanding Other Minds: Perspectives from Autism*. Oxford: Oxford University Press.

Ryle, G. 1949. *The Concept of Mind*. New York: Barnes and Noble Books.

Sacks, O. 1994. "An Anthropologist on Mars." *The New Yorker*, 27 Dec. 1993–3 Jan. 1994, pp. 106–125.

Samet, J. 1993. "Autism and Theory of Mind." In S. Baron-Cohen, H. Tager-Flusberg, and D. J. Cohen, (eds.), *Understanding Other Minds: Perspectives from Autism*. Oxford: Oxford University Press.

Savage-Rumbaugh, S., and Lewin, R. 1994. *Kanzi: The Ape at the Brink of the Human Mind*. New York: Wiley.

Schank, R. C., and Abelson, R. P. 1975. "Scripts, Plans, and Knowledge." In P. N. Johnson-Laird and P. C. Wason (eds.), *Thinking*. Cambridge: Cambridge University Press.

Schiffer, S. 1987. *Remnants of Meaning*. Cambridge: MIT Press.

Schmidt, C. F., and Marsella, S. C. 1991. "Planning and Plan Recognition from a Computational Point of View." In A. Whiten (ed.), *Natural Theories of Mind*. Oxford: Blackwell.

Shultz, T. R. 1988. "Assessing Intention: A Computational Model." In J. W. Astington, P. L. Harris, and D. R. Olson (eds.), *Developing Theories of Mind*. Cambridge: Cambridge University Press.

Shultz, T. R. 1991. "From Agency to Intention." In A. Whiten (ed.), *Natural Theories of Mind*. Oxford: Blackwell.

Siegal, M., and Peterson, C. C. 1994. "Children's Theory of Mind and the Conversational Territory of Cognitive Development." In C. Lewis and P. Mitchell (eds.), *Children's Early Understanding of Mind: Origins and Development*. Hillsdale, N.J.: Lawrence Erlbaum.

Slobin, D. 1990. "The Development from Child Speaker to Native Speaker." In J. W. Stigler, R. A. Schwede, and G. Herdt (eds.), *Cultural Psychology*. Cambridge: Cambridge University Press.

Smith, E. A., and Winterhalder, B. 1992. "Natural Selection and Decision-Making." In E. A. Smith and B. Winterhalder (eds.), *Evolutionary Ecology and Human Behavior*. New York: De Gruyter.

Smith, M. S. 1988. "Research in Developmental Sociobiology: Parenting and Family Behavior." In K. MacDonald (ed.), *Sociobiological Perspectives on Human Development*. New York: Springer-Verlag.

Sober, E. 1984a. *The Nature of Selection*. Cambridge: MIT Press.

Sober, E. 1984b. "Holism, Individualism, and the Units of Selection." In E. Sober (ed.), *Conceptual Issues in Evolutionary Biology*. Cambridge: MIT Press.

Sober, E. 1993a. *Philosophy of Biology*. Boulder, Colo.: Westview Press.

Sober, E. 1993b. "Evolutionary Altruism, Psychological Egoism, and Morality." In M. H. Nitecki and D. V. Nitecki (eds.), *Evolutionary Ethics*. Albany, N.Y.: SUNY Press.

Sodian, B., and Frith, U. 1993. "The Theory of Mind Deficit in Autism: Evidence from Deception." In S. Baron-Cohen, H. Tager-Flusberg, and D. J. Cohen, (eds.), *Understanding Other Minds: Perspectives from Autism*. Oxford: Oxford University Press.

Sperber, D. 1994. "The Modularity of Thought and the Epidemiology of Representations." In L. A. Hirschfeld and S. A. Gelman (eds.), *Domain Specificity in Cognition and Culture*. Cambridge: Cambridge University Press.

Sperber, D., and Wilson, D. 1986. *Relevance*. Cambridge: Harvard University Press.

Stalnaker, R. 1984. *Inquiry*. Cambridge: MIT Press.

Stich, S. 1983. *From Folk Psychology to Cognitive Science*. Cambridge: MIT Press.

Stich, S., and Ravenscroft, I. 1994. "What Is Folk Psychology?" *Cognition* 50:447–468.

Tager-Flusberg, H. 1993. "What Language Reveals about the Understanding of Minds in Children with Autism." In S. Baron-Cohen, H. Tager-Flusberg, and D. J. Cohen, (eds.), *Understanding Other Minds: Perspectives from Autism*. Oxford: Oxford University Press.

Taylor, M. 1988. "The Development of Children's Understanding of the Seeing-Knowing Distinction." In J. W. Astington, P. L. Harris, and D. R. Olson (eds.), *Developing Theories of Mind*. Cambridge: Cambridge University Press.

Thomas, R. K. 1986. "Vertebrate Intelligence: A Review of the Laboratory Research." In R. J. Hoage and L. Goldman (eds.), *Animal Intelligence*. Washington: Smithsonian Institution Press.

Tomasello, M. 1995. "Joint Attention as Social Cognition." In C. Moore and P. J. Dunham (eds.), *Joint Attention*. Hillsdale, N.J.: Lawrence Erlbaum.

Tomasello, M.; Kruger, A. C.; and Ratner, H. H. 1993. "Cultural Learning." *Behavioral and Brain Sciences* 16:495–511.

Tooby, J., and Cosmides, L. 1989. "Evolutionary Psychology and the Generation of Culture." *Ethology and Sociobiology* 10: 29–49, 51–97.

Tooby, J., and Cosmides, L. 1990a. "On the Universality of Human Nature and the Uniqueness of the Individual: The Role of Genetics and Adaptation." *Journal of Personality* 58:17–67.

Tooby, J., and Cosmides, L. 1990b. "The Past Explains the Present." *Ethology and Sociobiology* 11:375–424.

Tooby, J., and Cosmides, L. 1992. "The Psychological Foundations of Culture." In J. Barkow, L. Cosmides, and J. Tooby (eds.), *The Adapted Mind*. New York: Oxford University Press.

Trevarthen, C. 1979. "Communication and Cooperation in Early Infancy." In M. Bullova (ed.), *Before Speech*. Cambridge: Cambridge University Press.

Trivers, R. 1985. *Social Evolution*. Menlo Park, Calif.: Benjamin Cummings.

Tversky, A., and Kahneman, D. 1974. "Judgment under Certainty: Heuristics and Biases." *Science* 185:1124–1131.

Urmson, J. 1952. "Paranthetical Verbs." *Mind* 51:480–502.

Van Fraassen, B. 1980. *The Scientific Image*. Oxford: Oxford University Press.

Vogel, S. 1988. *Life's Devices*. Oxford: Oxford University Press.

Volkmar, F. R., and Klin, A. 1993. "Social Development in Autism." In S. Baron-Cohen, H. Tager-Flusberg, and D. J. Cohen, (eds.), *Understanding Other Minds: Perspectives from Autism*. Oxford: Oxford University Press.

Von Wright, G. H. 1971. *Explanation and Understanding*. Ithaca: Cornell University Press.

Weisfeld, G. E., and Billings, R. L. 1988. "Observations on Adolescence." In K. MacDonald (ed.), *Sociobiological Perspectives on Human Development*. New York: Springer-Verlag.

Wellman, H. 1988. "First Steps in the Child's Theorizing about the Mind." In J. W. Astington, P. L. Harris, and D. R. Olson (eds.), *Developing Theories of Mind*. Cambridge: Cambridge University Press.

Wellman, H. 1990. *The Child's Theory of Mind*. Cambridge: MIT Press.

Wellman, H. M. 1990. "From Desires to Beliefs." In A. Whiten (ed.), *Natural Theories of Mind*. Oxford: Blackwell.

Wellman, H. 1993. "Early Understanding of Mind." In S. Baron-Cohen, H. Tager-Flusberg, and D. J. Cohen (eds.), *Understanding Other Minds: Perspectives from Autism*. Oxford: Oxford University Press.

Werner, H. 1948. *Comparative Psychology of Mental Development*. Chicago: Follett.

West-Eberhard, M. J. 1992. "Adaptation." In E. V. Keller and E. A. Lloyd (eds.), *Keywords in Evolutionary Biology*. Cambridge: Harvard University Press.

Whiten, A. (ed.). 1991a. *Natural Theories of Mind*. Oxford: Blackwell.

Whiten, A. 1991b. "The Emergence of Mind Reading." In A. Whiten (ed.), *Natural Theories of Mind*. Oxford: Blackwell.

Whiten, A. 1993. "Evolving a Theory of Mind." In S. Baron-Cohen, H. Tager-Flusberg, and D. J. Cohen, (eds.), *Understanding Other Minds: Perspectives from Autism.* Oxford: Oxford University Press.

Whiten, A. 1994. "Grades of Mindreading." In C. Lewis and P. Mitchell (eds.), *Children's Early Understanding of Mind: Origins and Development.* Hillsdale, N.J.: Lawrence Erlbaum.

Whiten, A. 1996. "When Does Smart Behavior-Reading Become Mind-Reading?" In P. Carruthers and P. K. Smith (eds.), *Theories of Theories of Mind.* Cambridge: Cambridge University Press.

Whiten, A., and Byrne, R. W. 1988a. "The Manipulation of Attention in Primate Tactical Deception." In R. Byrne and A. Whiten (eds.), *Machiavellian Intelligence.* Oxford: Oxford University Press.

Whiten, A., and Byrne, R. W. 1988b. "Taking (Machiavellian) Intelligence Apart." In R. Byrne and A. Whiten (eds.), *Machiavellian Intelligence.* Oxford: Oxford University Press.

Whiten, A., and Byrne, R. W. 1988c. "Tactical Deception in Primates." *Behavioral and Brain Sciences* 11:233–244.

Whiten, A., and Byrne, R. W. 1991. "The Emergence of Metarepresentation in Human Ontogeny and Primate Phylogeny." In A. Whiten (ed.), *Natural Theories of Mind.* Oxford: Blackwell.

Whiten, A., and Perner, J. 1991. "Fundamental Issues in the Multidisciplinary Study of Mindreading." In A. Whiten (ed.), *Natural Theories of Mind.* Oxford: Blackwell.

Wilkes, K. V. 1981. "Functionalism, Psychology, and the Philosophy of Mind." *Philosophical Topics* 12:147–167.

Wilkes, K. V. 1984. "Pragmatics in Science and Theory in Common Sense." *Inquiry* 27:339–361.

Williams, G. C. 1966. *Adaptation and Natural Selection.* Princeton: Princeton University Press.

Williams, G. C. 1992. *Natural Selection.* Oxford: Oxford University Press.

Wills, C. 1993. *The Runaway Brain.* New York: Basic Books

Wimmer, H.; Hogrefe, J.; and Sodian, B. 1988. "A Second Stage in Children's Conception of Mental Life." In J. W. Astington, P. L. Harris, and D. R. Olson (eds.), *Developing Theories of Mind.* Cambridge: Cambridge University Press.

Wimmer, H., and Perner, J. 1983. "Beliefs about Beliefs." *Cognition* 13:103–128.

Wittgenstein, L. 1953. *Philosophical Investigations.* Oxford: Blackwell.

Wittgenstein, L. 1969. *On Certainty.* Oxford: Blackwell.

Zaitchik, D. 1990. "When Representations Conflict with Reality." *Cognition* 35:41–68.

Zimmermann, R. R., and Torrey, C. C. 1965. Ontogeny of Learning. In A. M. Schrier, H. F. Harlow, and F. Stollnitz (eds.), *Behavior of Nonhuman Primates.* New York: Academic Press.

Index